JUST SOME

GOOD THOUGHTS

(NOTHING MORE, NOTHING LESS)

JUST SOME
GOOD
THOUGHTS

(NOTHING MORE, NOTHING LESS)

TONY WASHINGTON

atmosphere press

TABLE OF CONTENTS

Chapter Three – Thoughts

Chapter Seven – Love

Chapter Eight – God

Chapter Nine – Happiness

Chapter Ten – Musings

INTRODUCTION

WHEN DID THE MUSIC STOP?

While watching the Grammys one night, it suddenly dawned on me that I barely knew any of the artists. It seemed that many friends around my age were coming to the same conclusion. So, I had to ask myself, when did we stop listening to the music? And, as I pondered that question, it seemed to take on a larger proportion. *Why* did we stop listening to the music?

Music has been described as one of the purest artistic mediums least subject to corruption. Music is often associated with the good times in our lives. Even as you read this, you can probably think back to certain songs that the moment you hear them again, summon a flood of pleasant memories to your mind. We play music at parties and at social gatherings. Movies and TV shows use music to illustrate and cultivate emotion. But, there's one thing that music seems especially attached to, and that is youth. I can remember as a young adult wondering how my parents could survive without music. Yet, here am I in middle age living on a music diet of just barely. Why did we stop listening to the music?

Young people have a zest for life and an enthusiasm that hasn't yet been dampened by the world. In our youth, we dream beautiful dreams of the future; living as we please; doing the things that excite us. But life, responsibility and pressure start to have their way with us, and before long we don't have time for music anymore. In fact, if we are honest, we don't have time for anything meaningful anymore. Go, go, go, night and day; ever rushing to this and from that, with no time for reflection and art. Music becomes a frivolity for people who don't have anything else to do. Yet, music is a metaphor for life. When it's playing, we are growing and we are flourishing. When it stops, maybe we have as well. Getting old isn't measured by the number of years or that aged image staring back from the mirror. Growing old is something that happens to our hearts when we become convinced that our dreams are no longer a reality and start settling for 'okay' and 'pretty good, I guess.' Most of us have some treasured items that are "old," but we tend to get the most excitement from the things that are "new." Why did we stop listening to the music? Because we got old...

If you think back, those of you who stopped listening to the music, there was a time when you refused to tolerate boredom and routine. When the tediousness of life set in, it was an emergency that needed to be fixed. You pressed for a new adventure and took immediate action to escape. Fast forward 30 years, and you found yourself accepting your condition as "just how life is" and, like an animal in the zoo, lowered your energy level to match your surroundings. You traded adventure for security (or so-called security) and decided that blasé was synonymous with being responsible. You couldn't take that trip or pursue that profession because it was just too risky. I mean, what if you didn't have the money you needed or, worse, failed? Yet, you didn't think that way when you were younger. If you came up short you would figure it out, and figure it out you did. The thrill of the challenge seemed to be far better than the comfort of the boredom. Why did we stop listening to the music? Because we became boring.

How many of you are working at a job and maybe even hold a high-ranking position but are bored to death? How many of you are in a relationship that has long since lost its spark? How many of you still feel the flicker of a one-time flame for some pursuit that you have buried under the guise of the "safe" route? How many? Why did we stop listening to the music? Because we became so safe.

Life, at least the life God intended, was not supposed to be "old" or "boring" or "safe." The word for *life* in the Bible literally means life in all of its multifarious variety and full manifestation. God is a God of infinite variety. As such, we all have passions and pursuits that turn us on. To think that the passion of living should be almost dead upon entering middle age is just plain crazy talk. Growing and flourishing aren't terms reserved for the young. The trouble isn't with God or with life. The trouble is in our minds and the things we have accepted as true. We only stop learning and growing when we stop learning and growing... The music that we surrendered is still there, waiting to be turned on again. All we have to do is turn it on. Make the time to listen to the music again.

It really doesn't matter how old or young you are when you read this. What matters is that you refuse to surrender the things you hold most sacred! You do have the time you need to start living again. Your heart hasn't molded over just yet. Instead, you simply stopped paying attention and settled for a lesser life. Don't settle for a lesser life!

You might need a little help to get started in breaking the chains of mediocrity, and for that I would highly recommend talking to God. But I can save you a little time and tell you that it is most likely based on fear. Fear is the number one killer of hopes and dreams, and if your dreams are almost dead, you know what is to blame.

I don't know about you but I'm going to start listening to the music again, not so I can recognize an artist at the Grammys, but rather so I can recognize life again. Why you stopped listening to the music isn't the real issue here, but instead, when will you start listening to the music again?

I wrote *Just Some Good Thoughts* to help you find that music and that life again...

CHAPTER ONE
Life

LIFE DOESN'T HAPPEN TO YOU
(YOU HAPPEN TO IT...)

Have you ever found yourself in a rut? You didn't see it coming. You didn't perceive the steps along the way. All you really know is that life isn't working for you anymore. Or maybe you suffered through some negative event, and now you can't seem to snap out of it. In fact, things keep getting worse and worse. It's like you're stuck in some type of negativity spin cycle, with each day offering another reason for you to give up all hope. Maybe, in order to cope with it, you've been self-medicating for so long that you don't even know what unmedicated feels like anymore. And in your despair, you ask God, what the hell is going on? Why is my life not happening the way I thought it would? Well, there's an answer to that question you may have never considered...

The vast majority of people are convinced that life just happens to them and that they are powerless to change it. They feel as if there's some big cosmic plan they're unaware of, which doles out in random fashion, good things and bad things at whim. In their troubles, they search their souls, looking for causes inside themselves for the hardships they're experiencing. In high times, they call it luck and good fortune. In low times they call it fate.

NOTHING COULD BE FURTHER FROM THE TRUTH! When we allow the circumstances of the world to move us to a negative space, we unknowingly begin to expect negative results. Tragedies, hardships, difficulties, or unresolved frustrations work first in our minds and then in our hearts to lower or even reverse our expectations for our lives. They jolt us or imperceptibly drag us into a doubtful position whereby we begin to question our views of how life truly works. They open the doors and our hearts to possibilities for difficulty we never contemplated before. And, each day honors our beliefs by presenting more information to corroborate those beliefs. Once the cycle starts, it's very hard to stop.

God, the author and designer of life, did not devise His creation by whim. He ordered it beautifully with breathtaking precision, replete with all conceivable love and goodness. He made his man, His precious man, to have full access to His instruction book on life! He's not a capricious God hidden away in the expanse doling out blessings and punishments by the same hand. He is only good, always, in every circumstance, every condition and all the time. He gave man complete control over his life by that which he (the man) chooses to believe. Absent the truth of God's Word, man is subject to the circumstances of life, never conceiving that he, the man, choosing and thus believing, is subconsciously working to bring about the circumstances he is experiencing. Your life, be it blessed or frightful, is the cumulative product of your own thoughts. When you find yourself in a rut, though difficult to get out of, the rut is the consequence of long persistence in negative thoughts unchecked. The shocks and jolts of unexpected tragedy, though not part of your own responsibility, serve not only to severely or mortally wound the sufferer, but also all those associated with that person. Difficulties and hardships, never from God, no matter how nobly explained, are a temptation; tempting you to come to the dark side and stay awhile. And, the longer you remain in the darkness, the worse your life becomes.

In this way, your life isn't happening to you; you are happening to it! You're not a victim in a grand drama playing a part you never chose. You are the lead in a play that you are writing. For this reason, you can change your character's role whenever and however you see fit. I don't care who you are, what you've done or what circumstance you find yourself in, arduous and severe or simply irritating and annoying, God has already heard your prayer! He will help you when and only when you begin to change your mind. There's no negative circumstance you cannot escape, no situation that cannot be resolved or healed if you will change your mind. "Dwelling on the darkness will not bring forth the light." The light comes as quickly as you turn on the switch! That is your one and only great power in this life; the power to choose what you will and will not believe.

Nothing about your life is happenstance. "You are where you are that you may learn and that you may grow." The negatives and hardships you are experiencing are not the way it is. It's not just life. Instead, it's life infected by darkness, and like any virus, it can be eradicated if the conditions are right. This isn't a simplistic view of life; it's the only true view of life. Truth is always simple. It's error that is complicated.

So how can you finally get out of the ruts in life? How can you escape from difficult and trying circumstances? How can you overcome and prevail against any challenge that comes your way? How can you live and realize your life's dreams and endless possibilities? How can you finally become the man or woman you always thought you could be? Change your mind! Change your thoughts from darkness to light. Stop confessing the negatives and confess the positives instead. Stop looking for and living in the trouble and walk out into the clear light of God's heavenly pastures, where you will find your rest. This life is too big and too fraught with difficulties for you to go it alone. Just because something looks true and sounds true and has every indicator that it is true, doesn't make it true. What's true is what God says is true, and you can bet your entire life on that!

Come out and join me in the sunshine where God has first place and see for yourself if your life isn't revolutionized in dramatic and delightful ways! Everything you ever wanted in your life resides in the light where God is! Won't you come and meet me there?

THE GOOD LIFE

There's something out there that all humans are after. It's something often talked about but rarely found. It's the inner heart desire of every person that draws breath. It's a goal, an experience, a journey and a destination. It is the pursuit of all pursuits, the good life!

If you've lived any amount of time, you know there are as many theories on the way to get there as there are people. One man's good life is a nightmare for another. One woman's unacceptable is another's acceptable, and even more, a victory. For some, it's money. For others, it's family. For some, it's solitude and quiet space. For others, it's opportunities for learning. Truth is, you have the privilege to decide your good life yourself. But there is one consistent thing that underlies all variations of the good life. It is the most glorious and delicate balance there is. It's called self-control...

If you're like me, you tend to bristle up when that "control" word shows up. Nobody likes to be controlled. And sometimes it's tough to control yourself, especially when that control involves the things you love. But, and you cannot find a larger *but*, self-control is truly the essence of life; the good life. Here's the paradox, the more control you exercise, the freer you become. Now, before you get besieged with sadness, self-control doesn't mean refusing happiness or good feelings or good things. Self-control is more about enjoying your happiness and producing good feelings, and maintaining your good things.

Have you ever had the experience of finally deciding to control some aspect of your life? If you were successful, i.e., lost the weight, stopped a behavior, brought some 'out of control' aspect under control, how did you feel when the job was done? Conversely, those areas that are out of control; those aspects of you that drive *you* nuts, the things you do over and over and over again and despise yourself when you do them, where do they leave you? You see, your feelings, though not 100 percent reliable, are trying to tell you something. They're telling you that you need to get a grip on you! And, sadly, you know it's true.

There is such a thing as too much of a good thing. Fun is always fun, but there is a 'too much' fun. Wine, the great mood enhancer, has an endpoint where it changes from a sparkle to a numb sedative. Tasty food is delightful, but the Thanksgiving gorge is over the top. Discomfort is the tell-tale indicator. Bad feelings are the barometer. If you really think it through, there should be no downside to a good thing. But the downside sometimes applies not to the thing itself but the quantity of the thing.

In every realm of life, there's an expectation of control. Control keeps you healthy. Control protects your finances. Control enhances your experiences. Control makes your highs higher and mitigates your lows. Your life depends upon your willingness to control it. I would surmise that whenever you observe someone who seems to be living the good life, behind that life is some element of control; decisions you might never be able to see.

Life is always about staying in balance. Work is good unless you work too much or too little. If you work too much, you allow it to compensate for other areas it was never designed to cover. It becomes a consuming force and begs for remedy. If you work too little, the penalty is found in dissatisfaction and angst. Even a day at work where your focus is not on work but on quitting time makes for the longest day ever. If you've ever lost your job, you know that time off is not really time off when your responsibilities aren't handled. But, how sweet is your vacation when the work preceded it?

Life requires both the things you have to do and the things you get to do. If all you have is things you have to do, you'll live your life in misery. Likewise, if all you do is things you get to do, you'll soon be found wanting. A lawn must be mowed before you can enjoy the patio. The bed must be made to make the night's sleep more refreshing. Food is eaten on clean dishes. Work comes before play, and play is made possible by work. The weekend comes at the end of the work week, not before it. The balance is the beauty of it all.

I think you may discover one day that the good life you were after was right there for you all along. But instead of being found in fame and riches, it is found in a thousand little choices; choices you make in defense of yourself. Choices that don't always feel good, but always feel good, if you know what I mean. The ability to sometimes say no, to yourself... The sublime, inherent ability to finally take command of yourself; your elusive self! That, my friends, is the sure steadfast definition of the good life - getting and then staying in control of yourself...

You don't know where to start, you say? Begin the next time you start to do something you really wish you wouldn't do. Listen to the gentle urging inside you when there's a decision to be made. Pay attention to that thought back there telling you something you have been trying to ignore. You already know where the control needs to be; you just need to make up your mind to do it. And when you do, notice how that feels and see if you cannot get a glimpse of the good life yourself...

LIFE MOVES IN ONE DIRECTION ONLY

*"Life moves in one direction only - and each day we are faced
with an actual set of circumstances, not with what might have
been, not with what we might have done, but with what is, and
with where we are now – and from this point we must proceed;
not from where we were, not from where we wish we were -
but from where we are..." ~ Richard L. Evans*

I came across this quote today and found myself immediately
filled with inspiration regarding its great reality. Your life, my
life is always an ever present 'now.' There is no such thing as
what might have been because what might have been hasn't
happened yet. Similarly, what we might have done is equally
deceptive in that we have not done it yet. Instead, in full ownership and without excuse, with full accountability, our life is
what it is today. We are where we are today and where we are
is the only place from which we can move forward. We cannot
move from where we were, nor can we move from where we
wish we were. Life only moves in one direction, and it can only
move forward and progress when we accept what is for what
it is, and resolve ourselves to change the things we need to
change.

As human beings, there will always be things in our lives
we know we need to change. Some things will come easy for
us and fade away like fog when the sun comes out. Other
things will not come out without a great and arduous struggle,

sometimes demanding years to overcome. But, make no mistake, nothing can ever change for the better until we come to full terms with what is. Our flaws, our foibles, our errors call aloud for resolution, and we are loathe to admit them for what they are. We excuse them, we justify them, we explain them away, secretly hoping we can someday gain a magical grasp on them and be that much better for it. But, at the end of the day, they are our problems, and no matter how they gained control over us, they call aloud for remedy.

It's not easy to admit our issues as, like a disagreeable friend, they have become a part of us. However unwelcome, they are a part of who we are today. But, they are not our friends, and the effects of their influence over us only lead to suffering and misery. They are our great hold-back and hindrance. They stymie our joy and blessings. They lead us down paths we never sought to traverse. They are bumps in an otherwise smooth road. They are ditches and well-worn ruts sent to defeat us. And we will never master them, though master them we must, until we allow ourselves to see them for what they really are - lies... There are enjoyments and pleasures in life to bless us, but when overdone and not controlled, they bring pain instead. But, you cannot control what you refuse to acknowledge. Nothing good starts as excess, but in excess becomes nothing good. What you fail to control eventually controls you. What you choose to ignore gradually gains ascendancy like a rock in your shoe ignored over many miles. The lesson required you to make a change the first time it hurt you.

There's a great freedom in accepting your life for what it is, both the good and the bad. No man is all good, and no woman is all bad. We are all shades and mixtures of both, with everything in-between. We may possess great strength and great weakness. We are all subject to like passions. We all feel and perceive deeply at times and other times are numb and without perception. We are both sensitive and have callouses over parts of our hearts. We have all been harmed at one time or another, and we are all in need of healing. But, in order to be healed, we have to once again recognize where we are hurting. We have to acknowledge what is... without judgment and self-chastisement. No man goes astray on his own without first being led. No one in their right mind would purposefully choose suffering and pain. But, we do suffer at times and need someone to deliver us. We need love, not a lecture. We need forgiveness and often first from ourselves. We need God!

In short, we need to be honest with ourselves and honest with God. Our relationship with God is not politics, whereby we seek to present all of our actions in a favorable light. Instead, it is a relationship based on trust. It is a willingness for us to see ourselves right as we are, no matter how dirty, confused or deceived we have become. It is having the humility to admit we have gone astray and an earnest desire for God to help us get back on track. He is not here to judge us or condemn us for where we have ended up, but instead, like a loving Father, welcomes us back into His arms with solutions we haven't yet been able to fathom. Discipline doesn't get the job done; love does! We need Him to love us back into loving ourselves again, not because we have only done right, but because He only does right, and He is love.

You're not going to travel very far in life before you find yourself totally screwed up over something. No matter what it is, that is not the end of the road. Be grateful it finally got clear enough for you to see it. You can't sink so low but that underneath, you aren't in the loving arms of God. Acknowledge it. Admit it! It is what it is, but it doesn't have to stay that way. Life truly moves in one direction only, and the only way you can move ahead is for you to accept where you are at this very moment and move up from there. Get back up! God loves you and so do I...

GETTING RID OF THE HURT AND THE DIRT
IN YOUR LIFE

You know, if you've lived long enough, there are things in life that serve no other purpose than to hold you back! No matter how hard you work to be successful and happy, those things are guaranteed to severely retard your progress. We don't hold on to these things on purpose, but somehow they manage to stick around and thwart our every move. It behooves us all to figure out how to get the hurt and dirt out of our lives.

All of us have been hurt by someone or something in some capacity. Maybe you were blessed to be a part of a beloved, spirit-based organization that really let you down in your later years. Maybe someone you cherished left you for someone else. Perhaps you gave your all for some important job only to discover that your value was fleeting and transitory. Perhaps you suffered some tragedy involving your loved ones that you are still scratching your head to try and figure out why. No matter what has happened to you, and some things are frightfully dreadful and incredibly painful, you have to find a way to move ahead.

Holding on to wrongs done and the multiplicity of injustices you've experienced does nothing more than to stymy and squash your current enjoyment of life. Your heart, in response to the hurts you are holding onto, has no choice but to resort to hardness to protect itself. And, once your heart gets hard and calloused, you no longer have the capacity to feel the things you are supposed to feel. The whole world suffers from this malady... People wander aimlessly their whole lives by searching and tirelessly pursuing the former heart they always remember with great fondness. Yet, they fail to realize that they themselves are doing the very thing that keeps their own heart hard! You absolutely must do whatever it takes to move ahead and let those things go. You have to move past the hurts in your life.

In similar fashion, we all have those parts of our lives we wish we didn't have. We are all human beings and, as such, are often easy to beat. We like things and then we like them too much! We cleave on to the very things that make our lives miserable. We know our excesses and propensity for more than enough, yet on we go traveling down the same roads over and over and over again! Certain behaviors, certain activities always turn out bad, no matter how they seem in the moment. Yet so goes humanity swirling and boiling in its passions leading wherever it gets led, never really taking the time to consider and thus choose.

If we really want to soar; if we really want to travel the high roads in life, we need to get rid of our dirt. We need to rid ourselves of those things, both subtle and obvious, that always return us woe. Why stagger between two opinions? We know those choices that bring us peace, and we also know those choices that cause unrest. It behooves us to simply recognize what is going on and change it. All humanity wrestles with this same conundrum. We want our cake and to eat it too! We seek to travel the roads of high endeavor with pockets full of sand, rocks and debris. We think we can somehow fool the system; straddle the fence; commingle truth and error. But, we cannot. We have to make a choice. We have to finally rid ourselves of our dirt!

In order to live life; to really experience all that God intended for you, you have to rid yourself of the hurt and all the dirt. Both, though very cleverly disguised, are thorns in your flesh, oil in your water, sand in your machinery. They are distractions and they are lies. Often your solution isn't to do something, but to stop doing something! Life can be more about the things you choose not to do rather than the things you should do. Holding onto hurts and wrongs done chokes and suffocates your life. Insisting on doing things you know always turn out wrong buries your heart in bad feelings and remorse. Both are crucially important, and both are matters of the heart.

In order to win at the game of life, you have to protect your heart. You have to make choices that encourage tenderness of heart. A tender heart; a heart that feels and loves and gives, is the heart of God. Once you rid yourself of the poisons, your heart begins to recover. Remove the cause and the body heals!

Decide now to get rid of the hurt and dirt in your life. You don't have to be perfect, but you do have to do your part... You have wings and you deserve to fly!

FIFTEEN TO LIFE...

I found myself again seeking to lose that same 15 pounds I've been working on for about 15 years. I lost all of it once and some of it many, many times. Yet, it always seems to creep back on. Funny thing is it's only 15 pounds. That got me thinking, why is it that my body would regulate itself just slightly higher than I would want? In fact, why do we seem to get certain things in our lives yet often feel like we need a little bit more? The house is nice, but I wish it didn't have bricks. The Ford Explorer works, but that Escalade is over the top! If you receive in life exactly what you have believed to receive, then why would our believing stop just short of what we really want? Or maybe, are we stopping short of what we really want or always wanting more and more? These are worthy questions for those serving 15 to life.

It was 1982 when I first took a class called, "Power for Abundant Living," where I learned that what a person believes in their heart is what they will manifest in their lives. I'm not referring to the reported "magic" outlined in "The Secret." Life wasn't designed for things to just appear out of nowhere, but instead the results we are pursuing show up naturally in direct accordance with our firm expectations! The Bible says, "As a man thinks in his heart, so is he." And, "Guard your heart with all diligence, for out of it flows forth the issues of your life!" Thus, your life, whether you like it or not, is a direct reflection of what you believe deep down in your heart. Similarly, the image that you carry of yourself is what you are. "How have you been picturing yourself for the last year, five years, 10 years? The image that you carry of yourself with clearness and concern is what you are." And the kicker? This law of believing works for positive and negative thinking alike!

A good friend complimented me yesterday on the back-splash I put up in the kitchen. I responded with thank you, then quickly pointed out that there were some flaws in the job and that I made some mistakes. Do you see where I'm going? Instead of just enjoying the positives, I felt the need to add in a "yes, but." Often, we limit ourselves in this life with our "yes, buts!" Somebody tricked us into believing that we have to take the good *with* the bad. Someone convinced us that we can't have it all. Something weaseled its way into our thinking and talked us into considering that we have to give darkness its place. Doubts, worries, fears, stressors and anxieties are the "yes, buts" in our lives. They represent a form of believing in the negative with just as powerful and specific results.

If you want to learn how to believe rightly, how to get positive results in your life, or how to get rid of the life-sucking negatives, the question to ask yourself involves your subject of focus. What is your subject of focus? What do you see most consistently? Does your good always have some "bad" in it? Would your friends describe you as positive or negative? Those thoughts you rehearse most consistently eventually find their way into your heart, determining how your life proceeds. You don't live how you *want* to live because you don't believe you can! You don't get what you want in life, you get what you are on the inside. In order to change the outside, you have to change the inside. You can change every circumstance of your life if you are willing to invest a little time in changing your thinking. Develop and build a crystal-clear image of something you need or someone you want to be, and hold fast to that image. Don't let anyone or anything change it! Keep your subject of focus.

At this point you may be wondering, "How does anyone know what is in their heart?" The answer is simple, what do you talk about the most? Out of the abundance of the heart, the mouth speaks. What does your communication consist of? Are you quick to notice and point out the negatives? Are you critical of other people? Do you use words that associate themselves with lack and struggle? Is your favorite topic the things that aren't right in your body? (If so, I'm guessing you have lots and lots of things not right in your body.) Or is your conversation pleasant, expectant, looking for the good in life? What you have been saying is what you have been believing and is exactly how you have been living! Good or bad, positive or negative, joyous or disastrous, are all your choice and within the realm of something you can control!

When it's all said and done, the reason I'm serving 15 to life is because my focus, the picture I carry of myself with clearness and concern, my expectation and believing has been completely centered on something I don't want rather than on something I do want. When I see myself in the mirror, I hone in on what isn't right rather than focusing in on everything that is right! And, you cannot do something for 15 years without being pretty damn consistent! The first place to make a change isn't addressed on the outside, but on the inside instead.

Fifteen pounds doesn't rank very highly on the life importance scale, that's for sure, but 15 years certainly does. Any time spent living life stuck in a cycle of something negative is too long, especially since you have the ability, by your belief, to change it. Don't settle for life's potluck or justifying your negatives by comparing them to other people's negatives. Choose the life you want to live, leaving no caveat for negatives, evil or wrong. You deserve that much because God gave you that much! Believe rightly! Choose life!

ARE YOU BORED WITH LIFE?

It's time for some interesting self-reflection. Are you ready for it? If you answered yes to the question, even secretly, then you are in the right place. If you answered no, that's cool, but you *are* reading this for a reason, and it might not be what you think...

I'd guess that most people equate boredom with a lack of activity. You know, like you've got nothing to do, so you're bored. Yet, have you ever been on a beach vacation? Beach vacays are full of nothing to do; serious lounging and maybe a choice, generally smuggled in, alcoholic beverage. (Why in the hell are beaches and pools alcohol prohibited when 90% of the attendees smuggle it in? - I digress.)

Before I wax philosophical on you, I decided to look up "bored" in the dictionary. Yes, it certainly includes a lack of activity or tedious events, but it has a component that deserves further inspection. It closely ties in with feelings of fatigue, weariness and a lack of enthusiasm. While a lack of enthusiasm may be obvious, fatigue and weariness are surprising. In other words, getting worn out in your mind engenders feelings of boredom.

There's an interesting phenomenon that's taking place in your mind, day by day. The phenomenon is called thinking. You are always thinking about stuff, whether you recognize it or not. Your mind is engaged in almost non-stop chatter, from you to you! No, it's not the Universal "I AM" communicating with you; that's called revelation and the topic of another essay. It's you telling you stuff about what is going on with you right now. Often, it's you instructing you on how you ought to be and chastising you for not being who you said you should be. Weird huh? Frequently it's you warning you about some potential pending danger coming your way, usually referred to as worrying. That's not to mention the incessant analysis and evaluation that besieges you because, well, you know, you, the adult, knows stuff! There's the critical you, thinking critical thoughts about others who are not you, and even though they are not you and you don't really know them, you know they are not you and therefore cannot be okay. You, you, you and damn it, it's exhausting to say the least! Now, back to that definition.

Some would argue that you feel bored because you're lacking enthusiasm for life. I would say that you feel bored because you are just plain ol' worn out. You've entertained so much stupid stuff by the end of the day that you've got nothing left. Your energy bank is on "E." Dale Carnegie used to say that hard work doesn't wear a man out, but fear and worry are what fatigues him. In these frenetic times of media overload and wrestling with well-planned and distracting issues (i.e., political absurdities or social issues that aren't really social issues), our minds are taking a hit. Everywhere you look and everything you read is pregnant with loaded messages, causing that chatter machine to take off. It's all run, run, run, get it done, work harder, be rich by age 30, get the house, the car, the model, write a book, run. Educate your kids, pay for a private school, get them in dance and sports and gymnastics and soccer. Make them the best, the fastest, the strongest, the most socially acceptable. Go, go, go, win, win, win, be the best, excel, dominate! And, while you chase it all, be sure to take your blood pressure meds, your anxiety meds, your fiber, your vitamins, eat less red meat and, for God's sake, wear your helmet! Then, sadly, at the end of the day, fatigue, weariness and exhaustion. Who told you that is life? The messages did via your own confused and over-worked thoughts.

Can you imagine how you might feel if you had some battery acid for breakfast, kerosene for lunch and Lime-away for dinner? I'm guessing you would be thinking you needed to eat better. Yet, when it comes to your thoughts and what you are feeding your mind, it goes unnoticed. Takeaway: You have to start noticing. You have to begin paying closer attention. Nothing will wear you out faster than worries and fears, then before you know it, the lethargy and lack of enthusiasm hold first place.

Boredom might be the polar opposite of enthusiasm. Enthusiasm is chock full of energy and excitement. It's not something based solely on the external environment, but more based on what you choose to think. I'm not talking about that overused phrase, "be positive," which people usually associate with foolishness, such as saying your leg isn't broken when it is. The word enthusiasm word origin is *"en-theos,"* and naturally, God is involved. But taking it a step further, I'm talking about choosing to think and consider what God says is true versus the deluge of messages you get throughout a day. Whoever said you couldn't get what you want and need in life? You did, albeit influenced, but alas, still you telling you. Who told you there was no point in (fill in the blank)? You did. Who convinced you that your life was so bad? You did. Who persists in chastising you and criticizing you, and shaming you? You do, that's who. All of the aforementioned stand in absolute contradiction to God's Word. Did you know that?

The problem with feeling bored about life is that by the time it happens, it has already happened. You got worked over and over and over, and your fruit got stale. If you weed-whack the bark of that fruit tree long enough, it's going to stop putting out. You can tell if this is you if you stopped putting out (energy, activity, life). When did you give up on the pursuit of your personal happiness? How did your definition of the good life become an electronic illusion you saw in HD?

The solution to boredom is simple but not quick or easy. You have to take charge of you, namely by making your mind your friend and then making it think what you want it to think. That is to say, make your mind behave more friendly towards you and not be a personal enemy. This isn't delusion. Delusion is spending time pondering that the earth may actually be flat. Instead, this is called controlling your thinking. You can do it if you really want to, and indeed you must if you want to be enthusiastic and happy and blessed. God is never going to take away your boredom, but if you cooperate with Him, He will show you exactly where your thinking went (and is going) south. He will help you learn what is really true, remind you of it and love you back into loving yourself.

Life is way too precious and way too short to live it bored out of your gourd. Grab and tame that unwieldy beast called your mind and see how quickly that dreaded boredom and lack of energy become a thing of the past. Oh, and unplug for a minute, for God's sake, to catch your breath.

IS LIFE RANDOM?

Imagine, if you will, that your life plays out on a field of pure potential. There's no predetermined destiny or well-developed course. You came from the factory with complete freedom of will to function within a complex, fully loaded network without limitation. You began with a mind and a heart as a means to tap into that potential and were given the ability to develop your own life as you saw fit. In the infinite field of potential (called life), you were provided with the choice to soar as high as the heavens or fall as low as the deepest valley. This is how your life started, and this is how your life functions to this day. There is no element of randomness involved. Randomness is a deception on a breathtakingly masterful level. Behind every apparent act of randomness is a carefully crafted plan.

In a world designed by God, there can be no element of chance. There is nothing without purpose or meaning. Often the meaning or cause remains hidden, and in a futile attempt to understand, man is forced to guess. Man is schooled to evaluate by cause and effect. When he fails to see the connection, as he often does, he foolishly assigns erroneous causes and, when played out to his exasperation, assigns nebulous causes which are not causes at all. The apparent randomness of life is such a nebulous cause. If you could see life as God sees it, you would be well aware of the complicated, unbroken chain of events that led to both your greatest accomplishments and your most tragic catastrophes. You did not land a good break nor did you run across a patch of bad luck. In the same way that a plant does not just appear, but first began as a seed, so your life and the results thereof began as a seed. And through knowledge or by ignorance, you planted and one day received. This offers you no consolation for the horrible things you may have experienced, but it is the truth, somewhat simplified, of course.

My purpose for attempting to explain this is not to condemn you for any negative events you are presently surviving, but rather to give you back something you have possessed all along. The sooner you stop guessing at the game of life and get back to life's Designer, the sooner you can change the course of your life and start manifesting the results you really want. God is quite adept at teaching you the truth and seeks only a willing heart. If you were paying attention, you would recognize where He was already at work. Whether it came in the form of an apparently random thought, or a close friend, or a teacher or your own attempt at evaluating what happened to you, God was back there igniting a burning bush to see if you might stop and investigate. No one is exempted from God's tender love and guidance if that person really wants to know. No one...

The notion that life is random serves only to take away reason and purpose and meaning. Without those elements, life becomes pointless. Logically there would be no point in what you think or what you do, or what you believe if life is random. It all becomes a giant exercise in futile existence whereby stuff just happens to you from a perpetual state of "look-out!" Now just observing your surroundings, you know that isn't true. Nature alone denies that theory, and it isn't anyone's mother.

There are reasons behind even the most insignificant events. Sometimes those reasons are good, and sometimes those reasons are bad, but how you vote determines the election (Dr. VPW). No person can control every aspect of life, nor should he attempt to, but he controls a *helluva* lot more than he thinks. He is playing in a field of pure potentiality with the potential to do or go or be whatever he wants. His only limitation is his beliefs and ignorance regarding the reality of things. God said, "My people are destroyed for a lack of knowledge." It's ignorance fostered by a world carefully manipulated to present an apparent order that is not order at all. It's a training program you have participated in without knowing you were participating. It is the systematizing of error that, once accepted, leads only to misery and hopelessness. Just think about how many things you hold as true that really aren't true at all. The doctor said your disease was incurable, but God didn't. The system says you cannot achieve without the right education, yet many achieve despite it. If you do this, you'll get that, and if you don't do this you will suffer. All erroneous, all systematized, all put forth as truth to a world starved for goodness and love and success, finally resulting only in evil and hate and failure.

This is your opportunity to break out of the myth of randomness and regain control of your life. This is your chance (pun intended) to chart a new course whereby you decide how things are going to turn out. This is the reality of the life that God gave you, complete with a full catalog of instruction if you want it.

Breaking free from bondage and limitation and ignorance isn't any more complicated than deciding in your heart that you need God to help you. You ain't smart enough to do this on your own, as your own experience exemplifies...

So as I wrap up these good thoughts, I peer into the sky where I see the moon mocking the sun by appearing to rise in the east behind the clouds, draped by the splendor of the mountains, and I think, "Thank you God that this wonderful sight isn't random either..."

WHY IS LIFE SO HARD?

I just sat down to write a little blog in the comfort of my living room. I poured myself a nice glass of Cabernet and stared at the screen, wondering what to write. Just then my son Chris popped in and, in a moment of impulse, launched a pillow into the table that formerly housed my wine glass, shattering the glass and splattering red wine on the recliner, the brand new upholstered, khaki-colored dining room chair and the white cloth lamp shade. We did our best to clean up the mess, including locating all of the glass. It seems the chairs are fine, but the lampshade may have suffered a fatal loss! And in that frenetic moment it came to me, why is life so hard, or maybe, is it really hard?

Maybe we humans make the mistake of assigning meaning to things that have no meaning and focusing on the material things while never really regarding the vital and necessary things. Maybe we have been deluded into putting such high importance on our stuff; maintaining our stuff and getting new stuff yet neglecting those parts of life that have true meaning. As a functioning and ambitious member of the rat race, I like to be somewhere near the front of the line. Oh, I don't do it on purpose mind you, but this old world sucks me in at times. Maybe it's my age, maybe it's something else, but I like my things to be a certain way. I clean, I organize (Lord knows I organize), and I get indignant when someone dares to mess up my stuff. There's nothing wrong with taking care of your stuff, in fact it is a quality, but sometimes the people should come before your stuff. Is that a justification for pillow slinging? Of course not! But maybe, just maybe, my obsession with stuff takes precedence over the people, and when that occurs, I may have missed the mark! I'm sure when I'm on my deathbed I'd rather have Chris there than all of the upholstered chairs and lamps in the world! Why is life so hard? Well, sometimes it seems hard because you are focusing on the wrong stuff!

If you lived any amount of time on earth, you are well aware of the many challenges and pitfalls that are right around the corner waiting for you. Life can seem to be really scary. There's a multitude of things that can go wrong at any time. Oh sure, you plan and prepare and do your best, yet still things go south on you, and before you can even recognize it, you find yourself faced with stress-producing situations. You just want to control what you can, and by God, you do your utmost. Yet, they still appear. Hopefully, somewhere along the line it finally dawns on you that you just cannot control everything. And, I'm loathe to admit, you really control an infinitesimal amount of stuff. Take, for example, your adult children (yes, this includes Chris). When they were little it was duck soup. You watched over them like a hawk and decided exactly what they did and when. Now, however, you are no longer in control. You see them heading south (no, not Chris), and there's not a damn thing you can do about it. You have to rely on them to make good choices, and like you when you were their age, they don't always choose right. You don't want them to suffer but they will, and in that suffering sometimes learn a thing or two. Why is life so hard? Often it gets hard when you're trying to control things you cannot control.

Now comes perhaps the greatest single factor in making life seem so hard. Recently I attended a birthday party for one of my closest friends. I was sitting next to another old friend and proceeded to lament about this and that and how I so wanted this to happen and wouldn't it be great if that happened, etc. In his one-of-a-kind manner, he quietly commented, "Isn't that God's job..." There, in 5 words or less, was the answer to all of life's apparent complexities! Life is hard because you and I are busying ourselves into oblivion trying to do God's job while neglecting our own job, namely trusting Him. We are so smart, ya know? So smart, in fact, that we have become experts in what ought to happen and dum-dums in regard to how things really happen. Life, absent a true belief in God's abiding goodness, is frightfully hard. You can figure it out, you say? No, you can't! The proof of that? Your thinking that life is hard! It's hard because you are determined to do it all by yourself. You think, *I don't need GodI will just make a lot of money.* Well, the money you made comes from God whether you ever choose to acknowledge it or not! He is just that good! The trouble is that the same world that has you wrongly focused on your stuff and trying to control everything yourself is also extremely persistent in talking you out of who God is! If you knew who He really is was and what He really does, you would never have the audacity to utter that life is hard. Yes, you would face your share of challenges and even maybe more than your share, but in the end, you would still have overcome because God's job is to teach you how to overcome!

Life is hard, my friends, but only because you've been talked into trusting in yourself and not in the One that made you! Stuff gets messed up; new stuff is always out there; you want to control everything but cannot control hardly anything; you're tired and frustrated and anxious and afraid, yet amidst all that you can learn who God is, and in a moment of time change your mind and begin to understand, life isn't really hard, but instead it is my heart that has gotten hard. Ask

God to teach you something new and in the process enjoy that new, tender heart He is helping you to shape! You can bet your entire hard life on that one!

THE IMPOSSIBILITY OF THE CUMULATIVE LIFE

I think if you are honest with yourself, and honesty is important in learning how to successfully navigate life, most of your difficulties come from your thoughts. You drag around this massive corpse of a memory of things long past. Since the past no longer exists in anything but your mind, it shouldn't have such an impact on the person you are today. Now, I'm not referring to pleasant memories or past learning. I'm talking about the bad things or the weaknesses or issues you doggedly assign to yourself in the present. Maybe you did have trouble standing up for yourself when you were 12, but to stubbornly cling to that worn-out notion at age forty makes no sense. The reason this mountainous weight of a stone clings to your psyche is because you keep it alive in your mind by trying to live a cumulative life.

Have you ever made a New Year's resolution to lose weight or exercise more and then failed miserably shortly thereafter? Say what you want about discipline, losing weight and exercising more, though producing a cumulative effect, cannot be successfully undertaken with a cumulative mindset. In other words, you have to decide to eat less or healthier or exercise right now, today. The fact that you did what you said for the past three days guarantees nothing. The fact that you didn't do what you said you were going to do for the past three days means nothing either. What matters is right now. What can you do right now? If you can get really good at doing "right now," soon you will experience a cumulative effect!

For some reason, people have the hardest time living in the present. Assuming we all have weaknesses and areas in which we don't do so well, how could we ever possibly expect to change anything living entangled in a spaghetti bowl of multiplied yesterdays? Add to that trying to live in some future day, and now you are just a sloppy Joe (poured over spaghetti)!

God, if I may speak for Him, designed life to be lived right now in succinct 24-hour periods (the evening and the morning were the first day). Imagine the idea of having a bad day if the day lasted forever. But that's exactly how people live; one perpetually long day. Instead, each day is cleverly separated by night (sleep), and in the morning a new day begins. "Well, tomorrow is a new day!" Every new day is an opportunity for you to begin anew, fresh. What you did wrong yesterday generally has little bearing on your life, that is of course unless you allow it to. You allow it to by granting it "airplay." Yes, sure, you need to learn from whatever, but you aren't playing that track for any learning. You are re-playing it because you feel bad and are punishing yourself. But now listen closely for a moment here. Does any amount of self-flagellation make you a better person? Does your incessant focus on yesterday or a year ago or 10 years ago or your childhood or "that one thing" do anything to change it? It only exists in your mind. Your cumulative negative past doesn't have a blessed thing to do with your life right now! So, my friend, just let it go. Stop persisting in your perpetual bad day and start fresh.

When you decide to live right now, in the new day, you give yourself permission to begin again. Remember the first time you played a certain sport? You probably sucked, right? If you held the thought of how bad you sucked and never tried again, you'd still suck, I'm guessing. But, if you had the courage to start again and again and again, at some point you got pretty good. Your life is like that. Those negative images; those frightful memories do not serve the person you are today. They do just the opposite. They hold you back. God does not want you to be held back! Every day, every single day, He is giving you another fresh start. Shoot, He even sent His son to pay the price for everything you ever did wrong! Everything! You aren't doing God any favors by living in your past. Instead, you are stubbornly refusing His gift to you; a new beginning!

Life was not designed to be lived cumulatively. You are not the sum of everything you have ever done and not done. Instead, you are who you are right now, in this moment. *Right now* you can be a tremendous source of love, compassion and kindness. Oh, you weren't that yesterday? So what? Be it today. Well, up to now you haven't had much success? So what? Decide to be a success right now! What if I forget tomorrow? You never have to deal with tomorrow, only right now! If you live to be 80 years old, that means you have 29,219.4 days to live. How many days have you already wasted, caught up thinking about something that happened on day 10,957.3?

If you believe what I'm telling you, and I sure hope you do, you will begin to understand that life is to be lived one day at a time. Imagine how much weight will be lifted off your shoulders when you agree with God and focus your energy on today. Imagine how sweet your life can become by making this day the best ever and refusing to let yesterday creep in. Imagine... huh?

The cumulative life is an impossible life!

You are who you are today. Don't let anyone (even yourself) tell you otherwise...

OUR MESSY LIFE

Our modern electronic era guarantees that we are going to be fed a multitude of images and words about how the ideal life should be. We become convinced of this image regarding how life should work what we should have and what we should be able to do. In this Hollywood version of life, difficulties are usually solved and almost everyone gets a happy ending (LOL, not that kind!). Yet, despite being daily bombarded with these images daily, life is really quite messy when you get right down to it. Things don't always work out as planned. There are obstacles, setbacks, and challenges. There are illnesses, frustrations and seemingly unsolvable problems. We face challenging detours, and changing environments, in a world that takes another form as soon as we figure out the last one. Real life is messy.

Have you ever wondered why things are the way they are? Seems to me that we could get along so much easier if we didn't have to deal with all this mess. I mean, imagine a world where there was no pain; no suffering. Imagine if everything you attempted was supremely successful and things always worked out. Think how awesome it would be if you got everything you ever wanted, and it came easily without stress and strain. Imagine...

It makes me chuckle when people think that because I love God, things always go in my favor. It's like, life with God means not having to deal with problems. Or worse, quote a few scriptures over the trouble and it immediately goes away.

Or, say a quick prayer and disaster is averted. That could not be further from the truth and perhaps a major reason the world thinks most Christians are nuts! We believer types face the same obstacles and challenges everyone else faces. We get pushed and pulled out of sorts; we get frustrated and at times even defeated. You see, God never promised that life would be without struggles. What He promised is that He would help you (and me) overcome any challenge that comes our way. In other words, He will help us clean up our messy life. God is love and, as such, is only good to people and incredulously just as good to "bad" people as He is to "good" people. Ponder that for a minute...

The reason our lives are messy is because we have an adversary, an opposing spiritual force that is ever at work to screw things up. And, whether you think he exists or not, is working on you to make a mess of your life. He steals your prosperity. He convinces you; that you aren't good enough for God or His blessings. He ruins your relationships. Every evil or bad thing that every person ever did was based on his influence. He is behind all sickness, disease and death. He makes the mental prisons you find yourself in and specializes in frustration. He gets you addicted and makes the ruts that are so hard to escape from. He promises you that things will be so much better if you can find this person or get that job or move to a new place. He convinces you that if you follow his ways, you will get the happiness you so ardently desire. The problem is that he is ALWAYS lying to you, and when you follow his advice it burns you 100 percent of the time, in every case, always. And still, behind all of his shenanigans, most folks don't even think he exists. Well, he does, and your life is only a mess because of it.

On the contrary, God is ever at work to show you what is real and to reveal the true source of your problems. The problem with problems is that we think we can use the same thinking to escape them that got us into them in the first place. Our difficulty persists because we haven't yet discovered the true cause. God is able to show you the true cause! Because God is all-knowing, He can completely and totally eradicate the difficulty. Yet we fail to get the answers we so desperately need because we either think we know better (according to our limited understanding); or dismiss the answers we do get in a variety of forms. When God answers the question or provides a solution, it is a full and complete solution. God's deliverance is very real and available to anyone who dares to believe. Don't you want to get things straightened out? I know you do.

This messy life we find ourselves living can be thoroughly straightened out. There are answers and deliverance from anything that ever plagued you. With God, nothing is impossible! Stop settling for life's "good enough." Stop concluding that every feeling and thought you have must be true. Stop rationalizing your problems away or distracting yourself from dealing with them. Instead seek; truly seek the real solution from God! He wants to help you more than you even want to be helped, but you have to meet Him halfway with some humility.

This life is way too short to live in a perpetual mess. Put away your broom and your cleaning rags and get the help you need. You owe yourselves that much, don't you think?

Just an anecdote to a messy life...

DOES LIFE REALLY THROW YOU CURVEBALLS?

Have you ever been warned to be ready for what life might throw at you? You suffer some huge disappointment and they say that's just life, right? "Yeah, life really threw me a curveball on that one!" Oh, I realize it is just an expression, like saying I've got sunshine in my soul, but you have to wonder what might be behind that expression. I mean, is there something about life we don't understand that leads to the occasional off-speed pitch being hurled in our direction? Nothing in the creation is haphazard or random, even if it appears to be that way. Everything in nature follows a distinct, well-defined order, and even though that order doesn't produce straight lines, it is still an intelligent order. So, in the midst of that breathtaking order, could life secretly be involved in disorder?

The answer to the question can be found in our understanding of how life came about. For example, if you think life is purely biological and somehow evolved out of nothing, you are likely to be deluged with wicked curveballs that don't just cause strikes but rather bean you in the head. Denying the existence of God and spiritual things doesn't change their existence any more than not believing in an as yet undiscovered species denies its existence. It already exists. You just don't know about it yet. Life in its most basic form is spiritual. The spiritual preceded the physical. As such, the physical always points back to the spiritual and not the other way around. Life is the creative expression of God, and He is the architect behind it. The absence of God means the absence of life. But if life is present, so is God. Haha, okay, before I lose you in my spiritual musings, let me explain it this way. Life as an expression of God's creativity is not in the business of throwing unusual pitches at you. (Are you happy now? We are back to baseball!) Life's order is very predictable, although almost infinite in variety. Life isn't happening to you; you are happening within it. So why do we at times feel like life isn't cooperating with us, or worse, is actually trying to hurt us? The answer is found in our understanding of the spiritual realm.

The spiritual realm is composed of two sources. One source, God, is life and light and love. He cannot ever be the opposite, no matter what anyone has told you before. In terms of existence, He always has been and always will be. (WARNING: DO NOT TRY TO WRAP YOUR MIND AROUND THAT ONE!) The other source is more of a Johnny-come-lately creature. He (it) hasn't always been around, but in the time he has been around (after choosing to separate from Light) has honed his skills as a pitcher to a magnificent level of expertise. He has learned precisely how humans tend to think and behave and uses what man thinks he knows or doesn't know against him to produce curveballs that would have earned him the Cy Young award had he been allowed to pitch. In fact, he has done such a fantastic job that you don't even know he is pitching and worse, blame life instead. Well, I'm here to tell you folks it ain't life that is after you! Fortunately, there is a way to still get hits no matter what gets thrown at you. That way is found by taking the time to learn about the spiritual realm.

The first and most important step is in learning who God is and what He will do for you. If your picture of Him is some weird, bearded guy with a large bat (forgive me) waiting to bash you in the head for running out of the baseline, you aren't going to win in life. If you have imagined He is some nebulous, mysterious being doing random acts of disaster (called acts of

God) or inexplicably killing off loved ones; never answering or even hearing your prayers, chances are you are batting .ooo. You just haven't done your research yet. If God is truly perfect, He cannot be contradictory. He can't be light one day and dark the next (as that would make Him partly cloudy-smile). Thus, you owe it to yourself to find out who He really is.

Once you finally start to get it, you'll discover that life never threw you a curveball; the adversary did! Life was never designed to be fraught with disappointment, heartache and tragedy! The problems came because of decisions that people made (with their sovereign free will) in choosing to believe what that *pseudo Cy Young* said over what God actually said. Then lots of people started getting beaned in their heads and still don't know who is really throwing at them and, as such, cannot charge the mound.

So, don't let that be your life story! For goodness sakes, take some time to learn. If you want to learn it (He) will be right there for you. Shoot, you will get so good that you will know what the next pitch is going to be before it even happens. And, for those times when you didn't see it coming, God will still be right there to heal you up and get you back out onto the field.

Does life really throw you curveballs? Of course not, but if one comes your way, why not knock it out of the park?

Thanks be unto God who always causes us to triumph in Christ!

And that pitch is outta here...

THE BEAUTY AND ENJOYMENT
OF THE SIMPLE LIFE

A great man once said that the zest of living is increased in simplicity. Yet, how often do we think it is just the opposite? Have you ever stopped to think about the things "you think" would make you the happiest? You see a huge house in the foothills and think, wouldn't it be great if I lived there? Would it? How much space do you really need in a house? Oh, I'm not promoting the tiny shoebox either, as there is such a thing as too little space. I'm talking about too much. My home has exactly 3,500 square feet of living space. During the holidays, we have been known to actually go into the basement, wherein is the magnificent mancave and stay there longer than 30 seconds. The rest of the year... not so much. So, what's the point? That no one should have 3,500 square feet? Hardly! The point is that the arrangement of the space (four bedrooms) worked perfectly when we had four kids at home, but not so perfectly now that we have no kids at home.

Okay, back to the gargantuan house in the foothills. Do you know what you would do with that 10,000 square foot home? You would use approximately 25 percent of it and the rest would sit there as a testimony to just how successful you are. You see, what you are really after is that symbol of success. But, to earnestly pursue it and then to pay $7,000 a month for it won't seem to make as much sense. It seems much of life in the United States works this way. The large SUV in the driveway is more of a status symbol than a practical form of transportation. I know this because it is almost too large for the garage; gets 12 miles to the gallon; has tires that cost $500 each, and requires very large parking spaces. So, should everyone scale down their desires, get the condo and a Smart Car? Definitely not! My manhood wouldn't let me buy the Smart Car even after the vasectomy. My (most likely lost) point here is that the beauty and enjoyment of life is ironically found in the simple and not in the complicated. Do you vaguely remember the old TGI-Friday's menu? There were about 20 pages grouped according to certain themes. The problem was that there were so many options we didn't know what to think. And, by the time I got to the salads, I had long since forgotten what I was leaning towards earlier. "Ummmm... could you give us a few more minutes?" There is such a thing as too many options. Have you ever taken a close look at your closet? I'm guessing (see, I don't even know) that I have about 25 pairs of pants. Wait, that doesn't include suit pants. I also guess that I probably wear about three to four pairs on a regular basis. There are those jeans I like; those 'casual pants' I like, etc. Towards the back there are all those pants I don't like. Why are they still there? Who knows? Dieters have all heard the catchy slogan that says, "nothing tastes as good as the first bite." How many times do we gorge ourselves trying to replicate the taste of that first bite? How many delicious entrées are available at the Thanksgiving Day feast? How many do you enjoy? And what about the desserts? By the time they show up I am a bite away from vomiting. How about my beloved red wine? I'm standing at the kitchen counter, steaks are grilling outside, and people are starting to arrive for the dinner party. I pour a glass of Cabernet and have a few delightful sips. The "sparkle" of the wine kicks in and suddenly, God is good, life is good, and I couldn't be happier. Then I finish my glass and have another and then another and then another. What happened to my sparkle? It is replaced by a numb glaze that I now must dutifully maintain the rest of the night. Is that what I was after? Not really. What I was after and am still after is the "sparkle" of the first glass. I think life is like that. Everyone seeking after the "sparkle" of those first, novel experiences.

Everyone loves to go on a vacation, right? What is the 'oh-so' glorious allure of a vacation? Well, for me when I go on vacation, I like to go somewhere that is warm and preferably has a beach. And, of the multitude of things you could do on a vacation, what do I personally want to do? I want to go and sit down on the beach, read my book and enjoy a cocktail. Simplicity!

Happiness isn't made in the many, it is made in the few. It is produced in simple enjoyment. A walk on the trail in the evening with someone you love; sitting on the back deck basking in the sunshine with a great book; a hike in the canyon on your way to the waterfall; these are the things that inspire beauty and enjoyment in us. A single man boasts that he enjoys being with many different women and that he can have a new woman every night. Yet, how much happier will he be with one woman whom he loves and who loves him, that he gets to share life's experiences with every day? You see, we all think we require so much when in reality we require so little. We buy a new home and sit down for dinner with our little family and think to ourselves, *could my life be any better?* Yet, all that changed was the location and design of our residence. In the midst of a very strict diet, there's nothing quite so tasty and so grand as a gummy multi-vitamin. But, when eating returns to normal, our perspective changes dramatically.

All of us should seek to get back to the simplicity of life. Simplify our desires, simplify our tastes and enjoy the little things. At the end of life, no one remembers the new car, the new house, the size of the bank account. What we remember is the smile on our daughter's face when we told her how pretty and smart she was or how proud we were of her for graduating from college. We recall the joy in the eyes of our son as he received his first offer to play Division One football, his lifelong dream. We think how could we ever love our second grandson as much as we love the first one, yet somehow, we do. We acquiesce and joy that our oldest son faithfully takes his siblings under his wing and steers them away from life's dangers.

Life is simple. Love God, love other people and rejoice in the beauty and enjoyment that is waiting around every corner for us when we look beyond the clutter and confusion of things and discover what life is really all about. So simple, really...

I HOPE YOU DANCE

I came across these beautiful lyrics today and was tenderly re-minded that no matter where your life may be heading with its twists and turns, there is always hope for a wonderful fu-ture. And, much of what has happened to you in the past exists now only in your memory, and even that is often undistin-guished and unreliable. Certain setbacks and hardships color your past experiences with unfair brushstrokes overly shaded on the difficulties. Childhood wishes and dreams were formed in the heart of a child and not within the ripened experience of an adult. So, no matter where you are today and whatever you are going through, I hope you find your life and your hap-piness again. I hope you dance...

"I Hope You Dance"

I hope you never lose your sense of wonder
You get your fill to eat but always keep that hunger
May you never take one single breath for granted
God forbid love ever leave you empty-handed

I hope you still feel small when you stand beside the ocean
Whenever one door closes, I hope one more opens
Promise me that you'll give faith a fighting chance
And when you get the choice to sit it out or dance

I hope you dance, I hope you dance

I hope you never fear those mountains in the distance
Never settle for the path of least resistance
Livin' might mean takin' chances but they're worth takin'
Lovin' might be a mistake but it's worth makin'

Don't let some hell-bent heart leave you bitter
When you come close to sellin' out reconsider
Give the heavens above more than just a passing glance
And when you get the choice to sit it out or dance

Dance, I hope you dance...
~ By Lee Ann Womack

All of us begin our lives in the same way. In front of us lies an enormous ocean of possibilities; we have only to find them and live them. Our young hearts, not yet distracted by the worries and concerns of life, are unshackled and free to experience. Our focus is singular and clear, unashamed and in harmony with our highest good. We seek in earnest the things that make us happy and shun those that do not. We believe unreservedly for the good in life, unaware of the alternatives. In childhood, life is simple and full of wonder. Yet something happens to people as the years go by, and what was once simple and free is no longer free nor simple. The challenges of life, when combined over a lifetime, can take away your zest for living and dim your gleaming shine. You can lose sight of the very essence of life and become encumbered in what might have been or what you could have done. The world is often a cruel teacher leading you to forget life's sweetest lessons and instead instructs and shapes your failures in the hopes of their continuance. But, the wonder of life, the passion, the opportunity, the promise hasn't gone away; it has just been obstructed from your view. What you felt once you can feel again when you become clear that life hasn't changed, you have. I hope you dance.

Of all of the frightful things that could happen to a man or a woman, nothing is more destructive and painful than giving up on life. Living your life, a shadow of your former self, banished to the sidelines, without God and without hope, is the most miserable way to live. Yet, people live this way day in and day out. They have sacrificed the joy of life for a paycheck or for approval, or to make someone else's life a pleasure. They willingly cash in their hopes and dreams for someone else's dream. They think they cannot so they do not. They become so accustomed to disappointment that they expect it and in expecting, live it. They rely on other people's judgments and no longer trust their own. Seeing a good thing that they love, that they could do, they refuse waiting for permission. And in so doing, they cease living. Your life is yours alone and what makes its appeal to you, to you alone, it appeals. You've lost your energy for life because you no longer seek what energizes you, but trade it in for another's life force. Finding your way back depends not so much on locating the path but on finding *your* path again. There is a way that exists only for you. To think yourself a part of the masses and conforming with those masses spells the end of you, the you, you seek to rediscover. No matter what complexities have enveloped your life, you will find yourself with simplicity in those things most appealing to you. Pursue them with vigor! I hope you dance...

Every day you have a choice in how you are going to live. To say you have no choice is never true. Life is full of new things to learn; things that take your breath away; things that bring tears to your eyes. The wonder of life cannot be over-worked or completed. There is infinitely more life to live than you have the capacity to experience. All of this God created for you. It remains there waiting for you to once again, discover it. Walk away from all of your disappointments and hurts. Let go of all the fears and insecurities. Take a chance that your life is worth the living. You have nothing to lose and everything to gain. Your memories, be they sublime or distressing, are just memories and do not hold the power to write your future. You do. And when you choose, I hope you dance!

Give the heavens above more than just a passing glance. And in doing so, I know you will dance.

SLOW DOWN TO THE SPEED OF LIFE

All of this social distancing and requirements to stay home have inadvertently provided us with some important clues about how we have been living our lives. Most of us are moving too damn fast. We have so many things to do, much of which are self-inflicted, too many obligations, too many commitments. We have been literally running for our lives from thing to thing, activity to activity, trying to get it all done, and by all, I mean everything we have read we should be doing. In between all of our "must-dos," we fill the remaining moments with our televisions, binge-watching Netflix series coupled with our incessant need to check Instagram and Facebook and whatever else pops us to use our every remaining moment. Like an addict, we have been convinced we need something else like non-stop activity to be okay. God forbid we should have nothing to do! The things we do, we don't do properly or give our full attention. We ram and cram and make do, ever trying to get to the next moment, the next fun time, the next vacation. And while we are being completely preoccupied, we have stopped thinking and dreaming and planning desirable future moments. We no longer have time to get to the bottom of our issues. We don't have time to think, or so we think. Someone convinced us we have to figure everything out for ourselves and work harder and do more, etc. We are driving ourselves crazy. We need to slow down and return to the speed of life.

There was a time when we didn't have the Internet or, for that matter, TV (or TV consisted of three channels, and they all went off around midnight). We didn't know what everyone was doing at all times, and it was good for us. The news we did get was very limited, reserved for the big things that threatened our happiness. Today we devour the bad news, filling our minds with it in excess under the guise that we are keeping ourselves informed. How much more do you want to know about the virus? How much more is there to know? It's not education; it is fear being fueled and fed by more fear. It's no wonder the world runs on anxiety. The world can appear to be a scary place, but how much more so when your mind is constantly being filled with all of the things that can get you? That's maybe why we are so dang busy. If we take time to slow down, we might actually have to deal with it all. But, dealing with it is exactly what you need to do. You have to take time to do something with your mind about the things that are bothering you. You HAVE to deal with them. I know you would rather not. Me neither. But, like any obstacle impeding your happiness, you have to take them on and move the roadblocks from your path. They aren't going to move themselves no matter how busy you make your life. Slow down, breathe and take the time you need to get things straight. Get things clear. TAKE THE TIME. You cannot get to the next place until you learn to overcome the challenges in your current place. Slow down, people and learn to live again.

Life was never designed to be this frenetic experience where you run from thing to thing, from pillar to post, hoping you end up somewhere good. Life is full of variables and things that need your attention, many of which aren't monumental. Sometimes I muse that God is more pleased that you took the time to fold your sweater than He is with all of your super accomplishments; that you took the time to organize that harassing evil called your sock drawer over all the money you donated. Don't you see it? Your only requirement is what the day demands of you, and whatever that is, that you invest your whole heart fully into its accomplishment. Call your mother. Clean out the closet. Write the poem. Tell someone who has been on your heart how much they mean to you. Buy someone a gift instead of the gift card. Think! Make time for yourself to think and consider. What has been eating at you lately? What, like a splinter, is under your skin? You can either get it out or wait for the infection. But, either way, it has got to come out. The unseen problem with the frenetic life is that you don't have time to handle you! You haven't given yourself an opportunity to get you straight. But, trust me on this one, you have to be straight before you can get anything else straight. Murky and confused isn't going to get the job done. Clarity and clear perception gets the job done. Slow down and get things straight.

Slowing down to the speed of life is about getting back on God's wavelength. God is not in a hurry. God doesn't miss anything, ever. He isn't running you around like a squirrel, herky-jerky, flitting around, full of anxiety and care. He is calm and relaxed and sure of everything. He wants you to feel the same way. He doesn't require that you know all the answers, but rather acknowledge that He does and, in so knowing, lay it all on Him. Everything that ever bothered you bothers Him when it isn't resolved in your life. Like any good parent, He wants you to be happy. He already knows what has been screwing you up and exactly what you need to know and do to make it stop. But, in order for you to know, you have to give Him a little time. You have to slow down in your quest for self and trust someone outside of yourself. You need time to think. You need time to pray. God is bigger than any virus!

Stop running, man. Stop dashing, lady. Stop letting fear dominate and rule your existence. There's an infinitely better way and you can find it (Him) by slowing down to the speed of life...

Y.O.L.O. (YOU ONLY LIVE ONCE)

Forgive me for overworking the *YOLO* cliché, but I've got something to say that I know will help you live a little better. If you think about how many times people use that cliché and its context, you'll find something very interesting. Almost every time we say it, we are making some reference to getting rid of our fear of doing something with a complimentary urge to "do it" right now. We are saying that life is too short to not do the things you really want to do. So, as you can imagine, that arrested my attention.

How much time do you spend doing things you really don't want to do? Or, how many things do you do because you think they are what others expect you to do? Or, stated in the positive, do you spend most of your time doing the things you enjoy doing, have passion about and want to do? And, of course, closely related to those questions, why are you doing the things you are doing?

As I've said 100 times prior, this old-world system funnels us into well-worn grooves of expectations. The subtle and not-so-subtle message is to get in line, shut your mouth and don't buck the system. Do acceptable work; make acceptable comments; have acceptable opinions (not your own opinions, but the popular ones); and for goodness sakes, don't start questioning things. If a thing doesn't make sense to you, it's not because it doesn't make sense, but rather because you don't understand it – so again, close your mouth and get in agreement (now!). The problem with that "go-along to get-along" mindset is that you no longer get to be "you" in the process. Now on the surface, you may not think this applies to you, so I ask you to give it a little more thought.

People are employed in a line of work they hate for decades. Folks are suppressed in unhealthy relationships or subject themselves to unhealthy family members for a lifetime. We laugh when it's not funny. We say the food tastes good when it doesn't. We nod in agreement to insane political ideas when those views couldn't be further from our own. We don't play the music we like when others are around. We get college degrees in subjects we cannot stand. We tip waiters for poor service. We devote time to reading books we don't enjoy. We trudge ourselves to tired church services and participate in nonsensical observances and even pray to a God we neither know nor understand. Why? Because we are afraid, that's why! Fear, wrongly confused with terror, is a subtle beast. We can all recognize the fright we feel when we see a tiger, but do we acknowledge the slipperier version that causes us to do all of the above? Why would a man work in a job he loathed for 20 years? He's afraid that he can't do anything else? He's afraid of what his family would say if he quit? He's afraid of what society might say if he stepped out of line? Why do folks put up with family members that are toxic and discourage their growth? Because they are afraid of what everyone would think if they stopped coming around. Fear. (Disclaimer - this does not refer to my family.) We agree, we cajole, we acquiesce, we agree because we're so friendly? Probably not when you get right down to it. Fear drives a multitude of things we feel obligated to do. Then there is obligation's close companion - guilt. Guilt is just another form of fear manifesting itself as something you need to do because of something you didn't do; should have done; or to avoid something because of what you did do (or perceive you might have done)! Fear...

I'm certainly not advocating morphing into a self-centered

douche, parading around town looking out only for number one! I'm suggesting rather that you take the time to consider why you do the things you do. There really are only two great motives in life - love and fear. Love works no ill to its neighbor (or to you either, for that matter). Fear starts bad, proceeds bad, and ends bad. Working out of fear leads to misery. Working out of love fans the flames of passion. Saying how you feel out of love leads to understanding, agreement and resolution. Saying how you feel out of fear leads to arguments and conflict. Doing things for other people out of love is the very heart of service. Doing things for people out of fear leads to slavery and bondage, and all kinds of mistreatment.

So, the simple acid test is to ask yourself why you are doing the thing that you are doing. Do you want to do it? If you had a million bucks, would you still do it? I'm sure we all have the fantasy of all the wonderful things we would do if we just became rich enough to do it. And the reason we cannot do it now? Fear... And while you are asking yourself these things in the solemn privacy of your mind, take solace in the truth that you can change anything you want to change. Sure, folks will deride you and chastise you and demand you get back to being who you are supposed to be! But what you owe yourself is to be the "you" you really want to be! Don't you think? People live frustrated, defeated, unsatisfied lives because they spend their precious lives living as someone else. Don't let that be you, my friend.

Cliché alert - At the end of the day, we all have only one life to live, and we all only live once (on earth anyway). Start today by asking yourself why and then get busy modifying and changing what needs to change. You ought to be able to be "you," doing "you" in the ways that make "you" the happiest! YOLO, my friends, YOLO!

WHAT ARE YOU LOOKING FOR IN LIFE?

Have you ever asked yourself exactly what it is you are looking for in life? What are you after? What do you want? Where are you going? Deep questions indeed, but are they? Some people, it seems, aren't looking for anything at all. Others are looking for something but in all the wrong places. And some blessed individuals are looking for and seeing clearly what they want and how to go about getting it. Which one are you?

Life in its basic essence is all about movement. Nothing that God has made stays the same. It is always in a state of flux, always growing or dying, always thriving or decaying. Nothing remains the same, and it is impossible to stand still physically or mentally unless, of course, you are dead. And sadly, some people die long before they are dead. Oh, I get it! I know what happens to you if you've lived long enough. The system of things sort of gets to you. You can get terribly disillusioned and disheartened by how things have turned out. Lost hopes, dissolved dreams, little or nothing to look forward to, mar the portals of your mind. Pretty soon and unbeknownst to you, all the doors and windows have been shut, leaving you alone in some empty, dark place with seemingly little opportunity for change. So, there you sit, exasperated and done with it all. You've checked out. You've cashed in your chips. You've played your hand and lost. But, have you really lost? Has life really stopped for you, or have you stopped doing life? Have the doors and windows of your soul been barricaded shut forever, or is it just an illusion? Has your fire been snubbed out, or is there still a flicker waiting for you to fan it? The system, the wheel of things may be iron clad, but there is still, and always will be a greater force, waiting for you to ask the right question, make the sincere request, and seek solemn help outside of yourself to recover your missing life. It doesn't matter how old you are. It matters what you believe and do...

Many people, busied, harried and distracted by things in life, are looking for their precious life in all the wrong places. They haven't stopped moving but instead are moving in the wrong direction. They are seeking things that aren't true, were never true and will never be true. They have believed the Hollywood version of life; a life where you can have your cake and eat it too; a life where your personal decisions and actions carry no weight; a life where you can do what you want, when you want, however you want without any regard for anyone else involved. They have foolishly put themselves first, second, third and every place thereafter. They think the "good life" is found in money and fame and fortune, which they pursue to their own demise. Oh, I understand them as well. The deception they follow has been artfully crafted. It is paraded on television, promoted on social media, wished for and worshipped. It is a life of ease and good times. It's a life where you no longer have to work and produce, but instead can tell your soul to take its ease and simply enjoy. But, can you really enjoy it? Like the poor folks that have stopped moving forward, seduced and deceived, you too will stop moving forward. Once you stop producing, however small, you will find yourself miserable and unhappy. The joy of life is found in the pursuit. You do not ever arrive to remain forever. You get to your destination to discover your next destination. There is nothing wrong with the money or the fame or the fortune unless they become your end point, unless they become about you and about you alone. All of us know how easy it is to get pushed or pulled off course, and all of us have done it. The measure of your life is not found in how many mistakes you made or didn't make, but rather in your willingness to get back on track, your willingness to find the right path, your willingness to admit you have gone astray. You can find it if you really want to find it...

Finally, we have all encountered that one guy or that one girl. They know exactly what they want and are busy about making it happen. We admire them, we feel jealousy towards them, we laud them and we revere them. We think they must have something special or enjoy favor we don't enjoy. We don't see that they are people just like we are people. We don't see their doubts and fears; we just see their results. We don't see their dogged persistence, but instead call them lucky. We don't regard their efforts, but instead conclude they must have had advantages we didn't receive. Their success comes because they move forward. They have setbacks, they have disappointments, they fail, but they keep moving forward. They have learned by trial and error, by steadfast endeavor, by strong beliefs, that the way to achieve, the way to acquire your dreams, the way to reach every goal is simply to never allow yourself to stop moving towards it. Oh, they might pause, maybe pushed off track, may feel disheartened, but they get back up and get themselves moving again! They don't have access to the secret or to some inside track; it is more simple than that. Any worthwhile thing in your life will require effort and sacrifice on your part to bring it to pass. Life requires effort, not thought alone, effort! You make no moves; you get no results. How many people are waiting for something to happen without doing anything to make things happen? How many people wish and dream and fantasize, but never get around to any concrete action? Life is about movement and effort, however small. Believing without any action is dead. If you want anything, anything at all, you have to act on it. You supply the effort. You don't get to see the second step until you take the first step. You don't start at the top; you start at the bottom. But, you have to start! God is so good that even if you make all the wrong moves trying to reach a goal, your movement will be rewarded with learning, leading to the right moves. But, make no mistake, you have got to move! It's there for you, it's there for me, but we have to make the moves.

What are you looking for in your life? What are you after? What do you want? Where are you going? The answers to these questions may not always be clear, but one thing is clear. If you want anything in your life, you have to supply the effort to get it. You have to move. You have to act. You... you... you! If you have been broken down and defeated, God can heal you, but you have to move. If you find yourself woefully off-track, God can get you on track if you are willing to move. Keep moving, keep acting, keep taking steps, even baby steps, because life, your life, will always be found in movement. If you are still alive, you always have a chance to win. Just move forward...

UNFULFILLED? MY LITTLE PRETTIES...

Many people nowadays are suffering from feeling unfulfilled. In other words, you feel as if your life isn't going in the right direction or is lacking in one or more categories. You aren't sure what exactly the remedy is, but you do know that you're stuck. So, the question of the day is, "What causes us to 'feel' unfulfilled?" Is it something that happens to us, like life? Or is it something we are doing to ourselves? Is there a problem with our expectations or our perceptions? Is it permanent and terminal? Or is there something we can do about it? Hopefully I can answer these and many more questions if you will just stick with me - my little pretties...

Picture that your mind is like a large warehouse. It's your own private storage place for your thoughts. There's temporary storage for certain thoughts, longer-range storage for important thoughts and beliefs, and permanent storage for things that you never want to lose. It is truly a marvelous thing - your mind. I mean, think about it. How many thoughts do you think in a day? A conservative estimate is 50,000 thoughts a day, 350,000 a week, 18,200,000 a year. And if you are my age, oh Lord, don't even do the math!

Now, of those 50,000 you are working on today, of how many of them are you even aware? My guess is very few. And to take it one step further, if you are not even remotely aware of them, can you tell how many are entering into your warehouse? Sure, it would be all peaches and roses if they just went away, but they don't just go away. They enter the shelves (un-marked of course) and seek to work their way into the more glamorous and important longer-range storage. From there they can take up residency as your beliefs and slowly but imperceptibly start controlling your life. Then you get all down and dissatisfied with the warehouse you control. You blame God and life and your spouse, your lack of opportunities, yet remain ignorant to the reality that the warehouse still belongs to you!

Day by day you think, "What am I doing with my life? What's the point of this? Why even bother? I'm never going to be anything or do anything!" Then, you think that over and over and over again. The more you entertain it, the more evidence you start to compile that seems to confirm it. Your friend Bill is doing so well. In fact, everyone is doing so well, except for Sally. I'm at least better than Sally (smile). Your storage unit is alive with a multitude of new products. But you didn't know they were coming, much less order them. Yet, there they are, seeking advancement. You see? You've almost unknowingly thought that stupid stuff for so long that you are starting to believe it. And to add insult to injury, while you are simmering and brooding, you aren't doing a damn thing to change the situation! After all, what's the point? So, I'm wagering that very often it isn't your life that is so unfulfilling, but rather your thoughts toward it...

Fulfilled is defined as *to be happy or satisfied due to fully developing one's ability or character*. That's worth thinking about a little deeper (50,001, 50,002, 50,003). Who the hell is ever satisfied these days? Your life is something your ancestors would have died for (and many did), yet you need more, more, more. It seems that another potential cause for feeling unfulfilled is never being satisfied about what you already enjoy. I know, I know, our American culture sort of did that to you! But good grief, stop pursuing every once in a while and take time to enjoy for a minute.

However, you may not be caught up in the more, more, more club. (♫ More, more, more, how do you like it, how do you like it? ♫) You may just recognize that you have so much more ability to develop. Now track with me here. If you know that to be true, it seems your focus should be on further developing your abilities. Storing up a multitude of bad thoughts of frustration and dissatisfaction serves only to halt your progress. Where should you start? What are you good at now? Start there and get busy developing. Did you catch that? The definition refers to you fully developing, as in a process that doesn't just happen tomorrow. Work on it now. You may be a good distance from your goal, but you are working on it and thus can feel fulfilled. What is crazier than whining about not feeling fulfilled and yet doing nothing to become fulfilled? It's your warehouse, by God!

I think you will find out quite quickly that the nagging in your soul is an urge to start doing something now. Don't worry about how it is going to end. Instead focus on enjoying the journey. You will always be develop-*ing,* so you may as well enjoy it. I'm sure when you are 85, you won't be angry with yourself for not reaching master perfection status, but you will regret never even having tried.

Feelings of frustration, discontent and not being fulfilled come from the eight million little bits of data you didn't notice or resist. Don't allow the mindless ways of today rob you from accomplishing all you could accomplish. You may not be able to control every thought, but you can dang sure confront the little liars and set them straight! Imagine what your warehouse might look like if most of its storage were thoughts that actually helped and encouraged you.

Feeling unfulfilled is not a terminal condition. It can and will change as soon as you decide it will, because, my little pretties, it is your warehouse...

DO THE PEBBLES IN THE BROOK
MAKE IT SING?

I'm sure you've heard the expression, "It's the pebbles in the brook that makes it sing," right? In other words, without those little obstacles located throughout the water, we wouldn't enjoy the sweet sounds of the water flowing downstream. And while I love the metaphor (who am I kidding, I love all metaphors!), there's something in that message we have to keep straight.

I recently read a post on a friend's Facebook page that basically derided our incessant focus on happiness for a more "realistic" focus on "real life," complete with sadness, difficulties and obstacles. In other words, without the hardships and negative sides of life, we could not be complete and whole. And that little beauty got me thinking... I mean, if the pebbles in the brook make it sing, maybe we need the negative side of life in order to enjoy the good? I mean, how would we know the good if we didn't know the bad? I mean, how can we appreciate our health without experiencing times of sickness and pain? Hmmm... Quite a conundrum, it seems.

"Don't get it twisted!" he exclaims with righteous indignation, spilling his glass of wine! Goodness is never dependent upon bad to do its job! The Yin and the Yang are a philosopher's invention that while recognizing the duality of life, fails to see the reality behind it. You see, there's a gross generalization that is sweeping the earth today, namely that everything that happens comes from the hand of God (or the universe or the earth), etc. And that generalization gains access to your mind by counting on the fact that you won't look any deeper than the cliché! How many times have you read something like, "God is allowing all this evil to come upon me because He knows I'm strong enough to handle it?" Or, "God must be using this horrible suffering to teach me a greater lesson!" Egads! God doesn't need evil to make you a better person. God doesn't use negatives to make us appreciate the positives. Again, egads! Wouldn't that be like me refusing to feed one of my children when they were hungry to make them appreciate the value of having food? People go to jail for that kind of behavior, and yet we say it about God without even flinching. Can you honestly imagine (think now, don't just go back to what someone told you before) that a God of pure love would purposely screw with you to teach you a lesson? Maybe give you a little cancer to make you humble? Or worse, kill the people you love for some mysterious reason you will understand later in the great by and by? Really?

God says His people are destroyed for a lack of knowledge. Not understanding the spiritual world leads to a lot of heartache and pain. There are **two** spiritual forces at work in the world today, one for good and one for evil. And it may be a bitter pill to swallow, but God never did anything evil to anyone ever. He is light and in Him is NO DARKNESS AT ALL! The reality is that we have all been sold a bill of goods. We have become trained to expect bad things to happen and thus, without knowing, open the door to all kinds of calamity. "Hey, you win some, you lose some." "That's just life." "Maybe it was just his time to go." What all these things have in common is a vague belief that life was supposed to be some good and some bad. Some happiness, some suffering. Yet, God is incapable of evil, so what gives?

In the beginning, God placed a man and woman in

paradise. There was no suffering. There was no death. There was no evil. There was no fear. Yet when they unknowingly chose an evil alternative (as folks often do), evil was introduced to the world. And we are still living under the effects of that evil to this day. But, there's a day coming when there will no longer be any such thing as evil, so how can we conclude that good needs evil to function?

You get it? The pebbles in the brook do make it sing, just as God is able to work with our many obstacles and challenges to help us sing. But, God doesn't need the pebbles, H; he just works with what is. God would never test you with evil to make you stronger or build your character. However, He is able to strengthen you against that evil which does build character. But, don't get it twisted, H; he doesn't need the negatives. In fact, He would rather we learn without all the pain, but we humans tend to be quite hard-headed (and hard-hearted). So, He works with what is. (Isn't God grand?)

So, I'm beseeching you, don't allow the logic of the world to convince you that suffering is normal, part of life or necessary! You don't have to pay the price or go through the bad to get to the good. You don't have to accept sickness and disease as normal. Evil isn't normal; it's an aberration! God intended for you to be happy, healthy, prosperous, vibrant and full of life! He doesn't need obstacles, harassment and suffering to get you there. He just needs *you* to believe what He says.

At the end of the day, what makes us whole and complete and entire is love. 'Whole things' aren't full of cracks and potholes. And while we may experience the negatives of life, just remember they are never God's will, and if you will look for Him, He will always show you the way back to love; back to peace of mind; back to His perfect wholeness.

Can you hear that gentle splashing of the water on the stones? Nah, it's just my wine I spilled earlier... (smile).

CHAPTER TWO
Self

THE SELF-FOCUS TRAP

Assuming you are a logical person, it would appear the more you focus on yourself, the happier your life would become. So much is written concerning the need to take care of yourself, refuel yourself and make time for yourself and most of it is probably good. But, what if incessant focus on yourself produces the exact opposite results than you intended? What if your focus on self can actually be detrimental? Is it possible that your sincere over-focus on improving yourself actually impedes you from making any progress? Are you looking in the right direction or have you unknowingly become distracted? Is perpetual focus on self a trap?

Most things in life that cause us to stumble do so because we are unaware of the true cause and effect relationship at play. We spend our lives trying to rid ourselves of some negative effect by focusing on the wrong cause. In so doing, our efforts are squandered away, chasing apparent realities that are not realities at all. We exert tremendous efforts to remedy our situation but find no remedy, not because life is too hard, but because we have the wrong focus. This is the very essence of deception. We fall prey to it so easily because we trust what people say and laud those opinions over the truth. We trust our *always* self-centered logic and conclude we can figure it out. We are loathe to admit that we cannot! If you have a problem, and let's face it, we all do to some degree, it is so because we have not yet touched upon the right solution. In earnest, we seek for a solution and subsequently apply a hundred-fold recommendations, never entertaining the idea that the solution escapes our comprehension. In this, we waste our lives, and our time is caught up in an endless cycle of error, working harder, trying harder, exerting more effort towards something that will never yield the right result. In short, our starting premise is wrong, as evidenced by our inability to find the answer, the real cause of our problems.

It has been said that the things man produces always reveal the imperfections of man, while the things God produces have no flaws in them. No matter the man-made masterpiece, closer inspection reveals imperfections. Conversely, the things God makes not only have no flaws in them but the closer the inspection the more perfection is discovered. Similarly, the more you seek to understand God, the more His perfection becomes apparent. Yet, the closer you inspect corruptible man and his ways, the more imperfections you will find. When you spend your time dwelling on and investigating your human ways, no matter how noble your motives, the more you will find your own imperfections and flaws. You will never find perfection within yourself, no matter your sincere efforts and arduous labor. Instead, you will find more and more not to feel good about and more areas of your life in need of revision. You think it is noble and pleasing to God that you spend your life trying to make your imperfections righteous, but your starting premise is already wrong; namely that you, by your human efforts, can make your imperfections perfect. In this, you waste your time, and in this you waste your life. How many Christians spend their days in endless self-examination, ever condemned and disapproved, ever conscious of their human flaws and shortcomings, ever defeated by an insidiously wrong starting premise? To the mainstream Christian, every action is wrong, every thought corrupt, every motive questioned. All enjoyments are to be examined, and all concepts of fun are to be rigorously discarded and rejected. Yet, in this they persist to their own misery and lack of true fulfillment, all based upon a starting premise that isn't true; that was never true.

God's job is to fix the things we cannot fix for ourselves. We were all born with a sin nature that is easily corrupted. Our natural tendency, after the fall of man and the introduction of sin to mankind, is towards error. It is in our blood. The more you search within yourself, the more apparent it becomes. Yet, instead of investing so much effort to fix it, we need to let God fix it for us. God's solution for us was to provide a perfect man, without sin in his blood, who, by the freedom of his own will, walked and lived God's Word perfectly. He is our savior who saved us from ourselves. He ended the need for us to fix ourselves; repair ourselves, and SPEND All OF OUR DAYS FOCUSING ON OURSELVES and everything we do and don't do right. God made it possible for us to stop dwelling on what isn't right with us and change our subject of focus to Him and what He did for us. We are right because He (not we by human efforts and damn hard work) made us right in His sight. And as contrary to human logic as it appears, our focus is to no longer be on what isn't right with us, but rather on God and what He made us to be.

Sounds so simple because it is true. Our job, your job, is to stop focusing on yourself and stop working so hard to figure out your own problems. Read that again! You won't figure out these life dilemmas; these life suckers by your human intellect and strength of will. How has it been working for you thus far? Instead, give your issues to God, one by one and let Him do God's job by getting you to the real solution. He already knows the real cause. In so doing, you are now beginning to think how God designed you to think. Self-focus and dwelling on self do not produce the results you desire. They just steal away your life, enthusiasm and energy on false causes you cannot truly affect. Get your focus off yourself and your issues and get God involved with your solution. Self-focus is a trap from which God will gladly help you escape... Change your subject of focus and free yourself!

BE GOOD TO YOURSELF

Have you ever had the experience where you think you are doing something the right way only to find out later that you're not? We humans get so caught up in our systems about how things work, and it seems to get worse as we get older. We already know, ya know? It's like we stumble into a methodology that worked a couple of times and start replicating it out over a thousand situations. That's all gravy if you got it right, but if you didn't... life gets crappy in a hurry.

One such system, well-rehearsed and approved as right, is the universally accepted notion that one can improve on his weaknesses and faults by analyzing himself. While 'thinking' is always encouraged (another forgotten aspect - smile), I'm talking about that dreadful analysis that only leads to one thing... the conclusion that you are not okay!

To understand this better, you need to understand certain realities. Everything that man does and is, is flawed. Not by design, but by some things you can read about in your Bible sometime. The more closely you inspect man's accomplishments, even masterpieces, the more imperfection you will discover. In stark contrast, everything that God does is perfect. You can put it under the highest power microscope on Earth, and the intricacy and perfection just multiplies. But I don't have to tell you that, right? It is literally (and beautifully) all around you.

So, how does this have anything to do with you and what

you are doing to yourself? Well, almost everything, really. In life you cannot really progress beyond what you think about yourself. If your opinion of yourself is poor, your results in life will be poor. Conversely, if you think highly of yourself and respect yourself, your results will be off the charts. So, what is one of the chief components that faithfully and regularly holds people back? Not being good to one's self.

You are, by your very nature, an imperfect being. You were born into this world with imperfection in your blood. You get it? You started out that way. You didn't start out all rosy and brilliant to only later to botch it up with all of your misdeeds. No! You began imperfect and you will remain imperfect until some future day when God sets it all back in order again. This is so vitally important for you to understand. The great Apostle Paul said (by revelation) that he knew that in himself (his physical nature or his body and mind) dwelled no good thing. Nothing, nada, zip! So, let me ask you another question. When you dwell on yourself and analyze yourself and deeply probe yourself to learn why you behave the way you do, what are you going to find? No good thing! You are only going to discover your imperfection again and again and again. The old familiar end will be that you are going to conclude that you are not so good; not deserving of good things; and basically, woe is you. You cannot reach any other conclusion. That old trick has been whooping mankind's behind since the beginning of time. But, and get this, my friends, it is always a trick!

The only way out of your messes is to stop dwelling on your messes. You want to teach a child how to be successful? You cannot persist in his mistakes, but instead, capitalize on his accomplishments. Seek out what he does well and laud it to the heavens. Build him up, build him up, build him up until he finally starts to believe he is worth something. Once that's in him, he is off to the races for success in life. If that works with children (and believe me, it does), then how about with adults? How about using that principle when you are dealing with you? Does that harsh taskmaster, referred to as yourself, ever lead you anywhere good? You know it doesn't! It just makes you feel like shit, and then you are ripe for the next set of errors.

Getting you to deeply analyze your faults and your failings is the oldest trick in the book. It's a rabbit hole with no rabbits inside. It's a black hole of epic proportions that leads surreptitiously to more and more darkness. And, dwelling on the darkness won't bring forth the light, as I love to say again and again. Now, lest you get all righteous on me here, of course, doing "bad" things is wrong. There's no free pass for hurting and damaging things. But logically, unless you're planning on doing some evil, I'm assuming your failings are in the past tense. They done already been done and done already got did. So, to stay in that dark place is categorically insane if you're trying to get to the light.

God's simple solution to help you out of your "no good thing" state is by giving you an opportunity to get His "every good thing" spirit on the inside. You don't have to work for it or change for it or become "good" for it. You simply believe in the Lord Jesus Christ and that God raised him from the dead (Romans 10:9-10), and you get it. Probably one of the greatest things God ever did. So profoundly simple, yet missed a lifetime by people. Once you get His spirit on the inside, He makes you every good thing. He does it. His son paid the price for every 'effed' up thing you ever did and ever will do. It's over; you win; you will live forever!

Make up your mind not to spend another millisecond analyzing your imperfections because as long as you have a body, your imperfections will always be right there. Instead, focus on what is the best about you. Focus on who God says you are and not what your old worn-out mind says you are. There's a new road for you to travel on if you decide you want it.

Be good to yourself. Love yourself. Accept yourself. Respect yourself. Focus on all that's good in you, knowing that in your flesh, or anyone else's flesh for that matter, dwells no good thing. Life is too short and fraught with too many dangers for your own mind to be your personal enemy. Become really good to yourself because it is the only way...

SELF-TALK

Human beings, unlike any other creature, contain this wonderful capacity to say things to themselves. It's called self-talk. Inside, where no one else can hear, you can engage in your own internal dialogue whereby you say things to yourself, about yourself, concerning yourself. We all do it. The question is, what sort of things are you saying to yourself? How are you treating yourself? Are you being kind and patient with yourself, or do you scold yourself for your shortcomings? Do you allow yourself the privilege to be human, or are you harsh and overly critical with yourself? It's time for some real honesty about the relationship you have been having with yourself! How is your self-talk?

As you move about in the world, chances are you treat people the way you have been treating yourself. If you find yourself being critical of everyone and everything, it is a sure-fire indicator that you have been levying that same criticism against yourself. If you have been angry and full of frustration towards others, you must be angry and frustrated with yourself. All of those emotions and negative feelings got their start somewhere. Their origin can be found within. Similarly, you cannot really love other people until you love yourself. You cannot freely forgive other people without first extending that forgiveness inward. Your behaviors and actions towards others are always a direct reflection of what is going on inside you. As crazy as it may sound, you are literally in a relationship with yourself. You aren't just you acting, absent anything going on inside of you. And, like any relationship, it is either maintained or damaged by how you communicate; by what you say. What is it that you are saying?

There is absolutely nothing positive that can come out of berating and chastising yourself. It just doesn't work. Who do you know that got any better as a result of being severely castigated and rebuked? Sure, we all need correction at times, but hurling insults towards yourself and outlining, in order, all that is wrong with yourself is a recipe for failure. If you chew yourself up and spit yourself out, who is left behind to pick up the pieces? If you insist on opposing your own self, who is left over to fight for you? In the final analysis it is aberrant behavior, and it comes forth from evil. Every single animal in the animal kingdom knows to fight for itself and protect itself. Animals do not work against their own best interests, but people do. But, when people do it, it is unnatural. Something, somewhere, has gotten to you. Something has been working to turn you against yourself. Once you finally figure that one out, you have a chance to change it. Here is a welcome newsflash - every wrong thing you have ever done; every mistake you have ever made; every hurt you have ever caused; every dumdum thing you ever got caught up in; happened because of evil influences outside of yourself. If there was no such thing as evil, those influences would not exist and absent their influences, you would always make a better choice. Don't you see it? All of that self-torture you have been inflicting upon yourself is wrong on an epic scale. It is not noble or humble or pious; it is evil working within you to defeat you! If God be for you, who can be against you?

You must, in the absolute honesty of your soul, stop doing that to yourself. Stop opposing yourself. Stop speaking and doling out cruelty towards your own self. It is enough to stand against the endless accusations and judgments of the world without cooperating by endorsing and supporting it. I think you wouldn't dare say the things you say to yourself, to other people. Yet, inside, it is just another thought, spoken without any real consideration. Well, consider it! See it for what it really is. Look, if you had a friend whom you loved, what would you say to them? When, in the honesty of their own soul, they shared the negative things they thought about themselves, wouldn't you challenge them? Wouldn't you encourage them and point out all their good parts? Wouldn't you extend your heart to them and offer how much you loved them? Wouldn't you? Well, what about you and your own heart? Couldn't you, at least, do that for yourself? Couldn't you remind yourself that you are a work in progress? A human being with flaws and weaknesses? Couldn't you give yourself a pass at times? Couldn't you chalk it up to learning and give yourself a fresh, new start? Of course you could, and you most assuredly should. You've got enough to stand against and oppose day by day to try and accomplish it divided against your own self. Can't you be a little better towards yourself?

One of the greatest defeats a human being will ever suffer is what happens when a person allows themselves to be talked into actively opposing their own best interests, to live in perpetual and active opposition against themselves. Every time you put yourself down; every time you speak harshness to yourself; every time you chastise and berate yourself; you are simply cooperating with your own personal adversary in severely limiting and hurting yourself. You have to learn how to be kind to yourself. You have to be patient with yourself. You have to get off your own back and encourage yourself towards a more worthy endeavor. None of us like it when we blow it, when we fail to measure up, when we fall short of the person we know in our hearts that we really ought to be. None of us. But, if you are honest, you know the only way to do better is to be better, and we accomplish that by choosing carefully what we say to ourselves. God is on your side, even when you aren't! Change what you have been saying to yourself, and let God clean up the rest. How has your self-talk been going lately? I hope it is full of love...

BE HONEST WITH YOURSELF – PART ONE

One of the great deceptions of the human race is that little thing called, "lying to yourself!" You know how it goes. You are afraid of something, and then you make those bravado declarations like, "I'm not scared of anything!" Yet on the inside, you know it isn't true. Now maybe you don't want to broadcast that from the rooftops, but come on now, really? You know if you are afraid of something, and the very least you could do is to be honest with yourself. You, my friends, are the only you, you have! You are the only person on earth that has to live in your head and you *ain't gonna* get into someone else's head (no matter what anyone says to the contrary). So let's just get honest, huh?

Maybe it will make more sense if I say it this way. Let's pretend your mind is like a big old house. (Come on, go with me now!) You probably paid a whole lot of money or owe a whole lot of money for your house (it's valuable). It's *your* house! It's where you live. It's where you go (hopefully) to relax. You can be naked in your own house if you know what I mean. You can sleep in your own house. You can talk out loud, sing songs, bungle the words, dance a little... hey, it's your house! No one is allowed in your house without your permission. You can share your house with others if you like them. You can decorate it how you want to and redecorate anytime you want. If it gets too hot, you turn on the AC. If it gets too cold, you turn on the heat. It is your house, you feel me? Now let's say you have a room in your house that terrifies you. That room just scares you to death. Every time you go in there you shudder and can't wait to get out of there again. "Maybe I will just avoid that room and not go in there," said no one, ever! You would march your butt into that room; declare, "this is my house blankety blank swear words," and take your room back in your house BECAUSE it is your house! Well, wouldn't you? Maybe it's not a scary room, but rather a scary creature that came in uninvited, like a wild dog or a hairy spider or a few million happy little ants. I'm guessing that no matter how much that wild beast scared you, you would do something to get it out of your house! Toss the dog some steak; smash a spider; or spray some 'bona-fide' ant killer fluid! Something, right? Okay, now stay with me... Your mind is a house. It is very, very valuable! You own it outright. You can modify anything in it; you can change anything in it; you can control what goes in there, and you can decide who gets to stay and who has to leave.

When you let things that scare you remain in your house and ignore them and talk around them and make excuses for them, you are lying to yourself! You are not being honest with yourself. You are putting on elaborate outfits when you would rather be naked. You are decorating on the top of dirty walls. You are locking the doors to scary rooms and refusing to go in them. Stop it! You only have one mind, and you only have one life to live. Be honest; have a talk with God and get those wild beasts out of your house once and for all. Make the decision to look them in the eye (àla James and the Giant Peach) and take it/them on. See what God says about overcoming fear in the Bible (He may just know a thing or two). Getting faded (slang intended) just prolongs your agony. Life is no joke folks, and you have to take this stuff seriously. People spend their whole life scared of something and end up missing their whole life. Their whole life!

If you have the courage to take back your house and everything in it, you will make an earth-shattering discovery. You will find that life is good (great name for a company). You will find that life is joyful and fun. You will begin to treasure your relationships and all those people in your life. You will appreciate the things God has blessed you with. You might even find yourself inspired to reach out and help somebody else (wink, wink). In short, you will begin to taste that life God had in mind when he came up with the whole idea.

It's right there waiting for you folks, if you will just be honest with yourself...

BE HONEST WITH YOURSELF – PART TWO

You know there's a whole lot more to being honest with yourself than simply getting rid of fear, though that is a massive subject of its own. Since we are on the thought, how about those other categories of our lives? You know what I mean, right? Those pesky little "hold-backs" that put roadblocks and obstacles in our path need a little further illumination. Here's a simple yet enlightening example. For about the last 10-15 years, I have been obsessing over losing weight. I'm older now (smile) and have carried an unfriendly companion with me for almost all of those years. You see, that gut and those love handles have been taunting me from the mirror for over a decade. Sure, there has always been something I could do about it, but somehow, I didn't. Like the now famous book said, I have been battling not with 50 pounds or even 30 pounds, but a measly little 15 pounds. How long does it take or how much discipline is required to lose 15 pounds? Not much, I imagine. So how can a man spend over a decade being unhappy with his own image in the mirror? Well, that thought is the subject of Part Two.

Why would we ever contemplate putting up with something for 15 years? Why does anyone live with the things they detest? Because we aren't being honest with ourselves, that's why. The reality of being overweight is that we consume more calories than we burn (simple physics, but not so simple when the human mind gets involved). Sure our "older" bodies burn calories at the speed of rats struggling in a sea of molasses, but still... 15 pounds? Okay, so we want to lose the gut, but we want to savor the flavor of the food (or drink) more. Honest! Chances are, if you are overweight, you like to eat and eating (desire) overrides discipline. Simple. We can say no. We can always say no! Truth is, we don't want to say no! We like to eat. Blaming thyroids, medications, genetics, etc., etc., is, most often, just not being honest with ourselves. That's not being mean; that's being honest (smile supplied to offset angry feelings). I'm not condemning folks that are overweight by any stretch. My message isn't get thin, be sexy. My message is get honest, do you! ? If you are okay with heavier, then be heavier. But for goodness sakes, don't play the chase your tail game for another minute. Up down, round and round, distracted, unhappy, yanked around.

You can track this 'not so nice pattern' through many areas of your own life. It's simple, what don't you like that you CAN do something about? I'm not talking about your brother, LOL; he is who he is. I'm talking about those perennial life suckers. Those "I wish" things. Maybe you hate your job, the boss, the company and all of your co-workers. Yet you stay there year after year. It's the economy, right? Good jobs are hard to find, right? Well, I mean, it is comfortable, right? Ding, ding, ding, see it? Lying to yourself. Truth is, you just don't want to deal with the effort (or perceived effort) required to change it. That's honest, unpleasant perhaps, but honest. Maybe you have always dreamed of being a __________ (fill in the blank). Well, considering your estimated time allotment on terra firma, you don't have that much time left. You dream of starting a business but continue working that job. You remember, the one that you loathe! You dream of writing a book, yet you can always start that next year. Why? Because as long as it is still future you don't have to deal with it right now. See, lying to yourself is really easy. You don't like your house because it is too small, too old, too confining. Hmmm...

so make some moves toward getting a different one. Wait, I can't. The economy is bad; housing is down, and; it's too risky. Here's a thought. You are going to pay to live somewhere, aren't you? Even welfare housing has a payment. Well, what if you can't afford the payment? Well, what if the sun crashes into the earth and everyone dies? What if aliens attack and happen to feed on mortgages? You see, we are lying to ourselves!

Being honest with yourself means looking yourself in the eye (not in the gut because you are working on that). Be 100 percent honest with yourself. Admit to yourself that you are afraid or lazy or whatever, but just say it like it is. Your old mind cannot function on negative realizations and has to justify itself. That's why we lie. It's hard to admit that I'm just too lazy to do something about something that has bothered me for 15 years. So, I make excuses, really, really, clever elaborate excuses. But alas, excuses nonetheless...

Get off the hamster wheel, folks. Get off the lying track where delusion takes the place of reality, and we go on living a life of semi-existence. As my great friend said recently, "quit being a spectator in your own life!" Talk truth to yourself. Take yourself by the mental bootstraps and pull! You really do "only live once," and you really do only have one shot at this thing.

So, as I pour another glass of the Pino Noir at the kitchen countertop and think, "my God, this wine is delicious," I remind myself to be honest. And in that honesty, I say, yes, Tony, it is delicious, but you are out of Weight Watcher's points, so sip it a little more slowly!

LOVE YOURSELF LIKE YOUR LIFE
DEPENDS UPON IT

In the beautiful words of Jen Sincero, "Love yourself like your life depends upon it, because it really does!" In our media-driven world, self-hate and self-loathing seem to have reached epidemic proportions. No one likes themselves anymore. If it isn't an obsession with being skinny, it's a compulsion with your hair or your skin. You are angry with yourself for doing this and not having done that. You think you aren't successful enough, smart enough or the deadliest of all, good enough. In the end you are just real hateful of that person staring back from the mirror!

As an individual living your one shot at life, imagine how devious and dastardly it is to not love yourself; you being the only self you've got! It's not natural, as even an animal knows to care for itself instinctively. Yet somehow, in some way, humans can be talked into actually hating themselves. If you're honest, something must have gotten to you! I'm sure when you were eight years old you didn't think that way, despite perhaps receiving perpetual correction from the people who loved you. Yet here you are today contemplating mean and hurtful things about yourself without even giving it a second thought. If you spoke to others like you spoke to yourself you wouldn't have any friends. But, because you are speaking to yourself, it is somehow okay.

A nation divided against itself cannot stand, and neither can an individual for that matter. The divided, beat-up you is not the real you. It is a shadow of your real essence. But, that essence cannot be seen by the world because you have already long since lost the fight in your own mind! Maybe if you knew you were in a fight you would have fought back, and that is the reason for this work.

Life is spiritual, my friend, and contrary to popular belief there is a spiritual force ever at work to defeat you. The battleground is your mind. The weapons are your thoughts. Ironically, you are always in control of your own thoughts. So, somewhere along the line that force got you to say and confess those horrible things about yourself directly to yourself in the solemn chambers of your own mind. "I can't help it!" you say... "It's just how I am!" you report. But nay, my man, my woman, it is not how you are, and you certainly can help it!

Real love is much more than an emotion, it is a decision. You decide to love, and that love must include yourself. Jay-Z famously said, "I cannot help the poor if I'm one of them. Well, you cannot really love anyone until you first love yourself. All of that constant chastisement you level upon yourself doesn't make you a better person. There's nothing humble about loathing yourself. All it does is weaken you and make you part of the problem instead of part of the solution. You walk around criticizing (in your mind) everyone you see and everything they do, never once stopping to realize that you are projecting out onto others the way you feel about yourself! You don't love them or forgive them because you don't love or forgive yourself! That's just how it works, and there ain't no getting around it...

What if God made you wonderful just the way you are? What if all of those imperfections you're obsessing over are actually a natural part of the human experience? I often muse that if you could get inside someone else's head, you would find all the same insanity you find inside your own head. At least then you would take solace in knowing you're just like everyone else! But this ol' world has done a number on you. Instead of being left to your own devices (and thoughts), there's a giant media machine that is glad to share with you exactly how you "should" look and how successful you "should" be and precisely how bad you really are for thinking and doing the things you do. Just stop buying it because it's a lie.

To escape this dilemma, you have to first become willing to admit that you're doing it to yourself, then take yourself by your thoughts and start loving that person again. Accept your limitations and weaknesses for being just what they are; limitations and weaknesses. How absurd to think you should be above weaknesses! Instead, change your focus to all that is glorious about you. If my gift to the world was being the greatest quarterback of all time, how nuts would you think I was if all I talked about was my lack of skill at soccer? Well, the same holds true for your gift to the world. Just do you, man, the good and the bad. Focus on what's awesome about you and stay there. No one overcomes weakness by focusing on it, but only by focusing on strength. Focus on your strengths!

Perhaps the worst on the sliding scale of bad thoughts is to think you aren't good enough. Newsflash! None of us are good enough; we came from the factory that way. Our great God has never loved anyone because they are good enough. He loves people because He is good enough. Most, if not all, self-loathing comes from the vague idea of not being good enough. And you got those ideas from some *whackadoo* parked outside an abortion clinic pretending to speak for God. God is love only, and that should settle every argument to the contrary!

When I listened to that statement from Jen that is the title, I actually shed tears. You know why? Because I, just like you, need to love myself. You are no different from me, and I'm no different from you. We're all on this trip together, and we may as well learn to love that dude or gal we see staring back at us from the mirror every morning! It just doesn't make any sense to do otherwise!

Love yourself like your life depends upon it, because it really does!

SETTLE IT. SOLVE IT. RESOLVE IT.

There are times in life when you are an avid believer in God and His Word, that God will open the eyes of your understanding and show you something that will absolutely change your life! Just such a thing happened to me this weekend. The subject of the teaching was accessing God's peace in your life and how, in order to experience and enjoy that peace, you have to take the time to settle the things in your heart that remain unsettled, unsolved and unresolved.

Peace typically occurs at the end of a conflict. It has been referred to as the absence of strife. Peace can follow accomplishment or a job well done. Peace is also defined as undisturbed wellbeing. It is knowing that everything is going to be okay. Peace is something God gives to us as His children. Yet for all the magnificence that God's peace is in our lives, we often fail to access it. We fail to access it because we go about obtaining it in the wrong way. We tend to believe that peace is something we have to work for by "living right" or by giving up something; by adding something; or by abstaining from something. Such is the life of the typical Christian believer, ever condemned and guilty, never measuring up, always unworthy! I cannot tell you how many Facebook and Instagram stories promote how unworthy we are before God, implying that if we only "did better" or worked harder we would arrive. Well, here's a newsflash for your weary soul - there will never be anything you can do that will make you worthy before God!

Making you worthy is something God had to do for you! The sooner you come across that realization, the closer you are to enjoying God's peace in your life. What a cruel, dreadful, awful trick the enemy of God has placed on God's people since the world began. Who the hell wants to worship and serve a God that is perpetually unhappy and displeased with His children? Are you perpetually displeased with your children? Don't you have a little forgiveness for their foolishness? Do you not extend them some mercy at times? Don't you just love them for who they are irrespective of their behavior? Well, it's fair to say the God of love can do even better than that! When you find yourself caught in that arduous trap, it isn't God that you are serving anymore, instead it is the commandments and doctrines of men, made by men in an attempt to access a God they neither know nor understand. There is no peace in living that way (and definitely no love).

Peace is something that God freely gives to His children. In order to access that peace in your heart, you have to settle things in your heart. You are not going to be able to settle all the things that aren't right in the world, but you can settle them in your own heart. You do so by believing and accepting what God says over what everyone and everything else says. You remain unpeaceful because you (and I) have all these things going on inside of us that are not resolved. God says that He gave us His son as a payment for all the sins we may commit in a lifetime, past, present and future. Accepting Jesus Christ's finished work for you leads to peace. BUT (and it's a *helluva* big BUT), your failure to accept that reality in your heart leads to a lifetime of dwelling on and living in every stupid thing you ever did throughout your life! Of course, the sin and error is wrong and leads to pain. You don't need me to tell you that. But, remaining in it is worse, especially when God, the only true judge, has already forgiven you in the life of His son. God solved your sin problem and mine forever. Our

Savior's work is finished; it's done. Until you resolve that in your own heart, you won't enjoy the peace God has freely given to you.

Another way believers get talked out of the peace God so dearly wants for His children is by living under the negative judgment of man, including yourself. You do not have the right to judge yourself. When you negatively judge yourself, you reject God's plan of redemption already enacted for you. Judging yourself and allowing yourself to be judged by other people is wrong. It is not humble to refer to yourself as a worm for God, lowly and defeated. Thinking this way not only robs you of God's peace, but it serves to work the purposes of your insidious enemy, the accuser of the brethren before God night and day. Similarly, living in the past, rehearsing and cataloging your every mistake, remembering and cleaving to your lowest moments, denies God's true opinion of you as His child and crucifies afresh His son that died for you. You may not be able to forget all the dumb stuff you have done throughout your life, but you can resolve to settle the matter in your heart. Leaving it unsettled and undone leads only to fear and an incessant focus on what is not right about you! (Have you ever been there?) Settle it in your heart. Forgive yourself and let it go. Let it ALL go and simply move ahead. Walk out a new man, a new woman, fresh, alive and vital for the day at hand. Walk out with your head held high, a son or daughter of the most high God! Once you really decide to let it all go and refuse to unearth it, you will find yourself living in the peace God has already given you. Resolve it in your heart once and for all.

The good life you dream of is not found in riches and cars and houses and more and more stuff. It is found when you know and understand Him, the God who so loved you that He gave His only begotten son for you. It is found in the joy and love and peace that only God can provide for you. It's not about you, for goodness sakes; it's about Him. You don't have to spend your life feeling like you don't measure up before God, which leads only to increasing fear and doubt and defeat. You have not been found wanting, and there is literally nothing you have to do in this life to be at peace other than fully accept all that God has already done for you. Settle the matter in your own heart. Resolve the matter in your own heart. Solve the matter in your own heart by believing what God says is true in every situation that ever confronts you. You will surely be challenged in this life, but God will make sure you always win! Always...

Get peace...

FOCUS ON YOUR GOOD BITS

If you are like me and I prefer to assume you are because then I will like you more (smile), you have learned to focus on those few areas that you need to improve rather than all of the things that make you awesome! It's sort of like a sickness, isn't it? You spend 16 of your waking hours doing what you are supposed to do and five minutes saying something you shouldn't have said and then spending another hour ruminating on why you said it and that you really shouldn't have said it. Sound familiar? Wouldn't it seem reasonable to applaud yourself for 16 hours of solid effort and to pay little attention to your one mistake? Indeed!

The world we live in, rife with media input, has done a masterful job of tricking you and me into obsessing over anything that may hint at imperfection. "My belly is too fat!" which discounts the fact that the ideal "belly" belongs to a 16-year-old with the metabolism of a racehorse. Or my hair or my eyes or my feet are too large or my cankels, etc., etc. Whether it be physical imperfections (assuming there is "physical perfection") or problems with our character or a propensity to sin (so-called), or just plain old ability to actually make mistakes, we have universally bought into a gigantic scheme that gets us to focus on what's wrong with us instead of focusing on our good bits...

So, you might be asking, why does it even matter? Well, it matters because incessant focus on what is wrong with you leads to one perpetually long, unhappy existence. "I'm no good," "I'm not okay," "Why can't I be like such and such," all presume a condition that may not actually exist. What if you are very, very similar to most human beings? What if the things you think and say and do are remarkably like the things most people think and say and do? What if, huh? What if that hour you just wasted obsessing over the "dumb thing" you said at the staff meeting was forgotten by everyone at the staff meeting five minutes after it ended? Pointless me thinks...

But here is another thing to consider that trumps even a wasted, unhappy life. If it's true that what you focus on expands, then focusing on what is wrong can only lead to more and more of "what is wrong!" Chew on that for a moment... If, unbeknownst to you, the things you focus on in life are conspiring to come your way, then it seems focusing on what you don't like can only produce more and more of "what you don't like." Are you beginning to see the large-scale scheme I was referring to earlier? Let's say you are a pretty good person, according to your own estimates, but you have a few weaknesses. But, you spend inordinate amounts of time working on your weaknesses. Sure, it seems noble because you are, after all, working on them. But, here's a thought, have you ever known a successful person that spends more time working on their weaknesses than what they are good at, who remains successful? Probably not, right? Successful people, while fully aware of their weaknesses, choose rather to focus on the things in which they excel. Obsessing over weakness serves only to exemplify weakness. How many good-hearted people have you met that can't go five minutes into the conversation without telling you something that is "bad" about themselves? Or conversely, how many people have you met that even dare to mention something they are good at? World-wide sickness, my friends.

A wise man named Eric taught me long ago in a conversation

about child-rearing that the way to get your child past their problems is by highlighting the things they do well! Think about that for a moment. Your child is sitting there quietly watching TV and you don't say a word, but as soon as they get rambunctious, you want to give them a lecture, thereby reinforcing the behavior you don't like! What works for children works for adults, except adults no longer have their parents to guide them in the way in which they should go.

So, the solution, weary travelers, is to decide to stop focusing on what is wrong with you. The Good Lord, who knows everything, is well aware of your imperfections and loves you just the same and always will! He's not unhappy with you, so you owe it to yourself to follow suit. Focus on the best parts of yourself. Focus on the good things you have in your life. Focus on the miracle that is your life and, in so doing, will begin to appreciate what you do have and not obsess on what you don't have.

If you will become determined to focus on the good, then you will find the good has actually been pursuing you all along. Let that good catch up to you by being so grateful for the life you already have. And for an added bonus, try focusing on the good in other people as well. Shoot, you may just find yourself surrounded by a lot of wonderful people.

Focus on your good bits!

ENTANGLED IN YOUR OWN WEB, SPIDERMAN

I've been fascinated lately with the subject of "mindfulness" and living in the moment. I just finished a great book about meditation and its benefits called, "Mindfulness ~ Finding Peace in a Frantic World." Now before I go any further, let me clarify what it means to meditate. Meditation doesn't mean emptying your mind of all thoughts because we all know what happens when there's a vacuum (things rush in to fill it!). True meditation means getting quiet on the inside. It means slowing down your thought processes and experiencing what "is" rather than your interpretation of what "is." In other words, it's about getting out of your own head.

There is an epidemic taking place today in that folks are no longer living and enjoying life but instead are spending their lives analyzing and cataloging and double-checking and over-thinking! It seems we have so much information available to us that we can't seem to get outside of our own heads. It's funny that we criticize young folks for not thinking enough and acting rashly, yet at the same time admire them for being spontaneous and free. It seems like the older you get, the more cautious you become and pretty soon everything is dangerous, everything is scary, and everything could bring some trouble your way! And while you are basking in your comfortable safety, avoiding all that might get you, life just rolls on by with you no longer a participant in it. You have become, in a sense, entangled in your own web. That beautiful processor that takes over your drive to work while you sip your coffee, adjust the radio and read a text message, also volunteers to take over your life.

Being mindful and aware is about getting outside of your preconceived notions of life and setting about to experience it anew. It's about taking a fresh look at things. And apparently, it's easy to take a fresh look when you are 20, but how about when you're 50? We think we know so much, but in reality, we don't know anything. It's that processor, man, that automatic pilot! It's habit man (or woman) that just does it the same way they always did it while expecting nothing to change. The problem with that is that life is dynamic and all about change. At some point, your old habits no longer serve you; you are serving them! Same old tired opinions; same old worn-out assumptions; same old soured and cynical view of life - ughh!

The remedy? You have to get outside of your own head for a bit. I don't mean turn it over to something else; I mean stop thinking and rethinking and get out there and live. What if something goes wrong? Ohh emm geee! What if there's a worse alternative - death by boredom! Change your habits; change your routines! Go hang out with a young person! They aren't bound by the clock or the day of the week! Isn't it more important to spend an evening with the people you love and not get enough sleep for work the next day than to stay at home and commit mental suicide with your DVR? (smile) Go a day without makeup! Dive in the water and get your hair wet! Quit obsessing over the fact that you have a one-inch bulge on your belly or that your butt is too big or that your legs aren't long enough, or that your hair is turning gray. Thank your wrinkles for reminding you how much you have laughed in your life and for reminding you that you may also have spent too much time worrying as well! Live man, just live. Oh, and while I'm on a rant, silence that inner critic that has fooled you into thinking that you aren't good enough for anything. Has that little voice inside you that magnifies everything you ever did wrong and is silent when you've done right ever really helped you get better? Do you know anyone that was ever successfully shamed into being a better person? Living inside your own head, all over your own back, only serves one purpose, and that is to keep you weak and afraid and defeated. Get out there and live!

There is a very simple way to do it. Quit making it all about you and make it about somebody else. You can stop "pretend" living inside your own head by making the decision to change your focus from you, yours to him, his and how or if you prefer her, hers and how! What can you do to make someone's life better? What can you give (that you have to give) to help someone else along the way? What warm, loving energy can you bring to the room or the conversation or the mood? Who can you go and visit? Who can you call or text? My barber told me the other day how God told him to pull over and talk to a young man walking down the street and give him a little cash because he needed it. And although he clearly heard it, he kept on driving. You know why? The same reason I, I'm ashamed to admit, have gone past that thing I was supposed to do as well, because I was too caught up in my own head and what I normally do and when I normally do it! (I mean, what would people think?)

You see, folks, the beauty that is this life is full of new things, new experiences, and new people, but we are never going to recognize those things while we are caught up in our own web of living inside our heads, analyzing everything from here to breakfast! Quit second-guessing yourself and make a bold move! Tell someone you love 'em! Talk to that stranger! Don't ask what everyone else thinks, but get back to what YOU think!

You've only got one shot at this thing, Spiderman. Break out of that web, of your own weaving, and take a breath, a new, fresh breath where it isn't always about you! See what's all around you and experience it to the full. Live your life now, Superhero, right now!

Breathe...

DO YOU LOVE YOURSELF, FLAWS AND ALL?

The other day I was listening to a teaching from my good buddy Mark Wallace. He told a story about an experiment where people were asked to describe themselves to a criminal sketch artist. Then, those same folks were also described to the sketch artist by their friends. Amazingly, the friends' description of the person looked much more like the person than their own description! Why, you ask? Because when people described themselves, they overly focused on their perceived flaws, resulting in an image not even close to how they really looked. So, the question that begs is, do you love yourself, flaws and all?

People tend to be brutal in their own estimation of themselves. They have been caught up in a culture that falsely represents who people are and, as such, have been talked into focusing on everything they are not instead of everything they truly are. They have forgone any recognition of all that makes them unique and wonderful in favor of an obsession with having to be something the world deems acceptable or beautiful or admirable. They magnify their "wrong behaviors" out of all proportion in comparison to their "right behaviors." In short, they have believed lies and accusations concerning themselves, failed to recognize them as such, and landed at a place where they don't even like themselves, much less love themselves.

The root of this dilemma stems back as far as there have

been people to trip up. The enemy of mankind knows that if you can divide people against themselves, they become weak and easy to defeat. If you can burrow deep enough into their psyche, they eventually become their own worst enemy, hurling internal insults at their own selves and perpetually shaming themselves, the end point of which is self-loathing and a complete loss of self-respect. Oh, no one is going to tell you this, much less admit it to themselves. But, it is a distinct reality of the human condition. There's so little love in the world because people don't even love themselves. Or worse, love does not prevail because people have a distorted view of what love is. They think love and self-respect accompany financial success or having a "perfect" body, marrying the right person or getting into the right school. They wrongly assign love-worthy acts as something they must do or be in order to be worthy of love. And, in never being able to fully realize those love-worthy acts or become, by their good behavior, love-worthy people, they eke out love to themselves as if it was a scarce commodity.

Loving yourself is a decision you make about yourself in the same way it is a decision you make about other people. When you have a new baby, no one has to remind you to love them. When you meet a potential life partner, though you hardly recognize it, you have made a conscious decision to love that person. You didn't "fall" in love; you chose love based upon certain criteria you already decided. In the same way, you make a decision to love yourself! You cannot say, as some falsely report, that you choose love as long as the behaviors are right, or the conditions are right, or the time is right. Love, real love, exists above behaviors. It is not fleeting, flitting around based on whether or not the sun is out or the vibe feels good or if that certain someone says the right things. Love is so much bigger and so much more important than that! Love is the most necessary ingredient of the human condition, and you need it more than anything else you could ever need!

Do you know where I learned this? I learned it from God. God loves me unconditionally, past, present and future. He loved me into finally loving myself. He continues to love me despite me, and for that I am forever grateful. He taught me that love isn't something you reserve for good behavior but rather something you decide to do no matter what. Love does not change and alter itself according to the ebb and flow of life. It is not dependent upon conditions. It is persistent and determined and never-ending. It is to be freely and liberally shared with others. In so doing, it finally persuades your stubborn heart to apply it to yourself; to love yourself!

You must learn to love yourself, not in a conceited or inflated way, but in the true depths of your being. You decide to love yourself, not because you are so good or so righteous or somehow have achieved perfection, but rather because you are imperfect and not always good and maybe seldom of your own works, righteous. You love yourself despite your frail humanity and weakness. You love yourself even when you falter and fail. You love yourself because your Father in heaven loves you and wants nothing less for you... ever!

You would be surprised to find that the weird stuff you do and think is the exact same weird stuff we all do and think. We are all in this thing together. Your secret sins are no worse than my secret sins. Your propensity towards error is no greater than my propensity towards error. We are all people, wonderfully flawed and unique, seeking in unending revolutions, endless expressions of love. Be yourself! Express yourself. Love yourself, not because you deserve it but rather because you need it. No one is worthy of love as love chooses its object first and not after.

Decide today to stop entertaining the accusations about everything you are not. Stop focusing in on what isn't right about you or what things you foolishly have concluded need revision. Instead, embrace who you are, who God made YOU to be, and give every piece of that loveliness to a love-starved and dying world. You are a wonderful, unique masterpiece formed, made and created by God to help other people love themselves too!

Oh, my friends, God *is* love...

HOW TO ESCAPE FROM YOURSELF

Life has many ironies which God seems to have thrown in for good measure, as if to say things aren't always what they appear. Ironically, sometimes the thing you need most to do in order to alleviate your present dilemma appears to be the exact opposite of what "you" think you should do. Today the world seems consumed with this notion of self and a myriad of things you need to do to best care for yourself. But what if many of those suggestions are based in error? What if your solution for your problem isn't at all what you thought it was? What if your best efforts to feel better (and let's face it, a lot of what we do or try to figure out is in an effort to feel better) are unsuccessful because the starting premise is wrong? Error only works when you are unable to see it for what it is...

We all want to be happy. We all want to feel good. We all are aware that life is filled with challenges, and we all understand that every day isn't necessarily going to be a blissful experience because of those challenges. But, we also all know what life is like when we feel good, and for that we are forever on a quest to feel good. When our mind feels out of sorts; when we feel agitated or troubled; when our experience feels boring or lacking fulfillment, we know that also. We accurately perceive when our energy is down; when our excitement is diminished; when our enthusiasm is missing, and; in our desperation we turn inwards. Our mission to feel good drives us further and further into ourselves, searching ardently for that thief, that hindrance, that devious bastard keeping us from our pure happiness. "Maybe it's because of how I have been acting lately. Maybe it's my diet. Maybe I'm doing something wrong. Maybe it's my wife or my husband or my job or my family or my..." Whatever we think it might be and however it affects us, the end result is the same in that our focus and attention is driven and pressed and steered deeper and deeper into ourselves...

The more you focus (or, more accurately are driven to focus) on yourself, the more miserable you will become. Oh sure, you think looking inward will lead you to some divine enlightenment you have heretofore been missing. You believe buried somewhere in your subconscious mind is a temple of knowledge awaiting your arrival. But, sadly, you are wrong. All you will find, if you must persist, is more and more unhappiness and the distinct absence of what you have been searching for so diligently!

Your problem isn't how you feel, though Lord knows it seems like it. Your problem is one of focus or where you are focusing your attention. If I may say it bluntly, you are inspecting your own imperfection and expecting perfection. You are considering your own weakness in an effort to find strength. You are searching for human solutions to spiritual problems, and by spiritual problems I mean the real source of your difficulties. As odd as it may seem to you, your challenges are being engendered by something outside of yourself. And that same damnable force behind your troubles is the same one pushing you inward, deeper and deeper inward, for a solution that doesn't exist within yourself. Your efforts are futile, no matter how well intended they may be. The answer isn't to look within but rather to look without.

When you finally figure this out, you will begin to see that you were designed to seek outside of yourself for help. Your focus is supposed to be on God, from which all good feelings like joy and peace and love, freely flow. In essence, you just give all of your human bullshit to God and leave it with Him. You have to get outside of yourself. You have to escape from yourself and all of your associated baggage. You must stop putting yourself and how you feel at any given moment ahead of everything else in life. It's not self-care; it's self-sabotage! It's a deception of gargantuan proportions. The world's remedies consisting of focusing on yourself and your happiness and your feelings and your problems don't lead you out of darkness but instead to more and more darkness. Happiness comes back with a quickness as you move the focus away from yourself! True happiness comes when you walk in the light!

If you've been around long enough, you know that when you stop moving forward in life and start slowing down and looking around you or within you, you are going to find more and more of that which troubles you. You will discern more and more darkness and more and more reasons to be distressed. Stop doing that! Get up mentally and move ahead. Lay your troubles on God and thank Him for helping you discover what has gone south on you. Ask Him to make it clear again and to restore your soul to that grand place you like to dwell in. It is that simple...

When you find yourself unhappy, disturbed, perplexed or confused, don't look within; look without. Don't spend another millisecond muddling through the heaviness. Unload it all as you were intended to do and change your subject of focus. Your answers are there, your happiness is there, and your enthusiasm and vitality for living are there, waiting for you to find them again. Don't look within; look without! Your happiness depends upon you escaping from yourself!

MAKE YOURSELF A PRIORITY

I know what you're thinking. You're thinking here comes another admonition to make yourself number one in a culture already deluged in narcissism and love of self above all else. Forget about other people and their needs because it's all about you! Yeah, those people do exist, but I don't think they are a majority. In fact, I think most of us are the exact opposite. Recently I had the most unusual insight concerning our personal happiness, and incredibly it involved making yourself a priority.

I know it sounds selfish and swims uphill against all we've been taught about sublimating our needs for others. It definitely challenges our well-worn "Christian" virtues suggesting we always place ourselves last in line. But, I think there's some honesty to it we may not have considered before, mainly because of what we have been taught. And, while selfishness is naturally frowned upon, making your own needs a priority isn't really selfish at all.

You, my friend, are the only you, you have got. You've got one you. There's no two *you's* requiring that you share you. When it comes to you, there is just you. When you do things that make you unhappy, you are doing it to "you" alone. When you make choices based on what other people think and what other people say that disagree with what you think and what you say, you are lying to "you." When you endeavor to live up to others' expectations for you while not honoring your own expectations for you, you are not taking care of you. When you try so hard not to hurt other people's feelings and to protect others' feelings, while running roughshod against your own feelings or worse, denying your own feelings, you are only hurting you. You are the only you, you have been given, and you have a sacred responsibility to so love and care for you that you will naturally and willingly love and care for others.

When it comes to serving God, I think people have gotten it all wrong. God does not require that we give until it hurts or that we burn ourselves out in service for other people. Nor does He expect us to sacrifice ourselves and our own happiness to make sure others are happy. Religion may have told you that, but God never did. Instead, the natural order is that God blesses us, and in proportion to that blessing, we bless others. The happier and more well taken care of I am, the more likely I am to help you. Oh sure, I can help you when I have needs too, but the real joy and love behind it will be missing. Think about it in terms of giving. The more I have, the more I have to give. Yes, I can give when I have little, but when I have been abundantly blessed, I want to give abundantly. The same principle applies to speaking God's Word. The proportion of how blessed I am will directly correlate to how much I want to tell other people about God. You don't have to tell super blessed and joyful people to go out and witness for the Lord. Their joy already got them out there. But, unhappy, unblessed folks will need to be prodded and goaded before they will go. Do you see it? Get yourself blessed first, and stop acting like it's an imposition on God or something or a selfish concept for your life. It's not selfish; you are the only you you have got!

Making yourself a priority is about slowing down from your busy and frenetic pace and daring to get back in touch with yourself. (See, even that sounded selfish....) Deep down, who are you, and what do you need to be happy? What things in life paint a smile on your face and add energy to your steps? In your interactions with others, are you with people you genuinely love and care about or are you "making it work" with drinks and fake smiles, playing a role until they go away? What goes through your mind on your way to work? What sadness or frustration have you been ignoring for years? What life flashes through your mind on those rare occasions, and why can't you live that life now? What drastic change or revolution might occur in your existence if you stopped being afraid to allow yourself to matter at least as much as you make everyone else matter?

The difference between being selfish and making yourself a priority is that you are not the only vote, but your vote counts as much as everyone else's does. It's not giving and loving and kind to get to the place where your vote doesn't count. With God, everyone counts. They matter and you matter. Their happiness is important and you do all you can to ensure it, but your happiness matters just as much. If you can supply their needs, whatever those needs are, do it. But, you also have needs, and they do not rank any less in priority. Every mother knows that although her infant is helpless without her, she will offer no help if she doesn't get what she needs to thrive as well. You don't always have to occupy first place in the line, but you don't need to step out of the line altogether.

Maybe it's time you rethink your worn-out ideas about service usually imposed upon you by people who needed to get some work done, and recognize that you are the only you, you have got, and if you fail to care for you, you won't be taken care of. God will always supply your needs, but only if you are willing to believe for in them for yourself! Life is short, my friends. Don't spend your whole life trying to live someone else's dream. You matter. Your needs matter. Make yourself a priority.

FIND YOUR WINGS BY TRUSTING YOURSELF

It's interesting to think that all of the famous or successful people you admire, be they a literary great, superstar performer, outstanding business person or even the President of the United States, all began somewhere. Maybe you read Shakespeare or Emerson with sublime admiration in your eyes. But remember, there was a time when Shakespeare and Emerson were just like you and me, beginners hastily penning their ideas into a journal at the dusty old library someplace. The reason these highly esteemed folk became so successful is that they learned to trust themselves. If you are ever going to discover your own wings, you have to learn to trust yourself.

The problem with our age, it seems, is that people have become so unoriginal. It's like someone put out a broadcast announcing that all of the things one may do, have already been done, so get on board someone else's train and figure out where you fit! And even worse, people have learned not to question anymore. Attach an authority figure or, better, a scientific study, and the whole world digests it as true without even giving it a second thought. The mass media machine has inundated us with so much information that we feel we already know the answer before the question is even posed. And most dastardly of all, we've learned to trust what the vulgar crowd says over the still small voice within our hearts.

You were designed to be an original. Observe nature and see if you can find any two things identical. You are unique in every sense of the word! So why should you trouble yourself so shamefully day by day for not fitting in with the organization of things? A society is made up of individuals and needs the best it can gather from each of them. A society that exists for the society is headed for disaster as group (mob) rule is always infused with danger. You don't need a government or a celebrity or even your family to tell you what to think! Sure, you listen to advice, but then you must think for yourself. What should I be doing? Where should I be going? What do I have to offer to the world? These are the only questions that matter. The reason so many people are drifting along, bored and unfulfilled, is because they are busy living someone else's dream!

Most of us shun our own insights because we have been herded and prodded to do so. Then, as Emerson aptly predicted, *"Tomorrow a stranger will say with masterly good sense precisely what we have thought and felt all the time, and we shall be forced to take with shame our own opinion from another."* We only half believe ourselves and that only half the time. We apply a strange method of thinking someone else always knows what is best for us, better than ourselves. Who should know more than I what is my duty; my obligations? Yet therein we travel down pathways and alleys seeking the happiness that someone else has promised us we'll find there. You alone, in your heart always know what to do and what not to do. You are conspicuously aware of what causes you both delight and shame.

Though there be a thousand reasons why you distrust yourself, every one of them is a thinly clad veil for of fear. If you are honest (and who would choose to be dishonest with themselves?), the only thing that ever stops a man from acting upon something he knows, is fear. And what great supremacy fear holds over the mind of man today! Fear whips you in line and threatens you with catastrophe for daring to step out of line! Fear drains the vivid colors out of men and makes them all gray-scale. Fear crushes your lofty dreams and orders you to settle for the status quo. Yet, fear is mastered in a moment of time when you choose to act upon what you and you alone know.

Each person living in the world has his particular gift to offer. And though time is required for its development, it is there; it must be there, as all of God's creation is never without purpose. To compare your purpose with my purpose is like expecting a salty taste from sugar. Salt is salt, and sugar is sugar, and both are required according to taste; with a million variations therein. Thus, your purpose must meet a need no other person can quite fill, else were all men the same and drudgery would overtake the planet. You find out your purpose by focusing in on your own delights. When I read Emerson, my heart doesn't quite know what to do, but when my wife listens to him, most words offer her no meaningful impact. What is it that passionately interests you? What thing, when done by you, is without effort and that for which time stands still? In that thing are your wings, though they still exist in embryonic form.

It's been said that if you find whatever it is you love to do and do it, you will never work another day in your life. I would expand that to say that if you find what you love to do and do it, you will be joyfully living the life God has personally called you to live. Your age doesn't matter. Your circumstances don't matter. How you've lived your life up to this point doesn't matter. What matters is that you pursue, with all that you are, your grand, unique purpose. And, that purpose will never appear written in cloud-like ink across the sky or be chanted by the convulsing masses. It won't be written by the finger of God on your wall. Instead, it will show itself in your interests; in those things you cannot get enough of; in the quiet, silent, tender regions of your heart from whence the still small voice gently urges, go this way my wonderful son; head that way my beautiful daughter...

You owe yourself the courage to stand up and masterfully take your place in this life.

"Insist on yourself, never imitate. Trust thyself, every heart vibrates to that iron string." (RWE)

WHEN THE DUST SETTLES

You know, it's no marvel that many folks spend the majority of their lives living from one turmoil to the next. The world and its negative circumstances, the impending and ever-present threats concerning the future, the agitation and tumults of daily life all loom on the horizon, assaulting folks' minds from sunup to sundown. And all of that turmoil and distress has one important object in mind, namely to prevent you from seeing clearly and discerning properly. Imagine how different your life might be if you could cut through all of the distractions and really see. What would you do differently? What would you do if the dust settled?

Most people, and you know it's true, live and subside on a steady diet of fear. Fear of sickness (got one in mind), fear of not having enough, fear of not measuring up or being pretty enough, or not having the right body. Fear of not getting their needs met, fear of something bad happening to them or someone they love. Fear concerning the planet or the sun or the melting icebergs. Fear of not being loved and feeling love and missing love. Fear of the future, fear of the past coming back to haunt them, fear of being present in the moment. Fear all day, every day, from the moment you wake up in the morning until you lay down your head to sleep at night. People have subsisted on fear for so long that they no longer even recognize its presence. Fear has been normalized as part of life. Fear drives and drags people around in its wake, pushing and pulling them in directions they never intended. If people manage to escape its grasp temporarily, they quickly fall back under its spell. Fear rules the world and the systems of the world. Often, very often, it has ruled you! Yet for all that power fear holds over people (and it's very powerful), at the end of the day, it is all a grand, cleverly designed illusion to control the hearts and lives of people. Fear is the dust that prevents you from being able to see.

Clarity of heart and mind is the missing ingredient in a tumultuous life. In order to move confidently in the direction of your dreams, you have to be able to see. You have to be clear about who you are, what you want, and where you are going. You have to cut through that mountain of clutter obscuring your view and discern just what the hell is actually going on. The world, with its teeming masses clamoring after this novel invention and that new threat to their existence, live the majority of their lives unclear and confused. They fail to get their honest questions answered. They live their lives perpetually attacked by an opponent they can neither see nor feel. They pray to a God they neither know nor understand. They plod along, herded and corralled into wrong-thought camps with no possibility of escape. It never dawns on them that there is a part of life they have yet to experience for themselves. They conclude they've already reached the end, figured it out and can choose wisely on their own. Yet, they cannot, and they cannot because they cannot see! It is only God who is able to make the dust finally settle so that you can see, and He does it with the light of his Word. Absent the Word and the truth in life, you are destined to a life of fear, whether acknowledged or not.

Once you begin to get some truth into your heart and life, things become very clear for you. It starts to dawn on you that many things that are said and done as truth are, in actuality, cleverly crafted lies. You begin to be able to discern both the good and the evil influencing your life. You start to understand how life really works and stop wasting your time striving for things of no avail. You quit working so desperately hard to fix yourself, or to improve your bad behavior, or to keep grinding at all costs to make something good of yourself. You see, the world presents to you a picture of life with suggestions on how to improve it. Yet, those improvements, those efforts, those arduous solutions are not solutions at all because they center on you for you and all about you, and they deny the God that made you! Absent God and His love, you will never be able to really see. You will simply be blown about with every wind of doctrine, clamoring to try this new source of help and that empty promise of the answer you need. It doesn't work, and it never has worked... Real life isn't all about you (or me) but is about the God who created you (us). He is your only true provider and your only genuine source of help. He has the answers you need. He offers the healing that has no limitation. He knows and understands your heart, has heard your every prayer, and wants to set you free from fear and its attendant misery. He is your promise of love and goodness and peace. He alone has the power to make the dust settle so that you can finally see clearly and can understand His wonderful, sincere and perfect will for your life!

This life, as you already know quite clearly, can be very tricky to navigate. You will daily be deluged with thousands of opinions, ideas and suggestions. You will be confronted with both evil and counterfeit good. You'll be presented with a myriad of potential beliefs, all offering something they cannot truly give. Yet, when all of the shouting and the clamor stops, when all of the fighting and tumult is ceased, when all of the falsehood and error goes away, when all of the pressures and the agitation subsides, behind it you will hear the still small voice offering you the clarity you have always dreamed of and then you will know the dust has settled at last.

ANNOYINGLY ANNOYED, AGITATED AND ANGRY

Have you ever found yourself just completely and unapologetically annoyed with people? Have you ever spent the day angry about everything? What is it that happens to us on certain days or maybe even for certain weeks when we have literally no patience left for circumstances and situations? What burr got under our saddle? Who are those thorns in the flesh? What has gotten us so pissed off? And, from whence does that agitation originate? Indeed, how did we end up so annoyingly annoyed, agitated and angry?

If you are anything like me, you know that sometimes people and situations just bug the living shit out of you! Oh, try as you might to return to your positive status quo; you just can't seem to locate it. Something happened to you. Something somewhere somehow got to you. Are you just grumpy or hungry or sleepy, or is there another variable involved? Your emotions, as varied and complex as they are, are still fed by the thoughts and feelings you are accepting or confronting. Your mind does not function in a vacuum. Words, opinions, and experiences all work to take you somewhere, be it good or bad. Words carry with them tremendous power to shape your mindset and encourage or discourage you. Opinions, though always personal in nature, work with you when you share them and work against you when you disagree. Experiences must be interpreted, and they are done so in the light of what you are thinking at the time. Some days we want to write off as bad days, close up shop and start fresh tomorrow. Other days we feel we have unlimited energy and can do anything we desire. Just what exactly is going on?

Every single thing you put into your mind has some kind of effect on you. Every. Single. Thing. There are no such things as benign thoughts. Every Facebook post, every Instagram meme, every so-called news report or article, every conversation, every skillfully crafted advertisement, every text string, every email, every LinkedIn posting, every single asinine campaign ad, every reality television program, makes some type of impact on your mind. You see it, you read it, you rehearse it, you contemplate it, ending in some type of effect on how you are going to feel. If you are not careful, soon you find yourself swept away and annoyed. For me, it's not differences in opinions that bother me; it's the general absence of any fathomable logic or common sense. It's group think. It's all or nothing processing where all choices are centered in either A or B. How absurd? There is good and evil and a whole world of choices in between. Americans, in particular, seem to have been lulled into non-thinking largely based on the cheap effects of social media. Empty words, empty ideas, completely illogical concepts and gross generalizations based on some bullshit someone else came up with. Reading it and considering it absolutely fries my soul! But, as has been the case since time began, the problem isn't all the outside influences trying to captivate and capture our minds; the real problem is in our consideration of those irrational concepts and lies. Lies, lies, lies, all craftily designed to dull and diminish our God-given capability to think for ourselves.

The solution to our dilemma is not to fuss and fume and fret ourselves over the latest line of insanity to assault our minds but instead refuse it. This precarious notion that being an adult means having to patiently sift through the garbage bin, politely agreeing to disagree, trying to find logic in illogic or acting as if everything is true, just a different kind of true, is abject delusion and nonsense! It was the consideration of evil that led to the first man's demise, and it will, without doubt, lead to yours as well. Your job, my job, is to separate ourselves from it. Stop listening to it. Get away from the people that promote it. Well, you can scroll past it they say. Yes, I can, but I'm worse off for having done so. Every small piece of poop you leave on your shoe is part of a collective larger piece of poop on your shoe you will be left within your mind. Stop arguing with them! Quit trying to interject something logical into something that isn't logical to begin with. Nuts is nuts is nuts is nuts! Walk away from it. The reason you are feeling so agitated is that you keep giving the source of agitation access to you, and it isn't your former friend that is behind it! Clean up your friendslist! Better, stay off the feed for a while. Figure out what it is that is upsetting you and remove its access to you.

Finally, recognize what it is you are saying to yourself or, worse, what you are saying about yourself. No one in their right mind is opposed to their own selves. By the time you are angry with yourself and no longer like that person staring back at you from the mirror, something has already worked you over. Something has succeeded in diminishing your worth to the point where you remain perpetually angry with your very own self! You are a human being, and like all humans will find yourself unknowingly participating in some absurdity from time to time. You are going to make mistakes. You are going to blow it, miss the mark, fail in your efforts and generally fall short of the person God called you to be. The nature of error pre-exists in your bloodline. Instead of being angry with yourself, figure out what it is that you are telling yourself about yourself. If it is causing you unrest it is probably not true. God, like any good parent, doesn't make you better by pointing out your flaws but rather by pointing out all that is right about you. He graciously provided the ultimate solution in the life of His son. God isn't mad at you; you are mad at you! After you clean up your friends list, take some time to clean up your own mind as well. Purge your thoughts of every accusation, every consideration of something being wrong with you.

These days we live in feel like the pinnacle of annoyance, agitation and anger, but they don't have to be. There's a better place to live. Calm yourself down a little bit and figure out what you have been feeding your mind that has you so pissed off! Anger and agitation do nothing but diminish your soul! Get above it on the high road where God lives. I don't know about you, but I feel better already!

I'VE BEEN BLIND FOR A WHILE NOW

In life, just because you cannot see something does not mean it doesn't exist. There are whole vistas of life and understanding to be discovered once you finally get the eyes to see. People trudge along their journeys lifeless and hopeless, never quite discerning; never really seeing; never able to make sense of life with all of its varied and manifold twists and turns. And because they have not experienced it, they don't believe it, and in not believing it, it escapes them. Often life is more about what has been obscured from your view than it is about seeing what is right there in front of you. Maybe there is more, much more, for you to learn still. Maybe you have been blind for a while now...

In order to see what is available to see, your mind needs illumination. Darkness is always the absence of light. You will remain unable to see what direction you are traveling as long as you are traveling in the dark. To think you are already illuminated yet continue in futility is a sure indicator that you remain in the dark. To grossly assume that your limited life experience or past education has provided you with all that is necessary to understand life is to cut yourself off from the very essence and fiber of life. You do not know what you do not know. All of the natural, breathtaking reality of nature surrounding you serves to capture your attention. Whether it be the brilliance of a sunset or the intricate depth of a flower, all are designed to lead you to a question; the next question. That question urges you to the light. In the light life, real life, is found.

The reason people live their whole lives in darkness is because they do not know or understand the truth. They have unknowingly lived in darkness for so long that they cannot even consider that light exists. The glimpses of light they have experienced are quickly chased away by the darkness. They are led away unmercifully time and time again, herded with the masses into uncertainty and fear. They do not seek light because they have been sold on lies concerning the light. Religion, posing as the light, feeds them error upon error, producing only more darkness. Religion informs them of all the things they must do to find the light, then chastises them for being unable to find it, attributing it to sins or hidden faults preventing them from finding, seeing or experiencing. Every wrong path pursued, be it intentionally or out of ignorance, leads only to more darkness. Error works to harden the hearts of men, and once hardened, can no longer perceive. Darkness is a cruelty that can only be remedied by the light. Otherwise man remains blinded and unable to see clearly.

Light comes from God and from God alone. The light is found in the truth of God's Word. Ask yourself how much of God's Word you understand and you can accurately predict how much light you enjoy. Most people, sadly, know very little about God's Word and worse, much of it has been manipulated and distorted to be something it is not. In place of unparalleled freedom, people are enslaved. Instead of being a source of encouragement and edification, it is turned into a touch point for accusation and criticism. People falsely conclude that life with God is all about their behavior and what they are doing and shouldn't, and aren't doing, but should. They make God the morality police and, as such, avoid Him like the plague. I'm pretty certain God already knows how you are living, yet like any good parent worth his salt, loves you anyway. You pray for healing to a god that supposedly made you sick. You endure unspeakable tragedies and console yourself with some mysterious higher purpose. You daily assign evil to the only good and live in abject fear of destruction and loss. Brothers and sisters, you have got it all wrong. God is only good always! God will never do anything to harm you, no matter who you are and whatever you have done! That is love, and that is light...

Once you begin to understand God's Word and His purposes, you find the light for which you have been searching your whole life. God's Word illuminates your path. The truth enables you to separate good from evil. God's Word helps you to finally see all the things you have formerly been unable to see. Once able to see, you become free to experience real life. You find the love and the joy you have only heard of before. You discover the peace of God that surpasses all human understanding and, in that peaceful state, are able to quickly spot the imposters when they arrive. You no longer have to live your life terrified about what tomorrow may bring. When you have a need, God, not your human wisdom, meets it. If you are sick, He will heal you. What you do not understand, He will explain to you. The parts of life that formerly enslaved you will no longer hold you bound because of the light that lives within your soul. Have you been blind for a while now? Well, now is the time to see...

If your heart is open and if you are willing to admit that maybe you don't know, you can learn. You can both see and experience all that God intended for life to be. You can live on the high road. You can escape the clutches of religion and bondage and walk in complete and total freedom, never again held in by anyone or anything! You can discern error for what it is, error promoted and espoused by evil to keep you away from the true light. God is not hiding any of this from you, but something else is, and you owe it to yourself to figure that out.

The life you are yearning for is yearning for you as well. Maybe you have been blind for a while now. The truth will make you see...

YOU VERSUS YOU...

After enduring another disastrous morning on the golf course, a good friend remarked something that really struck me! He said, "You are only competing against yourself." How profound... Golf, seemingly more than any other sport, is a mental game, and you win or lose right between your ears. Life is like that. The one you are really competing against is your own self. I know that life is spiritual and there is something behind what we see, but in its basic essence the most important struggle to win happens right inside your own mind. Will you win the battle of you versus you?

Inside all of us, a gigantic dichotomy plays out. We are literally two different entities living inside one body. One nature wants to seek out the good while the other nature seeks out the bad. It's the old adage of the angel on one shoulder and the devil on the other. And while that is not literally true, that scene plays out in a million variations. On the one hand we want to enjoy the best things in life, and on the other hand we habitually settle for far less. One side of us knows the value of working hard, while the other side seeks a quick fix. One part of us acts out of love and the other part acts out of fear. Almost instinctively, we know the man or the woman we ought to be, but we cannot seem to get there no matter how hard we try. We know what we should do to be successful, but we fall short of it. Instead of using words that are uplifting and encouraging, we blurt out hurtful words and wound the hearts of others. We find ourselves in a perpetual conundrum. When the opportunity to do good presents itself, we don't do it. But the things we hate, we do all the time. In the battle of you versus you, you have to fight. But, you are not fighting the world; you are fighting your own self based on the influences of the world. As human beings, it is our most important fight.

The reason we struggle to gain superiority over our own selves is because doing so requires that we learn to control ourselves. Self-mastery requires control. How quickly we lose ground when victory is assured because we give in on some principle. We don't see things through to their logical conclusion. We live inside bodies we no longer like, but are loathe to exercise the control necessary to set them right again. We fall for the false illusions of pleasure, offering us something they cannot give, then hate ourselves for doing so. We want to find the quick route, the shortcut, the workaround. We ignore the cautions because they don't apply to us, only to suffer the consequences down the road. We have the hardest time in the world learning that the wrong choice leads to the wrong result in every case, though it may not be readily apparent. We so desperately want to be happy but don't do the things that make for happiness. We want to have our cake and eat it too. We seek to blend the good and the evil and make them companions, hoping we can find a way to play in both leagues. The answer to our plight is only found in control, self-control.

Learning to control yourself is a difficult task. Yet the failure to do so accounts for most of the misery that is in the world. Every failure that ever thwarted man has its roots in some failure concerning self-control. Fear is a failure to properly control your thinking concerning some circumstance. Obesity is a failure to control what you eat. Alcoholism is a failure to control how much liquor you imbibe. Every character flaw, every weakness, every obnoxious habit comes about from a failure to control some aspect of your thinking and thus your life. Nothing is evil of itself. Things become evil in excess or overuse. Every aspect of life is to be enjoyed, and it's our job to recognize when our enjoyments are taking control of us. Anything that seeks to control you must be rigorously avoided at all costs. Once evil gets its foot in the door, it won't be long before it moves in, bringing more and more hurt and loss. Yet, your mind being the only thing you can actually control, holds the key to every situation you find yourself confronted with.

The good news is that you can learn to control yourself. But, in order to do so, you have to learn how to control your thinking. The temptation to do wrong, which comes as easily as weeds growing in the garden, is resisted not with so much discipline, but more by refusal to think in certain directions. You cannot tinker with the wrong ideas, but rather immediately reject them. You have to think about what you are thinking about. If you feel miserable, chances are you are thinking thoughts that lead to misery. You cannot get a good life from bad thoughts. You cannot win a race by looking back. You cannot win the next moment fixated on the previous moments. You cannot learn and grow and change by adhering to the same thoughts which you have been cleaving to in the past. You cannot win if you think you cannot win. You, my friend, have to stop saying the things to yourself that defeat you. You have to get off your own back. You have to dwell on your good and not your evil. We all have some combination of good and evil going on inside us, but we win in proportion to how much we can minimize the evil and emphasize the good. (God has already graciously covered the evil.)

This is a lesson that you have to learn for yourself. Try it out. Begin controlling some aspect of your life you feel has gotten away from you and see how good you feel about yourself. See how quickly your joy and enthusiasm for living come back. Self-control is not something to be avoided in order to live a fun life; it is the very essence of a truly fun and enjoyable life.

Even your golf game will improve if you can get ahold of yourself in the midst of going astray. If it works for golf, it will certainly work for you...

PULL YOUR WEEDS

Being an avid gardener and a lover of all things growing, I've pulled more than my fair share of weeds. No matter how much you endeavor to stay on top of them, they always come back. You take a little vacation hiatus and they've already taken over the entire garden. Life is like that. No matter how hard you work at it, there's always going to be challenges to overcome. Sometimes those challenges can get ahead of you and overwhelm you. No matter how big of a mess you may find yourself in at times, the only solution is to get back out there and pull those weeds one by one until they are all gone.

It seems awfully unfair that the weeds of life, the negatives, the personal problems, the difficulties, the challenges, and the bad habits, seemingly appear overnight while the good things take so much time and effort to build and preserve. Evil is truly relentless. It picks away at you day by day, ever seeking to take away some good, some happiness. Little things left unchecked quickly assemble and begin to strangle you. Unfinished business is the blight of mankind. Man, while endeavoring to enjoy good things, yet letting stuff go and overlooking things that need attention, garners to himself difficulties that could have been easily handled early on. As such, it is important to pull up the weeds as quickly as they appear. Waiting for a better time simply compounds the problem. The effort required to stay on top is significantly less than the energy required to dig out of the disaster. Pull your weeds.

Everything in life that you *let go* eventually turns back on you. The little issue you started recognizing, the thinking errors you haven't resolved, the vices you have employed, and your tendency towards procrastination with its associated stacking up and compounding, all stand as beacons calling out for you to act. Inaction, appearing as a viable alternative, simply works behind the scenes to bury you with worries and undue concerns. The elephant in the room remains and you are left worse off because of it. You aren't preserving precious time; you are squandering your future time. Fix the leaky pipe. Handle your overdue car registration. Pay the ticket. Replace your wiper blades. Pull your weeds. If you don't do it today, you are going to spend a lot more time doing it with its consequences tomorrow.

The origin of all of mankind's difficulties is found in the spiritual realm. (There was a time when there weren't any weeds!) The way that darkness gets on top of you occurs systematically, day by day, night by night. It chips away at you one weed at a time, counting on your inaction. Eventually, you find yourself so marred and overwhelmed that the solution is no longer apparent. Enter the method for every apparently unsolvable problem you have ever had. By the time you become aware that you are in trouble, you are already in deep. Thus, the solution to spiritual problems is to chip away at them one by one until they are gone. You cannot clean them up all at once, no matter how determined you are. They were unsuspectingly built into you over time, and they may require time to be resolved. Overcoming these kinds of problems will require God's help and loving assistance. Often, the problem you seek to address isn't the problem at all, but rather is an extension of another problem on top of another problem, masking another problem. You cannot clearly discern the problem (on your own), and that's why the problem persists. But, with God's help you can begin recovering yourself, pulling one weed at a time, weed by weed until the issue is at last resolved.

The weeds of life exist as the worries and fears that you unknowingly harbor; the negative outcomes you faithfully rehearse and consider, and the resultant inaction and lack of energy they produce. Thinking is not an action; it only precedes an action. In other words, you have to make up your mind to do something about the things that are bothering you. Do something! Take a step forward. Stop going down certain paths, either mentally or physically or both. Challenge your bad habits. Cease (or pause) doing something you are so desperately clinging onto as a need that isn't a need at all. The problem with bad habits is that they always begin as small and insignificant, yet gather power by your insistence on repeating them. After a time, as was secretly designed, you pursue your bad habits almost automatically until they develop enough steam to bring your entire life down to some terrible outcome. Fear produces inaction. The anecdote to fear is action, not more analysis. Once you begin to act, you will find more clues, more insights, and more valuable information about where and how you are being defeated. Until then, you will continue business as usual, suffering, churning, wishing for the answer. Get up and start pulling the weeds!

Life was designed by God and He already knows where you stumble and why. His Word already had the answer but you might not know that yet. Better than any good parent, He knows exactly how to rescue you. He sees all and cuts right through all of the facades and trickery. As you act, He acts. As you take believing steps, however small, He will provide you with glimpses of truth and flashes of light to guide you on your way. It doesn't matter where you came from or how you were brought up. It doesn't matter how bad your problem appears to be. What matters is that you decide to act, then act. What has been bothering you lately or for the past year, or even the last 20 years? What garbage can of crap assaults you day by day? What recurrent issues seem to keep popping up over and over again? That thing or those things are a good place to start! Start pulling the weeds up until you get back to the beautiful you, alive, thriving and unencumbered; the real you! Act now!

GETTING OUT OF YOUR FUNK

If you've spent enough time dwelling on terra firma, you know that at certain times in your life you find yourself deeply entrenched in a funk; an Americanism for feeling down in the dumps; which is related to a Dutch word meaning a mental haze; and in German a word for gloomy or depressed. No matter the language or the usage, all you know is that it sucks. It sucks away your life and enthusiasm for living. It's no happiness, no inspiration, nothing to look forward to, blah, blah, blah... Blah! But, there is something you can do about it! No matter how far entrenched in the rut you are, there is always a way out...

The place to begin when attempting to understand your feelings is first to examine your thoughts. Thoughts precede feelings. You don't wake up in a bad mood. Your bad mood follows where your mind has been. Most folks pay very little attention to their thoughts. They sort of let them come and go like the weather. They consider themselves blessed when their mental environment is sunny and cursed when it is gloomy. The weather never stays gloomy and you don't have to either. However, you do have to take some initiative with your thoughts. Letting your thoughts run makes you a victim to whatever circumstance is being engineered against you. Please read that sentence again! There are forces at work in the world plotting and scheming, persuading and manipulating to lead you and your thoughts to a certain place. You cannot see them but instead only register their effects. They gain access to you by the thoughts you allow and encourage. They cannot overtake your freedom of will (at first), but they can get you off track; way off track! They begin by getting you to consider some negative aspect of life, then work out circumstances and situations that corroborate your wrong thinking. And, if you remain stuck there long enough, you find yourself submerged and engulfed in heaviness from which it becomes very difficult to escape.

Life is spiritual in nature. It is not made up solely of the things which do appear. Ignorance concerning this will mire you in futility, chasing your own tail, searching yourself and your own feelings for a remedy. Yet, you won't find your solution in your own thoughts because the problem didn't originate in your own thoughts. You are not fighting against yourself, though it may feel like it; you are fighting against a negative spiritual opponent working behind the scenes to control you. To defeat this spiritual foe (behind all of the misery of mankind), you have to learn how to compete spiritually. You have to learn how to fight back. And, amazingly, the arena of competition is in your mind. You see, it's not as simple as deciding to be happy, though that is a good start. It is learning how and what to think and holding on to those thoughts though a monument of resistance be placed in front of you. If you find yourself today steeped in misery or unending gloominess, it is a good indicator that you are not winning the fight. You never want to get comfortable with those negative emotions or embrace them as some incredulously purport. Instead, you fight them, and you fight them, and you fight them with spiritual words that negate and overpower their authority. Refusing to fight back only leads to defeat. Or worse, explaining away those insidious attacks with man's wisdom will only serve to prolong the fight. You only win a fight by being stronger or tapping into something stronger than whomever or whatever you are fighting against. Evil has power but it is no match for God's power.

It certainly doesn't make for light conversation to learn about standing against evil. It probably won't be found in the self-help section of the bookstore. Public opinion poo poo's the notion of evil altogether, or portrays it as a construct of man. The movie media displays it as frightening and ghastly. But, no matter the babblings of the naysayers, it does exist and *it is your problem*. God does not want you to be ignorant concerning evil, nor does He want you to be afraid of it. Instead, He wants you to understand what is actually going on so you can direct your efforts appropriately and with great and lasting impact. People are stuck today ensconced in difficulties because they no longer understand or acknowledge spiritual realities. When Jesus stood against all the forces of hell, he did so simply, though not easily, by quoting and cleaving to what God's Word said. It is God's Word quoted on the lips of believing that defeats the powers of darkness. It is the only way.

You can be delivered today, rescued, set free by learning how to tap into God's power for your life. It doesn't matter how low you may have sunk or how entrenched you may have become. All you need is a little humility and a willingness to learn about spiritual realities. You can escape any of the chains that have been binding you; break free from any bondage; break out of the bands and fetters that have been controlling your life. You can learn again how to live and enjoy and be blessed. You can return to happiness and joy and peace and love. You can escape from the prisons that have been holding you in. Stop thinking that something is wrong with you or that you are somehow deserving of the misery you have been living. Stop settling for less than the best in your life. You don't need more medicine or more treatment or more of the expertise of men. You need God and His Word.

Finding yourself in a deep funk; down in the dumps; in a

mental haze; gloomy and depressed is a horrible way to experience life, and you do not have to live that way. There are answers and solutions for any malady that challenges your life. Won't you be willing to find your way out of your funk? I sure hope so...

CHAPTER THREE
Thoughts

DRIVING MS. DAISY

There's a little-known secret in the world today, and it involves what you think about the most in the privacy of your own mind. Your day-to-day thinking forms the building blocks of how your life turns out. What you consider, what you dwell upon, what you incubate in the chambers of your mind turns into your experience of life (not simply your reaction to it, but your actual experience). As such, and this is why it remains a secret, you have a duty to control your thinking. You are responsible to actively direct your thoughts as opposed to having them direct you! Are you driving Ms. Daisy going where you are told, or are you driving your own life?

Many, many people feel that their thoughts are something that just happen as they navigate life. They unknowingly just sort of let their thoughts run wherever the wind takes them. They wrongly assume "good" days and "bad" days are predetermined, with their responsibility being simply to make it through the bad days. They *hope* tomorrow will be better. And in thinking this way, they become victims, cruelly tortured by an opponent they cannot see nor discern. They are victimized because no one ever taught them how to control their thinking, much less any reason to seek to do so. A life lived with uncontrolled thinking is a life being directed by someone outside of yourself. It's a life filled with misery.

Your heart is the great citadel of your soul. Your heart must be guarded above all that you can ever guard because from "it" flow the issues of *your* life. Those things you have in your heart, be they wonderful or disastrous, will come to pass in your physical reality if they are allowed to remain in your heart. Your heart is made up collectively of the things you think about the most or hold most dear, like a treasure. The way that you guard your heart is by controlling what you will and will not think about. Failure to control your thinking, a human epidemic, leads to a heart filled with things you do not want, put in there by something that seeks to bring harm, defeat and loss into your life. Think about it for a second. If you aren't driving, who is? God doesn't do the driving for you, no matter how much you might wish He would. Instead, God admonishes you to guard your heart. He tells you to control your thinking. He asks that you, by your freedom of will, make the decision to think how He says to think. Committing to controlling your thinking and thinking in terms of the things God says to think about leads you directly to the abundant life He promised you!

Please allow me to clarify what I'm offering you in terms of your life experience! There's a whole world of goodness and love and blessings awaiting you if you are willing to do your part! But, you have to do your part! I'm certainly not suggesting that you walk around trying to find the good in bad things or simply putting a smile on your face when things go terribly wrong. Nor am I asking you to ignore negative events or act like things are okay when they are not okay. Instead, I'm suggesting that you fight to remain positive in your expectations. Allowing the world to define your experience and decide for you whether or not you are going to be okay leads only to more and more defeat. As such, your duty, your solemn duty is to not stake your existence on what things look like or seem like, but rather on what God's Word says is right; what God's Word says is true. Holding fast to what the Word says; to what God has promised you is the only way to escape your present circumstances and turn things around for the better. Your expectation for the future is just that, "your expectation!" You can expect for things not to work out, or you can expect that they will, no matter what is going on in your present experience. If you're honest you already know how negative the world is and the people and the circumstances. Controlling your thinking means knowing the preponderance of negativity, y. You still remain positive because God is bigger than any circumstance!

Controlled thinking isn't walking around all day holding onto a certain thought as life doesn't work that way. You aren't a robot! Instead, you go about your day-to-day experience and pay attention to what you are thinking about. When you notice you are afraid, for example, you think about some promise from God that counters that fear. Then, as your duty in controlled thought, you decide not to entertain those fearful expectations. Oh, it's not always easy as you will find yourself really tempted to consider those negatives, but controlled thinking refuses it. All of your reasoning and mental ability are no match for what's behind that stuff. You take it on by not taking it on! Refuse it. This pattern applies to every negative thing that limits and tarnishes your life. If you will commit yourself to doing as I suggest, you will begin to experience a joy and happiness you have not ever experienced before. You will find the peace that passes understanding and find yourself right in the middle of all of God's goodness, available for you...

Determine now that you will begin trying to control your thinking. Think about what you are thinking about. Thoughts that give you agitation or unrest are sure indicators you are thinking about things you need to stop thinking about. Don't overcomplicate things with your human reasoning. Simply refuse the negatives and replace them with the positives of God's Word. Do this faithfully moment by moment throughout your day. As you become more accustomed to it, it will get easier to do, and you will experience for yourself the blessedness.

Are you driving Ms. Daisy to destinations you didn't choose? Direct and control your own thoughts and arrive at the place where all *your* dreams come true...

LIFT UP YOUR THOUGHTS

The other day, a close friend (brother) of mine posted a quote from one of my favorite authors, James Allen, that truly resonated with me. "A man can only rise, conquer, and achieve by lifting up his thoughts. He can only remain weak, and abject, and miserable by refusing to lift up his thoughts." If you want to do life like you would like your life to be done, you have to learn to lift up your thoughts.

If you lived a little and experienced some things, you've begun to learn that the mindset you maintain is entirely within your control. Oh, crappy things still happen to you. Things go south inexplicably. Circumstances marshal together and bite you on the ass. But, what you do with your thoughts is always, always up to you. Sometimes you want to stay in your funk. Playing the victim has its own reward in absolving you from all personal responsibility. The reality that life is often unfair seems justification enough to stay down in the misty flats. But, at the end of the day, my friends, you know deep down that you are refusing to lift up your thoughts. Thoughts and emotions change at such a frequency that you might forget whatever clouds are blocking your sunshine, forcing you to willfully recall the source of your trouble and get back to acquiescing to it. In such cases, you are refusing your own happiness and reaping the results of your own decision.

The difficulty involved with lifting up your thoughts is not a matter of discipline or self-control, but rather a matter of being afraid. You're afraid that it won't matter what you do and that no matter what you do, things will continue as they are. You doubt the outcome. Fear has you ensnared and trapped. You wish and pray and beg God to change the circumstances but refuse to own the part for which you alone are responsible. You want to win the lottery or for some other miraculous event to solve your problems in one fell swoop. You want to lose the weight by taking a pill and still eating bad foods in excess. You want the happiness you have hoped for without doing the things that happiness requires. In short, you are not cooperating with your own solution. In stubborn rebellion, you want good from bad and blessings from cursings (your own mental cursings). In the immortal words of Emerson, "We need only obey."

Your thoughts connected to your mind, connected to your heart, form the basis of the life you live. If you want better you have to think better. You have to change your mind. You are waiting for God and God is waiting for you! God's part is to provide all that you need to be successful. Your part is to think accordingly. You can't hang around in the darkness and expect to see the light. God doesn't change. He is not found in the darkness. He lives in the light. You have to march your mental butt over to the light, where He is, and then you can finally see. Lifting up your thoughts means taking your thoughts to the light. You don't walk over to the light because everything looks good or feels good or because things are finally looking up. You walk over to the light in order to see the good and experience the good, and then and only then do things begin to start looking up. Do you understand what I'm saying? You act first. You take the initiative. You make the right move! Change your mind! Refuse the abject negativity and doom predictions and get yourself to the light!

Lifting up your thoughts is not blind faith or anything that cannot see what's ahead. Instead, it is a mental decision to think something different and stop thinking in accordance with the presentation engendered by the darkness. You may not realize it, but thinking negatively is actually a form of obedience also, but you are obeying the wrong source. You are cooperating knowingly or unknowingly with the wrong source. Cooperation with evil, even if you have never considered it that way, is a recipe for a life of abject misery! It is not how life is or being realistic or any other bullshit you have rehearsed in order to justify your wrong thinking. Instead, it is deception artfully crafted to make your life suck! And, if your life sucks, you know exactly what I'm talking about. Look, you cannot control the events of the world. You cannot control the economy. You cannot control the evil things that happen to people in this life. But, you can control your thinking. You can decide to lift up your thoughts, and you owe it to yourself to do so!

It is an absolute shame what happens to people in this life. It is awful and painful and terrible. People are blown about from pillar to post by an enemy they don't perceive. They feel helpless, lost and defeated. Yet, they fail to recognize the one thing they can control, their minds. They do not see or understand the connection. They wrongly assume that thoughts are just thoughts and, as such, don't put much stock in the importance of controlling those thoughts. God has not left you without remedy. Jesus was always successful because he controlled his thoughts perfectly and at all times. You and I will not accomplish that incredible feat, but we can sure as hell make an incredible impact on the lives we live on Earth today.

Lift up your thoughts! When you recognize that you are dwelling in the darkness, change your mind. Stop it! Stop rehearsing every wrong done, everything that isn't right, every problem that confronts you. Stop living in and getting comfortable with evil. Instead, choose light, choose love, choose good thoughts. "Finally, brethren, whatsoever things are true, whatsoever things are honest, whatsoever things are just, whatsoever things are pure, whatsoever things are lovely, whatsoever things are of good report; if there be any virtue, and if there be any praise, think on these things." Philippians 4:8 (and I didn't write the book!)

You can lift up your thoughts, thereby changing your heart and then discover every good thing God wants you to find! It's your mind and your thoughts. Cooperate with God! Obey!

GET BACK IN THE GAME

There was a time when you were incredibly enthusiastic about life. You had your dreams for the future and felt that your possibilities were absolutely endless. You woke each day excited about your future and what you might contribute to the world. Maybe your enthusiasm continues to this day. But for many, sadly, this is no longer the case. Many folks have resigned themselves to the sidelines, not dead yet, but not in the play. What happens to us that so artfully talks us out of our dreams? Who convinces us to give up on the things we so desperately want for our lives? How can we, no matter our years, get back in the game?

Everything you ever wanted in your life, you can have, if you can believe for it. Life and circumstance aren't responsible for the limitation. God isn't behind it, no matter how many Facebook memes claim otherwise. It isn't your background, your education or your upbringing. It's you, my friend. The limitation, if there is one, is you. It sounds simplistic, but it's true. In the final analysis, at the core, at the very root, is you and what you believe in your heart. The reason you don't get the things you want is because you don't believe you can have them. Your friend, who is 10 years younger than you and makes three times more than you, does so because he believes he can. He isn't highly favored or lucky, nor was he born with a silver spoon in his mouth. In his heart he believed he could and, in so believing, did. You can achieve the dreams you have for your life, many of which God put in your heart, if you believe you can. But, believing is a process and sometimes that process takes time. The devil cannot stymie your dreams or take them from you absent your cooperation. You cooperate by adhering to and believing all the evidence to the contrary. In short, you get talked out of it. Achieving your dreams will never appear to be easy, but will come with obstacles and challenges you must surmount. Neither the obstacles nor the challenges can stop you from receiving, unless you give up on what it is you want. You are not in the game because you gave up on yourself.

In the game of life, no one puts you on the sideline except yourself. The coach didn't bench you. God didn't bench you. You benched you! You gave up. You surrendered. You decided along the way that you were not worth (or worthy) of the things you wanted. Oh, you weren't functioning in a vacuum. Your ideas, your beliefs, your expectations were influenced. That influence, call it what you may, succeeded in getting you to believe and accept something that isn't true. It chipped away at you, day by day, week by week, year by year, until it convinced you to settle for something far less than God's best. Maybe it spent considerable time outlining how your previous bad behavior disqualified you from receiving something good from God today. Perhaps it persuaded you that your efforts were futile and that you didn't make any impact worth pursuing. Possibly it just distracted you and got you caught up in activities that wasted your time and didn't lead to anything. Whatever happened, however it happened, if you are sitting on the sidelines and not in the game, it happened. There's no point in lamenting how it happened to you. The solution is simply to get back in the game!

You get back in the game by remembering again the things that are most important to you. What is it or was it that made your heart race? What do you do well that is easy for you to do, that could benefit others in some capacity, that you fool-ishly stopped pursuing? Where and in what is your impact ob-vious? Start there... Maybe those things aren't clear enough for you yet. Instead, what parts of life do you no longer partic-ipate in? Life, if left unchecked and unguarded, has a funny way of reducing things down to the bare minimum. Over the years, a thousand interests turn into a 100 interests, then to 10 interests, ending in no interests. Who took away your in-terests? What gave you a reason to give up on your interests and convinced you that you had seen and done it all? Who stole away your uniqueness and individuality? What per-suaded you into believing that you had nothing left to offer; are now too old, or that it is too late for you? It's bad enough that we all have to die one day, but worse that we can die be-fore we are actually dead.

Your life, my life, is frightfully short. Frightfully short! You owe it to yourself and to God to live your life to the fullest. Get outside your own head. Quit stewing and brewing over what-ever has gone on thus far and check yourself back into the game. Challenge those age-old assumptions you have been making about yourself and your situation. Challenge those limitations that say you can't. Get up off the ground, dust yourself off and check back into the game! The same way you unknowingly checked out, the same way you can check your-self back in again. Try something new. Make a new friend. Pick up a new hobby. It's not really about your age or your energy level. It's about not giving up on yourself and believing to see where your life still has the capacity to make a lasting impact on someone else. Every single day of your precious life holds the promise of something wonderful. But it's not going to knock on your door and find you. You have to find it, though it was never really hidden from you to begin with. Have you been living on the sidelines hoping, wishing something would change so that you could live again? That something is you and it always was you. Get back in the game! We all need you...

BURIED FEELINGS

As far as I can tell, projections you may put upon your pets aside, human beings are God's only creatures that came from the factory equipped with feelings. That alone should have arrested our attention! Human beings have feelings, and those feelings are vast and complex. There are more feelings than there are descriptions for them. Some people say you should honor your feelings, while others say to ignore them. Some folks are described as emotional, yet others appear emotionless. Men attribute feelings to women and women demand more feelings from men. Have you ever wondered why people have feelings? What is the purpose for your feelings? Can you feel too much or too little? And most importantly, why would God have given you the capacity for all of those feelings if they didn't have any value in your life? You feel how you feel for a reason. But have you taken the time to figure out the reason? Or have you learned to bury your feelings instead?

The feelings that you experience are a barometer of your soul. And, like any good barometer, they provide you with important information concerning your internal weather patterns. Sometimes your feelings are sunny and warm, and at other times your feelings are gloomy and foreboding. Some feelings are turbulent and agitated, while other feelings are peaceful and calm. Feelings provide both warnings and confirmation. Certain feelings have no clear description associated with them, like when you feel something is right. Other feelings are painful and inform you something is very wrong.

You can feel anxious and apprehensive. You can experience feeling afraid. But, you can also feel confident and assured. Strangely, sometimes your feelings point out a lack of meaningful activity (boredom), yet also signal an overload of activity defined as stress. With all of the vast world of feelings at your disposal, there must be some intention behind them. Though infinitely complex to you, they are always understood, though sometimes needing further examination. Do you understand your feelings and receive the message they contain for you or have you learned to not give them much credence and go on about your merry way?

Feelings have been described as being no guarantee for truth. And while that is certainly true, feelings do represent the truth about where you are in your journey. Your feelings, both fleeting and long-standing, exist to act as a compass to guide you in the right direction. Feelings are not the "truth," but do indicate your position in relation to the "truth." When you are off track, you feel miserable and defeated. When you are right on, your feelings are light, pleasant and enjoyable. Feelings of apprehension do not necessarily indicate something is wrong but do indicate more thought and understanding may be required. To consistently ignore your feelings is to run headlong into the unknown, risking life and limb. You are feeling what you are feeling for a reason! Learn the reason. Most people don't feel their feelings because they have no feelings, but rather because the world has succeeded in numbing their feelings. A callous isn't formed from being tender, but instead from repeated rough treatment. Thus, having strong feelings isn't an indication of weakness, though it is reported as such, but rather points to a heart that is still tender, soft, and pliable. The more you understand your feelings and acknowledge them, the more successful a human being you will become. This insulting notion that a real man is devoid of feelings is an affront to his Creator. A man is a man because he feels, and a woman is a woman because she feels, though their feelings be as different as night and day. Burying your feelings as an act of self-preservation provides a completely opposite result than was intended!

Human beings are social creatures. Yet each creature feels independently. In order to get along, each other's feelings must be considered. Relationships do not end because of bad feelings, but rather because those feelings eventually go unexpressed. Every time you ignore the feelings that well up inside you and do not express those feelings where appropriate, you do yourself a disservice. While seeking harmony with another, you cause disharmony within yourself. To play a role as an actor or a politician while being untrue to your own feelings is to live a fraudulent life. You feel that you may know and you know that you may grow. Even anger, while feeling unpleasant and toxic, simply acts as a signal that something needs an immediate remedy. Anger ignored comes back with greater velocity until the pressure builds to a breaking point. How much destruction could be avoided simply by faithfully speaking up and expressing honestly how you feel?

To feel is to be human. Not feeling may aid a business endeavor, but eventually the one not feeling will have to come to terms with himself. You cannot be successful and prosperous while ignoring your feelings. Oh, you can for a while. You may garner for yourself much wealth and riches, but you will have paid the price with your very own soul. Listen to what your feelings are telling you. Feelings of boredom inform you of activities left undone, meanings ignored. Agitated feelings point to disturbances and call for a calming solution. How good we feel when we find the answer! Feelings of satisfaction point towards completed efforts. While feeling unfulfilled indicates greater purpose to be discovered. Use your barometer! Pay attention to the weather. It may be stormy today, but storms do not last forever. See your feelings for what they are - indicators, and adjust yourself accordingly.

Our great God equipped you with those feelings to help guide you on your way. Don't ignore them! Don't discount them as petty and meaningless. They are not your truth but will certainly help you discover it. Trust yourself. Trust how you feel though the whole world disagrees with you. Don't live in a world governed by other people's feelings. Instead, live in a world where you honor your feelings, right or wrong and adjust yourself accordingly. You feel that you may know and you know that you may grow! Don't bury your feelings! Feel them, experience them and see the message they have been communicating to you. It's never too late.

Feel...

CHASE THE APPEAL

Have you ever considered why some memories remain in your mind out of all proportion to other memories? (I'm not talking about the things that scared you or that time you got in big trouble.) Certain smells, a song from the past, a phrase or expression, carry with them some wonder; a warmth you find difficult to describe. Similarly, particular aspects of life like an abundant flower garden or a freshly mowed lawn seem to speak to something inside of you. Or maybe it's the feel of a hardbound book cover or the thin rim of your favorite coffee mug. Whatever it is in this world of infinite possibilities, those things are what they are and where they are for a reason. They make their appeal to an important aspect of who you are, and your responsibility is to pursue it. Catch the message. Chase the appeal.

Often, it seems, we fail to recognize our individuality and instead opt for conformity. It's like we cannot fathom our uniqueness and do our best to like what everyone else seems to like. We so desperately want to fit in, to our own detriment; to the sacrificing of everything we *and only we* can bring to the world. We don't trust ourselves. We don't believe in ourselves. When our bodies try to tell us something, we don't listen. We do not follow our own hearts but instead chase after whims and passing fancies. Ultimately, we should have the courage to choose our own paths. We should not be so afraid to upset the herd. In every situation of life there is one right way to go, and we can always find it if we pay attention. Yet, the circumstances of life are so loaded with distractions and alternate courses that we miss them almost every time. And afterwards we often find painfully that we already knew. In order to be consistently happy, you are going to have to learn how to be you; how to do you; to become the best version of you. There is only one you and no one else can bring what you alone can bring. What is appealing to you?

Emerson said, "The eye was placed where one ray should fall, that it might testify of that particular ray." As such, there is a distinct uniqueness to the things you experience, though they be quite dissimilar to someone else. The words of a certain poem, the feeling you experienced seeing the woman laughing on the beach, the high view of the lush valley below, all contain within them something specific for you. Follow after them. They are God's little clues for your greater experience; for your own abundant life. Don't lump them all together and chalk it up as oddity. Don't be so hurried and distracted that you miss them. The more you are willing to see, the more you will see. God is a God of specificity. Haven't you noticed? The One that made your eye with all of its complexity, made your mind as well with all its complexity and as such knows in great detail how to appeal to you. Follow the appeals.

"A man should learn to detect and watch that gleam of light which flashes across his mind from within, more than the luster of the firmament of bards and sages." (RWE) There are things in your experience that brighten your mind and fill and fulfill your heart. Similarly, there are things that serve to darken your mind and numb you to life's greater realities. Get yourself to the light. Notice the things speaking to your heart and investigate them further. They are not random and not happenstance. They lead you directly to the things that are for you. The appeal carries with it some deeper reality, some hidden truth for you that you need. Darkness also carries with it an appeal, but that appeal will always promise to satisfy some desire and damage you in the process. It's interesting to consider that God is not limited to church meetings or conventional settings, while absent from the grand majority of life. As the Author of life, He is in every aspect of life without limitation. Yet, many seem to think He is separate from the other aspects and, as such, miss the messages. Perhaps God wrote that line in the poem you can't seem to stop reading. Why does that song make you feel warm inside? What is that vivid flower communicating to you? All around you every day is intricate and unlimited beauty trying to tell you something, if only you remained willing to hear. Track down the appeal.

Life today is so hurried and frenzied that we miss it. There is so much at which to look. Things are confusing and distracting, overloading us with information and more things to do. But, one thing is needful. Return to the one thing. Live the day and the day only. Don't rush through the days trying to get to another day. Live the day. Experience the moments you are in. Be fully present. In so doing, you will begin to understand (again) that you aren't supposed to just get through life or reach some acceptable age before you die, but actually live life. There's happiness and fulfillment out there waiting for you to come upon it. Life is to be a period of discovery, ultimately discovering the One who made it all. Hold on to the good things. Savor those memories that stand out for you and make you that much better. Pay very close attention to those aspects of life that speak to you directly, even if you cannot fully understand them yet. There is something glorious behind it looking to care for you and love you. Slow down a little bit. Trim back all those activities. Turn off all the noise makers. Look around you and listen intently, for the best parts of life are right there seeking you. Chase the appeal!

SPREAD A LITTLE SUNSHINE

The Corona Virus pandemic has certainly done a fine job of screwing with everyone's minds in various proportions. Some folks have taken to buying 100 toilet paper rolls guaranteeing unlimited wiping for the foreseeable future. Others have seen fit to hoard bread and soup and even the spices. Salt anyone? Oddly, bottled water has reached an epic peak as preparation for Armageddon marches on! Some geographic locales have locked the populace down entirely for fear of an increased spread. Whatever the reactions, ranging from mild annoyance over lost conveniences to abject terror, ye old virus has done a dandy on the minds of Americans. So, what the hell can you do about it?

First, it is important to put things in their proper perspective. Things like this have been happening in the world almost since time began. There have been world wars and rumors of wars. There have been plagues and other health vexations for centuries. There have been catastrophes of unparalleled proportions. The threat of nuclear annihilation only just recently fell out of fashion. In short, there is always something going wrong, somewhere, to some people. It is all a million variations of the same threat, namely fear. Fear has no logical endpoint, because as soon as one fear is overcome, another pops up to take its place. Fear doubles down on bad circumstances and invites more and more disaster. Fear seeks to convince you there is nothing you can do about a situation; it severely limits your options and boldly asserts that God is dead! But, God is not dead, my friends, and He is infinitely bigger than any dreadful thing that rises up against you. Fear is a liar from the father of lies. Remaining in fear you cannot hope to win. Fear is negative outcomes accepted and believed before they come to pass. Fear is truly your only enemy!

In the midst of trying circumstances, you really have only one responsibility. Stop being afraid. Fear not! Fear will have you engaged in all kinds of crazy shit! (toilet paper anyone? - pun intended). Decisions made in fear are not decisions at all, but rather forced behaviors you neither chose or agreed to. Fear is a bully taking advantage of your mind and your human tendency towards futility. I mean, how much control do you really think you have over world events? What could you possibly do in your little reasoning machine to effect any change over what is going on? You cannot wish away negative circumstances, but you can sure as hell refuse to participate any longer. Do you really think that you or a scientist or the medical profession can have any serious, lasting impact over things that are based in the spiritual realm? The only thing that defeats spiritual negativity is spiritual positivity! In other words, instead of furthering the spread of negativity and fear, you must learn how to spread a little sunshine instead. Literally, shed some light on the subject. Be part of the solution. Wake up, stand up and get out there expecting something good to happen. You may not change the world, but you can change how things are going to work out for you. You are the only thing you can control. Instead of falling in line with the other sheep heading towards the cliff, turn around. Go the other way. Decide, "not me, boy," and get out there and live.

It has been my experience that God can turn anything around if enough people can get behind that notion. I'm quite sure God is very familiar with what is going on right now. I'm also sure He loves your loved ones at least as much as you do.

If you got sick, I'm quite sure He could heal you. Nothing that ever happens comes as a surprise to God. He has foreknowledge which means He already knows. And because He knows, He also has a solution for you. Your job is not to try and wrangle with fear, but instead trust God and find the solution. The alternative is almost certain defeat. God is infinitely bigger than anything you will ever come up against! Trusting God means making a decision to stop being afraid. Then, in response to that, let that shit go, Elsa! (Peloton reference). Walk away from it. Let it go! Don't worry yourself over it for another second. If there is nothing God can do when faced with a world pandemic, He certainly wouldn't be much of a God, would He? Well, there is something He can do, but you have to learn to trust Him and let Him do it! Start spreading a little sunshine...

This, too, will pass. One day you will look back on this time and wonder how you let it get you so shook up. But, you will have wasted a lot of time in churning and stressing over something you had no control over. If you think about it; I mean really consider it; nothing you have ever feared was ever within your realm of control. At some point, hopefully, you decided to let it go. Trusting God is always about letting it go. Just as you have enjoyed a beautiful day basking in the sunshine, put that sunshine on in your mind today. Inject some light into your thinking. Stop reasoning with potential catastrophes and walk in the light. Walk in the sunshine feeling the warmth of the One that invented sunshine. There's a reason sunny days make you feel so happy. It is God, don't you see it? It is God enlightening and uplifting your life. Sure, we may have some hardships to endure, but just as there are rains and storms in life, the sun always comes back out. It has to...

I, like you, am not sure what lies ahead. I have also considered economic collapse, sickness and mass misery in the days ahead. But I haven't considered it for very long! I decided I am going to continue spreading the sunshine, no matter how dark it gets, because my life isn't based on what things look like but rather on the promises of God. You, too, my friend, can spread the sunshine. Help somebody else out and get your mind off yourself. Bless people, love people and remember God is bigger, much, much bigger... There will always be a way out for us. Believe that and spread a little sunshine instead...

CHANGE DIRECTIONS

All of us get stuck sometimes in life. We are such creatures of habit, and those habits develop so deeply that sometimes they are difficult to change. At times, you might feel like you're sick of yourself; tired of struggling with the same issues, month after month, year after year. Maybe you're in a relationship that is heading nowhere fast. Perhaps you're weary of your job and your co-workers or the hierarchy and the politics. You can feel mired down in circumstances, smiling when you aren't happy and playing a role in a production you do not enjoy. Maybe you wish you were something that you are not, and the distance between the two is widening. No matter what has happened in the past, what is going on today, or your un-hopeful prospects for the future, don't fret, my friends; you can always change directions...

No person living hasn't experienced this in some form or fashion. It happens to us all. You get a few years under your belt and things dry up a bit. What was once gloriously hopeful and full of possibility can be eroded away through life and ex-perience, especially negative experiences. You get sort of grooved into certain paths, and it becomes hard to extricate yourself from the rut. It hasn't occurred because there is something fundamentally wrong with you. Despite the multi-tude of your private, negative self-talks, you are not the pri-mary cause. There are forces at work in the world whose sole purpose is to beat you down. They convince you to do the things you hate and prevent you from doing the things you love. They skillfully drag you down the same rotten roads where you end up at the same rotten place! They promise you liberty then enslave you. They use you against you. You are living in a spiritual world heavily influenced by things you cannot discern. Instead of settling into the mediocrity and the misery; instead of becoming angry with God; instead of giving up and giving in, you need to simply change directions...

Not understanding what is going on spiritually in life is your number one problem. You need to understand. You need spiritual understanding so you can finally see what has been happening to you. It's no coincidence that the whole world suffers from this as the whole world is being subjected to it. It's certainly not God's fault, and it is definitely not God's will. God, the God of life, is the answer to all of your questions. He is the satisfaction to your frustration. He is the fruitfulness to your futility. He is the forward progress to your feeling stuck. He is the way out, indeed the only way out. He is not chastising you. He is not judging you. He has not sentenced you to a crappy life. He is the polar opposite of all the pain and suffering, in ignorance, you have endured. But, we haven't always learned that just yet. We are on a journey and we have to learn it for ourselves. We have to be, at last, willing to learn or unlearn. Our lack of progress, lack of results, lack of fulfillment is always the first clue that we are chasing the wrong things and heading in the wrong direction. But don't let the apparent complexity of error cause you to faint. Truth is clear and simple, and in the end it requires only that you simply change directions...

No change can occur in life unless it is preceded by a decision. It doesn't first require discipline and force of will, as you have already long proven to yourself. You don't need a sudden stroke of luck or a miraculous circumstance to turn your life around. You need to simply decide. "You have to become sick and tired of being sick and tired." (Thank you, Fannie.) You have to finally consider, "Why sit we here until we die?" (Thanks, Bible.) In other words, you have to make up your dang mind! Stop waiting for the circumstances to change before you decide. Stop waiting for full understanding before you decide. Stop waiting for retirement, for your kids to grow up, until you find your person (thanks, Grey's Anatomy), until you've earned your first million, until you feel better and on and on and on. Change is only and always preceded by a decision. Then, the strength of your efforts will always match the strength of your decision. Strong, resolute decisions naturally supply the energy to carry them out. Weak "hope so" or "I'll try" or "I'll give it a shot" decisions will not be accompanied by any determination of will and will naturally fail. You're not stuck because there is no way out; you are stuck because you have not yet decided! Once you take the time to make the decision, you can simply change directions...

You will encounter tremendous opposition, of course. The same hidden forces that trapped you are going to fight like hell to keep you trapped! They are going to offer you counterfeit, alternate directions that sound so good and hopeful but still end in misery and defeat. In truth there is only one direction that leads only to victory, and God is more than willing to show it to you. "This is the way, walk ye in it..." Changing course is not about becoming super religious and swearing off booze and cigarettes, sex and anything else that feels good (smile). That route, often followed, and worse believed, is yet another alternate route that reduces God down to how good is man's behavior or how little he uses cuss words. How silly and insulting to God who invented mankind. Religion does nothing but salve the ego of man, convincing him that he can affect spiritual realities with human efforts. Changing directions happens first in your mind. You have to stop thinking and considering and entertaining the same old garbage that tied you up in the first place. You have to do something different. You have to learn to think differently. You have to simply change directions...

Don't fret; you can always change directions...

LIVING IN A DARK HOUSE

Being a lover of light, I've never understood how people could tolerate living in a dark house. They have all the blinds shut and the curtains drawn to keep out the light. Over in the corner is some old, dim lamp with a sad, 40-watt bulb throwing out yellow shadows. There's usually a bookshelf or two chock full of old books, covered with thick dust from years of neglect. There appears to be some type of carpet, but you can't really tell what color it is. It seems to lead down dreary hallways to even darker bedrooms. And, the people inside? They've got that look on their faces that says nothing goes on in here and it hasn't for a long time, and they seem okay with it. They have grown fondly attached to their darkness, however dim and blasé because it is familiar and feels safe. Are you living in that old, dark house?

Nature itself teaches you that the light feels good. There's nothing like a beautiful, sunny day to lift your spirits. People are happy in the sunshine and warmth and travel many miles to seek it out. But, when the weather is gloomy, people don't feel so good and sort of hang on until the sun comes back out from behind the clouds. Sunlight even has a positive effect on your body. It's as if all of creation is beckoning you towards the light. In the light you can see clearly. Colors are more vivid and details are overwhelmingly apparent. In the mornings and evenings, the shifting sun highlights the terrain and casts pleasant shadows on all of the other beautiful things. Without the light we could not live. Without the light, you do not live.

Although you may dispute it, you live your life from within the frameworks of your own mind. Your mind is your house. You have the freedom to decorate it as you see fit. You may fill it with bright, inviting artwork or pictures depicting misery and pain. You can adorn the walls with pleasant, serene colors or with dark, gloomy shades. You can open all the doors and windows to freely admit the light or you can close the blinds and draw the curtains, not allowing any light inside. Whatever you choose and however you do it, it is always your house, and the choices of decoration and lighting always remain with you. Many people, in ignorance, not willful, allow their homes to be decorated for them. Instead of choosing the adornments, they allow something else to choose for them. Once the negative and uninspiring images get inside, they permit them to stick around instead of immediately shooing them back outside. Through disappointments and false representations, they allow their windows to be closed and their doors to be shut. Little by little, their homes get darker and darker, drearier and drearier. Soon they become accustomed to the dreariness and expect it as just a necessary part of life. The darkness becomes familiar and safe, though it is slowly killing the owner inside.

The simple solution to this complicated dilemma is to turn the light back on. Turn the light on so that you are able to see what has been going on. The trouble with darkness is that once it gains entree, it is difficult to extricate yourself from it. Darkness begets more darkness. Darkness is never overcome by exploring and investigating the darkness; it is strengthened. Darkness may only be overcome by light. The light exposes the darkness for what it really is... a lie. Darkness paints a picture of life that is not true. Darkness convinces and persuades you to close your own windows and lock your own doors. It threatens and intimidates with the aim of getting you to retreat inside in the darkness and to remain inside without coming to the light. Scores of people miserably dwell in a dark house of their own choosing, completely unaware of the remedy found only in the light. It is not that the people no longer want the light. The darkness has discouraged them. The darkness has defeated them. The only way out is to return to the light. The light is always there, patiently waiting for people to open their blinds and their curtains and let the light back in. Many a frightful terror is easily dissolved in the light of day.

The light; the true light, is found in God's Word. It is the only light capable of defeating the darkness. You are not going to turn the lights on in your home with your human wisdom or your human logic. It's your human logic that has been defeated. Your human brain is no match for your spiritual opponent. God is light and in Him is no darkness at all. His Word is light. It is the answer to every question. The more you seek it, the more light you gain access to and the more your path is brightened. Things that have escaped you for years suddenly become apparent. You begin to see things for what they really are and, in seeing, can make real changes. Soon the role you have been playing in your own defeat enters your awareness, and you can finally stop cooperating with evil, leading to your own downfall. Only the light can deliver you from that darkness, and if you want it, it is there for you.

Decide today to stop living in that old, tired, dark house. Step out into the sunshine where life is good. Open the windows and doors of your soul and let that light inside. Let it shine inside of you and reveal every dark crevice and thereby set you free. You don't have to spend another night in futility as the day is at hand! You don't need a dim lamp to light your path; you have something brighter than the sun. Choose the light. Look for the light. Desire the light. Your days of living in a dark house are over. Choose the light!

JUST WALK AWAY

You've probably been a part of a situation where someone wanted to draw you into their drama or to get you to fight about something. Then, because of the advice of a trusted friend or maybe through your own thought processes, you decide it's not worth it and maybe you should just walk away. Many situations in life draw far more than their fair share of our attention and our focus when perhaps the best option might just have been to walk away. And sometimes even considering a situation or someone's words or words bouncing around in your own head becomes your problem when you should have just walked away from those thoughts. Just walk away...

It has oft been repeated that where you place your attention, your life moves. And life, if you haven't noticed by now, is chock full of little life suckers that appear like mosquitos nibbling away at your flesh, one irritation at a time. They don't represent life-threatening scenarios or circumstances demanding your full, focused attention. Instead, they are most often represented in annoyances, aggravations and frustrations carefully placed to rob you of minutes and hours, then days and years. They surreptitiously steal your energy, your vitality, your life force. They are raindrops at your picnic, the blowing wind while you are fishing, the clouds at the beach. They move with such subtlety that you rarely see them coming, only to recognize them after their work is done, leaving you depleted and lacking your original enthusiasm. They contradict life by occupying it and busying it until there is no joy left in it. They are not worthy of your attention or your time and are best dealt with by refusal or simply your decision to walk away.

While life demands at times that we must fight, not every fight is worth fighting for. Some fights serve only to draw you into the mud also where both parties have to get dirty. Some fights don't represent your cause but another's cause. Some fights are grounded in frivolity, not engendering sufficient reason. There is a fight worth your effort, unless that is, your energy has already been squandered on things that do not matter. How much time do we invest into things that do not matter? We allow words and opinions and judgments to push us off center, desperately defending ourselves against an idea or a concept that didn't accurately represent us to begin with. Yet there we remain, rolling around on the pavement getting scuffed and bruised, wrestling with someone or something that didn't really matter at all. Negative opinions and their associated judgment have never helped one person get better and never will. The only fight worth your time and effort is the fight between good and evil, whereby you do your part to choose the light and love and goodness in opposition to a whole world full of darkness. The rest exists only to waste your precious time. Just walk away.

The great competition of life takes place in your mind. The great fight is fought between your ears. You win and lose by the thoughts you choose to entertain. Wrong thoughts, negative thoughts, contrary thoughts, fearful thoughts, condemnatory thoughts, self-deprecating thoughts, accusatory thoughts, guilty thoughts, threatening thoughts all carry within them seeds of failure that in order to grow must be held onto and cultivated. Your consideration is the cultivation. They appear as reasonable in an appeal to your reason. They display themselves as truth but only have a kernel of truth in them. And no matter their appearance, their poison remains within. The more you sip, the more poisoned you become. And if you drink enough of them, they will kill you. These thought enemies appear harmless and beg for further inspection and consideration. And like the cat that curiosity killed, they clamor for your attention. They itch and ask you to scratch them. They tempt you and seduce you for the opportunity to remain, to exist, to have a place. Once you have given them a place they spread out and occupy, fixing little strongholds, seeking stronger attachments until eventually they bring down the entire edifice. And all along, while you fight and struggle and reason and worry, desperately trying to figure it out, their hold is strengthened and permitted and allowed. It never dawned on you that your solution was simply just to walk away. Let them go. Stop your consideration of their potential reality and just walk away.

Your time on Earth is limited. Your opportunities for an impact are finite. You have one and only one shot at this thing. You have got one life and not for very long. You owe it to yourself to maximize your existence. Your life demands that you learn where to place your efforts and when to walk away. There are a million worthy causes, but for you only one worthy cause. At the end of your days, you won't remember all of the petty aggravations and frustrations. You won't think of all the time you spent in useless worry and consideration over some awful thing that never appeared. You won't wish you had fought more and challenged more, and set people straight. Instead, you will reflect on all the good things you enjoyed and the time you spent rightfully on the things that really mattered. You will remember the people you loved and the people that loved you. You will rejoice over those times you got it right and helped people and lifted them up; your time spent on worthy efforts and the time you invested that impacted lives. You will have hoped to have left a legacy of love and kindness and goodness that no one will forget. And finally, you'll be so eternally grateful for the times you had the good sense to just walk away and no longer squander your precious life on the things not worthy of your time and effort. Thank God you had the good sense to just walk away!

Of all of the principles a man can employ in his life,
love is the most powerful.

CONNECTING THE DOTS

Life, as I have repeated often, in its basic essence, is spiritual. It originated from a spiritual source (God) who embodies love in every capacity possible. The creation is infused with order and laws that do not change. There are principles that cannot be altered. When the proper chain of reasoning is applied, you cannot fail. But, in order to be successful, you have to connect the dots.

The main reason that people suffer is from not knowing nor understanding the truth. In not knowing, they fall prey to a wicked despot working through the systems of the world to bring heartache and loss. He succeeds by introducing error, which, when believed and practiced, brings defeat. Though immensely intricate and well thought out, it can be summarized simply as those things that contradict the truth. Fear, which rules the world, is always error. Though it be justified and rationalized and even accepted as part of the human condition, it is man's basic enemy which must be defeated. In the proportion that men overcome fear, they enjoy health, prosperity and success. In those areas where fear is permitted to remain, they suffer loss. Fear is the primary weapon the adversary uses to control and enslave people. The opposite of love isn't hate; it is fear. In order to connect the dots, you have to recognize those areas where fear prevails and defeat it.

Fear feeds on and works according to principle; an unchanging principle that God set up for mankind; namely that those things a man believes in his heart will come to pass in his life. When operated positively, a man can overcome any challenge, achieve any result and see the impossible come into reality in his existence. However, believing also has a dark, negative side called fear. Fear is wrong believing. Fear is believing in reverse. Fear is becoming persuaded of some negative, potential outcome and holding onto that imaginary outcome until it too comes to pass in your life. The enemy parasitically leeches off this basic principle to bring evil and pain upon all people. The reason it has worked so successfully is because of man's ignorance of the truth. Worse, many people aren't even cognizant that they are afraid, as fear has many, many disguises. It shows up as procrastination, as anger, as settling for less than the best, as a loss of enthusiasm and energy. It produces stilted actions, shame and all manner of ingenuine behaviors and hypocritical stage acting. It is life that has stopped moving forward, frozen in place and unable to move freely. It is the antithesis of love and, as such, is only overcome by love. Properly connecting the dots means to choose love.

Of all of the principles a man can employ in his life, love is the most powerful. God is love. Love activates believing; positive believing which yields phenomenal results. The actions you take in love cannot fail. Love is the great overcomer, able to heal and deliver and rescue from any situation you find yourself in. Love, when properly applied from your heart, melts fear away, exposing it for the illusion it always was. Love isn't just warm feelings but more so warm actions directed towards other people and yourself. Love is a decision made not from repayment but as a free will offering expecting nothing in return. Love is the truth exemplified in actions. God so loved that He gave! We so love that we give. All men need God's love and until they receive it are unable to fully love themselves. God loves us into loving ourselves. He looks past our foibles and our failings. He loves us unconditionally without any 'merit on our part to earn it. He forgives the unforgivable and sets us free from guilt and condemnation. He gave us His son, the perfect for the imperfect, forever liberating mankind from a cruel and hateful opponent. In this life you triumph as you connect the dots that God is love, the source and the originator of it.

Connecting the dots in your life means opening your heart to the truth. It means applying God's system of logic rather than the world's *dog-eat-dog* logic. It is refusing the endless pursuit of number one in favor of the pursuit of helping meet the needs of numbers two, three and four. It is shifting your focus away from yourself, your unmet needs, your problems, your difficulties and frustrations and turning them over to someone else; namely God. It is choosing to give instead of always trying to get and then receiving because of it. It is the polar opposite of how the world propounds things work! It is unselfish because it isn't terrified its own needs won't be met. It places its trust in the hands of another instead of always trying to figure out everything for itself. Connecting the dots means doing things God's way, with God's heart of love and concern for all people.

In these tumultuous times we find ourselves in today, don't fret and get anxious or worry about how things are going to turn out. Learn to connect the dots spiritually and see for yourself that God is love and that in Him is no darkness at all. In so doing, not only will you enjoy the life that now is, but also the life that will never end. Connect the dots!

HOW TO GET BACK YOUR TENDER HEART

The number one reason people feel unhappy and unfulfilled in their lives is due to hardness of heart. Hardness of heart is subtle in that when your heart has gotten hard, you are no longer aware of it, much like a callous on your hand. You can no longer discern you are getting pricked! Today we focus on what you can do to get back your tender heart. I say back because your heart started out very tender, like the heart of a child, but the world and circumstances, disappointments and failures, as well as errors believed then practiced, rendered your heart hard and lacking feeling. It left you desensitized and numb to the true realities of life; those realities God wants you to experience. So, how can you get back your tender heart?

If you strip away all of the trimmings; get beyond all external appearances; get down to the very heart of things, all of us are the same. And although people are as varied and unique as the stars in the sky in multitude, we all want the same things. We all need love and acceptance; to belong and to feel needed. We have similar fears and dreads as well as similar aspirations for good health and prosperity. We all seek to get our needs met and the needs of those we love. Keeping this in mind is a good starting point for maintaining a tender heart. No matter how someone appears to be, whether abrasive and apparently heartless, aggressive and inflammatory, behind the facade is a scared, helpless person. At any given moment in time, all you may be exposed to is a version of that person, completely dependent upon where that person is coming from at any given time. Fear, which is error (also called sin or literally a stepping aside), is the number one hardener of your heart. Fear attempts to puff you up with a foolish disregard for things or people in an effort to protect you. Fear stops you from displaying the kindness and tenderness that is inherent inside. Fear of rejection or fear of not fitting in with the group leads you to all sorts of things that aren't really you at all. Getting rid of fear with all of its associated lies is the first place to go to get back your tender heart. There was a time when you weren't afraid of everything, that is until someone or some people taught you otherwise. Fear is a lie and, like every lie believed, it hardens your heart. Get rid of your fear...

Error in its most basic essence is the reverse of truth. The only sure way to discern truth from error is to know and understand God's heart for His people, which can be found in His Word. Error, though almost always appealing, carries within it the seeds of error that damage and corrupt the vessel. Something can look good and feel good; be completely accepted by society, but if its basic essence is based on error, it will only serve to hurt you. It will degrade and blunt your sharpness leading to more error and more heartache. All of us succumb to error in one capacity or another, but what matters most is what is in our hearts. Your heart will always respond favorably to goodness, to kindness, to love. And accordingly, your heart will always respond negatively to evil, to those being mean-spirited, to hatred. Thus, your responsibility is to make love your basic response. As a great man once said, "Love sees more but is willing to see less." Love covers a multitude of sins, because love comes from your heart. You want your heart to be more tender? Give people love! Bathe them in it. Love anyway... Practice kindness with absolutely no fear of a lack of repayment. Be tender in your approach and don't reserve that tenderness solely for your children or grandchildren. If you think that through a little, the reason we can be tender with a child is because we have no fear of our love being rejected. Well, here's a newsflash, no matter how that adult responded or how they behaved in the moment, they appreciated your expression of love at least as much as that child did. Trust me on that one. You want a tender heart, give out love to everyone. Once you know something is error, get rid of it. Love is at the basis of every good thing, so get rid of error and live love...

So, let's be honest with each other now. The reason your heart has gotten hard is because you have been damaged. You're not weak or too sensitive, as many would purport, but rather, living in the world today, chances are you have been assaulted many times by your spiritual enemy whom you cannot feel. You have been assailed often unfairly by a system setup to hurt you and break you down. Your adversary seeks only to steal from you, and as such he steals away your happiness, your tenderheartedness, your true feelings of love and compassion, and he does so because he hates God and all that is associated with God. God isn't your problem ever, but his opponent is. Thus, what you need most is God's healing. You need Him to right the ship. You need God to make your crooked places straight. You need God to heal your broken heart. God is able to restore your heart and teach you how to feel again. You need God's unconditional love. You need to know in His sight you are worthy and worth something, not because of what you do, but because of what He did for you. God and God alone can restore your heart and make life worth living again. God can open the eyes of your heart to the greater realities of life and make your path clear and obvious. Then, filled with His love and goodness, you can reach out and help all those other poor souls suffering and navigating a miserable existence. You want your tender heart back, get God's healing for your life...

A tender heart is the best kind of heart. Get yours back asap!

YOU ARE NOT YOUR BEHAVIOR!

It is common, in the highly philosophical world of social media, for people to have license to say whatever they think is true. Living in America, it certainly is their right. However, not all that is written is necessarily accurate. Some things, while sounding good on the surface, work against people's best interests. One such conclusion, usually stated in an attempt to confront hypocrisy, is the declaration that people "are" what their behaviors indicate! Are you the sum total of your behaviors? Read on...

To conclude that who you are is based on your behavior falsely assumes you are operating in a vacuum. It does not account for circumstances or the environment. It wrongly assumes that all human behavior is simply the individual acting, free of any outside influence. It does not begin to consider the vast impact of social media, which spreads negative messages like wildfire. It summarily discounts your upbringing, your difficulties and your troubles. It reckons in arrogance that all people have the same opportunity to make good decisions completely removed from the situations they find themselves in, whether arduous and perilous or delightful and easy. In short, it fails to take into account the human condition, the foibles, the errors in judgment, the emotions and passions, and the capacity to see the choices clearly and therefore choose wisely.

The spectrum of human behavior is vast and wide. What

is wrong for one person is right for another. The person who is hurting will naturally hurt people. But, the solution for "hurt" people is not to condemn their behavior but rather seek to remedy their hurts. People that steal and cheat and manipulate, do so because they have learned to do so, not because they are inherently bad, but because they learned no other way to get their needs met. And while their behavior is assuredly wrong, condemnation and judgment do little to offer a chance of escape. The person that consistently does "wrong" does so for a myriad of reasons. Simply demanding that they do better or assigning more and more punishments does nothing more than telling a beggar to get a job! Surely the person that begs, whether legitimately or as part of a deception, does so at the expense of their own self-image, shamefully begging as a last resort solution or in futility for not finding any other way to make it. Wrong behavior can be remedied, but whether repaired or worsened is not an indicator of the value of that person.

God's love for people is never based on their behaviors. God loves unconditionally, and He does so because that is what people need the most. God has the ability to see what cannot be seen and understands exactly what is behind the wrong behavior. He is all-knowing and, as such, knows who the person really is, absent all the evil influences. He looks on the heart. And in His provision for man, provided a way for men to escape the confinement of their own past behaviors. He gave man a Savior, a man subject to all the wrong choices possible for a man, yet without a failure to always make the right one. He gave him as a substitute for the man, so that the man could move forward according to the accomplished works of another man, thereby being set free from himself. In that acceptance of the Savior, His precious man could finally have the opportunity, the free will opportunity, to make a different choice. Then, men aren't simply the sum of their behaviors but instead a new creation.

In similar fashion, our job as fellow human beings experiencing the human condition, is to extend that same love and acceptance to other people. We must stop judging everyone and foolishly comparing their behaviors to our own in an attempt to feel better about ourselves. Though we cannot look on their hearts, we can at least acknowledge what stinkers we can be at times, complete with all of the past behaviors we would like to forget! People that act poorly or rashly or foolishly, do so from a lack of understanding, not an understanding of what is right, but rather an understanding of who they really are or can be. People need your love, not a lecture! People need compassion, understanding and kindness. The kid struggling at school or exhibiting bad behaviors needs love and forgiveness more than an extended restriction. Inside we are all the same. We need lots and lots of love and acceptance. We need people to think well of us despite our wrong behaviors and, as such, influence our behavior for the better. We need copious amounts of forgiveness which enables us to start again, over and over again if needed, free of judgment, resentment and long-harbored ill feelings.

Maybe you aren't feeling so good about yourself right now. Maybe you have made some mistakes and some bad choices. Maybe you have been choosing poorly for many, many years. Well, my brother, my sister, that does not define who you are at all. All it defines is where you are at this moment in your personal evolution and growth. Your life is not wasted. It isn't too late for you. God will give you a new beginning if you want one, and it does not matter what you did in the past. It is that big and God is that good! As a writer once noted, "You made a choice in the moment that seemed reasonable in the moment, but to look back upon it in your later years with new eyes is at a minimum unnecessary and foolish." Let your past be the past, even if it extends only five minutes ago.

You are NOT the sum total of your behaviors! You are a person subject to a wide variety of influences, some of which will have assuredly led you astray. The only remedy for being led astray is to rediscover the course. Remaining lost and lamenting is a fool's game. Know this day and every day that you can be exactly who you choose to be without any restriction. "Judge not another man's servant as God is able to make him stand!"

*If you knew how much your thoughts impacted your life,
you wouldn't be so frivolous concerning them.*

CLEAN UP YOUR ENVIRONMENT

Much can be said about your environment and what you choose to live in each day. Some environments are healthy and serve to promote growth. Other environments are toxic and slowly eat away at your core. Dark and dreary spaces rob your heart of the sunshine of living. While bright and cheerful abodes freely admit fresh air and revitalization into your soul. Clutter and unattended to accumulation choke and stifle. Well-placed and well-intentioned objects promote peace.

Human minds, like your living room, must be meticulously maintained and well cared for. Failure to do so will eventually lead to anarchy. Every non-beneficial thought you let go of will soon gain ascendancy over your life. Every unconfronted criticism, every darkening shadow, every unaddressed burden, every threat to your future will work together against you to suffocate your heart, rendering it callused and useless. Yet, most people only give a half-consciousness regarding their thoughts and even less confidence in their ability to control them. Worse still, only a tiny majority recognize that the space in their heads is theirs and theirs alone to manage and, if necessary, clean up.

I know it sounds trite and the expression is completely worn out, but you are the only you, you have got. Your mind is the command center of your life. Out from your mind and your heart come the issues of your life. I'll say it another way. That which you think about the most; that which you dwell upon; that which you choose to faithfully consider is how your life turns out. That person you pity at your high school reunion who seems as if life has gotten the better of him isn't so because of fate or bad luck, but rather because of a failure to protect his mental environment. If you knew how much your thoughts impacted your life, you wouldn't be so frivolous concerning them. Every negative seed "the wind" blows in will, if left unattended, produce a weed. And like every good weed seeks to do, will eventually ruin your garden. Your lack of energy, your absence of enthusiasm, your perpetual feelings of fatigue are more from your mental environment than any lack of sleep.

The circumstances you encounter, the trials and the difficulties, the weighty burdens come not first but after. Your thinking is the primary cause. And while the world may be engulfed in evil, irritation, suffering and annoyance, you don't have to be engulfed or submerged in it. There is a way out, and that way out is found in changing your thoughts. Feeling negative, frustrated and futile are temptations that must be fought against. Submission to the negatives in life is like settling down in a filthy home that you have the capability to clean up. Clean up your environment. Locate the unwelcome guests one at a time and replace them one at a time. Your goal isn't a vacuum (though you may need to vacuum - smile). Your goal is replacement. You have to locate something that is wholesome, edifying and true to replace that which is unhealthy, damaging and false. But, do it you must!

It may seem like controlling your thoughts is an impossible task given the sheer speed and volume with which we think. But your task isn't all of your thoughts; it is your next thoughts. When it comes to life, when it comes to your existence, when it comes to your personal experience, what are you saying to yourself? Are you being kind to yourself like you are to a dear friend, though despite his foibles, you continue to love? Are you exhibiting patience like you would offer to a child? Are you extending yourself a new beginning; a thousand new beginnings, like you would to someone that you've determined to forgive? Are you? Or are you faithfully engaged in berating yourself, criticizing yourself, comparing and weighing yourself against others? The Instagram model whose body you have been coveting may have spent a lifetime cultivating it, yet there you are actually hating your own wonderful flesh in response to it. You see, the beginning of healthy thought begins with the things you think about yourself. Are you really such a bad person or are you perhaps much like everyone else; battling absurdities and weakness and errors, yet continuing on in spite of them?

Building up your mind, and building up your heart takes time. You can't expect to change a lifetime of wrong thinking overnight, just as you wouldn't expect your body to show signs of change after the first few days of exercising. But persistence in controlling your mind will produce a lifetime of results. Controlling your thoughts doesn't just consist of the things you say about yourself, but also comprises the things you say about your life, your relationships, your job, your boss, you name it. Every negative viewpoint, every false assumption, and every rehearsed and expected failure you envision cannot help but to produce more after its kind. Maybe, just maybe, your life sucks because that's what you have been confessing for the past 20 years. Maybe you can't catch a break because you don't expect to catch a break, and then somehow that is God's fault. Your life is far, far from being destined or predetermined with our wonderful God having supplied you with the one thing you can control, your free will!

If you take nothing away from this but one solitary thing, know that your thinking is vitally and crucially important in determining how your life turns out. Clean up your environment. Don't allow anything to remain that pains you or causes you to feel unrest. Banish fear and worry as both have failed miserably in preventing anything from happening. Cleanse and purify your estimation of yourself by refusing anything that makes you feel bad about yourself or lessens you in your own sight. Thinking good things, expecting good things, envisioning good things is no harder than doing the opposite, with the only exception being breaking out of the things you have habitually practiced. It's all right there for you folks if you will only take heed and do it... Clean up your mental environment!

DO WHAT FEELS GOOD

Before you get started down the wrong path, this isn't some appeal to your hedonistic tendencies, wish as you may. Nor is this some modern-day philosophy that promises you pleasure in spite of future pain. Instead, this is about honoring your feelings for their true purpose, to lead you to something better. This is about de-numbing yourself from the grips of societal pressures and expectations. It's about recognizing when you feel good and wholeheartedly pursuing it rather than falling back to the circumstances that cause you to feel bad. If you have become weary of the see-saw; of the ups then the downs; of the heights then the valleys, this is for you!

Carefully constructed and intertwined with your mind are your feelings. God has designed for certain necessities to feel good to encourage their continuance and certain behaviors to cause pain demanding their termination. And as simple as it may seem, the world works feverishly to get you embroiled in certain patterns guaranteed to hurt you. Then, in the final analysis, there you sit like the alcoholic or drug abuser, buried and consumed by the very things that promised you liberty. You had many chances to escape, but in your numbness brought about by your error, you failed to be sensitive to your feelings any longer.

Life for humankind has one basic essence, and that foundational essence is control. Learning to control yourself is a class you cannot skip. Oh, you can spend a lot of time floundering around in the misty flats, but life will instruct you otherwise if you are still willing to hear. Everything you fail to control will eventually control you. Every "one too many" carries with it a penalty from which it is hard to escape. That which you refuse to control causes you to feel bad, just as everything you can control and do control causes you to feel good. A successful life isn't found in large batches, but is found in the multitude of little handfuls. It's not the critical decisions requiring your utmost concentration and effort that make or break you but is instead the seemingly minor decisions that confront you every day.

If you play it correctly, you soon learn there is a rhythm and a flow to life. The secret isn't to fight and argue in your rebellion but to acquiesce and adapt. It all falls subservient to one important question. *What is it that you need to do next?* What activity or behavior does the present situation demand? What thing should you do that will make you feel good about yourself? Do you need to clean the place up? Is there some nagging, aggravating, broken thing you know you need to fix? Is there some unresolved situation or conversation you know you need to have that you have been avoiding? Have you let yourself go in terms of your health or your finances or your creativity or your happiness? Have you settled into a life of mediocrity? Whatever it is, there it sits like a gigantic boulder impeding your path, and there you sit choosing to avoid it. The answer to the question of what you need to do next is painfully obvious to you, and you already know what it is!

The search to feel good is the supreme factor in finally becoming happy. Happiness doesn't come or, for that matter, last until you begin to make the right choices. When you stumble upon a behavior or activity that leaves you feeling good about yourself, that is an action to pursue. If the sight of yourself in the mirror causes you to flinch, there is something you can do about it. Like my barber said recently, "I control what

I eat so I can like myself naked!" (smile) You can substitute that phrase with anything that helps you like yourself. Self-esteem is only found when you do things that lead to self-respect. Self-loathing or self-hate come about only by a multiplicity of skipped, avoided or prolonged good choices. Take control of anything you can control and see for yourself how wonderful it feels.

Moderation in your life sees to it that you don't get too high and that you don't go too low, but there's lots of space in-between. There is a whole world of joy in-between. Sure, you will have times when you chased too much of a good thing. But not to worry, as that will always be very evident to you. Consequently, you will have periods of life where you foolishly sought after the wrong things, and they too will not fail to reveal themselves to you. The same moderation you employ in your behaviors is also required in the way that you think about yourself. Give yourself a break and embrace your new days. It is just as morally wrong for you to beat yourself up for some past bad behavior as it was to perform the wrong behavior in the first place. Moderation is the key!

Don't complicate things unnecessarily! As my Peloton inspiration often says, "It's not that deep!" Your requirement isn't to live your whole life in the next moment, but to live your "right now" life in the next moment. Do what in your heart you know you need to do now, next. Stop avoiding your life or waiting for some magical circumstance to make it all nice again, like when you were a kid. That ship has already sailed. But like that kid you so dearly miss did, live your life in the moment called now. Do the next thing, whatever it is.

I often marvel that the high road with God isn't found in complexity and complication, but is found in simplicity; in the many todays that eventually make up our best tomorrows. Grab your life by the balls and control it. Get back on top of whatever you are no longer on top of... You won't master it by tomorrow, but you will be on the right track, feeling good and doing good. My brothers and sisters, do what feels good!

THE WORLD NEEDS MORE NICE

As I was driving home from work the other day, I saw a billboard that said, "The world needs more Nice," and while it was likely an advertisement, it spoke a reality worth thinking about. What has gone wrong with people that has caused them to be so damn hateful? Is it the advent of the Internet? Is it the society in which we live or the current political climate? Or is it the natural consequence of a world mired in negativity and unmet needs? Whatever it is, the world definitely needs more "nice."

Social media seems to have spurned an environment of unparalleled cynicism or, at minimum, revealed it. Someone posts a problem they're experiencing and it's dismissed as a cry for attention. Someone else posts about the good that is happening in their lives and it is met with harsh criticism, as if it cannot be true or else it is a gross misrepresentation. Really? The question to be answered doesn't point back to the poster, but instead points to the hearts of the critics. What went so badly in *your* life or what unresolved issue do *you* harbor that made your heart so hard? What matter is it with you whether some person seeks attention? Why not give them the attention? If they boast of good times and happiness, shouldn't you rather be happy for them? If their words exaggerate, God bless them for it must be better to exaggerate happiness than magnify negativity! The issue isn't them; it is you...

The internet offers the world at your fingertips. You have the power to beat down and to lift up. Why not lift up? If you have been a person long enough, you know the trials and tribulations that accompany life. You know what it's like to suffer heartache and loss. You know how hard it is to overcome certain issues in your life. You likely know how infrequent are your successes, and in so knowing, you ought to rejoice when they happen for others. Your victories in life come not at the expense of other people, and when you win it shouldn't have to be because someone else has lost. If your life is so sad that the only way you rise is to cause others to fall, you need to ask yourself some serious questions! Your computer keyboard, though seemingly anonymous, is not really anonymous as the things you say point to who you really are...

The political climate in which we live is particularly arduous, but when hasn't it been? If you look to the world for your happiness, you will be waiting for a long time. The world, or I should say the systems of the world, are not designed to make you happy. They are designed to engulf you in a perpetual misery until you finally concede there is no way to escape. But, there is a way to escape, and it's not found in the ways of the world. It's found in kindness, in compassion, in love... It's found in seeking to make the world a little bit softer for your brother; a little easier to navigate. It's found in answers of peace and the promise of better days ahead. It's found in hope for the future and in learning a superior way. It's found in God and His Word with restoration, forgiveness, healing and love. Don't waste your time and your life trying to repair the evil, but instead do good and be good. What your brother needs from you is a break, a chance, an opportunity for a fresh start. If you are going to type something, give him that...

It is a sad testimony that most folks are typically negative. It's not so much their fault as they find themselves living in a negative society that feeds on what has gone wrong. People are so accustomed to what is wrong that they expect it or incredulously question when good happens to someone else. The good that you enjoy cannot be real good because of the shortage of goodness in their own lives. And instead of seeking the source of your happiness, they choose rather to discount your happiness as artificial because of their conditioning concerning what is wrong, or could go wrong, or will likely turn out wrong. Two or three wrongs do not make a right, no matter how many times you may have heard it. What makes something right is a change of heart. It is the honest recognition that when life sucks something is wrong and most often wrong in the heart of the sufferer. The purpose of suffering, if there is such a thing, is to encourage you to look outside yourself for the answer. It is to acknowledge that there just might be something you need to learn or understand. It is not to strengthen the walls of your heart in defiance but instead to tear down those walls with heartfelt humility, expecting a different result.

Somewhere, somehow, we have been talked into a futility. We think that unmet needs are normal; that prayer is just an exercise for the soul; that solutions don't really exist unless you are lucky or some other unexplainable nebulism. But, solutions do exist. Don't make your heart harder by tearing others down, but instead seek your own solution. Find out what made your heart so hard. Find out why it feels better to tear down than to build up, and make an earnest effort to build up. With all that you are and with all that you can ever be, find out how to make your heart tender again, like the one you had before the world kicked your ass. Be vulnerable. Take the risk. Offer your heart to others counting on the fact that they also have a heart, and if your blessing is unrequited, bless them anyway. Love people as you would want to be loved. Forgive people, understanding what a stinker you have been at times. Be a listening ear, a source of compassion, a place where judgment is suspended. That's what people need. They have enough of the criticism, but they haven't had enough of your love. The world needs more "nice." It all starts with you!

Be nice...

CLEAR EYES

There are times in our lives when we see with such unremitting, unobscured clarity; so grand and beautiful in its detail, so positively helpful and inspiring that we find ourselves awestruck, grateful, and wishing for more. The sudden jolt of an unexpected answer to a long-held question or being at last able to slice through the morass of confusion and pinpoint the direction to proceed, has no parallel in our minds or equal. Yet we sojourn most of our lives in lack of it, fainting and eventually surrendering ourselves from its absence. We begin to think not seeing and not knowing is normal, concluding that no one else can see either. Or, to our own demise, we trust ourselves to a false clarity, failing to even consider otherwise. In the end we grope blindly, victims of whatever will. We must find our clear eyes...

The trouble with not seeing is not seeing. When you cannot discern objects at night, you seek a light. When you cannot see things in the light, you need more light. It's the light that makes the hidden things visible. It is light in your mind that illuminates solutions, that clarifies obstacles, that lifts the scales as it were. Only the light can accomplish this, and without the light it cannot be accomplished. Our job when faced with challenges, fears persisting, frustrations and befuddlement, is not to press harder or think better or work smarter, but instead get light, pure light. "Dwelling on the darkness [problems] won't bring forth the light [true solutions]!" Clear eyes require great humility and the disciplined ability to set aside all of *our* plans and *our* solutions, and *our* remedies until we become first clear on *our* problem. Our human nature, our self-serving ego will send us around the hamster wheel, sometimes for years, scouring the planet's wisdom for a solution we will never find. Life is spiritual and spirit is light! Every undiagnosed issue, every lost solution, every corruption, every disease, every painful misstep has at its base darkness, spiritual darkness reigning supreme absent spiritual light. We must find the light...

The problem with darkness is the darkness. Darkness promises a thing but gives you another thing. Every offer presented by darkness carries within it more darkness. As darkness is indulged, in thought preceding deeds, it mystifies and clouds, producing more darkness. Fear of some dreadful event or circumstance, persisted in, invites the darkness in ending always in blindness and the inability to perceive it further. Now numbed by its effects, the victim no longer feels the pain of his wrong choices or the consequences of her unplanned decisions. It's the ultimate deception! It's a fool's game. It is an inescapable reality absent the light that reveals it. Trapped within it, man flails and flaps, desperately trying to break free only to find more chains with each disparate and uncoordinated action to escape. It never quite dawns on him that the effect is manufactured by a cause he cannot see. He remains buried in a riddle his human mind will never solve. We need to be illuminated!

The issue with man is the man. If he ever dares to step off his high horse, his so-called science and mathematics, his false sense of reality, his insatiable need for physical proof of spirit in a material existence, he would find the clarity he seeks is not where he has been searching. And in the place of foolishly concluding that man's wisdom is the end of all wisdom, trusting only what he can see, hear, smell, taste or touch, denying the great dwarfing, magnificent, miracle of creation, and instead using his suffering and frustration as a sure guide, he would at last reach upward for the light that reveals and clears up. And in seeking he would find as the door opens when knocked. And instead of finding a little man parading behind a curtain as that Great Wizard of Oz, falsely promising help and safety, he would discover the dust-covered Bible on his bookshelf waiting as it has always waited for the curious seeker to find the delights therein. We need to discover God's Word!

The light that God gives is God. Man's benefactor, His creator, had the foresight to write a book. In that book He placed words from Himself, infused with the light to see, as the guide, the solution, the source of His help. As a man considers those words and listens to those words, and dwells on those words, he illuminates himself. He shines a spiritual light no darkness can extinguish. He feeds himself pure words with no loopholes nor crevices nor breeches an enemy can exploit. As he remains in it, he finds himself healed from his maladies, built up strong where he was weak and repaired wherein he had been broken. The brilliant light, the only true light, the spiritual light he encounters, reassures his restless soul and offers him peace. And as that light races into every deep recess of his mind, he finds the answers he needs, the solutions he craves, the reasons and all of the real causes. He finds himself delivered! We need the light that saves us!

You may have just stumbled upon that which you have been stumbling upon. How incredulous in a vast world of knowledge and self-help and scholars, counselors, doctors and lawyers, the solutions you sought in many a weary and churning night, with unparalleled effort and commitment and tears, would be found nearby in a book you have heard about from long ago. Learn about that book. Seek help to comprehend that book. Find out what to think according to that book. Understand how to live in line with that book. Experience God's life and power and infinite, razor precision to cut through and discern between truth and error, between a blessed life and a miserable life, between all that is light and all that is indeed darkness. You need to understand that book...

No matter how many years you may have travailed, no matter the distances you may have traveled, no matter how many attempts you may have tried, there is one true way that, when found, will make your blind eyes finally able to see. And you will then proclaim fondly, "God has never forgotten me..." You need to find your clear eyes!

CHALLENGE YOUR ASSUMPTIONS

Can you imagine waking up one day only to find out that many things you thought were true were actually false? What if your tried and sure method of 'cause and effect' had effects based on unknown causes? Could it be that the images sitting right before your eyes have been manipulated to lead you and your human reasoning astray? Are all of the elements in your chain of logic real elements? What if you challenged your assumptions? Would it change your life?

If there is one spot where we humanoids get tripped up, it's in the assumptions we make about life. We have been so schooled to revere the information presented by "what it looks like" that we take hook, line and sinker the conclusion that has been presented to us in advance. If we live amidst a surface world alone, we could confidently take things at their face value. But what if we don't? What if there is a whole spiritual world working behind the scenes, all part of the grand drama of life? What if we are all participants in a contest, whether we know it or not, and are making decisions and drawing conclusions that will ultimately determine our outcomes? Finally, what if we had the ability to shape and form our reality instead of being victims of it?

The spiritual competition that rages day by day is a competition for the allegiance of your mind; your thoughts. What you think about, what you hold in your mind greatly influences the reality you experience. There are right thoughts and there are wrong thoughts. Some thoughts lead to good results, while other thoughts lead you down the slippery slope of error. All right thoughts come from goodness (God) who is seeking your allegiance. He needs your cooperation to do all the good for you that He has planned. All wrong thoughts ultimately come from evil (the devil); are always cleverly disguised as logical, reasonable or realistic, and when held onto, produce all manner of difficulty and defeat. The source of wrong and error also seeks your allegiance, and he gains it by getting you to think and act in opposition to goodness.

People today know relatively little about the impact their thoughts have on their life. For instance, people feel there is no need for any checks and balances in their thought life. They simply think whatever, whenever, however. They aren't able to discern a need to control their thinking and even falsely conclude that thinking cannot be controlled. You hear it with phrases such as, "My mind just won't shut off!" The responsibility to stop thinking certain thoughts or to decide when to think certain thoughts rests entirely with you, the owner of your mind. Your mind working at cross purposes with you is, in reality, your failure to take the helm and draw in the reigns when necessary.

I read the other day where a Life Coach stated that worry was beneficial because it helped you to resolve your problems. Well, here's a newsflash, if worrying actually helped resolve problems, then it would have a logical end point! But, it doesn't have an end point because the solution lies outside of your senses-driven mind, hence why it continues on and on and on. The only way to defeat worry is to stop scratching that itch! Resist the temptation to try to figure it out; you aren't going to be successful. Worry is part of a deceptive trigger that begins with doubt, is established with worry and culminates in fear which brings the hammer of destruction to you! Worrying, like being afraid, is wrong thinking coming from the wrong source seeking to bring you a wrong result! Refusing to entertain fearful thoughts is not being fanciful or unrealistic (lies); it is thinking properly and leading towards a sound mind. God doesn't need fear to keep you vigilant or safe. Instead, God needs your cooperation in thinking properly.

Though fear certainly holds the number one spot in beating people, there are other thoughts that serve only to drag you down to defeat and loss. Those thoughts are thoughts that take you out of the moment of time you are living in and either drag you back to your past or foolishly anticipate forward the potential difficulties of tomorrow. Whatever you did in the past, bad enough and terrible enough to demand space in your mind today, occurred in the past and lives on no longer except in your memories. In terms of redemption and forgiveness, Jesus Christ paid the price for every stupid or insane thing you or I ever got caught up in. Good thinking says the error is over with and should be forgotten. Wrong thinking, whether clothed in religious piety or required to pay the so-called debt, does not lead to resolution or recompense but rather drags the owner to a slow and painful death. Guilt has no other purpose than to break down its host to further decay. In similar fashion, worries over the future complete with grand, detailed pictures of future suffering, serve only to alarm the mind and, from its shaken-up state, lead to further miscalculations and conclusions. God can fix or repair anything! That is a good thought worth holding onto...

The optimum way to be a successful human being is to control your thinking. Think thoughts God says to think and reject thoughts that are in opposition to those thoughts. It doesn't matter what well-rehearsed reasons you have developed for holding on to your error. What matters is if you will obey goodness and get a good result. What I'm suggesting may go against all you have ever thought and concluded. Well, good! Maybe it's time some of those assumptions you have been doggedly clutching to should be given their exit! Maybe you need to rethink what it means to be realistic or practical or whatever other word you are using to justify the continuance of error!

You can live in peace with feelings of love and joy and happiness if you will learn to think how God says to think. Don't fight any longer for error; fight for the truth instead. It feels better...

THE SPIN CYCLE OF ERROR

Have you ever found yourself caught up in a negative spin cycle of error that ever picks you up and drops you off at the same place repeatedly, eventually draining all the life right out of you? Have you ever found yourself plagued by the same issues year after year? Have you ever decided to make a journal entry and, as you read some of your former entries from 10 years ago, realize you are writing about the exact same crap? If so, you might be trapped in the spin cycle of error...

It goes without much thought to recognize that error is always complicated. At its base it is simply a lie you've been talked into believing and subsequently experiencing day after day. However, its simplicity is masked and befuddled with extraneous data like the Tax Code, rendering its victims unaware of what is going on or how to ever change it. The only way that error can gain a foothold in your life is by getting you to cooperate by repeating and rehearsing certain thoughts, words and behaviors.

As a person thinks in their heart, they are, whether their thoughts are good, constructive and useful, or wrong, defeated and debilitating. Wrong thoughts or thoughts containing error hide alongside many other thoughts. In the milieu of thought, it is very difficult to discern what is going wrong or to isolate rogue thoughts that bring negative results. However, if you find yourself experiencing negative results, i.e., all mashed together in a damp heap, spinning and spinning amidst an ocean of the same junk, you have got some error going in your thinking that you must repair.

You can almost always tell what thoughts you are harboring in your mind by the stuff that spews out of your mouth. What negative views of yourself can your friends predict you will say? What line of self-deprecating humor is your 'go-to' laugh line? Are you disappointed with yourself or the person you have turned out to be and, as a result, say bad things about yourself to yourself? Those harsh views, bad jokes and negative self-image all point to some errors you have been holding onto inside.

Although always preceded by thoughts, certain behaviors serve only to thwart you and retard your progress. Certain pleasures conceal the poison contained within them, which is only discovered once the poison has taken effect. Some activities promise you fulfillment in one area only to pay a heavy tax in another. Behaviors that run at cross purposes with the Laws of Love always demand payment in pain and suffering.

In order to stop the murderous spin cycle of error, you must attach yourself to something that doesn't move around day by day. You must affix your purpose to something that is true and immovable. You finally find the hidden error by focusing on the truth. Focusing on the error; the *why didn't I see this coming* of the error; the *how did this happen to me* of the error; leads only to, and trust me on this one, countless journal pages dedicated to and salaaming error, inadvertently and unknowingly worshipping error (evil). You are not going to see your way out playing that game. The treachery isn't in presenting you with wrong choices and getting you to choose them. The deception is in what you've been talked into focusing on! If you've lived a little you already know that stepping aside or missing a step is easy. Everyone you have ever met has come up short in some capacity. The test for success is in getting back up, dusting yourself off and walking in a new direction, leaving all of the past behind you.

Error holds sway by wearing you out on the inside. In order to wear you down and eventually out, it must have access to your head and heart. It doesn't flourish by mistakes you have made here and there, even the egregious ones. It flourishes and tightens its grip by getting you to shift and *keep* your focus in the wrong place. Maybe you made a heinous mistake 20 years ago that ended up defining the life you live right now. How can something that happened 20 years ago define your present existence? It does so because you have held onto the damn thing like a cherished guest for 20 frikkin years. The fact that you did something wrong 20 years ago and still insist on bringing it to mind is the larger error.

God's way out of these mental prisons that thwart and defeat you is by you making the decision to no longer hold onto and cleave to the error! If your life isn't what you want it to be today, get busy changing it into something you like. Lamenting about what's wrong with it is just getting suckered into more of the same! If you've made some bad mistakes, you have beaten yourself up enough already. Jesus Christ paid for the sins, not your insistence on suffering and self-condemnation! (Do you really believe God wants you to suffer?) If you have some gnarly thoughts concerning your self-image, it's up to you to change those concepts and start seeing yourself as God sees you.

At the end of the day, just know and understand that you are doing it to yourself. Sure, there is an evil one, and yes, life can be very challenging at times, but you are only responsible for living this life one day at a time, forgetting all that is past and refusing to be afraid of the future. Change your life by changing your subject of focus! Get out of the spin cycle of error and move on over to the warm dryer where life is oh so good...

CONSIDER YOUR WAYS

The aforementioned title, borrowed from a verse in the book of Haggai (in the Bible), has oft been associated with condemnation from God for having bad behaviors. This, of course, fits with the common erroneous notion that God is *uber-interested* in your behavior and somehow takes pleasure in monitoring it and finding you, wait for it...... unworthy! Well, God already solved the bad behavior issue once and for all, for all of mankind! Instead, *considering your ways* has more to do with your allegiances and the subsequent results of those allegiances. Considering your ways leads to positive results if you're willing to consider. Are you willing?

Life doesn't suck! To think that life sucks is to be ignorant of the forces behind life and, rather than discover them, draw negative conclusions about life itself. Life doesn't suck! Your viewpoint towards life sucks. Your lack of willingness to learn and consider sucks. Your presumed understanding and subsequent refusal to look any further is what sucks. But life, as God intended it to be lived, is the polar opposite of things that suck! It's sort of maddening how humans, with all of their analytical skills; who can figure out why tomato plant leaves turn yellow; when a combustion engine is only functioning at about 70 percent power; how to calculate the mathematical trajectory of an object flying at thousands of miles per hour in space, cannot discern why things are not going well in their lives! Indeed, it is time, if things aren't going so well, to consider your ways!

Life at its foundational level is spiritual. It is not made

solely of the things you can see, hear, smell, taste or touch. Your life, whether you choose to believe it, choose to accept it or outright deny it, is spiritual. Your spiritual allegiances lead to the results, blessings or consequences you are experiencing today. Not getting what you want out of life isn't life's fault. Life was not designed to be arduous and hard. Life becomes arduous and hard again based on your spiritual allegiances. Pared down to the smallest level, there are only two choices. No sane person would choose the bad option, so the spiritual forces behind all negativity and pain must employ some trickery to gain allegiance; the greatest treachery coming from promoting ignorance concerning that which is good. Deciding not to choose is also a choice and, sadly, not a good choice. Again, consider your ways...

Absent holy spirit and a knowledge of God's Word (spiritual words), you will not be able to discern the differences between your choices. Oh, you can recognize the blatant stuff, but the more subtle choices will escape you. It's in the subtle choices where you find defeat and worse aren't able to even know it is occurring. God is well aware of your limitations and offers instead for you to consider your ways or, said another way, consider the results or lack thereof you are presently experiencing in your life! Have you planted with much effort yet only brought in a small harvest for your efforts? Have you eaten much but still don't have enough to eat? Have you had plenty to drink yet still find yourself thirsty? Do you have adequate clothing but still you're not warm enough? Does the money you make feel like it goes out faster than it comes in, like your purse or wallet has holes in it? Consider your ways...

The singular, most important maxim in life centers on who or what holds first place in your life. When God is first, as He rightfully must be, then He promises to supply your every need in every category and phase of life. When you or some other thing holds first place; when you take it upon yourself to supply your own every need; when you seek to the world or the things of the world to meet your needs, you will find yourself increasingly unsatisfied and unfulfilled! True satisfaction comes from God and from God alone. Other things promise us satisfaction, happiness and fulfillment, yet often leave us empty or seeking more and more. In our quest for more, we receive less and less, not because we don't work hard or aren't trying, but because we have allowed our priorities to get out-of-order. Considering your ways is simply an admonishment to check your priorities and to realign yourself with those things that are the most important, indeed God alone who is sovereign! Consider your ways...

Once you get things back in order, which is purely a decision, you'll find the sunshine where you used to find storm clouds. You'll find an abundant harvest far beyond your efforts at sowing. But most importantly, you'll find deep-seated satisfaction and fulfillment in terms of your hungers, your desires, and your thirsts, because you will have finally discovered the meaning of your life and its Originator's intentions for you! The world will keep telling you that you don't need God and that you can figure it all out, and you are certainly within your rights to keep doing just that, but the measure will always be found in your satisfaction meter (heart), and on the inside you always know whether your needs are being met or not. Unfulfilled heart needs are simply the result of seeking to get fulfillment from the wrong place!

Consider your ways, my friends, not to find yourself unworthy but to discover who you really are and how your life needs will always be met...

Are you willing to consider?

IT'S YOUR FRUIT

Whenever I see someone really living the life riding in the high places of the earth, after I change my mind to stop 'hatin' a little, I have tremendous admiration for them. I admire them because I know they have believed to be who they are and where they are and have received the results of their believing. LeBron James believed to be LeBron James. Sure, he came from the factory gifted with size and natural ability, but this whole "King James" business was his own idea. You can apply this with breathtaking accuracy to any successful person you see. You can also apply this with the same mathematical exactness to any failure you might observe, even your own. The life that you are living at this very moment in time is the result of those thoughts and beliefs you have held dear. Your frustrations, your sufferings, your pains have all come about as a result of what you have believed and continue in accordance with those beliefs. The results in your life, good or bad, are your fruit, and by your fruit you are known!

It's such a tragedy that so many people limp through life reacting to circumstances for which they have unknowingly accepted. They do not want those circumstances, but their thoughts and beliefs encourage them instead of thwarting and slaying them! The world, with all of its negativity, works you over day by day, without your consent or even your awareness. It's feeding you messages of struggle and defeat while at the same time lauding celebrities famous for being famous. It looks like the things you so desperately need are too hard or too far away. The goal? Talking you into settling for less than the best and accepting mediocrity and failure. Here's a simple experiment. Read the following statement: You deserve the very best in life. Say it out loud to yourself! "You deserve the very best in life, Tony!" Now, be honest and observe your reaction to that statement. Where did your mind trim that back a little? "Well, I don't need the best, but pretty good will work." Or maybe you don't feel you deserve the best. Or is it too late now for you to receive the very best? Whatever your mind came up with in opposition to that statement is a lie; a wrong belief that limits your success. Why wouldn't you, as the only you, you have, deserve the very best expectations from you, for you? Don't make this about God. This is about you in the realm that you control!

While you may find yourself a bit defeated in this life, or maybe you have had some wind taken out of your sails, be encouraged and comforted in this, namely that you can change your thoughts and thus change, remedy or repair your life. You're going to need God's help, but trust me, His first expectation from you is for you to change your thoughts. He's really, really, really good at His job, but He isn't going to do your job no matter how much you pray! Change your mind. You determine the speed and pace at which your life transforms. Radical life changes require radical thought changes. You see, this thought thing is so much larger than you may have imagined before. I'm not talking about thinking something positive from time to time; I'm talking about monitoring and reshaping your thoughts throughout a day, day after day, one day at a time. Find something true from God's Word that you can use to counter the darkness. Then seriously and diligently work on it!

Circumstances are not lined up against you; they're lined up against all of us. The difference lies only in what you will and will not accept as true. Things are not true because they look true or seem true, or are factually true; they are true if God says they are true. In similar fashion, you are not who you might see in the mirror, chubby or slim, or the results you have obtained in this life, or your successes or your failures, your mistakes or your good deeds. You are who God says you are, no exceptions! The only way to break the chains of previous results and former losses is to view yourself and your life in an entirely new light. No matter how it may look, you have control over those circumstances, albeit indirectly.

The fruit evident in your life at this very moment, delightful or rotten, is of your own making and owned entirely by you. Your life is like a full feature movie with you as the producer. You are the one deciding upon the beginning, the middle and the ending. You can write a dramatic success story, or you can write a sorrowful saga. But, make no mistake, you are the writer, the editor, the producer! You may choose to modify your story, or you can choose to ride the waves of circumstance. If you just go with the flow, then the flow may take you places you didn't want to go. How many times have you heard someone say, "I didn't think my life would end up this way?" The only way your life ends up in a place you didn't choose is by turning over the reins of choice and control to someone or something else. No action, no directed and focused thought is also an action, a passive one leading away from and not towards your dreams.

This incredibly short life with all of its ups and downs is one vast classroom whereby you may decide to learn how it works and modify yourself to fit within the existing framework, or you can continue to fight against the circumstances you created and blame God, the culture, the economy, your momma or whatever else neatly takes away responsibility from yourself! The choice is yours, dear reader. The choice has always been yours...

WHEN YOUR PROBLEM BECOMES
YOUR PROBLEM

By nature, in order to have a "problem," means there is some aspect of your life that you find yourself incapable of solving. You've done your best thinking. You've looked at it from every angle. In short, you've devoted yourself 100 percent to it, and yet your problem remains. You may have even resigned yourself to a life with the "problem." However, there eventually reaches a point where your problem becomes your problem!

We all have bad things happen to us. Some things that happen to people are so indescribably evil, there are no words to explain them. Other people just sort of get stuck with some dilemma they find themselves living a lifetime trying to escape. Catastrophes, extreme losses, losing it all, all have the potential to take away your lifeblood and reduce life to mere existence. Lower down the scale, many find themselves a victim, not to something that happened to them directly, but to the repercussions of some grand mistake; some error in judgment; some momentary lapse that became the defining factor of their lives! Again, the apparently inescapable problem became their life problem.

No matter what may have happened to you or what insurmountable problem you may face, there is always a solution. The trouble permeates when it becomes your sole focus in life. You can spot someone suffering in this way immediately because it is the only subject on which they speak authoritatively. They unknowingly dwell in it; they breathe it with every exhale; they consume it and drown themselves in it. Instead of being a problem from which they can still escape, it becomes their reason for living, their red badge of courage.

Ironically, the way to escape it is the exact opposite of what appears. In the words of a wise man, "You cannot solve your problems with the same thinking that led to the problem." Dwelling on what went wrong, what you did wrong, why something went wrong, all serve not to remedy the situation but rather to affix you, the sufferer, deeper and deeper into the problem. And sadly, if you remain fixated on the darkness long enough, your chances of escape become slimmer and slimmer. You are never, ever going to out-think the darkness by remaining in the darkness. Instead, like all people in the dark, your task will become more and more insurmountable. The reason people are locked into some tragedy or failing that happened 25 years ago is because they never let it go. You cannot overcome unless you eventually let it go. In fact, you aren't going to begin to solve your problems now until you finally learn to let them go.

Life was never intended for you to be the party of the first part, the second part and every other part. You are a human being, for God's sake, and much of life escapes your control. When the doctor says you have an incurable disease, there's not a damn thing you, the human being, can do about it. You are fighting against spiritual powers of which you may know or understand very little. Instead, you, the finite human being, are supposed to eventually admit you do not know what to do and beseech the help of the One that knows exactly what to do. Absent God and left to your own limited devices, you are simply going to lose. But, if you can get to the place where you wake up, you hand those life-long issues over to God and let Him do what He promised He would do all along!

Goodness knows that some of the things that may have happened to you are awful and painful and arduous at best.

That's not to minimize their grave impact on you at all. You're stuck because your problem is beyond your human capability to deal with it. Your solution is to let it go. Give it to God every time it lands itself back in your lap. Stop thinking it, fearing it, rehearsing it, addressing it and embracing it. The inescapable problem is bad enough without giving over your entire life and mind in defense and admiration of it. Your problem is not the supreme thing in life. It is not to be your primary thought in every situation. It may have become that, but it doesn't have to remain that. God is supposed to be your supreme thing and your primary thought in life. Dwelling on God and what He says is dwelling in the light. In the light, the solutions become clear and obvious. Maybe your solution is healing. Maybe your solution is to finally get past a terrible event. Maybe your solution is a radical change in your thinking and manner of living. Whatever your solution may be, it can only be found in one place and one place only - the light!

Darkness is a slippery character and is well schooled in how to defeat a human being. Evil and wrong don't just hit you with a sucker punch you never saw coming, but instead seeks to take away all that is important to you. Its goal, like trapping a bird in a cage, is to snare you into some mode of thinking that guarantees more and more trouble will replicate itself in your life. For this reason, you need something bigger than yourself to set you free.

All of us, at one time or another, have found ourselves trapped in some grand dilemma. Every one of us has had a problem whose solution escaped us. We've all been stuck, distracted and caught up in something that has been gaining more and more power over us. And like a rodent we seek to remove from our situation, in order to rid ourselves of it, we have to remove its food source. Literally, you have to stop feeding it! You have to steadfastly resist your human tendency and ego that is striving to figure it out and choose rather not to give it any space in your thinking. It's not easy to do but is required if you want to win. You have to seek God's help and continue seeking God's solution until you realize it in your life. God is faithful and will provide what you need, but you have to do it His way. Every time your problem presents itself to you by knocking on the doors of your mind, you have to give it back to God where it belongs. God will deliver you, my friend, with the duration dependent entirely upon your faithfulness to keep your mind fixed on the light! It can be done. It will be done!

How do you prevent your problem from being your life's problem? Make your problem God's problem and let Him figure it out. There is no other way...

IT IS YOUR INTERNAL CHATTER

The thoughts racing through your mind throughout the day, often referred to as your internal chatter, belong to you! And although it may appear to "just happen," the reality is that you are the one generating the thoughts. Those thoughts are heavily influenced by circumstances and conditions, but you still own them. You may have thoughts pop into your mind you did not consciously plan, again heavily shaped by internal and external influences, but the decision to entertain or persist with those thoughts belongs only to you! At the end of the day, they are just thoughts and can be carefully dismissed. However, those thoughts; the things you are saying to yourself over and over are not just thoughts, but actually form the basis of your beliefs. What you believe in life ends up being the life you are experiencing! Your success or your failure, in any category of life, is found amongst that infernal, internal chatter!

It would be well worth your time to begin paying attention to the things you are saying to yourself! Notice the thoughts going through your mind while you are speaking with someone or when you are interacting in a group. Are you able to engage a person with your full attention and heart, or are you simultaneously wading through your own thoughts spewing out negative things about you, from you, to you? Most people's internal chatter is horrifically negative to the point of being an enemy or a personal adversary. None of us would knowingly choose the option of being mean and harsh with ourselves on purpose. I mean, if I don't have my own back, who does? Instead, we are living in a world fueled and directed by fear and negativity. We are engulfed in subtle messages of inadequacy and how we don't measure up. We are drowning ourselves in the hidden messages of electronic media, carefully crafted to occupy our every waking moment. You thought the TV was a brilliant mass "idea" marketing machine? Well, add in the explosive rise of social media, and you end with a nation of captured minds, fully influenced night and day to generate thoughts in a specific, negative direction... It's pretty incredible to recognize but devastating in its effect on our minds.

In addition to starting a serious quest to pay attention to what your internal chatter is saying to you in public, also believe to hear and recognize what it (you) are saying to yourself in private. For example, I began to notice a habit I had of saying, "It's okay," to myself throughout a day. As I started in earnest to pay attention, I realized that I was speaking and entertaining accusatory thoughts towards myself. In other words, through negative self-accusation and internalized messages regarding my own worthiness, I was actually agreeing with and accepting those thoughts to the point where I was telling myself I was okay in response to me telling myself I wasn't okay! Do you see what I'm getting at here? YOUR INTERNAL CHATTER IS YOUR OWN THOUGHTS! Your thoughts are not the devil, and telling a thought to "shut the eff' up" is simply telling yourself to... The devil certainly is the source of evil in the world and the organizer of the "idea marketing" I referred to earlier, but his work is accomplished by influencing your thinking infinitely more than by some kind of imagined direct occupation! It is a slavery of epic proportion! What could work better than physically holding a slave in bondage? Get them to hold themselves in bondage by the wrong thoughts they're rehearsing to themselves all day long!

How many people do you know that are struggling with

their self-image? How much do you wrestle with your own self-image? How easy is it to move you off-center into doubt or concern about who you really are or what you can actually accomplish? Self-image is nothing more than the ideas you entertain about yourself, that you have been telling yourself since you were a small child. None of that stuff; those thoughts, had any basis in some type of truth, but rather messages you chose to believe were true. My mother convinced me I was exceptionally smart, and I believed her (and yes, I am - smile). Sure, there are genetic factors, tendencies, inborn strengths and weaknesses, but all are overridden by your beliefs, more specifically, what you believe to be true about yourself. Although it's not easy, you can change your self-image. You change it by changing what you are saying to yourself throughout the day. You can start to challenge thoughts instead of accepting them as true! Above all, stop berating yourself and rehearsing bad, negative stuff about yourself! Stop tearing yourself down. Cease searching for evidence that the garbage you've been dumping on yourself is somehow true. It is, for you, no more true than the good things you say about yourself. The only difference being that the good stuff we tell ourselves actually benefits our lives! I mean, good Lord, who are you to pass such severe judgment on your own life? That is exactly what you do every time you cooperate with the darkness by persisting in thoughts that only serve to hurt you. You're not "just being honest," you are being deceived with your own personal detriment and suffering in mind.

All that craziness besieging your brain during all waking hours belongs to you and comes from you. You can control your thinking. You can decide what you will and will not say to yourself. And, you can damn sure change anything about yourself, even if it is *who* you've been your whole life. You have a right to cultivate a mind, your mind, your one and only mind, to be your ally and not your enemy! You deserve a break from the great "idea marketing" machine for a chance at your own ideas about life. You can have success and satisfaction, and fulfillment like you've only dreamed of once you finally learn to get on your own side, where God is...

Hey, it's your internal chatter, but it's also yours to change for the better!

MAKING YOUR MIND A FRIEND

Years ago, I wrote a book called, "Making Your Mind a Friend." It was an amateurish project at best, but at the time I penned it, it helped save me from a world of suffering; suffering mostly self-imposed by wrong thought with a heavy, heavy dose of religious bondage. Somehow, in some imperceptible way, I had morphed (or had been morphed) into everything I hated in life. I became sickly religious, and when you get religious enough, everything you do or say or feel will be wrong. It's wrong because you have set up for yourself an impossible standard. And, before you know it, your worst, most pervasive enemy will be your very own mind. Thus, making your mind a friend isn't about splitting yourself into two separate entities and having positive dialogue with each part. It's about learning to extend kindness and forgiveness and friendliness to your own self in the same way you might extend it to your friend.

I remember years ago when my brother had agreed to watch our boys. When we picked them up, he explained incredulously that one of them was throwing rocks in the road, and when he told him to stop, he threw another one! He couldn't understand how that could happen. Of course, he didn't have his own children yet. He now knows that disobedience happens, but it is the parent's job to correct it. So, here's a thought. Disobedience happens with adults also. But, just like when you correct a child, no matter how satisfying the chastisement feels, all a parent is really after is an acknowledgement from the child that they did something wrong. There's rarely much to say after the apology occurs.

How many of you have spent years and years chastising yourself for some event that has long since expired? It's gone from life and is in the books. It only shows up again when you re-read the book. Stop re-reading the book! The things you do wrong and have done wrong were committed to the history book just as quickly as they happened. They are no longer a part of your life unless you allow them to be. The egregious errors, the scarring hurts, the bruising slights all have vanished from the present reality. You make your mind a friend by not subjecting your friend to the same old, tired story. Like your friend who might tell you it's time to get over it, it's time to get over it. You don't magically transform bad behaviors by punishing yourself; you know that! You transform yourself the same way your child transforms, by receiving your forgiveness. And don't you think for a second that God is bringing it up. God forgave you the FIRST time you were sorry. You have to "accept" His forgiveness also. Beyond that, it's all a bunch of egotism, and you can take that to the bank!

Once I heard a father say how dumb his kid was and that he didn't think his elevator went all the way to the top. How sad is that? To think that a father would say that about his own flesh and blood astounded me. All I could think was, he's your own kid! What the eff is the matter with you? Your child will be about as smart and talented and good as you can teach him he can be. You, horrible father, are outrageously defining his limit. Now as bad as I guess that made you feel, how about the things you say to yourself? Would you so easily tell your good friend that he was an idiot? Would you be so quick to focus on and point out his every weakness and fault? Oh, sure, you would see both, but out of love you wouldn't bring them up, would you? Do you know anyone on earth that gets better at something after repeatedly being told he sucks at it? Weakness is never overcome by focusing on the weakness. You win at life by focusing on your strengths; what you can do the best! Strength is built from strength! All you accomplish by acquiescing to an endless stream of negative chatter about yourself is to weaken and severely limit your true capabilities. And, the worst part? You are saying those things to yourself! You aren't just being honest! You are treating yourself like an enemy and not a friend. If you don't love you, who does? Well, God does, and He disagrees with your estimation of yourself. Again, beyond that, it's all just a bunch of egotism... and your own foolish persistence in self-harm.

Making your mind a friend is about choosing what you will and will not think about and choosing what you will and will not say to yourself. Your mind is your mind, and you may use it in whatever fashion you see fit. You may say, "I can't stop thinking about it!" But, oh yes you can! Like a lifelong smoker, the longer you've been engaged in the habit, the harder it is going to be to stop. The new non-smoker has to say 'no' to himself one 100 times a day at first, but the next day may only require 75. Eventually the thought comes up ever so rarely. The same with negative talk and condemnation; once you break the habit, it happens less and less. And like the smoker that quit, you brighten your prospects for a long, happy, successful life.

At the end of the day, you, my dear friend, are the only you, you've got! And, like your own heart would seek in earnest to console your sad, defeated child, you must learn to be good to yourself. You aren't serving God by behaving that way, no matter what some preacher may have told you, you are serving your enemy by your refusal to believe what God has already said. You aren't the evil one, but you just may have been listening to him. Be kind with yourself. Be forgiving with yourself. Learn to accept your imperfections and just be. It's okay. God knows all about you and loves you anyway!

TAMING YOUR WILD AND CRAZY MIND

I suppose it wouldn't matter much what you thought about if your thoughts had no effect on your life. If your life wasn't governed by what you believe and what you believe wasn't determined by what you think about the most, there would be no point in trying to get that unruly beast (your mind) under control. But alas, your thoughts do form the basis of what you believe and what you believe deep in your heart is the wellspring from which your entire life flows out (or lack thereof).

Of all of the things in life you can control, nothing is more important or potentially life-giving than controlling your thoughts. It's almost amusing to most folks, this insane notion that you *can* control your thoughts. In these frenetic times of visual, electronic images, overloaded and multiplied indefinitely, available in front of you, on your side and in your hand, calm, singular and controlled thought is highly discouraged or even considered boorish. Well, don't you believe that for a second!

Many people today just sort of limp through life. They drag along day by day, filled with anxiety, stress, depression, boredom and a general lack of zest for living. And sadly, they've done it for so long that they think that's just the way life is. They fail, disastrously, to make the connection between what appears in their life and what they think about the most. Subsequently, your life may be summed up in one simple question. "What do you believe is going to happen in your life?" If life for you is one continuous stream of things going wrong, negative events occurring, and disasters looming over the horizon, you have to ask yourself what kind of thoughts have you been incubating in your mind. Fear and anxiety are not a natural part of life; they are aberrations that come about by entertaining and focusing on the wrong things. Then when the catastrophe strikes, you exclaim, "I knew it!" Well, you did know it because you cooperated with "it" by allowing it to remain in your thinking. Disaster, catastrophe, hardship, difficulty and pain are not random at all, though they appear to be. They are pointed and specific and come about by man's cooperation with wrong by failing to control what he will and will not think about or failure to properly believe what is true. Man absent the truth is an anxiety machine ever churning out products to his own suffering and demise.

Life in its simplest form boils down to two distinct realities; light and darkness, love and fear, good and evil, right and wrong, truth and error; all an alternate way to say the same thing. As you live your own life, you are making decisions and choices every day. You don't get what you want, you get what you choose. If you choose to persist in something you know is wrong, no matter how rebellious, apathetic or careless you feel about it, you will continue to get the wrong results in your life. Oh, you can cling to it; get real damn angry about it, justify it infinitely, but it will still continue to bring to you what, at its core it is, whether you like it or not. Many times that inner turmoil you are experiencing doesn't need to be resolved by medication; it needs to be resolved by your decision to stop doing that thing (or maybe do that thing less) or stop thinking that thing, etc.! You decide what that thing is... This isn't some religious call to dissect and pick apart your life. That sort of thinking is just as bad (as you probably have already experienced). This is a sober reality check, pointing out that only good can come from good and only bad can come from bad. It doesn't matter what the world says; it matters what the truth is!

Worldly, so-called spiritual leaders always seem to shame and malign material prosperity, as if having an abundance is somehow not spiritual. Well, here's a quick newsflash for you. Life is a *helluva* lot easier with some resources than it is without them. Don't you kid yourself. If your car breaks down and costs $2,000 to fix it, it's hardly a flinch in your thought life if you've got plenty of money to fix it. If you don't, it's an emergency. Accordingly, God's will for you is abundance! So, back to the core issue, namely, what do you think about material prosperity? Does it elude you like a gazelle escaping the clutches of a lion? If so, that is a choice you are making in your thoughts. It doesn't matter that every previous generation in your family had very little. What matters is what you think or believe will happen in your life. Can you see it? The limit, the dividing line isn't the world; it's you.

Nowadays, disease is at an epidemic level. Almost everyone seems to have something. Sickness and disease are not God's will. Our imperfect bodies (not intended by God) sometimes fall prey to sickness. Fearful, worried, anxious thinking weakens our immune system and opens the door to illness. You may wonder why you are always so sick but fail to consider that your thoughts are sick. Your mind and your body engage in a delicate dance, with one responding to the other. Often your body is trying to tell you that something is wrong with your thoughts. Occasionally your body forces you to escape the frenetic pace you've engaged in and lays you up for a few days. Naturally some diseases carry a larger price tag. The "C" word for most threatens impending doom. Yet, even in the midst of life-threatening cancer, you still have a choice. For God, healing you of cancer is no different from healing you of a common cold. So even in that arduous, fear-inducing condition, you can choose to believe what God says and control your thoughts to keep the invader out. It doesn't matter how you feel. What matters is what is true.

You can control that unruly beast called your mind. You can also let it go, wherever it is being led. But beware, and know, that if you aren't leading it, something else is and that "something" does not wish you well. Instead, learn what to think and what is true. You have nothing to lose and everything to gain. You can turn your entire life around. You can change any aspect or part. You can acquire material abundance and be healed from everything that ever went wrong. You can, my friends, and you will if you'll only learn one thing - how to control your thinking, for your thoughts form the basis of your heart; the wellspring from which your entire life flows out! Make a good choice...

THE DEATH SPIRAL OF THE NEGATIVE MIND

A great man once said, "Negatives are like mosquitos on a blood hunt!" The world in which you and I live is ruled by negativity. The media is negative. Facebook is negative. The news is negative. Living in the world, we almost cannot help but become negative. So, you have to ask yourself, is all this negativity the natural way to be? Does being negative simply mean you are being realistic? Is it better to be negative and thus avoid getting your expectations dashed? Does negativity actually motivate you to become something good? Have you, my friend, become negative yourself?

What does it even mean to be negative? In math terms a negative is a number less than zero. To answer in the negative means to say no! A negative attitude is characterized as disagreeable. It closely ties to criticism and refusal. In photography it means to have the light and the darkness inverted. Now just stop right there for a moment. Deciding to be negative means less than nothing. You choose to say no rather than yes. You tend towards being disagreeable rather than promoting harmony (Facebook anyone). It enjoys criticism and refuses rather than accepts. It means you've got your light and darkness mixed up. Indeed, your light and darkness are mixed up.

Remember when you were a youngster? How long did your negativity last? Ten minutes, when Mom said no? Then you got back to your pursuit of happiness as quickly as you could. You somehow chose, with your innocent processor, to let disagreeable stuff go and change your focus back to the good. Then the world started mixing you up. It convinced you that you were less than zero. It taught you to say no to everything and be suspicious of anything good that showed up. People tried to tell you, but you disagreed because you knew better. You got really critical of everything and everyone and mostly with yourself. Finally, you started to confuse the darkness with the light and even preferred it. You refused the goodness as fanciful and believed the darkness is what is real. Thus, you entered the death spiral of negativity with no hope on the horizon. Is this not true? How many people just expect things not to work out? How many folks are afraid of good things happening because they won't last or something is going to take them away? How many good people spend their lives looking over their shoulder and waiting for the other shoe to drop? How many kind hearts live in perpetual fear of what might happen hasn't happened yet, but is surely going to happen one day? The Death Spiral...

Once you allow yourself to become negative, your focus shifts to the negative. You start looking for the negatives. You're just looking for trouble and almost always find it. Then, one negative event leads to another negative event, and the cycle is in full effect. The problem isn't life and the reality that bad things happen. The problem is that you got talked into shifting your focus away from what you want to what you don't want! Your dreams and your prayers went from, "I want" and "I need" to "Please don't let" and "Please take this away from me." Instead of being thankful, so extremely thankful, you dwelled on what you don't have and why you don't have it. Negative... less than zero, can you see it? Here's a newsflash that you might find unsettling. Your life will continue on the death spiral until YOU decide to change your thoughts. YOU have to get YOUR head out of the garbage can and look up. Look to where you want to go and go there! Stop looking back and rehearsing the hurts of the past. Stop dwelling on the things that didn't go right. Stop blaming, criticizing, refusing and ruminating, and just move your mind to a positive place. Until you do, this old world will just eat you alive... every day... until you die.

The opposite of negativity is being positive. Now, because people have their light and dark messed up, they want to chastise you for being positive. You stick out like a healed thumb! You're not being realistic. You're not thinking maturely. You're being all Pollyanna and foolish. As if expecting the worst of everything makes any sense. As if the reality of life is suffering and never blessings. As if grown-ups are supposed to be miserable. As if being lighthearted and jolly is worse than feeling melancholy and depressed. As if...

People who say those things don't yet understand life. Life isn't some predestined ride ending in a destination you don't get to choose. God does not have the dice loaded against you. If anything is loaded against you, it is your misunderstanding of the control you have in your life. It is you not clearly recognizing that your tendency toward negativity actually produces bad results as your tendency toward positivity actually produces good results. It is YOUR life and YOU are producing something. Seems only reasonable that you would want to produce something good.

Why not separate yourself from the herd and start expecting good things? Look, do the math! If you expect something good 75 percent of the time and the good only happens 50 percent of the time, I'd say that beats the hell out of below zero! I'll bet many of you would pay good money for something positive happening 10 percent of the time. And, while you are separating yourself from the herd, start separating yourself from the negativity. Stop watching the stupid news. Stop getting caught up in racial, political and economic debates on Facebook. Stop letting people and friends and relatives convince you of things that aren't true. Choose the light. Choose the things that encourage you and help you. Choose to believe that there is another way; God's way, and He is the one who dreamed this whole thing up...

Once you start smacking at the mosquitos, they start to overwhelm you. Just go inside; it's easier...

THE PERPETUAL STOMACH ACHE
OF THE RESTLESS MIND

Have you ever visited the digestive aids aisle at Walgreens? Man, there's more stuff for your stomach than almost any other ailment, except cold medicine, but that's another story. Heartburn, acid reflux, indigestion, gas, bloating, diarrhea, upset stomach, constipation and on and on it goes. (Oh, Mylanta!) Sure, we eat weird foods nowadays, but John the Baptist ate locusts (spiky legs and all). And yes, we are in a perpetual hurry so we eat fast, drink fast, work fast, talk fast and think fast; so fast we don't think. We all know we need to slow down, don't we? But a better question might be, what has us moving so dang fast? What in the world happened to us that made us need an endless supply of Tums? Rolaids spells relief, but only addresses the symptoms, never the cause. So, I'm thinking (belch) we better find out the cause.

One predominant idea centers on our minds; specifically our thoughts. Have you ever really gotten serious about what thoughts you are revolving around in your head? Here's a shocker for you - you are 100 percent responsible for the thoughts that you think, whether consciously or subconsciously. Shocker #2 - you can control your thoughts! Shocker #3 - you can control EVERY thought. Shocker #4 - most folks see no connection between the thoughts they think and the perpetual need for antacids! In case you just stopped reading and reached for your Tums, here's some spiritual insight:

Overthrowing reasonings and every high thing that lifts itself up against the knowledge of God, and leading captive every thought into the obedience of the Christ; 2 Corinthians 10:5 (Darby Version)

Shocker #3 revealed! God surely wouldn't tell us to lead captive every thought if He only meant some of our thoughts. Plus, I love the words, "leading captive," meaning sometimes those ol' thoughts just seem to appear, but you don't have to let them stay! So now back to Shocker #2 (waiting while you go back to read it...) A mind may be a terrible thing to waste, but even more specifically, a mind is a terrible thing to just let drift where it wants to drift. An open mind is a beautiful thing indeed, but not open to whatever or whomever, whenever! Okay, back to your thoughts... What are you saying to yourself throughout a day? Are you being kind to yourself? Do you give yourself a break and allow yourself to be a human? Do you forgive yourself? Or do you spend most of your "private" thought life mercilessly beating yourself to death? Oh, you don't do that? Really? I can assure you, unless you have been taught otherwise (and who the heck ever teaches this stuff?), that if you take the time, you will make a frightening discovery! I would surmise that no one is meaner to you than you are to yourself! You think Daddy or Mommy didn't say nice things to you? Haha, trust me, they got nothing on what you say to yourself! Most humans (and yes, I am also human) spend their days comparing themselves to others (and coming up short); evaluating themselves (and coming up short); judging themselves (and coming up short); dwelling on themselves (and coming up short); and just flat-out hating themselves because they aren't this or that or don't have this or that or don't earn this or that or don't look like this or that. Come on, admit it. Why the obsession with earning money or dressing in style or losing weight or having this kind of hair or getting some work done (an odd expression meaning body reconstruction?)

or driving this car or living in that house, etc., etc.? There's nothing wrong with ambition or nice things, but there's something wrong with having that perpetual stomach ache. In short, we just don't pay attention to that gnarling, persistent, attacking, insidious, agitated, never-satisfied inner voice that we have mistakenly confused with ourselves. And, we wonder why we have indigestion again? If someone sat across from you and hurled insults your way all day long, chances are (unless you are really passive or on the football team) you would get up and leave. I mean, really, you don't have to take that! But when it's you talking to you, somehow it must be truth. Well, it ain't truth, folks. It's "drifter mind" being let loose on itself. The enemy of mankind has a real slick trick up his sleeve, and that trick is your own thoughts. He takes advantage of what you let go of or don't maintain. Have you ever seen a house that is abandoned? It doesn't take long for the place to start decomposing. Well, how long does it take for your mind to start decomposing? Well, let's see, how old am I? (I'm kidding!) But I trust you see my point. In life, whatever you can control that you don't control will soon start controlling you. Have you ever wondered why you don't get the big break? Make the serious cash? Get into the wonderful relationship? Well, what do you think about all of those things? "I just don't get any breaks!" thought enough times IS your reality! "Making serious money is really hard!" and we wonder why it seems so elusive? "All men are assholes!" hmmm, and those are the ones I keep running into. It's you and it's me, folks.

So, do you want to get out of the digestive aids aisle at Walgreens? Would you rather visit the candy aisle? Then, you have to learn how to control your thoughts. Some of those thoughts that now define you are, in reality, well-worn tapes that YOU play over and over again! Pop the tape out and buy a CD (already outdated)! CD=change direction... (Clever, huh?)

Notice what nasty thing you just said to yourself and start changing it around. You'll never get to the Skittles unless you are willing to give it a shot. (Hey, maybe you like Tums!) You see, the reason we are so restless and dissatisfied isn't because our lives suck so bad, but rather because what we think about our life sucks so bad! Change your thoughts, change your life. No, not by tomorrow morning, but eventually. And hey, the life you are living in the present will get better immediately. Challenge those old stories because they were never who you really are anyway! The real you is satisfied, happy and contented, knowing that everything you will ever need will show up when you need it, once you get out of the stomach ache trap.

So, at the end of the day, remember, the reason I know about the digestive aids aisle at Walgreens is because I was there... I, like you, am a work in progress, but I'm okay with that. I hope you will be okay with that as well...

CHAPTER FOUR
Relationships

COMMUNICATION –
THE KEY TO A GOOD RELATIONSHIP

The secret to any good relationship is being able to communicate successfully. Have you ever been in a relationship with someone and felt like you were fighting all the time? Well, fighting and arguing isn't what kills a relationship! What kills a relationship is when you decide to go into silent mode. As long as you still feel it is worth the effort to say what you think, or disagree with what someone else thinks, your relationship maintains the potential for good. But, if the relationship deteriorates to the point where "it just ain't worth it," or you no longer care to say what bothers you, then the relationship is on the slippery slope downward and destined to end badly.

All of us want to have sweet, meaningful relationships with other people. When our relationships are mostly sweet, life becomes a joy. So, how can you have a "sweet" relationship with another person? Well, you have to take the time to handle the issues that threaten it. Let's say you get home from work feeling pretty good, and you are met with a bad mood from your partner. You recognize that they are in a funky mood and now your good mood is being threatened. Instead of getting mad or matching mood for mood, why not take the time to find out what is wrong with them? That's called having a conversation. Now, let's say every time you come home in a good mood, your partner is in a bad mood. Well, that's another conversation. It bothers you, right? So, why in the world would you spend your days with things bothering you when you can talk it over and get it straight? If you do it well, you can do better than straight and get to sweet.

The problem with most people is that they do not take the time to get the "air" cleared. And worse, they let stuff go day after day, quietly seething and thinking evil of the other person. The best time to talk about things is as the things are happening. Right now, in the moment, say what you are thinking. Say what you like. Say what you don't like. Say it, say it, say it! You're not looking for a fight; you are looking for the sweet. If you delude yourself and say things like, "I don't want the drama!" - you are setting yourself up for a big volcanic eruption. How could it not turn out that way? Have you ever heard people say, "I just need to get some things off my chest?" The reason they have to get them off their chest is because they cannot remain "on their chest" for them to be okay. If you bottle things up, hold things in, stop talking, and let things go that you shouldn't let go - you are going to blow! When you blow, you are going to bring up 300 issues that you have been saving, and you will bring them up in a way that is all out of proportion to the incidents! In short, you will sound like a crazy person; a stark, raving *looney tunes* person. Chances are your anger is going to result in saying a whole bunch of things you really didn't want to say. Then, despite your heartfelt petitions towards the other person, your words are going to cut them like a knife. Slice and dice - and there's hardly any coming back from that.

So, what should you do instead? Get into the habit of saying what you think. Emerson said, "I ought to go upright and vital, and speak the rude truth in all ways...." Get it? Upright and vital means stand up and wake up. But remember your goal is sweetness, not victory over the other person. You can win an argument but lose the relationship. You can browbeat your partner but find them getting the final say on the way out the door. It kills me when people say awful, dreadful things and then justify them by saying, "I'm just being honest." That's not honest. Being honest doesn't mean you have to say every silly thing that runs across your mind. Just because you thought it doesn't make it valid. Don't let anger have its way. Anger always follows another emotion anyway, so why not be "honest" and speak up when you are experiencing the other emotions (sadness, fear, frustration, guilt, etc.)? It seems to all boil down to having some healthy self-respect. In other words, respecting yourself enough to acknowledge that your feelings are just as important as other people's feelings, not less important. Your *likes* and *dislikes* are just as valid as someone else's likes and dislikes. Again, I am reminded of Ralph Dubya (RWE) -

"I must be myself. I cannot break myself any longer for you, or you. If you can love me for what I am, we shall be happier. If you cannot, I will still seek to deserve that you should. I will not hide my tastes or aversions. I will so trust that what is deep is holy, that I will do strongly before the sun and moon whatever inly rejoices me, and the heart appoints."

That, my friends, is honest. There is nothing wrong with "going with the flow" or being "yielding on insignificant matters." That's how we all manage to get along. But on those matters of the heart; those things that are important to you - you have to speak up! People who really love you aren't going to stop loving you because you spoke up about some issue. If you can't speak up about anything to them, you need to re-evaluate that relationship. You may surprise yourself and find out something you didn't know before. You might even actually learn that you had it all wrong and that the other person wasn't thinking what you thought at all... (smile).

At the end of the day, life goes by way too fast for drama and hurt feelings. Your life and your relationship are worth it!

RELATIONSHIP RESCUE

Nothing can get you more twisted up than being in a relationship that isn't going well. People talk about falling in and out of love as if love involves gravity. In some homes the tension is so thick you can feel the chill in the air. What happens in a relationship that makes it go so terribly wrong? What changed from the original proposition? What the heck happened? And, how can you rescue it from the danger of failing altogether?

In order for any relationship to work successfully, there has to be some underlying form of goodwill; a willingness to make it good. Spending all that time engaged in pitiful diatribes about what the other person isn't doing to make you feel a certain way is a frightful waste of time. Although your feelings are no doubt sincere in every way, it fails to address the real issue. The real question is, why is your partner acting the way they are acting? Why are they ignoring you? Why don't they want to talk with you? What thoughts and feelings are they carrying around concerning you? You began on the sound footing of goodwill, a sincere desire to make the other person happy, then something happened to change the dynamic. You need to find out what changed the dynamic. It always amazes me when engaging in relationship counseling how clear and obvious the issues are when completely alien to the people involved. Somewhere along the way, each person began developing a narrative about who or what the other person is (or became), and they are loathe to let go of their narrative. And, the narrative they have created for the other person always, always, always fails to include the part they are playing in the story! Step one in rescuing your relationship is acknowledging the part you personally are playing! You can't send out rejection vibes and expect love vibes to return. You can't discourage honest conversations by getting all outraged and angry and then complain that your partner won't talk! If you want love, you have to give love. If you want kindness, you have to give kindness. Waiting for your partner to go first will be a very long wait...

Warm, loving feelings follow warm, loving thoughts. Dragging around the world history of everything your partner ever did that you don't like or how they wronged you or don't get you (whatever that means...) or how different they are than from you are is a surefire recipe for disaster. People do wrong things, ever notice? Surely you have made a few blunders in your days, haven't you? Rehearsing the one time they did *this* to me or when they said *that* to me is relationship poison. It was evil enough the first time it happened, was it not? So, why on earth would you drag about that corpse of a memory with you now? Forgiveness means stop bringing that bullshit back up! Further, if you really want your partner to *get you*, you have to do a good job of communicating who you are to get. Feeling like they should somehow instinctively know who you are is madness. Say what you love, and do not hide your aversions. If you spend your days modifying yourself for others, hiding the real you; the real you will be really hard to get. Get it? Surprisingly, relationships thrive more on differences than on similarities. Fretting over not having all the same interests is equally insane. Relationships aren't about turning into each other. How weird? Relationships are about two people with different backgrounds and different upbringings coming together to form a union that works together. Relationships complement each other by one strong area compensating for one weaker area in the other, and we all have both involved.

Love is not something you fall into or fall out of over time. Love isn't some magical spell someone casts on you that is only as good as the spell lasts. Love is a decision. Your soul-mate is simply someone who meets most of the expectations you have set for yourself. I'm certainly not trying to take away the beauty or the romance of love. Rather I'm trying to point out that true love is a decision you make and keep making. When things go south, it isn't that mythical love has left the situation, but rather you have left the situation. Instead of good thoughts towards your partner, you harbor wrong thoughts. You are no longer focused on making them happy or helping them feel good but focused instead on how you are feeling and where you suffer lack. Your feelings are valid and matter much, but harboring the wrong thoughts about your significant other is making the decision to love no longer. You may proclaim the magic is gone, but it wasn't magic to begin with. If you want to rescue your relationship, get back to your decision to love.

I often muse that any relationship could be brought back to life if both people simply acted as if it was brand new again. Instead of carrying around all of those preconceived notions, start fresh. I can assure you, just because you have been to-gether for 25 years does not mean you already know where the other person is coming from. You barely know where you are coming from, right? How often do you allow yourself the privilege of changing? Can you not put aside the undesirable parts of yourself and go another direction? Well, can't they as well? Don't you see it? We all need the opportunity for a new day. We all need the chance to reinvent ourselves. We all need a fresh start; many, many fresh starts. Just because your wife always does such and such doesn't mean she always has to do such and such. Just because you struggled early on with such and such doesn't mean you have to struggle with such and such now.

Maybe you can't rescue every relationship given whatever may have occurred, but you can surely rescue yours if you really want to do it. Take your long-time partner on a date and find out what they like. Hey, they may just surprise you! Put some love in the air; it just feels better.

HAVE THINGS GOTTEN BITTER
BETWEEN YOU? (ADD SOME SUGAR)

Relationships are often complicated because people are complicated. When a long-term relationship begins to dissolve, it's not usually due to a big mistake made or some epic past failure, but rather in response to a multitude of minor slights adding, multiplying and blending into one large, bitter whole! Relationships fail due to words not said, important things not remembered, genuine care and concern not demonstrated. It breaks up and splinters first in the mind, then in the heart from too many missed opportunities to communicate love. And despite all of its associated complexity, it can be repaired quickly by adding a little sugar.

The problem with us humans is that we tend to hold on to the negatives and easily forget the positives. How many people still rehearse the cruel words spoken to them by their partner during a big fight from five years ago? How easy it is to compile a list of a spouse's failings, then read those failings into future scenarios that soon become present. How many of you have simply made up your mind about who your significant other is and, as such, offer zero possibilities for a new way in a new day? Your boyfriend, your girlfriend, has little chance to demonstrate proper behavior while being chained by you to the mistakes of their past.

Understanding relationships is understanding how each of us grows and evolves. People can and do change even after they may have shown you who they are. The point being that who they are isn't always defined by who they were. Priorities change. Desires change. Happiness and contentment are based on varying stages of life. Change is good unless it is met with a refusal to see the person through a different lens. Maybe your ex-husband is so happy with his new wife because he finally was afforded the opportunity to be someone else. Maybe you needed to get away from your ex-husband so you could be someone else. Wherever you are or whatever you may be facing, you must have some capability to modify your thinking; to get out of your rut; to reframe your expectations.

I think if you are honest, you have to recognize that relationships require commitment on both parts. I'm not referring to your decision to commit yourself to the relationship, but rather your decision to commit yourself to stop drawing negative conclusions. You have to change your own mind, your own beliefs, your own long-held preconceived notions. You have to cease from being mired in perpetual negative expectations. No matter your justifications, your righteous rights, your standing up for yourself and your other stories you've made up to justify your shitty approach, you have to flip the script. You have to realign your "self-defense" mentality to one of alignment and loving mutual respect. You cannot make someone else be something else, but you can damn sure make yourself be something or someone else.

In order for a relationship to thrive there has to be some element of love involved, and love is best characterized by sweetness. To think that sweetness is somehow weak or pitiful or acknowledging inferiority is to be deluded in regard to the essence of human relationships. Now I recognize that people have hurt you and maybe done and said all manner of terrible things to you, but that doesn't negate your ability to be kind; to be tender; to be sweet. The alternative is simply to keep living and reliving the same nightmare over and over and over again. Your escape isn't in finding the perfect guy or the ideal woman but rather in relocating your heart; the one you had before the damage occurred. The real you wants to give love and receive love no matter how far down you got knocked. It seems risky, but in reality there is no risk because love never fails!

Real love; true love; abiding love requires a new beginning, a fresh start. Just as you forgive yourself for your own absurdities and foolishness, you have to be willing to offer your love interest the same privileges. You have to learn to make your evaluations and draw your conclusions based on today, in the moment called now. Today is always a new day and carries with it unlimited new beginnings. Sure, stuff is going to happen that drags you back to yesterday, but in like fashion, you pull your own self back to today. You treat your partner like someone you love in spite of yourself. Just as a soft answer turns away wrath, a soft approach can remedy a whole world of failings. If your love is always based on proper behaviors and the right words, you are setting yourself up for a misery that will not be overcome.

Decide right now to be that warm, loving person you know you really are already. Stop with your defensive approach, your self-preservation, and ever hedging just in case. End your failure planning and plan to succeed. In spite of what is going on and what you are experiencing, be sweet; so lovingly, genuinely sweet. In doing so, you will find that sweetness and kindness are irresistible and almost impossible to slight. You will find yourself on the high road, unshaken and unaltered in your thinking. You will find yourself living love and giving love from which there is never any need to retreat. You will be loving people how God loves you, unconditionally and without a change of heart.

No matter how bitter or jaundiced you may have become towards him or her, know that there is something you can do.

Don't go to the counselor with an expectation of confirmation for the things you have seen for years, but instead with an open heart regarding what you can do with you to effect a change. Maybe, just maybe, it's you! And if it's not you, you still have the solemn responsibility to guard and nurture your own heart, which is never accomplished in anger, fighting and bitterness of soul! Oh, my friends, choose sweetness! Add some sugar and see how much better it all tastes!

HE WHO SMELT IT, DEALT IT

Forgive me for grabbing your attention with a foul metaphor (smile). While you are likely familiar with the saying, thankfully I'm going in a different direction. Many times in life we can get so caught up in what other people are doing to us, how unfair they are and how insensitive they can be to our own needs and wants. Yet, it is easy to forget about our involvement in the equations. Your life, my life, is really about being the best version of ourselves. It's about choosing our own thoughts and actions and taking full ownership of our lives because ultimately, he who smelt it probably dealt it!

Have you ever stopped to consider that you play a key role in every relationship you have, be it foul (there it is again) or fair? The one constant in every relationship you have is you. When you find yourself confronted with the same challenges or the same unwanted judgments, or the same faulty conclusions about who you are, maybe it's not because the people you deal with are all idiots (been there), but rather because of what you are giving off. Maybe, just maybe, you are sending a consistent message, accurate or not, about yourself that isn't really true. Perhaps you have been so accustomed to playing a specific role with others that you are loathe to let it go, even if you don't enjoy the results thereof. Many of us become familiar with a certain performance we put on for others; one they faithfully enjoy and demand, which leads people to a false understanding about who we are. The world is not always a nice place, and its inhabitants not always offering us the benefit of the doubt. It's not easy to be authentic in our interactions, and in so doing, we set up circumstances and conditions we do not like. The first requirement in building lasting relationships is to be an authentic person.

In a relationship, it is incredibly easy to hone in and discern the faults of others. Whether it be mild annoyances or full-on agitation, it is surprisingly effortless to figure out things about other people you do not like. But, sadly perhaps, it is very difficult to recognize the things we do that others may not like. That's not to say we should mold and shape our character to meet the demands of others, but rather that we should become humble enough to admit we've also got some unpleasant bits. Maybe we aren't as funny as we think? Maybe they should know we mean no harm, but after they have told us otherwise a 100 times, we should have perhaps gotten the message by now. There are, it seems, certain people that have the capacity to drive you nuts! They have found your buttons and joy exceedingly in pressing them. But, have you ever considered that maybe before they sent you a message, you already sent them one? Sometimes your tone of voice, your facial expressions, your approach, already communicated your thoughts about them being a moron and in like manner they have rightfully perhaps decided to assault you back. Naturally, you are aghast at their behavior yet cannot conceive you began the conflict yourself. In relationships, it makes sense to pride yourself on being altruistic, but often, imperceptibly, we may be the one that needs to make a change.

In marriages or lasting relationships, couples often spend a lifetime wishing their partner would only listen to what they are telling them and change, yet refuse on the grounds of principle to change themselves. Or they dutifully carry a lifetime of assumed responses based upon "knowing their significant other" without really knowing them at all. How could they know them after deciding 20 years ago exactly who they are?

Bitter, long since burned out couples could not hear a good thing from their partner if it slapped them in their face! They have already concluded and, in so doing, have already closed the door to change. The other person can scarce bring up a topic without their spouse already knowing where they are heading, requiring them to head it off at the pass. Bad relationships are seldom not formed by the actions of the present but rather on the thousand-fold actions of the past. No couple can honestly survive such closed-mindedness! The answer isn't found in the other person; it is found in yourself! Someone has to stop the madness and it may as well be you. So, you find yourself divorced and finally living out your dreams, yet never considered that you might be treating your "new" person in all the ways your "old" person would have loved. You gave your new person a chance...

What should you do when you find yourself in such a dilemma? Stop assigning responsibility for the relationship to the other person because the responsibility rests with you. You change you! You be the best you, you can be. You give the love first. You decide to be sweet, loving and kind. You decide to listen and really hear the messages with your heart. You'd be surprised what can change when you change. You may find out the person whose faults you have been faithfully cataloging for years has qualities you never before imagined. You might just discover true love, not based on endless expectations but rather on your decision to love first. You may at last recognize the love you have spent a lifetime searching for is right there waiting for you and has been all along. Take ownership of yourself first, and in so doing, stop making it always about them. Sure, they will still have faults and failings and blind spots, but criticism never ever cured them; only love can.

Whether your relationship is a marriage or dating or people you work with or your family members, the success of them all is first dependent upon you and the hidden messages you are transmitting to them. Seek to change the only thing you can change - you! Because two people are involved, it may not always work out no matter what you do. But, at least you will have done your honest best. Remember, usually, he who smelt it likely dealt it!

REWRITE YOUR SCRIPT

Your successful relationships with other people form the basis of one of the most needful, necessary elements in your life. Your happiness, your personal feelings of fulfillment, your peace, your love, and your joy all rely heavily on your ability to successfully navigate your relationships. So, what can you do when your relationship lacks some of its original luster? Is there a way to escape the mundane and rekindle the once-present emotional availability? Can you somehow steer the ship off the rocks and back into the deep water? Is there even anything you can do about it? Is it really all about your partner, or is it maybe about you?

Any couple who have been together for many years can tell you that things change over time. Goals change. Priorities change. People grow. People regress. The hopes and dreams you held in such high regard in high school are barely recognizable in middle age. Your body ages and things you once took for granted don't come as easy as they used to do. You're generally smarter and a little more assured about how things work. And, like anyone that has done the same thing for a number of years, you develop habits; many, many habits. Habits are built for efficiency. But, not all habits are good for you. Habits tend to be morally neutral. In other words, you can engage in certain habits for a lifetime and never feel they need any revision because of how long you've been holding on to them. Relationship habits can make for heaven on earth or make life a living hell. But, at the end of the day, they are your habits.

In order to have a successful relationship, you have to embrace the reality that people change. Your spouse is not the same person they were when you married them. Chances are they have grown, evolved and need different things to be happy. You also have changed, grown and evolved. Your needs are now different as well. To hold your partner in some sort of time-lock is categorically insane. To continue to think and rehearse that same old, tired, irritating version of them is also insane and entirely unfair to them. To perpetually strengthen and maintain in your mind all the things they have not done that they should have done or the things you didn't like about them when you first met them or the person you wish they were when you were first building your negative pictures of them, is to drag about a weight of epic proportions! In life, every day is a new day. Every moment is a new moment, unique and one that has not existed before. Your partner is also afforded the opportunity of a new day, a new moment. You have to be able to give them the same chance at doing better that you give yourself. You have to encourage the reality that they, like you, can change. You see, things start going south not because of your relationship reality, but instead because of your rehearsed, mental reality! Things become worse and worse because your thinking has become worse and worse. You couldn't see the things you so desperately want if they slapped you in the face because you are stuck, trapped in rehearsed negative feelings and memories from past days! In order for things to get better, you have to get better.

Many, many people like to play the victim in their relationships. Poor old, unfulfilled me. "I just need someone to love me." "I just need someone to accept me for me." "If only they were nice to me, then I would be nice." "If they ever took time to offer me love and affection, then I would offer them love and affection back. But, they never do that for me, and they're not going to, so poor, poor me living my life in misery." Sound familiar? The problem with this mentality is that you are playing a role in a drama that you are writing. You are acting in a play as the main character that you and you alone have assigned as the victim. And, as the victim it feels good to dredge up all the wrongs done to you and to fantasize about how good life could really be. But, would it really be good for you? How could it be? In order for your role to ever change, you have to change the script. You have to write a new story. Look, if you found a new relationship, you would likely change the script and start thinking and acting like the person you wanted to be, which in turn would probably return to you the feelings you wanted to feel as well. Well, your solution is that you can do that now in your present relationship. Rewrite your script. Edit your character. Stop rehearsing and ruminating and harboring and cleaving to every single thing you haven't liked for the past 20 years and start fresh. Give your partner a chance to be someone else as well. I can assure you that they have some tremendous qualities waiting to be shared with you in your life once you finally give them the opportunity to do so. Don't remain stuck in yesterday; live today.

One of life's strangest dichotomies is found in relationships with other people. When you change towards them, they change towards you. You have to give love to get love. You have to show kindness to receive kindness. Waiting for the other person to change is a perilous waiting game. You might be waiting for a long time. Maybe you don't feel fully accepted for who you are because you are spending so much time rejecting who they are. Maybe, just maybe, you don't feel like they like you because your behavior says you don't like them! You cannot make other people do anything, and you know that. The one person you can control and change is you. Are you doing for that person you are so upset with, what you would like to be done for yourself? Are you willing to let them be something other than the negative picture you have made them to be? You can become so accustomed to your habitual way of thinking that you don't even recognize it anymore. Change your mind. Change your script. Change your bad habits of negative thinking and negative expectations.

Relationships take work to be successful, but it's not the kind of work you need a vacation from. The work is in learning to think properly. The effort is in refusing to harbor and maintain negative stories, likely only partially based on reality. Your energy is used to build and bless and help and warm, which is always reciprocated when done from your heart. You can recover any relationship that has gone astray if you want to, but most of the work to be done will involve yourself first. That's not to say that every relationship is worth preserving or repairing, as some relationships need to dissolve. In those scenarios there will be no doubt. But, it's still worth your time to work on yourself to avoid it the next time.

It certainly takes two to tango, but the only dance moves you can improve are your own. Life is short, and your chances at happiness are sometimes fleeting, but a loving, warm, mutually committed relationship is worth every ounce of your effort! Decide to live love; it's irresistible... Decide to forgive; it's refreshing. Decide to make every day a brand-new day; it is life changing...

Rewrite your script.

RELIGION AND HOW IT CAN RUIN YOUR RELATIONSHIP WITH GOD

If you are born again of God's spirit, your relationship with Him should be the sweetest thing this side of heaven. However, for most, it seems, it is just the opposite. Well, there's a reason for this, and that reason is called, "religion." Sounds like quite a contradiction, I know, but being religious and having a vital relationship with God are often miles apart.

The issue isn't the sincerity of the believer or their heartfelt desire to walk with God. The crucial issue centers around what the believer "thinks" is required in that relationship, which, when religion gets involved, contradicts the Bible on every front. Religion, in its thousand-fold forms, always, always, always puts the emphasis on what man is or isn't doing. Conversely, true Christianity's focus is always, always, always on what God has done and will do for you, the believer. Now, just let that simmer for a minute...

Look, I'm not trying to bash your religion, whatever that might be. I'm just trying to tell you some stuff that I know is true from the Word of God, which, if you dare to believe and understand it, will completely change your life and your relationship with Big Poppa!

First and perhaps most important, God is not following you around monitoring your behavior. He's not condemning you, making you feel guilty or convicting you by the holy spirit (whatever the hell that means)! Surprise! God already knows your behaviors and thoughts aren't always righteous and, as such, made a way to make you righteous before Him without it being based on your (and my) ever fluctuating behaviors. His son, Jesus Christ (who, by the way, didn't have a sin nature in his blood), walked perfectly by his free will, so you wouldn't have to! Your job is to believe in his sacrifice for you and thus God reckons righteousness unto you, because you chose to believe! Come on now, do you really think your sincere commitment not to cuss or smoke would really make you righteous in God's sight? It's just silliness; a silliness promoted by religion that ever seeks to make it all about YOU and not all about God! Note* Insert whatever foolishness you've been taught in place of no smoking and no cussing!

Who in the world wants a Father who constantly abides to criticize you and point out what you aren't doing and should be doing or are doing that you shouldn't be doing? Lord have mercy, do you do that with your kids? Well, if you do, stop it, because that crap is evil. There is someone who is accusing you day by day, but he isn't God! And, just for the record, almost the entire book of Romans focuses on this issue because it's that big! (Book of Romans... in Bible.)

Next, I have to address the Facebook meme frenzy, whereby God is doing some dastardly shit to you to make you better, somehow, someway! Like... God saves the toughest challenges for His strongest people or God's testing you to make you better or anything that implies that God does negative stuff to make you worthy or humble or strong or whatever! This, my friends, is a lie from hell! God doesn't need the stupid adversary or evil to perfect you. Where did you ever get that insane idea? From religion, that's where you got it. It comes from a lack of understanding regarding evil and in that ignorance attributing everything that happens back to God. What possible purpose could God have in causing a disaster where people are killed? It's nuts, if your brain works, but somehow acceptable in religion. You know, God is mad at _______ (insert who you are mad at today), and that's why that happened. Again, the focus is on what? The people and what they are and aren't doing! What a fantastic delusion! Get rid of the true source of the problem, blame it on God and totally screw up the sincere believer.

God is light and in Him is no darkness at all. No darkness... at all... ever! Just for the record, supposedly giving people sickness is darkness. Killing people is darkness. Making life generally hard and annoying for some vague, unknown lesson is darkness. Threatening people with a life lived in perpetual torture called, "hell" is darkness. There's no hell as described afore in the Bible. Who the hell (pun intended) would run it forever? So, who told you all that garbage? Religion did, that's who! To help you, you ask? No, to control you! It has nothing to do with your relationship with God and everything to do with your relationship with the people who seek to control you! Maybe that's too blunt for you, but by God, it's the truth, and if you are ever going to feel good about your relationship with your Heavenly Father, you need to know the truth!

Time fails me to speak of bead counting, chanting, lighting candles, repetitious prayers, going without, kneeling, going to this place at that time, avoiding that place, sacrificing, not drinking, not cussing, not smoking, no sex, no caffeine, no medicine, no, no, no, no - arghhhhhhhhhh, misery! No wonder you don't want to talk to God except on Sunday when it's required. No wonder the mention of His name makes you uncomfortable. No wonder why you don't share your heart with Him; after all, He might figure you out. Newsflash! He already knows all about you (duh) and still loves you. He is God, for God's sake! Do you really think there is some aspect of your humanness of which God isn't familiar? Really?

Religion really is the opiate of the masses, but unlike other opiates, it doesn't make you feel better. You have to give God more credit than that. Seriously? Beads? Chanting? Saying the same crap over and over again? Would any of that bless you as a Father? Mother? I think you really might be after, above all else, their heart. Well, it may surprise you that God is after... wait for it... your heart; your free will; unforced or coerced; just because; for love's sake; heart... God wants to give all of His goodness to you! He wants to help you and heal you and restore you and make you smile. He desires to give you life and that you have it more abundantly.

As I said, I'm not mad at your religion, or whatever your allegiance is to, or what your folks taught you or what your pastor said. My aim is ever and always your freedom to live and enjoy this life. I didn't make this stuff up. This is God's Word of true Christianity for you!

CLEARING THE INVERSION

Living in Utah, we are often subjected to inversions. The inversions occur because we live in a valley, and all of the pollutants get trapped in the air making it difficult to breathe. There's not enough airflow, absent a storm, to remove the gunk from the atmosphere resulting in a serious health risk! So how does this apply to your relationships? Before we proceed, read the above again...

For a relationship to be healthy, you have to be able to talk; talk about anything. And generally, it's best to talk about the offending situation the moment it blips across your radar screen. You know exactly when that remark or that attitude or that look sent you a message that didn't agree with your mental harmony system. You know, right? So why would you put that message on the back burner or worse, fear the repercussions of bringing it up? In fact, with people you care about and especially those you love, you owe it to yourself and them to always bring it up. Often young married couples, for fear of offending or worse, losing the object of their affections, choose silence, only to discover later that the initial offending issue not only comes back, it comes back with hair on! Bring it up. If it leads to a big argument, so what? It's better to have the mother of all arguments than to pretend you are okay when you are not okay. It's better to have the war and come to an agreement than to avoid the war and live amidst the constant skirmishes. Peace often comes after the war, right?

Like an inversion, allowing pollutants to stay in your mental air risks the health of your relationship. Maybe you need a quick storm or two. Maybe. People often seem to think that harmony in a relationship comes from letting things go. Oh, sure, there's nothing wrong with compromise, as compromise helps maintain a relationship, but letting things go is always bad news. Being married for many years now, I can tell you with complete confidence that every issue you bury under the guise of keeping harmony is going to come back with a vengeance and unreasonably all together in one moment of time. That one fight on that one bad day will turn into a floodgate of unresolved issues seeing the opportunity to finally get out of your heart. And like a pressure boiler that takes on more pressure than it can handle, it's going to blow boy and blow at catastrophic levels. So, take my advice and speak up often.

None of us want to hear the things we have done wrong or hear in minute detail our faults and our failings. None of us look forward to that conversation ever. But always hidden within that conversation, if we have ears to hear, is some gem of truth that speaks to our hearts. In the middle of all that anger and yelling and accusation sits a little minuscule, almost unnoticed piece of truth that alerts our battered heart of some wrong done; some sensitivity walked over; some selfishness we have engaged in. And when we see it; when we finally see it and feel remorse over the thing we have done, healing takes place; a healing that transcends many, many infractions. That, my friends, is the point of the discussion, the fight, the argument, or whatever. In a sense you are kicking up the winds that will eventually blow that inversion out of your way so you once again can see clearly. How many relationships have come to an end because we didn't love enough to say what needed to be said? How many breakups could have been avoided if we had the honesty to say what really was?

Now to those of you who have already loved and lost, I offer the following. There's a bible verse that tells husbands to love their wives and be not bitter again them. Bitterness comes unannounced from a multitude of unresolved hurts, be they ever so slight. Bitterness is born of the small many, not of the large few. But once bitterness takes root, it takes on a life of its own and permanently blinds a heart that once could see and feel and experience. In its bitter state, it is now poisoned and goes on poisoning everything it comes into contact with until it ruins the person completely. Don't let that be you. Stop rehearsing the past hurts, the wrongs done to you, the pain. Stop carrying around in your memory those unbearable weights. Instead, allow yourself to start again; to start over. Resolve in your heart that you will never allow that to happen to you again. If you can still speak those words you have buried for so long, speak them, though the hearer be long past listening or understanding. If not, speak them to God alone and be now done with it, forever... You are worth that.

Inversion air is hard to breathe and puts your health at risk. Poison cannot exist where there is fresh, clean air. Clear the air between yourself and the people who you care about. Speak up about the things you hold most dear. Forgive where forgiveness is needed, and be the person you always wanted to be. You can. You should. You owe it to yourself.

Ah, what is that I'm feeling? The feeling that comes from finally breathing a breath of clean, pure, fresh air... And it feels so good!

BLESSED PEOPLE BLESS PEOPLE

Recently I came across a post proclaiming that true followers of Christ don't need health, wealth or prosperity and that they should content themselves with Christ alone. And those statements, while dripping with religiosity, could not be further from the truth! Oh, it sounds noble enough, so humble, so pious, but is that how life works; indeed, how human beings work?

For the life of me, I cannot understand how people think a life with God involves going without the things that make life a blessing. If God is all-powerful, all mighty, all good, why would we allow someone to convince us that His will for us was anything less? Do you have kids? How did you treat them? Sure, you needed to teach them some tough lessons at times; maybe you even spanked a butt or two, but did you ever take it upon yourself not to supply what they needed? I'm guessing, and I know from my own children, that you did everything in your power and sometimes beyond your power to make sure they lacked no good thing. Come on; you know that! So, why would you ever accept that God would not only do less for you, but even require that you went without your prosperity or worse, your health for some grand unknown purpose? You see, that's the problem with religion. It doesn't make sense, and God, in His perfection, isn't allowed to not make sense.

How life really works, and you know this in your heart, is that blessed people, bless people. When people are prospering, they want to share their prosperity with other people. When people don't have enough, which is never God's will, they cannot afford to help other people and trying to do so just adds more pressure to their lives. When your health is good, and you feel good, you have the energy to reach out. When you're sick, which is also never God's will, you are forced to focus on yourself and whatever it takes to recover. In short, when you are enjoying God's blessings in your life is when you are most apt to reach out and help someone else. It is just how life is, and God knows this. To tell people who don't have their needs met that they are being selfish in their focus, doesn't help them at all. What they need is to be taught how to believe to get their needs met.

A relationship with God, as your Father, is all about you learning how to receive and enjoy God's blessings. The first person you have to prove God to is yourself! If you personally never got blessed by God or received His help in trying times or had access to his healing during times of sickness or affliction, then what on earth would you ever witness to anyone else? Who or what are you promoting? If I'm God's child and still have to suffer all the garbage, all the suffering the world goes through, if I cannot get the help I need when I need it the most, if I'm just supposed to perpetually suffer for the glory of the Lord, then what the hell kind of life is that? Yet, that is exactly what people preach and teach. In reality, people have just not yet learned how to receive from God.

I know, I know someone is going to say this sounds selfish. I mean, God-forbid you get your needs met, right? Well, supplying all your needs is something God promises, not me. God is more interested in helping to meet your needs than you are in having them met. God wants to prove His love for you. You don't initiate the goodness; God does. You simply respond. You simply give God a try... Religion, always man-made, seeks to make the irrational, rational. It adds principles and policies that contradict life. It suggests behaviors and practices that have no foundation in logic or reason. In fact, it promotes a lack of reasoning as a basis for faith, a conundrum from which people have a hard time escaping. God, life with God, is the exact opposite. It is completely logical and sensible. It fits with life and nature and everything in our existence. It feels so good because it is so good. It's warmth and love and tenderness and everything you always knew intuitively it should be. Don't doubt yourself... Don't let someone talk you out of things you know for sure. Keep questing, keep seeking, keep learning.

You know how you can be the best kind of human you can be? Learn about God and start getting your needs met. Learn how to receive God's blessings. Learn how to believe. In doing so, you will open yourself to a world of possibility and potential. You'll discover a realm where for God nothing is impossible and that He will use His power to help you. You will find that smile you left in childhood returning with so much more to feel good about. You will find the life God intended for you to find. God always works in individuals, not organizations. Get blessed! Blessed people bless people...

Are you blessed?

THE MEASURE OF A MAN

This is a story about your life. You know, the one you are living right now. It's about where you're at today. It's about your successes and your failures. It's about how much money you make and where you work. It touches on your relationships, your togetherness and your loneliness. It reaches into every facet of your life, and there's no part of your existence that it doesn't explain. It's not about how you measure up, but rather how you measure yourself.

I got into a discussion the other day about the term "realistic." I'll spare you the details but suffice it to say that most people who utter those words use them for limitation and not for endless possibility. My key point centered around the question, what is realistic? You see, the world but half expresses itself. The things you see are not made up of what is really back of them. But, on we go wrestling on the outside with a world defined by our inside. The circumstances you encounter scream for supremacy as the first cause but in truth are, in reality, a result. They align themselves perfectly with your expectations. If they are pervasive and miserable, it is no one's fault but your own. Likewise, if they are glorious, spontaneous and grand, for that you may take some credit as well.

The question that concerns you most is not what hand the world has dealt you. The question of utmost importance is, what do you think of yourself? What do you expect for your life? What things do you think you can have in this life? What is the measure of yourself? The answer to those questions is played out amongst a million precise variations in the life you are living right now. Look around you. The environment you are in, you chose. The proof is in the pudding. Whining about not having enough money is foolish because you make exactly what you think you can make. No more, no less. The only way a man raises himself from mental poverty is in finally convincing himself of his own value. I say finally, because a man is knowingly or unknowingly in a contest day by day; a contest between what apparently "is" versus what may actually be. How he votes determines the election. The more highly he values himself, the more he expects for and from himself. As a man seeks to improve himself and does, he begins to grow out of whatever confining conditions have seemed to hold him back. He cannot help but succeed the more because he is more. In this, his life solemnly testifies to the man he has become.

The most ironic yet heartbreakingly sad "reality" is that man is free to decide upon his own estimation of himself. His self-esteem, his self-value is decided by himself. It's not for no good reason a man aims so low. He aims low because he lives in a world constantly whipping himself out of himself. His behavior is bad; his desires are bad; his decisions are bad. But are they? Those in advantage methodically make plans to ensure the so-called lesser man remains lesser. Is he lesser? God has made from one blood all nations of men that dwell upon the earth. A man, in order to be a real man, must raise his estimation of himself. He must consider and take to heart whom God says he is. God's men cannot settle for second best.

The people of the world exhaust themselves in the endless pursuit of success; success measured by boats and houses and leisure time. Television celebrities are not real people. Yet, you have to commend them on how they have made themselves indispensable. The estimation they make of themselves being clearly evident. So, whether your success is measured in boats and houses and leisure time or by love, relationships and legacy, the measure will always be found in yourself. The way to success is found in the value you place on yourself. You must find the way to do what you alone can do and in that which you have no rival. Instead of investing pointless energy in comparison, you must spend your energy on your estimation of yourself. It can never be called selfish to think highly of yourself because those who love themselves love others, and for that the world will always be in need.

No matter what you have gone through; the mistakes you have made; the blunders you have done, each day offers the bright and shining hope of a new day. And as the sun ebbs the horizon offering light to all the inhabitants thereof, you awaken offering your light in your way, to the world. Start where you are, as you must, but know the limitations you have imagined are your own and hold no sway in a world created by infinite possibility. You wish to be a man of courage and boldness, be that man. You desire to be a man of magnanimous wealth and supply, be that man. You dream of earning the respect of all around you, respect yourself. No circumstance, no condition, no predetermined fate can stop a man who knows who he is and values it.

God has graciously granted man the chance to be whomever he wants to be and has done it without limit or check. Check yourself and see what measure you have placed on yourself. Throw off the chains of genealogy and circumstance and be exactly who you always knew you could be! The world is waiting for you to be who you were already supposed to be. Your past has no bearing unless you make it so. Your background, your education, your job, your track record is nothing more than an account of the man you used to be. Be whomever you want to be today and see if the great God does not honor your desires at every step. See if He will not back your every effort and toil with a handsome reward; the reward that follows every man who believes.

What is reality? Reality is exactly what you expect it to be!

ALIGNMENT AND HARMONY

Many moons ago I learned about this thing called, "alignment and harmony." Basically, staying in alignment and harmony refers to your relationship with God and you, the variable, doing your part to keep your head in the space that God occupies. Remaining in alignment and harmony is where all of the believer's joy and happiness come from in this life. Being out of alignment with God is the number one source of misery and defeat, and leads to an inability to tap into God's power or to get your prayers answered!

It has been my experience, as sad as this is to say, that most Christians seem to be living a fairly miserable life. They're usually submerged in sin-consciousness, overly concerned and focused on the so-called rules for Christian living. They're born again and have God's spirit within them, yet they lack the power promised by God to make their lives abundant. The reason for this is that through either ignorance concerning God's Word or wrong teaching regarding God's Word, they are out of alignment and harmony with God. You can be uber-religious and totally out of alignment with God. You can tell if you're out of fellowship with God by how you feel. If you are full of anger and frustration, you are out of alignment. If you have no love for yourself and other people, you are out of harmony. If your mind is filled with bitterness and complaining, you are out of fellowship. If you spend your days working hard to make yourself approved and righteous before God, you are in the wrong place and will suffer as a result of it. You are not in alignment and harmony with God.

This old world works night and day to get you out of that good space where love holds first place. It seeks to make you negative and chips away at you day by day with subtle and not-so-subtle attacks on your thinking. It wants to fill your mind with worries and fears. It presses you to focus only on yourself and have little or no concern for others. It wraps your mind into various media events hell-bent on dividing and causing angst. Then, as you indulge it, you get further and further away from God and your own happiness, joy and contentment.

Your personal relationship with God, your Father, is your most important relationship on Earth. As such, you cannot allow misconceptions and wrong ideas to cloud the beauty of that relationship. You are on this Earth to find out who God is and how to get His spirit within. Then, to learn how to operate that spirit producing power and joy in your day-by-day life. You have to cut through the error of religion and see God for who He says He is. A lady reported the other day how God uses people and often has them doing things they don't like! To which I responded with a hearty "bullshit!" It's lies like this that keep people away from God. The only being that uses people and makes them do things they don't like is the devil and his host of evil companions. When things people tell you don't make any sense, they're probably not true.

Staying in alignment is no more complicated than deciding to walk in the light. It's recognizing when you have gone south, for whatever reason, and getting back to the light. It's not days spent in guilt and condemnation, begging God for forgiveness. It's simply a recognition in your heart that you may have mis-stepped and a decision to get back to the light. Walking in the light isn't following some strict creed of rules for living, but rather keeping your mind in the right place. It's deciding to love and be kind and patient with people and to love and be kind and patient with yourself. It's cultivating a tender heart like God's heart and, through modifications to your thinking, keeping your heart soft and pliable. A hard heart doesn't show up overnight but comes from years of wrong thinking and unresolved issues.

Alignment and harmony are really relationship advice. It starts with God, of course, but applies to every relationship you have. Husbands and wives can get out of fellowship with one another. Carrying resentment and refusing to forgive lead to walking in darkness where there is no sweetness of living left. Thus, it is your duty, for God's sake, to get those relationships repaired if you can and be the one who initiates the light. Married couples, out of fellowship with one another, have no power with God and miss out on a golden opportunity to believe together for great things!

Perhaps the worst thing; the most dastardly of all, is when the darkness persuades you to be at odds with yourself. It's when you are no longer in alignment with your very own self. If you are not even for yourself in this life, what chance could you have at happiness and fulfillment? Those harsh words and negative ideas about yourself do not come from God. The accusations, the perpetual reminder of past mistakes, the questioning of your character and goodness are weapons in the enemy's arsenal that he has been using for years and years on mankind. Don't believe it. Get your head to the light, where God is and see if that doesn't completely revolutionize your life!

Being in alignment and harmony with God is the greatest thing in the whole world! It's an unparalleled sweetness and joy like you may have never experienced before. It's walking with confidence and power, knowing that God will answer your every prayer. It's being so tight with God that nothing can make you afraid. It's riding on the high places of the Earth!

It's God's will for His children in order for them to live the more than abundant life He promised them. It is the way, the truth and the life!

Stay in fellowship... it works!

FATHERS AND SONS

You would think that by being a man, it would be inherent that you would know how to raise a son. You would think... But, all you really have to go on is how you were raised, right or wrong. So, this is a story; a story about raising that boy you always wanted to have. The Mommy part? Well, that's another story.

Many men, it seems, want to raise the next NFL star or the next NBA legend. No matter the sport, we daddies want that little fella to be a "man's man." We want to go to his games; grunt, scratch and watch boxing with him; teach him how we men are supposed to act. But, mostly we want him to be well-adjusted and fulfill the roles that he will be called upon to fulfill; being a provider, a protector, a leader and so forth. This is where the misinformation conundrum begins!

Somebody, somewhere, imbedded into men's heads that you make your boy tough by ridiculing him. For example, you see your son playing with a doll and God forbid he plays with dolls, right? (smile). So instead of recognizing that there is nothing wrong with a boy playing with a doll, you make a grand production and say things like, "What are you, a girl? Put that damn doll down, you sissy!" Okay, now stop and analyze that for a minute. You, the Poppa, are so afraid your son will grow up feminine that you choose to ridicule him in the "hopes" that he will somehow internalize your twisted message; discard it and choose to be macho instead! Crazy, ya think? Crazy, I know!

You Dads need to recognize that what your son needs most from you is your approval. His developing confidence in himself and his relation to the world comes directly from the things you say to him. Directly! Assuming you want him to be confident in himself, you need to carefully watch over the things you say to him. Ridicule only leads to a lack of self-confidence that will manifest itself in a nervous, afraid son behaving in all the ways you hate. That's for real, folks!

Your real job as the daddy is to mold that boy into the best he can possibly be, and you do that by words of encouragement; a multitude of words of encouragement. I once read that we should offer 10 positive encouragements and compliments for every one word of criticism. And, while I'm on a rant, criticism never made anyone better. Often critical and hurtful words come following frustration and anger. Don't allow that to happen. Take a breath; count to 10, do something before you lodge those awful words into his heart.

Practically, maybe you want your son to be good at sports (because you weren't and would like to live vicariously through him - ha). So the first time he gets out there and plays catch with you, you notice he sucks. Well, of course he sucks because everyone sucks the first time they do something. So, you have an important decision to make. Will you allow him to suck at first while you load him with encouragement, or will you get angry because he throws like (God forbid) a girl? Have you ever thrown a ball with your non-dominant hand? Exactly! If you stick with it, you will quickly see that he gets it in direct proportion to your level of encouragement. The better you say he is, the better he becomes! Voila!

Young boys, like all human beings, have hearts and feelings and emotions. To say that a boy shouldn't cry is ludicrous. Again, is it really the crying you are reacting to or your own terrible fear that your son is going to become feminine? Babies cry; young boys cry; adult men cry! Sure, you don't want him bursting into tears every time something goes wrong, but there's a better way to send your message. My son Josh tells his son, "You're okay, bro, dry your eyes or walk it off!" No ridicule needed!

Those little boys idolize their fathers and whether you notice it or not are constantly watching and analyzing how you react to things. You want them to exhibit calmness? You exhibit calmness. You want them to be fair? You show fairness. You want them to watch boxing? You watch boxing...(LOL).

When my boys were coming up, my golden rule (and by God, I stuck to it) was that I would never call them any name that diminished their value or made them feel inferior, weak, etc. Oh, sure, I pointed out dum-dum behaviors, but never called them names directly as people! Never! And today, those boys are the boys you wish you had! Trust me on that one!

I think some of the toughest guys on earth play in the NFL. Have you ever noticed how many of them hug and kiss their fathers? A man's man is made from love - and no other way!

Do you want to see a grown man cry? Ask him to speak about his father! Yes, it's that serious...

ADVICE TO A YOUNG BROTHER

Life is not easily mastered, and happy is the man who is able to discern its clues. The responsibility of the older is to pass along that which he knows to the younger. This advice, inspired by Emerson in his essay, "Compensation," seeks to impart that which may be known but not yet experienced; to those who have lived but have not really lived yet. Resist any argument to the contrary knowing that I too was once a young brother...

Success - Everything one may gain has a price, and one must be willing to pay it in order to get it. Trying to obtain without payment is a futile endeavor. You may be sitting at your job dreaming of better things, but better things will elude you while you yet dream. Promotion only comes with excellence, and marginal work is reserved for those in the margins. Honesty reveals that your job is crappy because you are yet still crappy. The successful man didn't become a success because of whom he knew, but rather when the chance encounter matched his already mastered skills. There is no value in overcoming your weaknesses until you have first exploited your strengths. The musician performing to sold-out arenas first sold himself to his craft. The respected business mogul began with a lemonade stand. The athlete earning millions to play his game learned early the discipline required.

Pitfalls - No man ever fell into a pit that he could see. Instead, the trap was hidden, concealed in a promise of never-ending pleasure. Every man has his vice, but until his vice is cornered it will soon defeat him. Wine brings forth gladness in moderation, but uncontrolled brings dimness of wit and a thousand foolish decisions. Every crime exacts its punishment, but its effect is often far removed from its cause. There is no "getting over!" Getting over at work, if persisted in, ends in termination though maybe for different reasons. Shirking and slothfulness require less effort but are nothing compared to the cost of recovery. Each man recovers himself as he recognizes the greater laws and finally submits himself to them. The world is founded on justice and though oft hidden, still prevails.

Women - A young man, clothed with genetic disadvantage, is programmed to spread his seed. He is crazed over urges that perpetually prompt him and seldom has the discipline to say no. But, as each part is connected to another, when he hurts another, he hurts himself in the process. A woman used as an object for sexual gratification, though willing, defies the laws of nature, as both must benefit in the process. In so taking, he wounds other souls, which carries its own penalty in suffering and discontent. There is no play in being a player, as the sting of deception does not discriminate its participants. The beasts of the field don't discriminate their partners but there's a reason we call them beasts. Proper sexual expression always has love in it, for which there is no downside. Anything you must hide in the cover of secrecy and darkness will always find its way to the light, whether in actuality or inside your own heart. Goodness stands upright in the light of day. Happy is the young man who carefully chooses the one as the one is all that he needs.

Associations - A man does not choose his companions as his companions choose him. He attracts that which he is though it be only for the moment. A true friend is one in whom you may bear your soul and not him for which you must play a role to be accepted. Bad associations with bad ideas must be avoided. A friend is one who tells you the truth and seeks your ultimate happiness over the fleeting. A right association is willing to be both teacher and student. A man should choose his friends as carefully as he watches over his bank account, as he will never rise beyond the level of those with whom he associates the most.

Play - Play and fun are vital components of the human experience. Life without fun is not life. But fun always follows the work and never precedes it. A vacation is enjoyed only after a period of work. The unemployed does not enjoy his time off as his mind is worried about his future. Only when his future appears secured does he revel in his free time. Persisting in play at the expense of work is reserved for the children. In order to be happy a man must work, but his choice of work is always his own. All work is honorable that offers no penalty to those it affects. Engaging in illegal activities for gain, though never caught, reveals itself in negative, impoverished circumstances. Justice will always win out over illicit rewards, and there is no satisfaction that parallels gain obtained by honesty and industry.

God - For a man to become a man, he must admit that life is bigger than himself. He has but to look around him at the perfection within the creation; the breathtaking order and unparalleled intelligence behind it. He has to step down off the pedestal of self-knowledge and youthful ego and see what is literally surrounding him. Yet, it's not until he has been severely pricked and awakened from his lethargy that he begins to contemplate the spiritual world behind things. It's not until he finally concedes there is no way that he considers "The Way" that has been waiting for him all along. A man becomes a man when he becomes body, soul AND spirit and not until then. It's not until he finally realizes his abilities, his gifts, were given to him in advance for him to maximize to his own and everyone else's benefit.

You young brothers hold the future in your hands. You will knowingly or unknowingly shape the world your children will live in. By your choices and decisions, you will lay the foundation for a thousand generations. Choose wisely, young brothers, and listen to your elders...

THE MAN YOU USED TO BE

Recently we had some old college friends over for a barbecue. Thank goodness I'm not as old as them (smile)! When I casually told one of them I was the clinical Director for my organization, he couldn't believe that the guy he knew in college was the director of anything! I could see his point as my only objectives in life back then were to chase women, play basketball and find different methods to anesthetize myself! (smile). But that was a lifetime ago... Afterwards, I couldn't help but think how sad it would be to be the same person you were 35 years ago. None of us is the same person we were back then, nor should we be. This life is all about growth and finding out the obstacles that stunt our growth. Are you ready to find out some things that may have been stunting your growth?

By far, the number one culprit for impeding your progress in life, as Emerson aptly stated, is "carrying about that corpse of a memory." What you did at any given point in time reflects how you thought at that point in time. It means nothing else. To assign your future course in life to a hodge-podge of foolish past decisions is the height of insanity. In fact, you are completely free to be today whomever it is you choose to be. Your past served only as the preparation ground to grow the person you are today. You needed your mistakes as much as you needed your successes. The difficulties you are experiencing right now are remnants of a course you have yet to complete. Figure it out so you can take the exam and move on.

Dwelling on the past, even yesterday, is a pointless endeavor. Learn whatever you can learn from it and immediately move forward. Spending your days incubating some failure serves only to guarantee future failure, like a runner looking back in the race. The hotshot swimmer in the Olympics was so preoccupied with his opponent that he failed to even medal. Staying your mind on your past is being preoccupied with your opponent. No matter your inherent goodness or practiced virtue, you are going to fall prey to that spurious *alternate power* at times, and for that you owe God nothing but a commitment to move ahead. How many good-hearted folks do you know who are locked into some past event, imprisoned in the decisions of yesterday? Let it go and move ahead!

Another impediment to future growth is the overuse and abuse of those squirrely little vices that promise you transport to another time and place. Do you remember the commercial where the 30-old is extolling the virtues of smoking marijuana when his acquiescence is suddenly interrupted by his mother's voice in her home, in which he still resides? Drugs and over-indulgence in alcohol press a perpetual pause button on your life, stymying future growth while waiting for you to move out of that phase. Fun and games are all fun and games while your life is fun and games, but every man's life has a day when he has to forgo fun and games for the work he must do. Indulge if you must, but find a way to balance your fun with the stuff you have to do! Go to work!

Of all the opinions that matter in life, the most important one is the opinion you carry of yourself. Enter your circle of friends and family that work together in unison to define just exactly who you are and where you fit. And again, in the words of Emerson, you are loathe to disappoint them! If you were "always" the joker, you must continue to be the joker. If you were ditsy and scatterbrained, that moniker must stay with you for life. People in their estimation of you allow no room for growth or change. Of necessity they cannot because of their compulsion to fit your present life into their past estimation of you. But, growth demands the change, and your responsibility is nothing more than to allow your present life to speak for itself! The fact that you were "never" the smart one is only a limitation in their minds, not your own. My dad still thinks I'm not mechanical though I've repaired my fair share of broken stuff. Once I configured an Oshkosh B'gosh buckle into a door latch, but now I'm just bragging! The point is, your only limitation is within yourself. Answering to public opinion; to your friend's judgments; to your family background is like blaming your unmowed grass on the sunshine and water. Mow your own grass and no defense is required!

People's opinions are in reality a judgment on their own lives. If they are callous and unforgiving, then you must be also. Their suspicions of you are a testimony to their own motives. No man can possibly know another's motive and until that person has lived in your shoes, they have no opinion that matters at all. We don't fault the poor mother who steals so her children can eat, nor can we fault another man for his hidden poverty we cannot readily discern. Underneath it all, people are basically good and kind and seek a means to express their goodness though a thousand voices scream to the contrary! Be your own self doing your own stuff that you know you must do. The value of your choice is determined by you and you alone... Other people cannot stunt your growth unless you allow it. Refuse it and grow!

Your life has a specific design in a specific place at a specific time. Your job is not to find out what the world wants, but rather to find out who you are and what you can best offer to the world. If you can do that, your life will grow in unparalleled dimensions.

You are not the man or woman you used to be, thank God. Instead you are the sum total of all the lessons you have mastered thus far. I say, get your PhD...

A REAL MARRIAGE

I posted a beautiful little expose on marriage the other day, and it was well received. It was sort of the 'real deal,' if you know what I mean. But, despite all the kind words towards me, it was written by someone else! So, ready or not, here's my version.

Having been married now for over 35 years, I can let you in on a few dirty secrets. Marriage isn't about feeling happy all the time with your spouse. It's about figuring out when it's your turn to add the happiness back in. You can't always control where your partner is in their mind, but you can sure control where your mind goes. What you want so desperately, you have to give. You can spend a whole lifetime mired in that mud. You wait and wait and wait to receive the kindness, yet refuse to share any of yours first! Marriage is a reciprocal deal, but you always have to go first. How you feel about your spouse is a decision you make and make and make. Choosing not to love someone anymore is also a decision. You don't feel the love because you aren't thinking any love. Rehearsing everything you don't like about someone is foolish at best. The trick isn't to struggle to find something good. The trick is to stop thinking evil!

If you've been married for any significant amount of years, you can fall into the "cycle." The cycle is a perpetual, spinning narrative where no matter what you say or what you do, it ties back into some former thing you said or some former thing you did. When couples get to this place, and it doesn't take long, their communication virtually ends. Instead of listening to each other anymore, the communication quickly dives into the rabbit hole of "I already know where this ends." In this disastrous scenario, neither party has any opportunity to be anything else. No one can change. No one can modify their behavior because you "always" do this and "always" say that; thus I already know where you're going and am not listening anymore. Lord, I hate that! Each day is a new day! Every moment is new in time. The stupid stuff you did three years ago no longer applies unless you've been in a coma for three years! Stop and truly listen to what your spouse is telling you. You don't have to like it or agree with it, but you do need to hear it. The great marriage killer is the silence that follows a resignation from speaking up!

Speaking of speaking up, if there is one thing I can tell you that almost stands above everything else, it is to keep speaking up. Keep communicating what is bothering you. You serve no one by keeping silent for your marriage's sake! Keeping silent runs at cross purposes with your marriage, or at best, delays the inevitable. In marriage, as in life, you have got to be honest with yourself. I don't mean negative and miserable. I mean honest. You have got to be able to have honest conversations with your spouse. In some areas, you will be tempted to quit speaking up as you perceive nothing is changing, but speak up anyway. Any anger you feel towards your spouse is a sure-fire sign there is something that needs to be resolved. So hey, have the damn fight! Do some yelling, add a little screaming and get it straight once and for all. Simmering within yourself or rehearsing every past injustice is emotional cancer and it is going to kill you! But one caveat, you have to fight fair. Your emotions can help you, but not when you resort to attack mode. The stuff you say in attack mode lasts long after the fight is over. Fight fair...

A common mistake in marriage involves compatibility.

People think that in order for the marriage to work well, there must be many common interests. The only required common interest is the other person. Marriage isn't two people turning into one person (usually the more dominant one). Marriage is two separate, distinct people figuring out how to head in one direction (while remaining distinct). The more difference between you the better, as long as you come together on the important stuff. (This is why married couples need two TVs - smile.) You also have the joy of figuring out your own arrangement. Don't copy Mom and Dad because you aren't married to either one of them. Do individually what you're good at individually. You already know and you may as well make it work for you!

If I could diagnose one shortfall where people go south today concerning marriage, it would encompass one word - commitment! You have to decide first to remain married, then work out how to make it all work. You don't remain married because everything feels good, the sex is fantastic and your spouse maintains their ideal weight. You don't stay married as long as there are no fights, no difficult circumstances or no challenges. (Two people can kick much more ass in a challenge than one can!) You don't remain married with an expectation that your spouse won't change or grow or evolve. What turned you on at 25 is going to feel ridiculous at 50. Side note - no one really gives you any insight into the weird stuff that happens as you age; you just sort of have to arrive there together. Okay, back to the point! You stay married because, by God, that is the decision you made! You may want a divorce today, but as long as your spouse doesn't want one on the same day, you will be okay.

In the final analysis, the reason my wife and I have remained married for so long is because we both love God and rely on Him to help us get our stuff together when it has fallen apart. We need Him to heal our hearts and make them tender whenever they get hard. We need someone bigger than our-selves to lead the way. Marriage was designed by God for His people. That's a union you cannot easily dissolve. That is a real marriage...

HOW TO FIND A MAN (FROM A MAN)

Before you get suspicious about an endless stream of sexism involving high heels, lipstick and bedroom antics, rest assured I'm not going there. Instead, I was pondering what I think are some common mistakes women make in dating. Of course, I'm no expert, but I am a man old enough to get past the usual sex-crazed silliness. I got married at the tender age of 22 while my bride was only 18, and while I wouldn't recommend getting married that early (i.e., starving college kids have no cash), I did learn some valuable insights.

If you had the fortune or misfortune of meeting me when I was 22, you would have immediately discovered that I was a work in progress; in fact, a huge work in progress. I had no job; no ambition, and no clear plans about who I wanted to be. (Funny, I look back on that with fondness.) I digress... If my wife's goal was financial stability, she got the wrong dude (then anyway). If she was looking for a guy who had his stuff together and was going places, she would have to wait awhile to do that. Instead she got a bundle of raw potential and, of course, stunning good looks (hey, it's my story!). My actual proposal was laughable (read former description). My plans nonexistent. But doggone it, she married me anyway. She must have seen something that I couldn't see. That brings me to the point.

It seems like many women nowadays are looking for the perfect guy. You may have seen him on the Bachelor or a reality show or somewhere else, compliments of the media. But sadly, unless you are actually marrying Jesus, he doesn't exist. The TV and movies present this mythical creature that is non-existent; he's smart, funny, brilliant, successful, accomplished, chiseled and hot. He adores you, even worships you and still has time for business acumen, poetry, playing the guitar and romantic pursuits. Sadly, that's not the reality of us dudes. At least, not in the beginning.

Finding a good man is sort of like making a business investment. You're betting heavily on something you believe in with the grand hope it pays out later. But trust me on this one, if he's not all the things you want now, try giving him a minute. Womenkind are sometimes neglectful of the impact they have on us dudes. You know, you can actually get him to stop doing behaviors you don't like. You can gently nudge him into something called ambition by simply expressing your belief in him. Now obviously you can't change the total loser, but sometimes, oh, sometimes, you can. I should add that I'm not saying we guys are like some sort of trainable horse that can eventually be made to do anything. What I'm saying is that you have to look for potential. Look for a kind heart. Look for what can be over what is. Look for, as my daughter aptly proclaims, love!

I'm reminded of a friend I had on the east coast who was part of our Bible fellowships. She was having trouble dating guys and it never seemed to work out. One day she told me about her last date. She said, "He was trying to talk to me and get to know me, and so I told him (loud voice inserted here) I'm all about the Word of God, and if you want to be with me, you better be about the Word!" Gasp... LOL. Can you imagine? When I met my wife, I was already about the Word (foolish, but loved God), and she was already my girlfriend before I brought *that* up. Us dudes are easily freaked out, and that statement would have sent me running as well!

My advice to you, though I know it's not always this simple, is stop looking for the perfect guy. Sometimes manners and respect still need to be learned. Maybe, just maybe that guy you like who, as the saying goes, isn't doing shit, just hasn't gotten started yet. Possibly there is something you see there that no one else could see. You can't trust your parents or your friends on this one. What you can trust is your heart, so listen to it even when the circumstances strongly disagree. Treasures of gold aren't found without much digging.

Enough on us bumblers... How about you women? What should you do? Be yourself, be yourself, be yourself. If you don't like sports, you don't have to. Who made up the rule that good couples have to have everything in common? How absurd! My wife and I have lots of things in common, but we didn't always. You couldn't bribe my wife to watch a football game when we first got married. Now she not only watches them but even gets it! (She has the t-shirt to prove it.) What I'm getting at is that lots of things change as time moves forward, and just because he does something today that annoys you doesn't mean he always will. And here's the bonus thought - even though I have a lot of my stuff together now, I still have absurdities that would require a saint to look past. Yeah, I think I married a saint!

Do yourselves a favor and don't make it harder than it really is. Even after you get married and have been married for many years, you're still going to hate his ass at times! That's just how life is. Just find yourself someone that floats your boat and has at least the potential to one day add a motor!

Disclaimer: That one guy who is hell-bent on making your life a misery ain't the one!

CHAPTER FIVE
Time

IT'S TIME

It is high time we talked about time. It's time to make a move. The time is right, and the time is now. We are running out of time. Time waits for no man, yet there are times when time stands still. There is always a first time, and this just might be your last time. There is never enough time, yet sometimes we find ourselves killing time. Time flies when you are having fun, but moves like molasses during tough times. You make time for the things that are most important to you, but you *ain't* got time for things that don't matter. We may not have time to get into all of the details, yet on certain matters we have all the time in the world. Ladies and gentlemen, it's time...

If you have a little extra time, I think you'll find that time is one of the most curious aspects of God's creation. Time never travels in reverse though we often wish it would. There are times in our lives that we hold in such high regard we wish we could return to them. There are other times we wish never existed and gladly we move ahead. Yet, time remains the one constant that only moves in one direction - forward. Time trudges onward whether we like it or not. The question is never how much time you have in a day, as that never varies for anyone. The question is, what will you do with the time that you have?

In a world governed by the laws of time, time only exists in the present moment. We cannot return to the past even if the past was only five seconds ago. Similarly, we cannot live in a future time, even a mere three seconds from now. Human beings suffer from their failure to understand this simple yet profound law. Much of the fear and anxiety people experience comes in relation to some future time. We can generally handle what is occurring in the moment, but we can scarce handle all the potential dreads of the future. Conversely, we spend our precious present time trying to move ahead to some future time. Instead of reveling in all the beauty and possibility a day may bring, we foolishly skip ahead to the weekend or to our next vacation or to any other future event we excitedly anticipate. And while anticipation is a good thing, it can make our present time feel unbearable. Whenever we shift our attention away from the moment called now, we rob ourselves of the time we have to experience now. As such we only half live, raided of life's pleasures by our focus on the future. For others, their focus is centered on past time; a time that no longer exists except in their memories. How many people trade away a lifetime in the present for some enduring failure from their past? Some sad souls are still reliving some awful, dreadful mistake from 40 years ago; a time they can never retrieve though they search the world over to find it. The past can only ever be the past, though you be reminded of it forever. No matter whether your past be littered with mistakes; involve some catastrophic event or loss; or even contain some life-altering event, it can only be and always will be in the past. The only reasonable solution is to come back to the time called now. Your life is now...

Time exists as a commodity for you to use and to use wisely. There's a time to work and a time to play. There's a time to plant and a time to harvest. There is a time to exert effort and a time to relax from your efforts. There's a time to rejoice and a time for sorrow. But, through it all, it is your time to steward in the manner that you see fit. People often confuse time for labor with a time for respite. There is no rule that states all useful time is time spent working or that all useless time is spent not working. Human beings were designed to work with purpose, but all work and no play, "makes Jack a dull boy!" It isn't so much what you do with your time as much as it is whether or not you are rightfully choosing where your time is spent. Wasting time; time spent floating along wistfully with no purpose, is generally a bad time. If you are at work wasting time waiting for a future time when you are not at work, that time will always be most miserable. It is better for you that you throw your whole heart into the work at hand and later throw your whole heart into your leisure time. Likewise, mulling over your myriad work problems during time reserved for your family is equally distasteful. You spend your finite commodity called time with the whole of you participating in the whole of all there is at the present time. Otherwise, you will live your life distracted from your present by your illusions of the future and remembrances of the past. The time to live is now...

Time is finite in terms of human existence. We all are going to age, and we are all going to have to come to terms with the loss of our youth. The problem with aging is the same as the problem with youth in that you are not familiar with either while you are experiencing them. When you are young, your time is unlimited and not worthy of undue consideration. When you get older, your time is no longer unlimited yet is also not worthy of undue consideration. This is so because no matter your age, you cannot live in another time. Spending time lamenting the loss of your hair or your cheekbones or your physique is wasted time; time wishing for another time. Likewise, times of youth spent dreaming of future safety and security is also wasted time; time that could be spent moving towards your destination today. You can only live your life in the time called now.

At the end of the day; at the end of your days, it will become very apparent where you decided to spend your time and what you spent your time on. Your successes and your failures alike will not encompass your dearest thoughts, but instead how much you experienced and treasured the journey. You will remember with great fondness those times you lived fully with those you love the most, and that will make it all worthwhile. Now is the only time you can live, my friends, and that time is now. It's time...

WIN THE MOMENT, WIN THE DAY

Did you know that by the time you are full of anxiety and fear; when you feel like something is wrong and you can't seem to get it straight; when you feel out of sorts and disconnected, confused, bamboozled, lost, defeated, chances are you have been losing the day, day after day! It happens to all of us at times. We get distracted by the world and all of the things that assault and perplex our minds. We get overly focused on our future and perpetually dragged back to our past. We have failed to live in the moment and win the moment. We have failed to win the day.

Your mind was designed to function within a 24-hour period. The great processor, your brain, was built to handle all of the demands of the day. It was never intended that you would tax your brain cells to decipher and figure out a future you could not possibly discern, nor waste its resources on a past you can neither change nor modify nor improve. Instead, you function best devoting your full attention to the moment at hand. The moment at hand is always something you can handle. Otherwise, you quickly find yourself losing track of the moments, rapidly forging ahead when you needed to slow down or slowing down anxiously when you needed to move ahead. It is in the moment that negative thoughts hit your awareness, and it is in the moment that you must handle the challenges with which you are presented. Anxiety, for example, is simply misplaced fears that whittle and carve their way into your thinking. Once misplaced, they surface as feelings of fear that you can no longer put your finger on, much less address! Confusion and feeling lost don't happen today, but during a 100 yesterdays you failed to recognize appropriately. Feeling out of sorts and disconnected doesn't just fall upon you suddenly but develops slowly, imperceptibly over time, with one misconnection following another. The reason you cannot get something straight is because by the time you are experiencing the dilemma, its cause has long since hidden itself. You cannot track backwards and solve your issues. You solve your issues by winning the day.

The source of your troubles works in secret. The less you know about your opponent, the better success your opponent enjoys. Every thought stone you leave unturned turns again to rend you. Your opposition works by distraction; by overloading your awareness with worries over the future and regrets about your past. Your enemy convinces you to let things go you should not let go and instead focus on things that do not really matter. Your opposer cooks up a gigantic spaghetti bowl of confusing and distracting thoughts which, when completed, leaves you wading through the noodles, in vain searching for solutions you are long past obtaining. It counts on your lack of attention and sneaks in again and again until it renders you defeated. You will never find it in the collective, but only in the singular. Alone, those thought assaults can be overcome, but fortified in your awareness they gain strength. The intensity of the contest demands your full awareness; your full attention. And your full attention is found only in the moment in which you find yourself. You need to win the moment.

You learn to win the day by learning to win the moment. What negativity or threat just hit your mind? What prediction of doom or future danger just took a swipe at you? What accusation about who you are; the motives you have; who you really are as a person, just took aim at your heart? When you live, as best you can, in the moment, you are much more likely to see what just happened to you. And, in seeing and hearing, there is something you can do about it. Like any good fight, you have to learn to fight back. Just as you would not tolerate (for long) someone punching you repeatedly, in the contest you have to fight back. Sure, you don't feel like it, but it doesn't matter as long as you are getting hit. Yes, you can lament and wish it wasn't this way, but it is this way, at least as long as there is evil in the world. So, you fight, in that very moment. You confront the wrong thoughts. You challenge them. You take a stand against them. In fact (or better in truth), you fight back until it/they shut up. You are in a spiritual fight so you don't try to fight with your human logic or by being rational. You fight by countering the negatives with the positives of God's Word. Don't try to be so smart! What does God's Word say that counters the evil consideration? Say that! If your opponent threatens your health (i.e., Corona Virus), you counter by proclaiming God's promise to keep you healthy or forever heal you when you need it. Somewhere in that Good Book, God says often fear not; be anxious for nothing; you are not wrong, and He will make all of your paths straight. He says you are always connected; have the answers you need; have been found when you were lost; are not confused, and definitely have not been defeated as He always causes you to win! It's all in there, folks, and is the perfect answer to every challenge you will ever be confronted with.

Learn to slow down a little and live in the moment. Take on the obvious challenges of the moment. Deal with what is standing right in front of you. Recognize what is traveling through your mind in the moment and decide whether it can stay or it can go. Take it on in the moment. And, as you win the moment, you decide to win the next moment and the next and the next. Pretty soon, you find yourself able to win the day. Tomorrow is tomorrow, and yesterday was yesterday. No matter what happened or where you may have fallen short, win the next moment. Soon, you enter the realm of the kick-ass human that God always intended for you to be.

Don't you want to win the day? Win the moment that is now...

THE WONDER FILLED PRESENT

I learned through trial and error that you can give your growing vegetables too much water. You'd think that more water meant a more abundant crop, wouldn't you? Veggies need some water and some time to dig their roots down into the soil in search of water. If you make it too easy for them, they don't dig down and they don't grow. If you make it too hard by neglecting them, they wither and die. As humans, our joy is found in discovering how the system works already and co-operating with it. We were never asked to invent the process, but rather work within the frameworks previously established for us. Sure, we can spend many years bucking against the system, trying and erring, trying and erring, but it's always a wonder filled day when finally, we learn how it works and work with it!

Your mind and, more specifically, your thoughts are also a system. The system was designed to produce something for you. It is neither random nor whimsical. It's not happenstance, nor is it something outside your control. You can neglect the system and it will begin to wither and fail. You can overload the system and it will start to break down. It, like all of the systems that exist in this world, is always a delicate balance that requires an effort on man's part to learn and master. You begin to neglect the system when you stop thinking and deeply considering in favor of habit and rote behaviors. It happens when you think you already know and have the audacity to conclude there's nothing new for you to learn. The system becomes frightfully overloaded when you burden it down with worries and cares. One central theme of worry will overshadow all of your thinking and suffocate the life right out of you. Thoughts of your past failures and anticipating the doom of some future state, short-circuit the whole operation and reduce your vitality immeasurably.

Thought processes, though highly debated, have been estimated to number between 50,000 and 70,000 per day. Clearly, the system was designed with a large capacity in mind. However, the Wisdom behind the massive system planned for the thought processes to be managed one day at a time. The reason we miss the "wonder filled present" is because our minds are all over the damn place! Our minds have been schooled to flick around like dragonflies, changing directions frenetically, running from thing to thing to thing! We can barely tolerate the present moment without some additional source of information streaming into our consciousness from devices we must recharge every hour. In interactions with other humans, we half participate at best. We nod and reply with 20 percent agreement having only partially registered what was said. With reverted eye we drift in and out of the moment, scanning backwards and forwards like radar, yet missing the target in the center. And as we faithfully miss the mark, our personal fulfillment suffers a mortal blow.

The precious moment called "now" is not found only in moments of quiet repose in a shaded wood or glimmering off the surface of the ocean. It's not location-dependent nor reserved for sunrises or sunsets. It's not something saved as a celebration for the hard-won fight or worthy goal accomplished. It is life happening right now in the midst of the 50,000+ with the whole sum participating each one by one by one. It is your next idea, your next activity, your very next move. It is you waking, preparing, eating, walking, driving, parking, entering and working. It is the work to be done next in priority. It's your opportunity to do good for your co-worker and his co-worker and hers. It's in noticing her furrowed brow and asking if everything is okay. It is looking at the faces in the meeting and seeing them all one by one. It is pausing to think whether those words should be said out loud and choosing silence instead. It is observing the whole drive home then arriving with a determination to bring light and happiness to those with whom you interact the most, despite your familiarity with them and every previously imagined insult. It is your glorious opportunity to win the moment, the hour, the day, and in so doing honor the God that made you!

SO DANG BUSY

Good question, right? Everyone is so busy nowadays... And, if you don't appear too busy, they assume something is not quite right with you. Have you ever stopped to ponder why we are so busy? Busy, busy, busy; no time for anything! Is it good to be that busy? Does busy mean we are getting things done and making progress? Maybe. Maybe not. Maybe this old world has taught us that all that frenetic activity means we are making moves and getting closer to our desired state. Here's a thought. Many of us dream of being rich, right? With that lofty idea we imagine a life where we can do just whatever we want, when we want. We don't picture ourselves running from this thing to that thing. Definitely not. We see ourselves vacationing with friends and family, relaxing on a sandy beach. Or we visualize pursuing things that really interest us that we "never had time" to do before. Hmmm.

It might just be that we are getting our leg pulled. With the advent of electronic media and our ability to know everything going on everywhere; or social media where we follow each other's lives replete with "likes" and "comments" and status updates, we can become overwhelmed with information. As soon as we finish one house project, we start another one, patterning the project after that home makeover show. We go to work all day and carry out our responsibilities, then get home to carry those out too. Saturday becomes the day to do all the stuff you couldn't do all week. And, what you didn't get done on Saturday you can do on Sunday. Then it is time to start all over again. You can discern our prevailing mindset with the language we speak. "It's time to get back on my grind," implying that success follows a continual "grinding" until we reach some goal. Or, "every day I'm hustling, hustling," which carries the message that good things must be hustled after until they reluctantly come to pass. Now, I'm smart enough to know that 'real' life isn't about sitting in the chair all day. Sure, we need to go to work. Absolutely we should fix the leaky sink or the hole in the wall. There's cooking, dishes, chores, cleaning and laundry that all cry for attention. Everyone has many things to do in a day. It's not so much the work we accomplish but our mindset while we are doing the work. The reality is that most folks are so dang busy that they don't have time to think. There's no reflection concerning which direction we are heading. There's no quiet time to consider, to pray, to invest our hearts into things we want them invested into. Instead, we scramble around stressed, anxious and not even aware that all of this is going on.

Our core problem is that we have bought into a man-made doctrine that states that you must almost kill yourself to achieve things in life, and if you are not overly busy, you are heading for a disaster. It's like relaxation is some kind of curse reserved for the lazy; the failures in life. And, we wonder why folks die so early. What good is the fortune grandpa made if he died at 52? Maybe there is something behind all this mad dash for things; for status; for supposed success. Maybe, just maybe, if something can keep you busy enough, you won't take time to think (something only us humans can do). Without thought you may just spend a lifetime mindlessly fulfilling supposed obligations with only a brief respite to the mountains or the beach. Why do we love camping so much? Is it the s'mores; the booze by the fire pit at night? Or is it the absence of all that stuff we "have" to do? You decide.

While we get to enjoy comforts formerly only dreamed of by people, we have also allowed ourselves to become too stressed out. In short, we have gotten it all backwards. Our minds; our thinking; our beliefs are the very essence of the things we achieve in life. It isn't the grind of the 100 hour work week that makes you successful; it's the beliefs you have associated with your work; with your life. A little believing and positive expectation go a long, long way. But hey, who has time for that? Life was not designed to be a helter-skelter of anxious activity that concludes in an untimely death. Life was meant to be a time for enjoyment, for reflection, for learning. Life is to be lived with love and care for our fellow man. So many people say they lack purpose, but in reality, they just haven't taken the time to "see" their purpose. How could they? We want to control everything, fix everything, worry about everything... Maybe if I am hypervigilant and stressed and eternally busy, bad things won't happen. Maybe through my obsessive effort, I can ensure all will be okay for everyone involved. Maybe not.

Let God control the world, people, and just relax... Maybe the things you want most in life; your hopes, your dreams; maybe those things want you as well, if you will just slow down enough to see them coming. You are killing yourself digging in that hole for the gold, and it's not even there. Slow yourself down and relax. Let some stuff go. Live in the moment and enjoy it. Take time to reflect on your life. Take a quiet walk outside or a drive. Turn off the TV, unplug the laptop and silence the notifications on the cell phone. Make the time you need to think and think deeply. You may just hear some things that change your life.

Oh me? I'm just relaxing on this beautiful Saturday morning...

THE SIMPLE JOY OF LIVING TODAY

Think back to the last time you were on vacation. Whether it was lounging on a sandy beach or taking in the gorgeous views during a mountain hike or languishing in your hotel room in a beautiful city, or the smell of bacon frying in the morning while camping by the side of the lake; what made your vacation time so much better than the rest of your time? You may argue that it was so sublime because you didn't have to go to work. But many folks exert as much energy playing as they do at work, and sometimes more energy. You may conclude that it is the change of environment; the sand, the trail, the room, the water, etc. Certainly, there are many factors involved with vacations that cause us to feel joyful, but there is one common theme that is the subject of this story. On a vacation intended for relaxation, we shift our focus from the past and the future to the wonderful present. We purposefully don't think about the bills that "will" be due or the work we need to finish later or what the boss said to us in anger last week. No, we make some loose plans and then get busy enjoying the wonder and beauty that is today. It is as if we free ourselves from all the illusory burdens of time and focus ourselves on "right now!" And since right now is all we can experience, we decide to thoroughly enjoy it.

There is a way to live your life that escapes the thinking of the masses. There's a way to make the most of your experiences. There is a simplicity to life that is so simple we have missed it all our lives. The culture of our world is ever seeking ways for us to move faster, get more done, accomplish more and maximize our time. We laud multi-tasking and efficiency and "to get err done..." Just do it and do it and do it again is the mindset of today. And for all of our inventions and efficiencies and time savers, where has it gotten us? Are we happier? Are we joyful? Do we feel blessed and content? I would say no. Yet it's not the speed at which we move that bogs us down. It's where we have learned to put the focus of our minds. Humans were designed to live in one time period and one time period only - right now! The only time we have available to us is this present moment. Yet how much time do we spend focused on the present moment? While we are at work today, we focus on getting home. During the week we focus on the upcoming weekend. During the work year we focus on the coming vacation. While we are at school, we are thinking about being done with school. While cleaning the house, we are thinking about how great it will be to sit down and relax after the house is clean. But the real joy of living is found in 100 percent commitment to the present moment. It is persisting in a state of experiencing and enjoying right now. If the duties of right now call for some house cleaning, so be it. If it's time to go to work, go to work and be 100 percent involved in your work while you are there. Don't spend one idle moment wishing you were off work, as that shift of focus will make your work a misery. What is the best way to experience school? Don't mentally leave the classroom before you physically leave the classroom. In fact, don't mentally leave any moment you are still in, as departing from the present moment takes the enjoyment out of it.

Interestingly, the vast majority of our concerns and our anxieties and our fears are found where? In the future! Unless a large tiger is currently gnawing on your calf muscle, you probably don't have anything to be afraid of right at this moment, correct? So, do this moment and refuse to do the future moments. Can't you see how huge and life-changing this is? Uh huh, but what about the future? Am I supposed to just let everything go now and make no plans for the future? Well, of course not, silly! Make the most grand and glorious plans that you can, then do today, today! Maybe in your future you see yourself as an author? Then take some time to write today (smile)...

And what about the past? How do we handle all those times we zigged when we should have zagged? Or that one big thing? Well, the past is ummm past... We can't go back to those moments, can we? Shoot, we can't even go back to 15 minutes ago when we were eating those three donuts and refuse to eat them, right? Haha. In reality, the past no longer exists. It's gone, man! Over. In the books! Thus, imagine the sheer FUTILITY (yelling now) of spending any of your present moments regretting your past moments. Sure, encourage your sweet memories; your times of love and success and appreciation, and remember the people you cherished, but do it while you are wholeheartedly choosing to live today.

I realize the simplicity of this is almost too much to take. But if you have ever believed anything I have ever said, believe this; living 100 percent in the present moment will cause your "joy" and "appreciation" levels to go off the chart! And while you are seriously giving this a try, take a look at your children or your grandchildren. Notice the joy they experience by living in the moment? Oh, they don't have to pay bills! Maybe not, but neither do you at this present moment! (You are reading, right?)

So how can you thoroughly enjoy the simplicity of living life today? Get your vacation mindset working for you. Decide to be fully alive and observant and mindful of these very moments you find yourself in today. Don't go back in time, and don't go too far ahead in time. Do, be, live, love and enjoy today, as tomorrow will have its own issues for you to deal with "tomorrow...."

Mmmm, is that the smell of bacon by the campfire? No, it's the smell of many minds that just came back to life!

UNTANGLE THE SPAGHETTI BOWL

A good bowl of spaghetti gets there one noodle at a time. No matter the size of the bowl, each noodle is a single entity that only gets tangled when it's added together with the other noodles, one noodle at a time! Remember that intently because you will never untangle the mess in your mind until you do.

If you are like most people, you tend to put off unpleasant tasks until you are forced to deal with them. It can wait, right? But, sadly, all the little things you put off slither into the bowl unnoticed. Imagine how many random thoughts you think in a day. How many of those thoughts are hurtful feelings of inadequacy? How many are seething with self-criticism and condemnation? What tired notions repeat themselves over and over, begging for resolution? The worries, the doubts, the fear? What "what-if" dramas clamor for your attention? Oodles and oodles of noodles...

It's been said that your outer world is an indicator of your inner world. Have you ever visited someone with a messy house? Or (haha) is it your house? Well, how did it get so messy? It became a mess one messy, misplaced thing at a time. All of us are confronted with the mess, but not all of us choose to clean it up. The best time to vacuum up the popcorn on the carpet is right after the popcorn hits the carpet. That's not being anal; that's cleaning up. Conversely, how do you feel when you visit the clean house? You feel relaxed, don't you? You see, someone invested their effort in making the environment peaceful, and you got the benefit of it. I dare say none of us really enjoy the cleaning up process, but we probably treasure the cleaned-up feeling!

When it comes to your thoughts, sometimes you have to take the time to clean up. I mean you have so much to do in a day, right? You're busy, busy, busy, and there are many demands clamoring for your time. Well, that's nothing compared to the time you spend sifting through the madness to find your car keys. In this 'live in the moment life,' generally the best time to do something is now. You feel yourself getting a toothache. You don't like the dentist (who does?), or you don't have dental insurance, or you don't have time to go. So, you decide to wait. Maybe it will go away. Maybe it will resolve on its own. Maybe? In reality it will probably get worse until it hurts so badly that you cannot do anything else until you get it fixed; not to mention the two months you put up with the agonizing dull ache in your jaw. Can't you see it? We have been lulled into a complacent state where we don't handle what we need to handle. We foolishly think we can wait, but really cannot afford to wait. Each moment we spend unresolved is a moment we don't get to really live!

If you are honest, what you really want is clarity of thought. You want that noise to quiet down. You need your mind to slow down and take a breath. You need some peace. But, peace normally comes at the end of the fight. You have to win the fight. Unfortunately, you don't get to choose not to be in the fight. The fight is there every single day. God never promised you wouldn't have to fight; He said He would help you to win it. You win the contest by winning the battle in your mind. When a nation wins a war or a football team wins a game, they have to do it one battle or one play at a time. You can't skip plays, nor can you overlook key battles. The contest starts every single morning. You decide what you will think and challenge any opposition to those thoughts. It doesn't matter how long it takes; what matters is your willingness to fight!

One day, when it finally dawns on you that your mind has become a hot slithering menagerie of pasta, and your persistent sense of fatigue and depression begins to overtake you, remember you can clean up any mountain of mess if you take it on one small mess at a time. You can't spend time thinking of the outcome; instead just think of the next play. What thought or series of thoughts are causing you the most stress? Start there! Challenge those inane thoughts. Just because you think something does not make it true. Where did we ever get that idea? Probably from the same source as the thought.

This life we are blessed to live is best lived in the moment called "now!" You have 24 hours in a day, maybe 16 waking, perhaps eight after work, five after meals and maybe 30 minutes after the television. But no matter what is clamoring for your time, whether work or sleep or mealtimes or electronic mediums, you can only work with the time called "now!" The time to deal with the troubling thought is now. The time to vacuum the carpet is now. The time to repair the broken appliance is now. The time to do the task that's eating at you is now. The time to get things sorted out in your mind is now! Now, now, now!

That peace of mind you are ardently seeking is seeking you as well. It's there for you, always right there for you, waiting for you to stand up and get into the fight, then win it... WIN THE FIGHT! You are worth that much.

Everyone loves a tasty bowl of spaghetti, right? But a peaceful mind trumps a bowl of spaghetti every single time.

BE... PRESENT

It seems of all the futilities possible in this life, there is one futility that tops the list. It is the futility of trying to live in a moment that isn't now. Think about that for a moment. The only moment you and I can live is the moment called, 'now.' But we don't do that, do we? We spend all of our 'precious now' living either in the past or in the future.

The past exists only in your mind. Those moments, good or bad, are gone forever. Sure, you have memories, but in reality that time is gone forever. And, whatever happened that lives on so vividly in your mind is no longer anything but a memory. Humans are a very peculiar bunch. You may have spent years doing good things, yet you foolishly cleave to those fragmented times when you didn't do so well. It seems if you played the odds, you would give yourself a little credit. But you don't. And, to make matters worse, you rehearse those fragments and feel the hurt and pain all over again. Those annoying ghosts serve no purpose but to make your present life miserable and distracted. Instead of rejoicing in the possibility of today, you exercise your demons again and again and wonder why you aren't happy or why your life feels lousy and stressed.

The flip side of the equation is trying to live in the future. How many times have you discarded five days while waiting for two? Or pushed to make it through several months while waiting for that dream two-week vacation in the summer? And how about the "put-off" epidemic? Once I get done with college... Or, when I get that dream job... Or, when I find that special person... And that doesn't even account for those times you feel afraid! You are so sure that such and such a bad thing is going to happen that you waste days on end only to find out it either didn't happen, or when it did happen, you could actually handle it?

The ultimate problem with not living in the moment is that you miss your life that is happening now. Life is pregnant with possibilities waiting to be born, but you will never see them until you slow that *monkey mind* down and learn to live in this moment. Otherwise, you won't see it. Here's a thought. How many of you feel restless and anxious? Now ask yourself, is your restlessness or anxiety based on now, or is it based on your past or on your future? Again, we humans are a peculiar bunch! We are so worried about the long-gone past and not yet arrived future, that we can't even relax and enjoy right now. What if I'm not successful? What if my life goes to hell and I spend my latter days in misery? Really? Really? Call me crazy but it seems that my success in life depends on what I do right now! Misery, like happiness, doesn't just show up unexpectedly. It shows up based on what preceded it. And what precedes it is the moment called, 'now.'

Life really isn't as complex as we have imagined. You're worried about your relationship because things have been bad lately (the past...). You think that things may be going to hell in a handbasket (the future...). But, in truth, you have 100 percent control over yourself in this very moment. You want happiness. You want love. You want warmth. You want harmony. So... Do happiness now. Do love now. Do warmth now. Do harmony now! Yeah, but what about the hurts of the past? (Memory.) What if things don't work out? (Imagination of the future.)

This may come as a surprise to you, but God really designed you to live in the present moment. His instruction book clearly tells you to forget the past and quit worrying about the future. And, because He knows all about how your mind works, He tells you that He has forgiven your past (and paid for it - take that karma!) and promises you a wonderful future. But, neither promise can be fulfilled while you persist in that dastardly past and future focus.

Children are the best example of being in the moment. When my grandchildren come over, Braylon sits on the couch next to me and plays with my iPad. (He said I'm the Grandpa that likes to sit down - smile.) Wherever I move to, he follows. He doesn't say much. He doesn't need much. He just wants to sit next to his grandpa, feeling the love in the moment.

In microcosm form, that is what life is really about. It's about people being fully present in the moment and sharing love with one another. Don't you see it? We are all the same. We all want the same stuff. It's not about chasing this and avoiding that; running from this and trying to hold on to that. It's about being present; living fully in the present moment. And when you finally get it, you are going to find that everything you ever wanted is going to show up, right at the perfect moment; not a minute too soon or a minute too late. The reason it hasn't happened so far is that you aren't here yet.

Just be... present, and see if things don't appear out of nowhere, because they have been there all along.

CLEANING OUT YOUR CLOSET –
ONE THOUGHT AT A TIME

Did you know that your mind (emphasis on YOUR mind) is not supposed to be full of fear, anxiety and stress? Oh sure, most people are living that way, but it's not supposed to be that way. The problem is that we have become so accustomed to living that way and feel like it must be the norm. If you notice, we say things like, "welcome to life" or "life happens," and even, "shit happens!" And, by saying that, we are openly declaring or admitting that we have accepted something, namely - that's just the way life is... Well, what if that's not the way life is? What if you have been seduced into a mindset that, once established, goes on defeating you for years and years? What if there is something out there operating within a vast network, secretly, to convince you and me of a gargantuan lie?

Believe it or not, that something or other does exist and is presently working within the systems of the world to do just that. Everything around you is negative, with subtle fear trappings in the background. And, the more you buy into it, the more fear you experience; the more anxiety; the more stress, which are all more or less alternative names for the same thing.

If you have ever taken the time to monitor those wieldy thoughts of yours, you'll see just how consistently this is occurring. But hey, who has time to monitor their thoughts? I mean, life is sooooo busy, right? Well, I submit to you that it's so busy because you have bought in. How much of that crap you do day by day, do you really have to do? Look at our obsession with health (in America, of course). You have to eat this and ingest that and add this and supplement that. After all, you don't want to get cancer, right? You see, you bought in, man. You became convinced that your only shot at living a long, healthy life was to do what the TV and Facebook and the media told you to do. And the clincher? You are doing it all out of fear. Now this doesn't even account for the requirements to exercise. Gotta get your cardio; your weight training; your Pilates; your yoga, or else you will surely die! The Bible says that bodily exercise does profit you, of course, but the real source of your good health is God. Absent God, get on the fear train!

You can't eat this or have too much of that. Sugar is outlawed and everything must be low fat. Butter kills, bacon kills, red meat kills, fried food kills, high cholesterol, heart disease, diabetes and on it goes. Generations of people ate those things before us, but we are so much smarter now. I'll bet you never considered that all that advertising wasn't designed to make you healthier but rather to make you buy something. And bought it, you did! (As did I.)

So, it is high time to get off the fear train and start cleaning out your closet. You feel the need to clean out your closet because it has become chock full of stuff. What about your mind? Chock full of stuff. And like with your pesky closet, you can only start clearing it out one thought at a time. But even before you can start cleaning, you have to decide you want to. How many things in your life are sitting out there unresolved, cluttering up the background? It's no wonder people feel overwhelmed. So why don't we resolve things? We haven't got enough time between the gym and Pilates and healthy food shopping and getting stuff done! No, I mean getting everything done! Today! Bought in...

Healthy thinking involves getting problems resolved. It

means taking the time necessary to get on top of whatever is on top of you. If it takes a week, so be it. If it takes six months, so be it. Why put up with problems? You put up with them because you think you have to. I often wonder just how many health issues we face come directly from our own frenetic minds being pushed and pulled all over the globe and back.

Next we need some time to get quiet. Just get quiet. Whether it's prayer or meditation or simply turning off electronics, just get quiet. You will be amazed how many things come up when you give your mind a chance to get quiet. You may just find that thing you have been doing for the last 10 years because you are disciplined really gets done because you are afraid. Here's a test. Try to stop doing it. Just let it go... Seems to me that God can do His job pretty well without all my incessant meddling! When you stop doing all of that crap, it is like you are saying, "Here I am and I have stopped running!" Indeed...

My good friend once remarked, "I find that my mind is at peace when I focus on right now, and whenever I start to feel stress it's because I have either gone back into the past or moved ahead to the future." So, try to live just for today. Or better, try to live just for right now. Did you know that God designed life to be lived in 24-hour compartments? (God, not Dale Carnegie....)

In order to even have a chance of living that "good life" you have often imagined; you must first get control of your mind. Take the mental time you need to get things straight. If there's something you need to say, say it! If something is undone and driving you nuts, do it. And, for goodness sakes, stop being afraid of everything! So, what if a disease shortened your life? Well, what if you are shortening your life by living in fear? You can only do what you can do, right? And the way I see it, the only thing you can ever totally control is your mind; or more specifically, your thoughts!

This short little go round the sun doesn't offer you enough time to live another moment that way. Get God involved and stop trying to be so smart. He's infinitely better than your best thinking and worth checking into (unless, of course, you are content right where you are...).

The "normal" way to live, though long hidden, is to be unafraid. The absence of fear introduces you to a world you only thought existed in childhood. But, as a kid, you knew you weren't that smart. Hmmm...

You are worth the time...

NOW IS THE TIME TO DETERMINE HOW YOUR LIFE WILL TURN OUT

There is an interesting phenomenon that takes place nowadays called *living in the future*. You begrudgingly go to work all week because you can hardly wait for the weekend, right? (Thank God It's Friday and everybody's workin' for the weekend....) One day, when your ship comes in, everything will be okay. Buy the lotto ticket because when you finally win, man-o-man life will be good. You know how it goes... "When I get that new job..." "When we finally sell this house..." "When I find that one special person... (my soul-mate specifically created to make MY life complete!)." ...and so on and so on! But, did you ever stop to think that your life actually is this moment of time that you are in, right now? You can't go back to yesterday to change something (trust me, I've prayed for that one a lot). You can't ever arrive at the future; you can only live this day. SO, what are you going to do with this day? Will you trade it for the illusory promise of a better tomorrow? (That tomorrow that never comes because it will always be tomorrow?) When you pray to God for something (which, by the way, He not only hears but wants to provide for you), is it future tense? Some folks spend their whole lives praying for some future event that never leaves the future. Or, will you finally leave the land of self-deception and get into the here and now? You see, the time to determine how your life will turn out is now.

If you were going on a very long journey, one that was

going to take a long time, the most logical thing to do would be to take the first step. Sure, it's a helluva distance, sure, it seems like it is going to take forever, but if you make up your mind to take a step (right now), you are going to be at least one step closer than you were yesterday. And if you follow me, you are going to get there at some point. But here's where the self-deception kicks in. Because what you want is in the future, you fail to start the journey. You keep waiting and waiting and waiting. "It's too far, man!" "I just can't see it happening yet!" And, at the end of the ride, you haven't moved forward one inch. Every one of us is at some location in this journey of life, and I imagine every one of us has some other destination in mind. So, what in the world are we waiting for? The secret is to simply start! Take a step; make a move; get off your "butt."

Lately, I have been challenging myself to do some visualizing. Oh yeah, I know it works (intellectually), but when do I do it? Never! It is so much easier to dream of some future state that will make my life complete, as long as it remains a dream. But to actually take the steps to make it happen is a whole different story! So, I broke out my trusty iPad and put together a PowerPoint presentation called "Visualization." Then, I put pictures on there of my "future life" so that I could get a clear picture in my mind of what that life looks like. Then (and here's when I departed from the land of self-deception), I made (and am making) myself study it every morning and every night. I know, I know, you don't have time for that, right? But somehow you have time to live the same life day after day, peering into the horizon watching for that ship; that one ship that will make everything okay! I digress... Now, here's where it gets interesting. My house that we have been selling for three years now is on there with a cleverly photoshopped picture of a "sold" sign on the banner. (Future plan – sell house.) After all, when we finally sell this house, we will be able to live again... Well, today we got an offer. Glory be, an offer! Do you think there is a connection? As soon as I decided to make that future goal a present-day reality, it became a present-day reality. I'll say it again; it became a present-day reality! It wasn't the "magic" of visualizing that made it happen; it was my personal mental shift from the future to right now.

What dreams do you have for the future that you would like to enter the present tense? Well, get off your "butt" and get busy making it happen. Tomorrow? No, now! Get a crystal-clear picture of what it looks like and see it and see it and see it. You are not getting any younger. That future you earnestly desire is not going to move towards you until you move towards it. MOVE TOWARDS IT! (yelling intended... smile). Even if your grand and glorious journey took three years, in three years you would be living it. That's worth it, right?

Now, I should add an important point here. Don't think for one moment that the stars will align and all of life will harmonize to help you as soon as you start. In fact, circumstances and events are going to do their best to talk you out of what you just decided. (There's a reason for that called "the adversary" who is never in favor of your personal happiness.) Do it anyway.... Stay the course and keep moving on your plans. If you keep moving forward and refute those false appearances, you are going to arrive just as surely as the sun is going to come up tomorrow. And, as you steadfastly set your mind, you will discover another fantastic reality. You will start getting to the place where your dream is no longer a dream but instead, a reality that no one can talk you out of. You will find yourself in places and circumstances that are going to help you get to where you are heading. Why didn't it happen before? You weren't moving towards it before!

Now, you are left with an important decision. Will you continue your futile attempts at staring into the horizon waiting for that ship; that circumstance; that indicator that it's time to move, or will you put on your big-boy briefs (and your big-girl panties) and take a step? Will you decide that the time to determine how your life will turn out is now?

I sure hope so...

WAITING TO LIVE

Imagine you found yourself with just three months left to live. After you got past the dread of it all, what would you do? It seems you would seek to spend your remaining time on the things that mattered most. In the front of your mind would be all of the people you love, with you most assuredly making the commitment to make sure they knew just how much. Your moments would all become precious and you would take nothing for granted. Putting things off for the future would quickly become a thing of the past. You would endeavor to live your last days with all that you are. Well, my friend, you don't need a death sentence to stop waiting to live...

Most people have become adept at the waiting game. They are waiting for the conditions to be just right. They are waiting to have enough money. They are waiting to reach a certain age or get married or have some kids. They are waiting to feel good or safe. They are always looking for some future day when all they ever wanted will have finally arrived. They are waiting until they get off of work or for the weekend or for that grand vacation next month. But sadly, the majority of your life will be lived in the spaces in-between. Life is found in each new moment of the day. It's getting ready in the morning. It's driving to work. It's getting ready for bed. It's in the mundane and the routine. It's in happiness and struggles, joy and pain. It's feeling at ease and feeling threatened. It's having what you need and not having what you need. It's life and all that goes with it.

It seems logical then, seeing we are all in this thing together, that your job is to learn how to live your life. Your task is to embrace the struggle. Get into the fight. Stop putting off and putting up with everything. Quit waiting for another day. Do the things that matter now. Capitalize on the moments that are now. Use your time available now, not when you get past the next big problem. Choose good thoughts right now, not when it looks like things are lining up. Be happy and uplifting and kind. Love people, bless people, help people! In short, be that wonderful person you really are inside today, not later when circumstances get better; not after you get the promotion; not when people finally treat you right, but right frikkin now, today!

You see, the grand deception is that you will always have more time. You can do it tomorrow, figure it out tomorrow, get better tomorrow. And while you are living with unlimited tomorrows, nothing worthwhile gets done today. Oh, you can do important stuff, serious stuff, but do those things really impact your life in meaningful and fulfilling ways? Are those things you focus on today the things that will take your focus when your life becomes very short? None of us have unlimited days (at least not in this life), so our number one priority is to make our days count. Live with purpose, on purpose with all that you have and all that you are! Learn new things. Pursue new goals. Those things where you already excel, excel all the more! Give what you have got to give. All of you! All of the time!

Every one of us is unique and has a special place in the world. No one can duplicate you and all that you are. But, you have to get busy doing you! You have to move beyond the endless distractions and threats and worries, into something new, namely what you have to offer to the world. What good part of you have you been holding back? What loveliness, what deep love and concern, what passion have you been extinguishing while you wait and wait for that day that never comes? What supreme goodness exists inside of you that you keep waiting to give out? Give yourself! Pour yourself out! Produce what only you can produce. Write it, paint it, sculpt it! Do it! Do it now! If you don't do it, it won't get done, at least not in the way you were supposed to do it.

Your mind was designed to thrive in the moments called now. All your energy, your perceptions, your insights, your love, are there for you right now. The thrill in the vast unexplored life exists now. The untapped learning, the excitement of new things, the beauty and unparalleled variety are here right now. But, you can only begin to perceive them when you finally decide to stop waiting to live, waiting to love, waiting for the future, but instead live now. Why not be the best employee; the best husband; the best father or mother; the most loving, kind person now? Why settle for a 60 percent version of yourself? Why be satisfied with a C? Why fool yourself into believing you could be all you ever wanted to be while still holding the best part of you back? Indeed, write the song, invent the tool, start the group, but do it now!

You don't have to wait to navigate the uncertainty of your time running out soon, to make the decision to live. You can choose to live right now, today. You can go all in. You can leave it all out on the field. You can say what you have always wanted to say, be who you always wanted to be, do all you ever wanted to do right now with all that you are. Don't spend another day waiting for a future day to live. Live right now, in this moment, as if it was your last, because in a sense it is your last as you can't ever get those moments back! Be the person you know to be today. You can. You must. Stop waiting. Live life; your life, now!

BE PATIENT

We live today in the culture of hurry. We want our food fast, our internet fast, our weight loss programs fast, our test results fast. We tend to seek out the quick fix, the shortcut. We don't want to invest the time, just get it done; the sooner the better. Microwave beats stove top and temporary repairs are preferred over lasting solutions. We just don't have the time to invest in doing things properly or the right way because we have to get to the next thing. Can't we just pay a guy or order it on Amazon and get it done already? And while technological advances have certainly made life easier, we seem to have lost our ability to exercise a little patience. The best things in life always seem to take a little time. Do we even know anymore what it means to be patient?

If you have ever watched a craftsman at work, it becomes apparent rather quickly that there is always an element of time involved. The craftsman isn't just trying to get the job done, but instead is seeking to get the job done where the result is perfect and beautiful and pleasing. People are willing to pay more for that person because the quality of the work speaks for itself. And as much as our frenetic world says otherwise, quality always makes the lasting impression. It's quality, not quantity, that we are after. The lowest bidder's work generally reflects a lower quality because of the time and effort they are willing to exert on the task. If you pay less, you generally get less. The cheap clothing doesn't last, and for every dollar you save on your purchase, you pay for in terms of its longevity. It is better that you spend more on the front end than count on the bargain to stand the test of time.

In life, the best things take time. Relationships take time. Raising children takes time. Perfecting a skill takes time. Success takes time. Learning to live life the best way takes time. There are no shortcuts. Shortcuts always promise a faster result but fail to deliver, though they appear to do so at first. Whatever is easy generally isn't worth it. That's not to say that everything good is hard, but rather that good things require an investment on your part. Expecting good things without investing your own personal time and energy into those good things cannot fail but to produce loss. You may be able to count on the conveniences of technology to make things happen faster, but the real things in life, the most important things, require time and, with time, patience.

Patience is a lost virtue in the helter-skelter of life today. We have been seduced by technology into thinking that there is always a way to obtain a result more quickly. We carry that mindset into our important life activities and expect a similar result. We seek to get the degree quickly in order to advance, but leave off the learning. We pursue important changes in our lives by employing the method that seems to get us there the fastest. We are all hat and no cowboy. We look good not by patient training and self-control, but by the cosmetic surgeon's scalpel. We want the diet plan that offers to burn the calories via a pill that requires neither exercise nor portion control. We want to have our cake and eat it too. In terms of our mental health, we don't want to invest the time in discovering where our thinking patterns have gone astray but instead seek for a diagnosis with its subsequent promised medication fix. And while medication is a beautiful addition to life, the goal was always that we arrived at the good place naturally, even if it took a little time. Modern advances certainly succeed in making life easier, but sometimes the ease and the convenience are not what we really need. It's the pricks and the obstacles and the difficulties of life that really put us on our toes and awaken us to life's more important lessons, as Emerson masterfully noted. Give a man a serious challenge to contend with and note how quickly he engages himself fully until a solution is at last found.

The reason we do not exhibit patience in life is that we have bought into the illusion that we have no time. We fail to recognize how forcefully we are being pushed and pulled towards activities that have little impact in helping us to live our best lives. We feel as if we don't have time to think things through, much less the time required to actually solve our problems and make strides towards a brighter future. We are loathe to engage in something uncomfortable or new, even if that new thing might serve to completely revolutionize our lives. Instead we go to work expending our best efforts for someone else and leave ourselves and our happiness undone. When we try something new or endeavor to move in a different direction, we feel that we don't have the time or the energy to make the necessary changes though we only gave it a minimal try at best. Living this way, we soon find ourselves at the end of this brief life, full of regrets regarding the man or woman we always knew we could be. And all along, all we had need of was a little patience. All we needed to do was step off the hamster wheel and take ourselves to account. We only needed to slow down a little and give our lives a little more consideration.

It's never too late to begin practicing patience. Patience isn't as concerned in getting the job done as it is in getting the job done properly. Patience knows that all good things take time and allots its time accordingly. Patience is required to live a successful life and to allow yourself the love and the space you need to get it right! Be patient with yourself and extend that same patience to everyone and everything that you love. Be patient.

CHAPTER SIX
Fear

WHAT IS WRONG WITH ME?

Have you ever arrived at the place where things don't seem to matter much anymore? You are tired of the routine of life and there's nothing new under the sun? It's sort of like life has lost its point somewhere, or if it has a point, it somehow snuck by you. You are stuck in a deep pit of "who cares?" and can't seem to navigate your way out of it. You search for clues in the physical realm, like maybe you aren't getting enough sleep or you're dehydrated or something. No matter what words you use to describe it, it feels like "blah" and calls aloud for a remedy. What the hell is wrong with me?

Life is best summarized by two giant life forces working behind the scenes influencing people to decide to move in a certain direction. One force for good is always working to provide you with clues about how to think and where to take your thoughts, while the other one seeks to hijack your thoughts and move you forcefully towards a certain path. One motivates by love and the other motivates by fear. Imagine that life is like a race and as long as you keep running you will arrive at a good destination. Your pace of life fluctuates with your mind. When your mind is functioning properly without fear or other constraints, you are able to run effortlessly towards your hopes and dreams. But, when fear forces its way into your existence, there's an immediate drag on the system and life begins to slow down. Lowered energy, lowered vitality, low capacity to give a damn, all point to fear that has forced itself upon you. You may feel your situation is much more complicated than that, but it really isn't so there's no need to perplex your mind any further. More rest isn't going to fix it. Eating better is not going to solve it. Exercising and losing a few pounds isn't going to correct it. It's fear, fear, fear and it will suck your life right out from underneath you!

Fear is a slippery character, and it's hard to put your arms around it. It moves in quietly without fanfare in the form of a few doubts and maybe some worries here and there. Then, as you unknowingly give it space in your thinking, it gains a little traction and starts occupying a place. It's like a breeze blowing in your face while you're running. It's not enough to stop you, but it is enough to slow you down. You can tell that you've slowed down because you are no longer looking forward in your life. You're no longer focused on your destination, but instead you begin looking all around you. The more you slow down and the more you start looking around, the more potential difficulty you begin to see. It's like your life is a huge room with an infinite number of doors you can travel through to get to different destinations. Fear starts closing off the doors, one by one, until your life seems to have very few options or remaining opportunities. The doors aren't really closed, but fear gives the illusion that they are, and as long as you sit there in "it," you aren't going to see the way out.

Fear at its basis is pure illusion. It isn't the negative, disastrous outcome, it's the threat of the disastrous outcome! It's the ultimate energy suppressor. It feeds on your energy like a parasite as it has no real life of its own. It exists by permission only which its host is unaware he has given away. It can only gain energy from you by your insistence on letting it stick around. You don't willfully allow it to remain, but you feel compelled to give it mental space as it has suggested some unreasonable outcome from which you wish to escape. Its illusion shines the most brightly as you foolishly decide to engage it with your human logic and understanding. It's a wrong starting premise which cannot end successfully in any scenario. In the middle of his nightmare Job said, "I have no ease, I have no quietness; I cannot rest; turmoil has come upon me." The hallmark of fear, if you are still in denial, is no ease, no quietness, no rest and the feeling that trouble has landed upon you. What is wrong with you? Fear has descended upon you and you need to escape its grasp!

If you want your life to return to you. If you want to experience your former energy and vitality, you have to rid yourself of fear. You have to eradicate it from your life like the plague. You've got to clear out both the obnoxious and the subtle. You've got to learn to hear its words inside your head and begin the process of refuting them. You must find some promise of God that overcomes that fear and hurl it on the fear thoughts like dry chemical carbon dioxide on a fire. Maybe there is some action you need to take or some course you need to attend, but whatever it is, take that action! Then, once you've refuted it and coated it with God's promises and taken action against it, let the damn thing go! Nothing kills off fear faster than your personal decision to refuse it access to your thoughts. Resist the urge to reason it out, it has no reason behind it. Quote the Word and let it go.

What is wrong with you? It's the same thing that's wrong with the whole world in its quest to recover its former existence. You've fallen victim to fear in some capacity and it is eating away at your life. Get rid of it. Squash it! Stomp it out! Get back to running in your own race of life, effortlessly toward the things that matter most to you. Your condition isn't permanent no matter how long you've been living this way. You not only should get rid of every fear, but it is your birthright as a human being to do it. Your life without all of the fear is your real existence. It's the way God intended for you to live.

Let Him take on all the so-called threats to your existence. Let Him do what He said He would do – carefully watch over you. No more fear... none.

THE PSYCHOLOGY OF FEAR

It's ironic to me that fear, which exists only in the mind of man, has such a powerful influence over the American people of today. Good old America is literally scared to death. When fear is introduced, logic leaves the building. There's no more sound thinking, rational thought or anything that even resembles a normal cognitive process. And, during the woefully sad circus called election season, the only real threat to so-called "ruining" our country is fear.

Fear in its true essence is nothing more than false evidence appearing real (F.E.A.R.). It's false evidence because that which people fear has not happened yet. But, in order for false evidence to gain a foothold in people's minds it must also appear real. Fear has not always been a part of man's existence. It first entered the scene when the original man (Adam) separated himself from God and in so doing allowed entrée to a manner of thinking which formerly didn't exist. And, ever since that fateful day, fear has been hard at work ruining people's lives. Fear demands you react to a problem which isn't yet a problem. The choices you make in response to fear are almost always wrong! However, the illusion of fear, once accepted and subsequently believed, is on its way into becoming a reality. What a person believes, they will receive into their life, positive and negative alike. False evidence then, frightfully, turns into real evidence.

Nothing lights a fire under the American people (or any people) faster than fear. The message of fear threatens your existence, your happiness, your peace. So, if you want to garner votes, simply scare the hell out of the people. Tell them of dangers that don't exist. Carefully craft your messages and add in unhealthy doses of pending doom and disaster. When someone questions your message, accuse them of lying and then get back to the business of fear. Sound familiar?

The tenuous threat of fear aside, the ultimate trouble comes from the illogic that naturally follows it. Absent logic, the only choice left is insanity. Insanity and illogic are exhausting. Every parent knows that reasoning with a child who's not yet capable of reasoning is a foolish endeavor. Yet, that's exactly where we are today! What would be considered horrible or distasteful or just plain wrong, somehow becomes acceptable because fear and illogic are at the helm. Without sound reasoning in place, up becomes down, left becomes right and black morphs into white. And, in a world where things no longer have meaning, what would you expect?

What I'm setting before you today folks is much bigger than politics. This is about your life, your freedom, your ability to pursue happiness. The reason America became great is because of the collective beliefs of its citizens. Its forefathers had the holy boldness to pursue a new way. They weren't afraid to break away from the regimes of fear and bondage. They envisioned a land that would be tolerant of all people and all beliefs and fought hard to obtain it. And now, this great empire is threatened, not from factions of terrorists or illegal aliens or even racism, but more directly from the individual fears of the citizens united together to become collective fear, which however false, will become reality if persisted in. The psychology of today's America is fear!

The solution to this grand dilemma is not found in arguing, fighting and threatening. However much you want to slap the good sense back into people, it wouldn't matter anyway. Once people are afraid and continue to feed on that fear, their minds have become unstable. Just look around you. It's pretty obvious isn't it? Instead, your job, your only reasonable job is to refuse to be a part of their fear. Once fear exits the picture, sound thought returns. I certainly don't purport to be the smartest person around, but one thing I'm not, is afraid! The only true solution to your own fear is a return to love; to compassion; to sound thinking. Stop being so damn worried about some segment of society that's going to get you! Nothing is going to get you if you trust God. It really doesn't matter if the whole damn thing goes to hell if God's got your back! He'll make a way for you, no matter what it looks like.

You sir, you madam, have to get out of the fear business! Put love back into your heart. Return yourself to kindness, to encouragement, to love. Quit letting the great societal fear make your decisions for you. Stop stockpiling your weapons and preparing for Armageddon. Cease your doomsday preparations. The wheels haven't fallen off the bus yet, they just want you to think they have. You, in your life, decide the wheels are still on the bus. Be honest with yourself. Is your life, the way you have been living, really so awful? Is your corner of the globe really a "disaster?" Is the America where you reside truly being ruined by a neighbor that wears a turban? Do someone's different beliefs threaten your beliefs? Is the truth of God somehow negated by another person's error? Illogic people, you must rid yourself of the insanity.

Our great God that made America great isn't out of business. But, your fear will negate His ability to protect you and help you. Don't allow false evidence to turn into real evidence. Stop looking over your shoulder for something that is going to get you. Instead, walk out boldly with your head held high knowing that it is God who watches over your life. Refuse the psychology of fear and return to the true essence of being an American. Be a badass!

It is election season, so get your butt out there and vote.

But, more important than deciding on a candidate, decide on what it is you will and will not believe. The individual believing of one person can turn the whole world right-side up. Imagine the possibilities if the majority of us believe.

Replace the psychology of fear with the psychology of love. You won't be sorry. You'll be blessed!

THE QUINTESSENTIAL, ULTIMATE, IRREPLACEABLE, TRANSFORMATIVE, FEAR ELIMINATOR

What if I told you there is one simple, surefire way to remove fear from your life? What if it was quintessential in its perfection? What if it represented the ultimate solution? What if it was irreplaceable in nature? What if it was so transformative that it would change your entire life? What if...

Before I reveal this life-changing secret, let's get clear on something that is vitally important. Fear is your number one enemy in life and the cause behind your every failure; every disappointment; every aspect of life wherein you suffer and struggle. By the same token, the absence of fear only leads to success; to happiness; to the end of the struggling and the pain.

Fear is a rather curious and sneaky animal. It's rarely obvious and upfront. It weasels its way into your heart building nests of which you are completely unaware. And, once its stronghold is established, it asserts its way into your life, robbing you of life's enthusiasm and joy. Fear must be eliminated at all costs!

In order to apply the secret, first you have to understand the process whereby fear gets to you. It is not, nor was it ever intended to be a "normal" part of life. It's not being "realistic!" It's an aberration; an outside force seeking to act upon you. It's something that isn't a part of you seeking to become a part of you. Fear is positive expectation working in reverse to bring about a negative outcome. It approaches you as a doubt, gains traction by worry and finally settles in as fear.

There you are, living your life and enjoying your day. Your mind is in a nice place and you feel pretty good. Then, in a moment in time, it happens. Some negative potentiality enters your consciousness. How it enters and from where it enters is a bit of a mystery. But alas, it happens and there it is. Now you have a choice, whether you realize it or not. Doubt has knocked on your door and it's up to you to answer. Because the thought is alarming, you think perhaps that if you take the time to consider it, you can figure it out. Enter the weasel! The consideration of the evil thought prolongs its access to your mind. But, by golly, you are a smart person and you can figure it out. So, you begin to foolishly run it through your analysis center, hoping for an answer; a solution that puts your mind at ease. And, the more you consider the possibility, the more nervous and distracted you become. Your doubt has now progressed to worry and is making a play for your heart. Grimly, if you persist in the evil consideration, it will move in as fear, poised to bring about, by your own wrong belief (fear), disastrous results into your life. That's how it works; how it's always worked, from the beginning of time.

What is the secret to eliminating fear? QUIT it! Do not allow it access into your head. Stop considering it and worse, trying to figure it out. The confusion enters in because you've been taught to confront fear head-on, which is technically true, but usually applied to things like skydiving or riding scary roller coasters. Sure, ignoring the things that scare you is generally a bad idea. But, I'm talking about that day by day battle that's going on in your mind. The fight between happy and unhappy; energetic or depressed; joyfully expectant or miserably bored. As a side, it may surprise you to know that boredom is also a result of fear or being talked out of the fullness that is life. Fear must be challenged by something bigger than it, like one of those over 900 promises in God's Word. But, once you challenge it with the truth, you have to let it go. Don't continue to run it through your mind because if you do, you will lose 100 percent of the time and in every case!

In order to defeat fear, you have to starve it out. If you don't feed it, it cannot live. It's very simple, though never easy. It takes a real discipline to give an issue to God and refuse to take it back. You see, your human logic just desperately wants to claim its superiority and insists, even demands that you think the negative thing through. Have you ever heard people say they cannot let something go? Well, they can but, old familiar Mr. Ego won't allow it. It takes humility and trust to just turn something over and refuse to take it back. But, if you can do it, you will find that fear loses its grip on you fairly quickly. Oh yeah, it will be back with a new idea shortly, but you just apply the same principles in every case and you will win every time. Before you recognize it, you will be overcome with that radical, unusual feeling called, "peace..."

There are some other gnarly thoughts to be addressed as well, such as guilt and condemnation, but that's maybe the subject of another writing. But, for today, work on starving out fear and see where that takes you. You'll see how it is the quintessential, ultimate, irreplaceable and transformational solution if you will just make up your mind to QUIT fear. QUIT it!

IS THERE FEAR IN YOUR FUTURE?

As I wrestled around with the notion of fear in the darkness, suddenly it dawned on me, all fear exists only in the future. That is precisely why fear is always an illusion, because it exists only in a time that has not yet arrived. Even fear of the past is in reality fear of its effect on your future and potentially your present moments. Is there fear in your future?

Of all the things in life, in all the details, in every aspect and facet of living, the number one enemy you must fight and overcome is fear. All that you do not have or cannot do or are unable to overcome is always based on fear. Fear is the great killer of ambition and desire and your future. Fear persisted in will bring with it all the defeat you have ever imagined. As long as you have fear, whether it be in the form of anxiety or worry or concern falsely named, you cannot have peace. Fear is the great antithesis to love, not hate. Fear is a falsehood, a lie at the very core of life, robbing it of its vitality and enthusiasm. Fear is wrong and most unnatural. Fear is sin.

The problem with fear in your life is that it is a form of believing, but is its opposite. What good things you can believe for without limit, have their parallel in what awful things you can fear (believe) without limit. The longer you hold onto your fear, the greater the likelihood of its appearance into your life. And, even if you never quite arrive at all the terrible things you have imagined, you will have endured a terrible ride along the way. Your fear encourages and invites disaster. And just as your positive believing invites God and His blessings into your life, your negative believing; your anxiety and worry and fear invite the adversary into your life in all manner of misery and sickness and suffering.

Fear isn't real because it is always a threat to your future. It growls of some impending disaster. It roars predictions of future suffering and lack. It shouts how your needs will not be met. It cannot know this of course, as only God knows the future, so "it" is counting on you to help make the threat a reality. The way you ignorantly cooperate is by accepting the lie as truth and holding onto it instead of discarding it. It's a really sticky trick. Your human ego, once threatened, will insist on trying to figure it out. Thus, it will demand you think about it and think about it until you can solve it. However, you are not going to figure it out with your mind, as its origin is spiritual. Instead, your ego-driven insistence will result in keeping the wrong thought in your mind, which is all fear needs to take hold. It begins with a knock at your door called doubt. It gets a foot in the door as you worry. Finally, it gets inside fully once you are afraid. At that point you've been captured! Then, fear's companion anxiety is knocking on your door and your windows and your garage all at once. It returns as the many fears you have misplaced by your refusal to deal with them, one by one, in the moments they approached. You have to deal with your thoughts. There is no other way.

All throughout history, men and women have been admonished to fear not. In order to beat it, you have to depend upon something bigger than yourself. On your own, you won't really get the job done. Oh, you can muster up all the bravado you can imagine, but in the end, you need spiritual power to defeat spiritual power. You need Someone that exists in your past, your present and your future, all at the same time. (Don't even try to wrap your head around that one.) You need to be able to give all that care to someone else. And therein is your solution! You have to hand it over, and once you realize you have taken it back, hand it over again. Prayer isn't, as I read recently, just some psychological process to help you feel better. The idea behind prayer is that God will actually do something about that which concerns you. Otherwise, why even pray? When you finally let God preserve your future as He promises, you will find yourself at rest. Unrest is thus a signal that there is something you need to handle or resolve, even if just within your heart. Often your solution is simply to stop persisting in your dreadful considerations. Refuse to scratch that itch. Letting it go isn't negligence; it's wisdom. In terms of the fear thought, sure *that* would be awful on an epic scale, but it hasn't actually happened, right? (Notice I left out "yet.") It's false evidence! Not worthy of your mental considerations... You have to let it go! Now...

It may seem simplistic, but God's solutions are always simple and clear. Error is complicated! Error is what produces the mind boggle and keeps you up all night. Lies, artfully presented, designed to hold your interest based on some vague possibility in your reality, are still lies. They began as untrue and will remain untrue if you can get this right. Dread or worry about some potential future day has never, in the history of existence, helped a difficult situation get better. Help is found in the quiet. Answers arrive when you settle down. Solutions come from the "still small voice."

Is there fear in your future? Get rid of it today! Find that promise of God that negates your fear and say it to the thing until "the thing" retreats. Say it today, my friend... Today!

FEAR IS A DECISION

I know what you are thinking... Man, how much can you say about fear? Well, that's for good reason. The number one problem you have, recognized or not, is fear. Fear is the ulti- mate hold back. Fear is the great *thwarter* of dreams and plans. Fear is the cause of your negative effects. Fear! So, in- dulge me yet again and hear what I'm saying. Fear has ruined more men's lives than all other things combined. Fear isn't something that just happens to you and you have to find a way to survive it. Fear is a choice.

Shocking statement number one - believe it or not, fear is actually a decision. That's right! It's not something that just happens and you have to wait it out. Nope. It's a decision you are making. You (your mind) is presented with some negative variable; some dreadful potentiality, and depending upon how well that threat relates to you as being possible, fear follows. You aren't really afraid of the mountains blowing up while you climb them, but maybe so if it is a volcanic mountain. So, how fear hits your mind will always be somewhat relatable to you and your experiences. That shows you that something sinister is behind it. Anyway, when you get confronted with that fiery dart of negativity, you have a decision to make. Oh, you don't feel like you need to make a decision, but you do. You have to decide IF that thing can happen to you. And sadly, the more you mull it over in your mind, the more ground it gains and the more believable the fear becomes.

To win the contest, and it is a contest, you have to believe that whatever is being negatively presented is not going to happen to you. This is where God enters the picture. If you believe in God and His love and protection of you, you can dismiss that fear by claiming a promise in God's Word that counteracts that fear. Side note - every potential fear that you will ever be confronted with has an antidote in God's Word. Or, if the promise escapes you, you can always pray about it and even ask God for an answer of peace. Without God, the world is going to be a very scary place. In fact, absent any belief in God's ability to do things, you can pretty much be assured of a life full of fear.

There is another aspect of fear we should consider. Those particular fears that have been plaguing you or have been following you around for a lifetime, are the worst types of fear. You can spot them fairly easily because they represent the sole cause of where you struggle the most. It's not the circumstances, your upbringing, your family, your lack of money or your gene pool. It's fear! The reason that they are clinging to you like a hair shirt is because they have gained a stronghold in your thinking. Yes, they started as a foothold, but because of your insistence on allowing them entrée, they became a stronghold. In the military when we speak of the enemy having a stronghold, we mean he has a strengthened, fortified position. Well, fear in like fashion, is an enemy (something sinister) that has built a fortified position in your head. Now, hear me out because this might make you angry. The reason that you still have certain fears is because of your own insistence. You are stubbornly clinging to what you think you know is true, because you just know! Even if God Himself told you audibly that it was just a lie, you wouldn't believe it because you know better. I mean after all, haven't you heard the news reports? Have you not studied the latest scientific research? Are you asking me to completely disregard the current medical findings? Yes, yes and no, of course not! What I'm asking you to consider is that there is something, someone far greater in ability than men and what men say. Isn't it even remotely possible that what the world promotes as true cause and effect isn't really the cause that produces the effect? (Let that simmer...) The reason certain fears defeat you on an epic, chronic level is because you are refusing to let them go. You, my friend, are refusing to change your mind and just decide they aren't true.

Fear is always a lie; always wrong and always an illusion. The enemy works hard to get you to fear because fear is believing for something to happen in the negative. And believing equals receiving, as the saying goes... Thus, the first step in overcoming fear is to admit you have it. If you catch yourself telling some scenario over and over that you aren't afraid of it - you are. Once you acknowledge it by being honest with yourself, you are finally on the way to overcoming it. Next find something good that God says concerning it and cleave to that. Every time you think of your situation or condition, claim that promise until the fear is gone. And finally, get sick and tired of being sick and tired. Make a decision! Decide you are over being afraid of _____________, and move ahead. You will find, surprisingly, that once you stop giving "it" airplay, it just sort of dies out. It dies out because it was a lie to begin with.

Now, if you are still saying you have no fear, I hear you... Say on my brother! Preach my sister! But, a life of peace, tranquility, abundance and health is waiting for you on the other side of that mountain; that mountain made of clouds called fear. Make the right decision.

FEAR – THE SILENT KILLER

In our frantic world today, people have lost sight of the core essence of what it means to be a thinking, human being. We run from this activity to that activity; we have never-ending "to do" lists; we are so, so busy with our requirements, that we rarely have time to sit down and consider what is driving our decisions. We are bombarded with news media, social media. We have computers, iPads, iPods, iPhones, cell phones, droid phones and a host of other devices to keep us connected to everything, everywhere, at all times. We find ourselves left with one large, looming consequence; we don't have time to think. We have become collectively distracted and, in our distraction, have lost sight of who is in control of our lives. And by surrendering control we "all like sheep have gone astray." We have secretly been funneled with the masses of society into well-worn paths that always lead to misery and futility.

There are really only two great motives in life; love and fear. All of humanity is basing their decisions; their plans; their thinking on one of the two... Love comes from God and has nothing harmful in it. Love empowers men and women and gives them back control in their lives. Love puts the energy into a life and, like a gently flowing river, is refreshed day by day. Fear is just the opposite. Fear comes from the enemy and has nothing good or useful in it (Nothing!). Fear controls people and binds them down like slaves. Fear stops all forward movement, and as the lion roars to freeze its prey, fear roars and brings our lives to a standstill. "Fear is sand in the machinery of life." (Eli Stanley Jones.) Fear stops all forward movement. Fear harasses and attacks and controls. Fear is the hidden power behind all the suffering in this world, and if allowed to continue without being rigorously and thoroughly purged, will lead to ruin and defeat in EVERY situation and in EVERY case. Fear breaks our minds down and, in that divided state, makes us insane. Fear wrecks marriages; destroys our businesses; invites sickness; welcomes catastrophe; ensures poverty; murders, steals, hurts, harasses, controls, ruins, and reduces us down to a mere fraction of the person we once were. In short, fear torments.

So, how can we overcome this seemingly insurmountable enemy and bring restoration and wholeness to our lives? How can we get back all that has been stolen from us? How can we get off the treadmill and step out of the rat race? How can we regain control of our lives and once again live peacefully and confidently? We can do it by making a decision. Our life isn't just happening to us; we are happening to it! And in contrast to our former ignorance when we sat there frozen in the bushes waiting for the lion to strike, we can now make the decision to get the hell out of those bushes and get on with our lives. Fear, like every other slippery deception must be dealt with swiftly. We don't answer fear; entertain fear; dialogue with fear; rationalize with fear; try to understand and analyze fear; or, for God's sake, make friends with our fear. The moment we take that approach we lose. We don't proclaim to ourselves over and over, "I'm not afraid! I'm not afraid! I'm not afraid!" Instead, we simply move forward with love. Mature love casts out fear. We decide adamantly that we will not think the thoughts of fear. Oh, I know, it's very tempting to try to figure it out. "Maybe if I just run this scenario through my head one thousand times, I will be able to figure it out." So, ummm, how's that working out for you? Getting any closer? Almost got it? NO! Hell no! All you get when you do that is more fear, more fear, more fear... Sure you're smart; sure you're logical; sure you can figure stuff out, but when it comes to evil, you ain't that smart! You lost before you began. The moment you entertained it (in your wisdom), you lost. And you know why that trick always works on humans? Because your enemy makes an appeal to your human logic. He is banking on the fact that you, like all humans, will try to figure the dang thing out. But, fear has a spiritual basis and your human mind is not capable of figuring it out. So, like every other deception the enemy tries to work us over with, our job is to simply do what God said to do about it and refuse to engage in a discussion otherwise. When Eve paused to consider what the devil asked her to consider, she lost! When you keep running that fear through your mind over and over, you lose! Soon you will become a walking, talking anxiety attack, mentally threadbare and defeated.

God does not want us to live in fear. God wants to deliver us out of fear. How would you feel as a parent if you had to watch your child being controlled and bullied and beaten? Do you like it when your children are afraid? Do they think soundly when they are afraid? Are there really boogeymen? Of course not, but when you are afraid aren't you doing the same thing? And what do you tell your children? "Well, don't be afraid, son"... end of story? No! You tell them something to counteract that fear. You give them something to put in their minds to replace it. "Mommy and Daddy protect you, son, and we won't let anything get you!" Sure, you might point out there is nothing under the bed, but you don't suggest they sit in the darkness and try to figure it out. You turn on the light before you do the inspection. Well, that's how you overcome fear. You turn on the light before you do the inspection. What does God say about the thing you are so afraid of? Turn on the lights! Things aren't so scary when you turn on the lights. If you hear a potential intruder outside your house, you turn the lights on. The light might not make him go away, but in the light, you can figure out what to do next. That's what love does; it turns on the light so you can figure out what to do next, ultimately leading to God's solution, which is infinitely bigger than any intruder!

Let's just get honest with ourselves when we are afraid and seek a solution. Call a thing, a thing! "I can't leave this job I hate because I need the money!" = Fear. "I can't tell him what I really think because he will leave me!" = Fear. "I cannot forgive her for what she did!" = Fear. "I cannot get past this big negative thing that happened to me!" = Fear. The reality is that you can do all of those things, but fear has you under its control and is feeding you another story. Decide right now that it ends today! You decide because you are worth infinitely more than that to God!

Where you have been, I have been also. What you have tried to figure out, I have tried to figure out also. The anxiety you are feeling, I have felt too. So, trust me when I say there is only one way you can escape that fear. Don't be so smart and instead "let" God show you otherwise. You'll never get to the other side of that fear and experience the sheer joy of deliverance until you are willing to humble yourself and do it God's way. Are you afraid? Turn off your electronics, log out, log off and think; take some time to think. Take back the control of your life and for goodness sakes, don't do it alone... God loves you and so do I! Be not afraid, only believe...

THIS IS YOUR BRAIN ON FEAR

Have you ever seen the bumper stickers that say, "No Fear?" Great advice for living, but saying it and living it are two totally different animals. Fear is perhaps the most detrimental thing that can happen to a human being and in order to succeed in life you have to learn how to beat it. I'll say it again, you have to learn how to beat it! If you don't learn how to overcome it, your life will be a fraction of what it was meant to be. You will never enjoy the peace God envisioned for you to have in your mind. You will unknowingly bring hardship and difficulty upon yourself. You won't say what you oughta' say or do what you oughta' do. You will always settle for less than you deserve and you will be a slave to what might happen next and what might go wrong later! The hardship involved with being a slave is that slaves are subjected to forced labor and don't have any say about what happens next. Slaves don't decide anything. Slaves do what the master says and if they don't, they get whipped and forced into submission. If you have fear you have a master that decides for you what your life will be like. So, it seems only reasonable that we should want to learn how to escape fear; not deny it exists, ignore it or puff up and vow to fight it, but actually escape its grasp.

Part of a former job involved teaching a course on Mandt. Mandt is actually the name of the gentleman that developed the course. Mandt training is all about learning to develop strong relationships that help us in de-escalating situations that lead to aggressive behavior in the customers we serve.

Part of the material I review talks about fear. Fear is described as a normal human emotion. Further, it is described as something that was built into humans to help them defend themselves. I always struggle with that part of the presentation because there is nothing normal about fear. When I am afraid, I don't think clearly. I choose expedient options not necessarily the right options. Caution is helpful; fear is not. I am cautious about mountain lions because they have the potential to kill me. But if I let my mind get overcome with fear during my dreaded big cat encounter, then chances are I'm going to lose. So, just how exactly can I learn to overcome fear?

To understand fear, you have to understand the basic spiritual competition that all people are in that live in the world. In the beginning, back in the days of Adam and Eve, originally, there was no such thing as fear. Fear came after the fall of man when man decided by his own free will to believe something contrary to what God said. In essence, man chose to believe his five senses' reasoning over what God said was reality. Whenever you and I choose to believe our five senses' logic over the logic of God's Word, fear is on the way. The adversary, that dark opposer of all that is good, works out circumstances and situations that seem to contradict what God says, and those circumstances and situations are damn convincing! And since we are pretty smart folks, we start to believe something that isn't true and if we persist in that thinking, we bring into our reality the thing we were so dang afraid of! Then we say, see, I knew it! (As if it was true all along.) That being said, fear isn't always so obvious. Most fear is very, very subtle. People are afraid of not succeeding and will unknowingly sabotage their own efforts. They may even be presented with an opportunity that would lead them to success, but they turn it down due to the 35 reasons they came up with (and 34 were based on fear). People are afraid of everything. There's no criticism from me, however. I personally have been the most scared man on earth! Instead of criticism, I have empathy for people. Empathy because it is so sad what happens to people when fear gets involved, and if you are over two years old, fear has gotten involved.

Fear is a present-day reality that we all have to deal with and had better figure out. So how are you supposed to overcome fear when fear is such a formidable, frightful feeling? The key word here is feeling. Newsflash! Our feelings have nothing to do with whether or not something is true. Oh, our feelings can function as a barometer to clue us into something like hmmm, maybe I shouldn't go there, but at the end of the day (favorite cliché included on purpose), feelings are no guarantee for truth. In fact, your feelings are what bring that fear to life. You consider some dreadful possibility, your heart speeds up, you piece together the facts and they all add up to one thing - it's true! Hidden in that last sentence was another clue. You considered it. You're smart, I'm smart, we consider! Ahh, but that is precisely where we go wrong. Considering a negative or a fear is like taking a little nibble on the bait. It looks so inviting. It is hard to resist (i.e., thinking about it). But, that is exactly what you HAVE to do. Back in the beginning, the fall of man started with a tiny consideration of an idea that was not what God had said. But the defeat didn't come there; it began there. The consideration is the bait. Don't take it. Don't entertain it. Don't try to reason it out. Don't! Instead of taking the bait (and you know this already if you have ever tried to reason with fear), immediately replace that idea with something true that God said. If your health is being threatened, what does God say about your health? If your finances are being threatened, what does God say about your finances? Your happiness, your future, your needs? What does God say about those things? That is the key, my friends. Refuse the lies by finding the promises. I know what you might be thinking. Are you saying I should just ignore life? Put my head in the sand? Pretend like bad things don't exist? No, no and no! Don't ignore life; ignore fear, which is NOT life! Pick your head up and put your feet in the sand by finally relaxing. Don't pretend anything because you know bad things exist; just decide they won't (future tense) exist for you!

Now that you are clear about your responsibility to refuse to consider those fears, is replacing them by God's promises enough? Believing is a verb, and a verb connotes action. When you believe, you act. Act on what God said. If God promised to take care of you, walk out like someone who is taken care of. Do your life. Have your fun. Get up out of that "worry" chair and live!

Unscramble your eggs man! Respond how I always respond. "If you've already 'got me,' why are you spending so much time trying to convince me that it's true?" No one has to put up with fear, and it's certainly not God's will. Don't go by your feelings. Don't take the time to consider, no matter how tempting it is. Act on the promises of God and you'll learn something new. Peace...

This is Your Brain on Peace!

ANXIOUS FOR NOTHING

There's a thing going around in the world today called anxiety, and almost everybody has it in one way or another. The question isn't whether or not anxiety exists, but rather can you do anything about it? Feeling anxious and troubled is not just a normal part of life, but instead is a learned behavior. You may never find yourself completely free from anxiety's assaults, but you can learn how to overcome it and its effects over your life. Be anxious for nothing!

It likely seems incredulous to you that you could live today without any anxiety about anything. Imagine getting to a place where feeling anxious was the exception rather than the rule. Anxiety in its lowest common denominator is fear. However, it's not an overt fear that is in your face threatening you with some negative outcome. Instead it is a hidden, veiled fear. It is fear misplaced. It's a foreboding feeling of doom based on nothing you can put your finger on. It is feeling unsettled or uncomfortable with something, somewhere, somehow. At best it is unpleasant and people do all kinds of things to minimize its effects. Anxiety leads to avoidance and procrastination. Anxiety, the wayward stepchild of fear, promotes inaction! Anxiety suggests it is better to do nothing about something that is troubling you rather than to take it on. Anxiety presumes defeat or hardship in advance and proclaims loss before the contest starts. Anxiety is not the negative result; it is the threat of a negative result. And sadly, for many it is debilitating. Feeling anxious is "just" a feeling. It's not a reality, it is a feeling. It is an internal dread about something that has been cleverly designed, then hidden to frighten you. But, like any unpleasant feeling, it can and must be overcome.

If you were to carefully and thoughtfully trace back your thoughts that led to anxiety, working through the layers and the subtle promptings; the pieced together misinformation; the false connections and associations, you would see it for what it really is - a lie. It doesn't seem untrue because of how you feel when you experience it. It can be very, very convincing. But it isn't pointing to some pending reality heading in your direction. It is highlighting something you have let go. Anxious feelings are always an indicator of something you have let go. The first step in overcoming anxiety isn't to dig through the jumbled spaghetti bowl of feelings and sensations. It is to confront the negative possibility the first time it shows up! By the time you are experiencing anxiety, the seeds have long since been planted. It happened long before you started *feeling* anxious! In the midst of anxiety, you have to ride it out; changing your thinking with perseverance until your feelings catch up. We are so schooled to revere our feelings that we accept them as truth rather than indicators. Anxious feelings communicate that you have let something go.

The cure for anxiety is action. Take action on whatever it is you are letting go! What's the point of all of that thinking and analysis if you aren't going to do anything about it? You can think yourself into a full-on panic attack! What things in your life are you ignoring? What do you need to handle that you have been putting off? And, why the hell are you putting it off? It will not go away on its own... Take it on! Solve it. Try to solve it. Bring it up. Handle it. Be honest with yourself! Be honest with other people. Take the time to get "it" fixed. Resolve it in your own mind. Answer the damn question once and for all. Quit drifting. Stop putting up with it. Cease waiting around for something that isn't going to happen. Put an end to endless prayers that involve no action on your part. Get sick and tired of being sick and tired. Have the conversation you have been avoiding. Make a move. Pay the bill. Look for the job. Go to the doctor. Do something! Otherwise, you will find yourself living in a riddle that will never be solved on its own. You don't have to know what to do already. But, you do have to do something!

It is not God's will for you to be anxious all the time or, for that matter, anytime... God, His Word, His love is the only real lasting solution to your anxiety. Look, life is big and chock full of scary shit! There are a multitude of things that could go wrong. You and your human mind are no match for what you are really up against. On your own, you are not smart enough or strong enough to measure up to the fight. You will not be able to reason or logic your way out of the potential downfalls. You won't be able to do it. As long as you think your victory is all on you, you are guaranteed to lose. God did not design life that way. You can't pull up enough bootstraps to get the job done! The solution, the best solution for anxiety is to stop trying so hard to figure it all out and give all of that crap to God to figure out. Just hand it over. Tell him about your situation (that He already knows about) and leave it with him to solve. Then, get busy living and doing and taking actions. Ninety percent of your defeat lies within your persistent consideration of that dreadful outcome. Read that sentence again! Your problem isn't what is going to happen; your problem is what you think (fear) is going to happen! Hand it over and make some moves. What is the worst that could happen? Have you ever met anyone that worried themselves out of their problems? Be anxious for nothing (no thing), but in everything (every thing) let your requests be made known unto Him (God) and enjoy the wonderful peace that follows!

Be anxious for nothing. That is living your best life...

STRIVING ABOVE NEGATIVITY

No matter how gloomy the day is, above it all the sun still shines faithful and sure. In similar fashion, no matter how gloomy our minds feel, no matter what circumstances we are facing, no matter how things appear to our sense's minds, we must continue to strive until the sun reappears faithful and sure.

The world lives and thrives on negativity. The systems of the world have all been craftily designed to submerge us in negativity. Whether it be the news reports or any number of the fear crazed people of the world, our primary job is to endeavor to live above it. If we acquiesce to what things look like or if we hang on the sincere words of the so-called experts, we will find ourselves miserable and defeated. Life is not good because it always seems so, but rather because we know the goodness and blessings are there, despite what things appear to be. We aren't defeated until we accept the forecast. Don't accept the forecast.

What happens in your life, whether it be good or bad, largely happens because of the things you choose to believe. You decide what it is you will and will not believe. However, your beliefs must be founded upon something true. To base your beliefs and actions on the appearance of things leads only to being blown about by every wind of doctrine! Sadly, this is exactly how most people live. If the world says it is hard to find a job that pays good money, thus believing, the people settle for less money. If the news report predicts tough times ahead, expecting so, the people anticipate difficulties and find them. If the doctors and scientists say this activity leads to this disease, people curtail the activity and still get the disease. You simply cannot believe everything that you hear! Health and prosperity come from God and the truth has no caveats nor exceptions.

The problem with negativity is that it fashions and forms your expectations. Being negative, with the rest of the huddled masses, leads you down a predictable path that always ends in defeat. Just as nothing can come from corn but corn, nothing can come from negatives but more things to be negative about. You can't keep wrapping your mind in darkness then wonder why you can't see what's going on. You aren't being realistic or responsible or whatever other rationalization you've been talked into using. But instead, you are simply being deceived. You have become a cooperator with ignorance, working against your own best interest under the guise of being "realistic" or in today's terms, "real!" What is real or actual or true is what God says is real and actual and true. To consider otherwise is to slide down the same greased path with the rest of mankind to your own destruction, hurt and loss.

Positivity isn't fanciful or foolish or whim. Positivity is the basis on which your whole life has been conceived. What is foolish is to look around and draw wrong conclusions based on appearances. I can tell you this with all certainty and confidence, the things that mean the most to you, those aspects of life wherein you seek success, will never look as if you are about to get them until you actually overcome and get them! This is the contest and the mystery of life. The whole world lives and suffers amidst frustration because of their learned negativity. Being positive; being determined to think positively, expecting the best no matter appearances opens the very portals of heaven to help you live upon the earth in the moments of your life right now.

In order to be a positive person, you must strive. You have to fight for what is right. You have to contend in order to get the things God wants for your life. If you had no spiritual opponent, the things you ardently seek would come to you easily, effortlessly. All that you pursued would turn into gold with minimal effort on your part. However, you have an opponent and the way he steals from you is by convincing you of things that aren't true. He sours your disposition and leaves you cynical and bitter. Through the systemization of error, he makes the right ways seem wrong and the wrong ways seem right. He convinces you that your attitude, though negative, is proper and fitting given the circumstances that surround you. He persuades you to expect the worst and even when good happens, to view it tentatively as fleeting and bound not to last. Add to that all manner of superstition and rituals that mean nothing and do nothing to preserve your happiness. Yet on you go, knocking on wood and modifying your expectations, hoping good things will last and bad things will stay away.

The only sure way to secure your own happiness and refute negativity is to determine within yourself to be a positive person. People flock towards a positive person like they seek out the sun. Drowning in negatives, people need good words and good deeds to restore their beliefs. They need an alternate viewpoint. In continuing to be positive, not ignorant but positive, you set a pattern for the things you do want in your life, which serves to root out the things you don't want in your life. Just as a room doesn't become fresh until you freely admit air and sunshine into it, your mind won't become fresh and alive until you admit sunny thoughts and blessed expectations into it. Life works out better for the positive person, not because everything always goes well, but because despite what is going on now, in the end it will all be well.

Whatever storm you find yourself besieged by, know this, above the clouds of doom and despair the sun is still shining, ever shining as you strive against the negativity and find the Love and Goodness that has always existed for you...

SOLVING YOUR ANXIETY ISSUES

Living in the world today, you have likely been convinced that it is perfectly normal to have anxiety and that it is actually a natural part of life. And, although our overtly negative society has normalized and rationalized the experience, it is completely unnatural and is something you should seek to exterminate each and every time it encroaches on your life. Imagine that something or someone greater than yourself would purposefully design life to be an overly anxious affair and leave you no recourse in overcoming its daily onslaughts and attacks. Well, imagine no further because it simply isn't true. Learn to rid yourself of any and all anxiety, code name vague fear, secret name, defeat!

Growing up as a particularly scared individual, I completely acclimatized myself to anxiety and couldn't have even comprehended what it meant to have true peace. I, like you, I suppose, found methods to cope, beginning with whistling, humming and chewing gum as a child, graduating up to self-medicating and other escape seeking behaviors as a young adult. In short, I was running from that feeling; the apprehensive, something is going to go wrong or something is going to get me or, what if I end up here or there or some other undesirable destination? feeling... It was never clear enough for me to wrap my mind around it, but it was distinct enough to take away my rest. Then, right in the midst of my ego-driven, perpetual desire to work it out on my own, a nice guy named Jon taught me about God, loved me and introduced me to a class called Power for Abundant Living that changed my life forever.

PFAL, as we affectionately called it, taught me about my number one enemy, fear, and how to overcome it with God's Word. The class showed me the source of fear and anxiety and that it certainly wasn't something I should embrace or learn to accept in my life. It taught me that I needed to control my thoughts and, maybe, for the first time in my life, learn how to think properly. And the result was one of the most unusual, odd things I had ever experienced in my life. Suddenly, unexpectedly, my heart was completely at rest and I was experiencing true peace, the kind that surpasses understanding. Wow! There is truly nothing like it in the world. It is the absence of all conflict. It is knowing you have absolutely nothing to fear in any capacity, in any way. It is how human beings were intended to live. In fact, we were supposed to get so accustomed to the peace we enjoyed that any threat to it or any disturbance was immediately detected, so we could act, so we could win.

But sadly, that is not how life works for most people. We live our lives pushed from pillar to post, hurried, exhausted, overworked, overtaxed with outrageous expectations for ourselves that we foolishly call success. Meanwhile, our day collapses if we eat a donut for breakfast, or miss morning meditations by six minutes, or aren't earning six-figure salaries by the time we are 28. There's nothing wrong with self-improvement, but is it ourselves we are improving or some fictitious version of ourselves we got from an influencer or Instagram or some other well-known spokesperson for society? We can't even sit down in the evening to relax without some "don't waste time" expectation nagging us to get back up. We've got work to do, by God, and if we don't get it all done now, some almighty total collapse is looming on the horizon! We work full-time, have work that needs to be accomplished at home after work and work to be handled on the weekend. If we stay in our PJs all day on Sunday, we feel terrible because we've lost valuable yardage in the race of the rats! And you know why we are killing ourselves to get it all done? Because we are afraid! Because we think we must carry the entire load of living on our own backs, and every step missed has the potential to spiral our lives into failure! We are party of the first part, party of the second part and party of every damn part in between! We think we are God Himself, but instead of enjoying love and peace, we are chock full of anxiety! It's no wonder, folks...

Philosophize, self-aggrandize, get more education, pull yourself up by your own bootstraps, seek more opinions, more Google searches or more WebMD, you aren't going to rid yourself of this persistent malady on your own. You need spiritual truth to combat the abundance of spiritual error. You need to finally concede that God never intended for you to figure it all out for yourself. He never wanted you to drive yourself into a frazzle making sure things always worked out. God only wanted to be party of the first part ensuring all of your second and third parts worked out. If you're honest, your anxiety is always related to some fear you have about something that you need or might need in the future. Or, your anxiety is based on some unchangeable, unrepairable mistake from your past that only lives on in your mind and not in actual reality. In both cases you are playing an "away game" you cannot win because neither time period presently exists. Anxiety, solely based on the present circumstances, prompts you to make changes, which you are fully able to do. Now, you're playing "at home!"

Do yourself a solid and stop being so smart. Accept your limitations like children do and simply ask for what you need.

Getting your needs met may involve some work, but good old-fashioned work never made anybody anxious. Cease from trying to carry a world of concerns you were never meant to carry. Stop pretending to be God minus all of the infinite spiritual power and intelligence and ability! In fact, stop pretending to be okay and blowing past that anxiety as if it's normal, choosing to use your mouth to ask for assistance instead of using your mouth to ingest or swallow or inhale something to make you feel a little better. You, my friend, owe yourself and your Creator that much, don't you think?

Someone or something sold you tornadoes and hurricanes so you might be satisfied with thunderstorms and gale-force winds, while calm, blessed sunshine was not listed as an option.

INNER DISTURBANCES

Having just traveled back from beautiful, warm southern California, I can certainly appreciate the blessing and reverie that accompanies a calm, sunny day with absolutely no weather disturbances. Far less frequently, perhaps, I've been a part of turbulent storms deluged with rain, howling winds and general upset feelings of turmoil and unrest. During storms, the accepted notion is to get through the disturbed weather and back to the calm; the sooner, the better. Our ideal state of mind is also found in peaceful, pleasant warmth of thought, and as such it is our duty to track down and eliminate all sources of disturbance and turbulence that seek to assault us day by day...

You might be surprised to learn that we all have a mental environment that we maintain day by day. Our mental environment might be best represented by the weather. Our mental weather, like physical weather, is not a permanent condition but rather something that ebbs and flows depending upon where we live (mentally). However, unlike the physical weather, we have complete control over our mental weather no matter what is going on around us. The trouble is that many of you have lived in the bad weather for so long that you have resigned yourself to it, considering it "normal." You've accepted it like a thunderstorm and concluded it is just a part of life. You believe it is to be expected as a human to have persistent anxiety and perpetual worries blowing your mind around like chance gusts of wind! Instead of getting to the bottom of the disturbances, you wait and wait for the sun to come back out or produce some artificial sunlight through chemicals and other distractions. You are so disturbed you are no longer aware you are disturbed.

Think back to the times when your mind wasn't a helter-skelter of confusing thoughts and unusual sensations. Try to recall when you didn't rashly assume your job was to think your way out of looming disasters, thereby eliminating the need for constant fret and worry. Picture yourself fondly consumed in the moment with no particular inclination to find the surreptitious beast looming behind every corner seeking to bring you woe. Do you remember? You may have been a child or even perhaps a young adult. In some cases, you might have even been in middle age yet delightfully caught up in some combination of sublime conditions. No matter the time period, the age or the conditions, those times of sun-drenched days came around and persisted because you were making proper use of your mind. There should be nothing associated with adulthood that requires living amidst perpetual shitty weather! Boiling up with worry, anxiety and fear are not traits associated with maturity or heightened awareness of the pitfalls of life. They are instead just that... worry, anxiety and fear! And like any good student, you learned their ways and adopted them for yourself. Someone or something sold you tornadoes and hurricanes so you might be satisfied with thunderstorms and gale-force winds, while calm, blessed sunshine was not listed as an option.

The good news is that your weather forecast is entirely changeable, dependent upon how serious you are about getting above the clouds. You can learn, no matter what has assailed you in the past, to develop a calm, peaceful, settled mind and experience a clarity that formerly eluded you. However, you, similar to your dealings with the physical weather, aren't going to be able to do this on your own. You aren't going to brace yourself up by your own bootstraps and get the job done. Do you know why? Because your limited, finite senses' logic is not capable of getting the job done. Welcome to humanity! The slippery tricks that planted the storm clouds in your noggin' planted them there based on what you did not know! Instead, if you want to get to the sunshine, the sweet repose, the perfect day, it is necessary for you to get back to the Source of light and sunshine directly. I don't know what it is about people that compels them to figure everything out on their own. Remember when you knew you didn't know? How sweet that time was...

Your heartfelt conversation with the One that invented thinking is as simple as, "Lord, I read a thing today that said I didn't have to live with all this turbulence in my head. (You know how I hate turbulence!) Help me to get back to that sweet place and show me how to do it!" With God, it never needs be any more complicated than that. You'll discover a fantastic thing when you finally figure out how hard you have been making everything and just ask for help. Children have the good sense not to accept mental disturbances, and on those rare occasions when they are troubled, they are going to let you know about it fairly quickly. You see, they are still children of the sunshine!

Today is the day to get your head to California! Now is the time to seek something better for yourself. Stop succumbing to the fear and terror that ravages the planet and your mind. Quit accepting anxiety as a normal condition and the medications that go with it. Believe to experience life as you were intended to experience it. Get to that place because that place exists, and it's not reserved for those who do anything other than believe! Ask, believe and see...

When confronted with the storms of life, declare, "Peace be still..." and then go back to sleep... ;-)

THE INDECISION TRAP

Have you ever had that nagging feeling that there is something else you need to do? I'm not talking about the time you left the iron on or forgot to close the garage door. I'm talking about the larger decisions you make; the ones that define your life and your contribution to the world. All of us have that special something that we alone can give, and that won't come into evidence unless we give it. Well, that feeling has besieged me lately and seemed worthy of further exploration...

None of us climb the hill to success without first making a decision. Before anything worthwhile can take place in your life; before any real overcoming; before any victory over the things that formerly held you down; of necessity comes a heartfelt, fully persuaded decision. Absent a decision, your life will continue to flounder around somewhere between distraction and mediocrity. Sure, you'll be very busy and have little time for extra activities, but you will end up missing the mark; the only mark that ever truly mattered. So, with all that is at stake, why don't we make the decision?

One slippery tentacle in the indecision trap is the old familiar "waiting for a feeling!" It seems in America, the land of feelings, we've all been mesmerized by the promise of strong, passionate feelings clearly marking the way that we should go; some grand purpose that causes our eyes to well with tears. Some folks call it inspiration, and while we all need to be inspired, we might be surprised to learn that feelings follow our decisions and not the other way around. The stronger your decision, the more powerful your emotions that accompany it. While you are so patiently waiting for your ship to come in, your ship is out at sea waiting for *you* to decide! Decisions don't need to be accompanied by feelings; they just need to be decided with adamancy!

Often indecision appears not because we cannot see the value of making a decision but because we are stuck with too many different choices. We would like this, and we would like that. This would make us happy and shoot, so would that! Remember when you were looking for a new job? Chances are you broadened your options to sort of increase your chances for success. You started enumerating things that "could work." At its core, this also is a trap, albeit a subtle one. The odds are hugely in favor of you getting what you want the VERY most! Otherwise, you scatter your forces on a giant dartboard hoping to stick somewhere with something that could work... And because you aren't God and don't know the future possibilities contained in different circumstances, you certainly make application broadly, but in your heart, you hold fast to what would be the best for you. Minus all of the fear and doubt, you know what is the best, because you know you, don't you?

Now, there is one area in decision-making that encompasses all of the rest of the tentacles and maybe the mouth full of sharp teeth as well. At its root, indecision is always based on fear. Let's say you know you have something special just waiting to be capitalized. You know when it comes to such and such, you've got it going on! Yet, you don't take action. You vacillate on making the decision. You rationalize with, maybe I won't be successful, and it is far easier to just keep quasi-planning and dreaming and scheming without ever really making a choice. If you don't make a wholehearted decision, you can delay and delay and delay. Put it off. Maybe next year.

Perhaps when I get this other thing worked out first. After I've finished such and such. One day when I have enough... (money, free time, energy, lack of stress, warm weather, ideal settings, etc., etc.). This is the definition of indecision. It feels (there's that word again) so much safer. It's like having one foot on the bridge and one foot in the water. It's hedging your bets. It is doubt, hesitation, wavering and vacillating. It feels painless, but it guarantees you one thing and one thing only. You aren't going to get what you really want to get! It's not going to happen! It isn't in the cards! In order to win in your life, in your way, with your own results, you have to either get all the way in the water or all the way on the damn bridge. Don't you see it?

When it comes to this decision-making process, there is a great possibility of you making the wrong choice. Well, so what! Indecision is also a choice, and unlike a wrong choice, it won't provide you with the learning you need to make the right choice next time! Just imagine how great your life could be if you made a habit of deciding what you want and, by God, sticking to that choice! Picture your life being lived on your terms, with you being the leading actor. Have you ever watched some movie star or famous athlete that seems to have it all and secretly thought, I wish that was my life? Well, I submit the only difference between your life and theirs is that somewhere along the line, they made some choices that you, heretofore, have yet to make...

The good life isn't reserved for the lucky or the fortunate or the blessed. The good life is waiting for the people who make decisions, and there's no limit on the choices you can make. Don't spend another day lost in indecision and fear of the future. Get busy designing your ideal life, then make some decisions about how it is going to turn out. Don't wait and see. Don't wait on God; God is waiting on you. Decide!

CALM DOWN

I remember a time when my wife and I were talking to some friends, and she said something that sparked my happy meter and forever etched itself in my heart. She remarked, "Tony isn't like me, he has a calm mind..." What a nice thing to say! And I have to admit my mind is generally very calm, despite the occasional times I'm like a duck on the water, appearing serene but paddling like hell underneath (smile). So, as you may have already guessed, this story is about cultivating a calm mind.

Before I highlight some key principles, I think it's important to understand the why. Your mind is the center of your life. It's not just part of your experience; it is your experience. It's the largest determining factor in how your life progresses. And, as the central hub from which your life proceeds, it has to be in order. Imagine trying to run a business with a thousand random papers and files all over your desk. Picture your warehouse operation functioning properly with no system in place. Instead of success, you would experience chaos which may be an apt description of many people's lives. Good things, great ideas, quiet, gentle guidance, self-control, and the ability to problem solve all come from a calm mind.

An agitated, upset mind is like your mouth when you leave the dentist's chair. You're drooling and biting through your tongue; your face is sagging and you are completely unaware of it. Or said another way, all kinds of junk is happening to you; affecting you; harassing you, but you are too distracted to see what's going on. It's similar to trying to find your ring at the bottom of the pool while the water is agitated. You've got to wait until the "agua" settles down before you can see. You get it?

You're not alone in your anxiety because the whole world is in turmoil. People suffer in silence because they think it's normal. Some have never experienced true peace. But, you should know that you were not designed to live that way. You were specifically designed with a mind so that you could direct your life. You're not an animal with built-in instinctual behavior. You're a human being who needs a calm mind. Interestingly, letting everything go; being perpetually distracted and overwhelmed actually reduces your life to the level of the common beast. You sort of sniff around seeking to get your basic needs met with no thought about what you could really accomplish or experience if you got your base of operations in order.

Stop for a moment to consider how many thoughts go through your mind in a day. How many of them are negative, critical or fear-inducing? If you are inexperienced in controlling your thinking (and yes, you can control your thinking), I would wager many, if not most, of your thoughts fall into these categories. "You're an idiot for forgetting that meeting." "Look how fat you've gotten, you big slob!" "Why don't things ever work out for me?" "No one gives a damn about me." "My stomach hurts. I hope it's not cancer." You can multiply these thoughts out indefinitely. What runs through your mind isn't the biggest issue. The crucible that separates calm from chaos is what you do or don't do about those thoughts. You can't crap on yourself all day long then wonder why you feel anxious. And trust me, it is occurring even if you don't recognize it. You don't recognize it because you are distracted and if you add up enough distraction, you feel overwhelmed! Simplistic? Maybe. True? Likely.

In order to find your way to tranquility, you have to do some work with your mind. The peace is already there for you, but you aren't experiencing it because of those rogue thoughts you are letting go. Your primary job is to fight back. Challenge that assertion! For God's sake, don't just resign yourself. You may be a pacifist. You might be the most non-confrontational person on Earth. But, if someone keeps punching you in the nose every day, at some point you'd have to punch back. Not fighting back parallels the distress affecting your nose region. You've heard of the calm before the storm, right? Well, there's also a calm after the storm. Peace comes at the end of the fight. You can gauge your success rate by how you feel. But make no mistake, like it or not, you have to take it on. It's like quitting smoking. It feels impossible at first, but day by day, it gets easier. At some point you may even forget you ever smoked.

Once you begin to win that battle in your mind each day, your calm returns like that feral cat you've been feeding. In that space of calmness; of tranquility; at peace, you can finally see. Not the cat silly (smile), the trouble when it shows up. You're at last in a position to handle the issues on the front end. As you cultivate this habit, you get more and more accustomed to the peace. In your peaceful state you can sort out the issues; recognize your triggers; think through your problems objectively and best of all, hear that still small voice ever able and willing to give you a solution. You're no longer distracted by the 100-fold fears that assault your mind. You cannot be overwhelmed because you've been handling your business in the only time period you can affect - now!

Tempest-tossed souls, wherever ye may be, under whatsoever conditions ye may live, know this, in the ocean of life the isles of Blessedness are smiling, and the sunny shore of your ideal awaits your coming. Keep your hand firmly upon the helm of thought. In the bark of your soul reclines the commanding Master; He does but sleep: wake Him. Self-control is strength; Right Thought is mastery; Calmness is power. Say unto your heart, "Peace, be still!" ~ James Allen

Maybe then, the best way to get that real life you've been pining away for, is to stop seeking it so exhaustively and work rather on getting rid of the stuff that is taking it away from you.

REAL LIFE IS THE ABSENCE OF...

One of the most grand, important and hugely significant realizations of our times seems to center on life; a REAL LIFE! Let's face it, we are all trying to get a life. We want a life filled with happiness and love. We want variety and vibrancy and delight. We want to wake up in the morning excited for the day, with our hearts full of love and joy and peace. And all of us, yes, every single one of us, are seeking the exact same thing in infinite variations. So, the million-dollar question is, is the real life we so ardently desire something we can get or rather the absence of something we've been getting?

The cheap answer would appear to be finding that special "something" out there that promises to heal all of our wounds; solve all of our dilemmas; straighten all of our crookedness and infuse us with lasting vitality! But, the vastly more costly answer is found on the other side, in the absence of...

Life, behind all of the sense knowledge coverings, always boils down to two things, good and evil. But, here's where it gets interesting. Life's greater realities are not really two distinct entities, but rather one true entity and one illusory entity. The illusory entity is not anything in itself except the absence of the true entity. Wow, crazy talk, huh? Let me explain... The opposite of life is death. Death is simply the absence of life. Darkness is merely the absence of light. Fear is the absence of love, or to put it another way, love is the absence of fear. Peace is the absence of trouble or the end of the struggle. All of life's negatives represent the absence of something good; something we were designed to have!

As I mused this idea, I thought about how many of us are seeking and toiling and searching for that special something, never considering that, that "special" something is already here for us. It's quite literally all around us. It's found in the mighty oak tree and in the most delicate orchid. It's in the warmth of the sunlight and the sound of the ocean. It's in the eyes of your grandchildren and the smile from your mother. Life, beautiful life, real life just is and requires no help from you or me. And when you see life, there is no mistaking it for what it is, that is unless you've allowed the darkness to hold sway.

The other side of life, the absence of it, seeks to blind your eyes from the real life God intended for you. It makes you afraid and anxious about life. It steals away your peace by introducing agitation and unrest. It robs you of your enthusiasm and energy by getting you to dwell on its negative illusions. It works to occupy your mind with nothingness and pointlessness and would, if allowed to, reduce your life into one long, useless travail on an empty road leading nowhere! It's behind every sickness, every sorrow, every lost hope, and every miserable thing that ever happened. Its work is displayed in every murder, every suicide, and in every rape. And all of it, every single piece of it, is nothing more than the absence of goodness and love and light!

Maybe then, the best way to get that real life you've been pining away for, is to stop seeking it so exhaustively and work rather on getting rid of the stuff that is taking it away from you. Instead of searching the world over for love, get rid of your fear. Love comes from life who also goes by the name, God! And, before I continue let me give you a sidelight which is really the whole light. You are not going to find that real life you are after without God's help. You know how I know? Because you haven't found it on your own yet, have you? Oh, you can try, and you can fill your mind with endless theories, but in the end, you won't find life because you haven't yet found God!

Instead of doing all kinds of shenanigans to find peace, why not work on eliminating the agitations and the trouble. Trouble cannot exist without your cooperation because it's a parasite feeding off your thoughts. To become agitated or maybe stay agitated, you have to continue entertaining the evil thought. Thinking it, or often in my case, analyzing it, only serves to permit its entree that much longer. The solution isn't to clear your mind of all thought, but rather to replace agitating thoughts with thoughts of peace.

If you feel depressed or bored or just plain weary, begin to track down which thoughts are sucking away your energy. Your energy comes from the life force and is always there for you. However, certain thoughts, certain activities steal away that precious energy and leave you life-less! There's almost nothing more energizing than to begin a new day with new thoughts and a renewed anticipation.

If you don't know what to do or where to go or how to navigate your way, turn on the light (God's Word). Dwelling on the darkness won't bring forth the light because darkness is and always will be, the absence of light. The reason so many people are profoundly stuck in life is because they spend almost all of their precious days dwelling on everything that isn't right. Dwelling on sickness won't bring forth health. Dwelling on problems doesn't engender solutions. Dwelling on lack never forces prosperity.

At the end of the day, to the end of your life, you have one thing you can control and that is your mind. Your mind is where all of the good things live. You should no more allow evil to permeate your thoughts than you would allow a poisonous snake to hang out in your living room. The only way to make your house safe again would be to get rid of the "thing" making it unsafe. It doesn't require long prayers or voodoo doctors or snake charmers, it requires a decision in your mind, namely, no more snakes!

The one and only "real life" is already there, waiting for you. It is infused into everything that life is... To find it you only need to once and for all rid yourself of everything that is blinding you to its reality. The time is short my friends, so short. You've got one shot at this thing. Learn how to get rid of everything that holds you back. You know how to do it? Ask God to teach you. If this made any sense to you, just imagine how good it would be to get it from the Source!

Real life... man, what a concept!

THE YOKES ON YOU

Fear is the silent epidemic that thwarts all hopes and dreams. Fear is the great hold-back and reason you procrastinate. Fear is the imposing wall between you and everything you ever wanted. Fear rules the entire world and few escape its grasp. Fear is your worst and most pervasive enemy. Fear is a yoke of slavery and the yoke is on you!

Nothing in life retards your progress like fear does. Fear stops you dead in your tracks. Fear will make you turn back when you need to move ahead. It works to silence the voice that is truly yours and ever seeks to make you into someone you are not. And although all these things are probably very obvious, folks just march on frustrated and working hard, pretending and faking; trying and trying; hoping and wishing, with little or no results.

You would think that the hardest thing in the world was actually getting what you want given the amount of energy you have spent trying to arrive. Now, I don't mean getting some needs met here and there. I'm talking about being and doing everything you ever wanted to do. I'm referring to that "more than abundant" life God promised His children. I'm getting at the A+ life! That dream life; however it looks to you, is waiting around for you; not to figure everything out but to get rid of the obstacle, the blocker, the real effin' problem... fear! Funny (peculiar), everyone denies its existence and everyone lives under its yoke. Again, the yoke is on you!

It's time to get honest, folks. It's high time to recognize the real issue. It's not the economy, racism, where you live, your upbringing, the police, your education level, climate change, the terrorists, politics, money or lack thereof, your IQ, EQ or Ps and Qs; it's you! Just let that sink in for a minute... Everything you really, really want but don't have is because of your fear. Obliterate the anxiety-ridden doubt. Cast off the heavy burden, worry. Kill off every semblance of fear and you will find every good thing you desire. You'll find it because it is already there, well hidden by the obscuring, deadening clouds of fear.

If you really want to live the A+ life and find the contentment and fulfillment you know deep down you desperately need, invest yourself in eliminating fear. Nothing good can come from bad no matter the disguise. Bad begets bad and fear is bad. If your motive is fear, for anything you do, the result can only be more fear. If you work hard out of fear, you won't succeed. If you give to others based on fear, you won't enjoy a harvest. Fear is an illusion. Fear is an expectation of defeat. Fear, through deception, brings negative results into your life. Fear is always about you. And, the only lasting solution to fear is love.

Love is the light that illuminates your path. Love isn't blind, it's just willing to see less. Love nurtures and encourages and builds. Love is never discouraged or impatient or frustrated. Love heals and revitalizes. Love warms and softens. Love removes every yoke. Love knows that what it seeks always comes to pass and there's no power on earth greater than it. Love never fails. God is love.

The only possible way you can finally escape from the yoke of fear is by making the decision to love. So simple, yet so profoundly difficult. Real love isn't all about you, it's all about everyone else. Love doesn't have time to sulk and brood and feel sorry for itself. Love doesn't take what it already has for granted. Love doesn't judge and criticize and condemn. Love seeks to relieve the suffering in others. Love wants to lend a helping hand. Love gives and gives and gives expecting nothing in return. Love speaks lavish words of kindness. Love forgives everything and everyone, knowing the true source of the wrong done. Love is tender-hearted and not afraid of revealing itself, for there is nothing wrong of itself. Love is the only enduring answer.

When you head out into the world tomorrow, instead of bracing yourself to be bold and brave and courageous; taking on fear wherever it shows up, do something different instead. Stop making it about you and make it about someone else. Quit pursuing your life's dreams and help make someone else's dream a reality. Love those people around you that you take for granted every day. Love those people all around you. Just love them. Speak words of kindness and encouragement. Let your real heart out without fear of someone hurting it. Give your goodness to those folks at work. Have compassion on them and forgive them. Look deeply into their eyes and honestly seek their good. Heal them, help them, love them. Perfect love casts out fear.

The funny (peculiar) thing about love is that when you do it with all of your heart, all that you ever wanted for yourself comes to you without effort and striving and trying so hard. The door will open without you knocking. The opportunity will arise from the place you least expected. Your place, your purpose will find you because you finally found it, by deciding to love. So "funny" that getting everything you ever wanted was never based on pursuing everything you ever wanted, but rather by changing your focus to someone else.

The yoke's on them, so why not help to remove it?

CHAPTER SEVEN
Love

THE LOVE FACTOR

There is one thing the whole world needs, and there is one thing the whole world seeks, and that is love. Love is the unifying power of the universe. Love is the answer to every heartfelt question. Love is an unstoppable force. Love is the reason and motive for every human life. Love never fails and God is love. When your life feels off-track or unfulfilled or empty, the cause is always a lack of that love. In order to live a real life, you need much, much love. You need to employ the love factor!

Life absent love is not a real life. Days spent earning and churning to succeed and get ahead; to outwork and outproduce; to lead the pack; to be the top dog, when lacking love as the motive, end only in a material gratification amidst an empty soul. Rewards gained through arduous effort and toil without love behind them leave a man desolate and unfulfilled. The ambitious drive for success is not wrong, but becomes so in the heart and life of the man without love as the only alternative to love is fear. Fear motivation, though powerful, cannot help but produce more of the same.

People today exist in a world that repudiates love. Love is somehow viewed as soft or weak. Love is considered too vulnerable and is reserved only for the closest of family and friends. Love freely given seems to come with a risk, the risk of possible rejection, ridicule or shame. In order to properly insulate your tender heart, you think it plausible to armor your heart with hardness, a tough exterior impenetrable to outside jabs and assaults. You wrongly conclude that a hardened heart cannot be reached and in so doing close yourself off to life's greatest reality. In your hardness and calloused response, you fail to recognize the true sensitivity of life and in no longer feeling, miss everything. On your deathbed all that will matter to you is the people that you love and the people that love you. Your life begins and ends in love.

God in His basic essence is love and accordingly, if you lack love, is the sole thing missing from your life. You don't need more relationships; you need ONE relationship from which ALL relationships take shape and blossom! Your relationship with Him is not one of faultfinding and bondage under the hand of the moral police, but instead one of unfathomable love, unlimited forgiveness and unending, unearned, divine favor allowing you to at last prosper and thrive! God is the life you once dared to imagine unfolding in infinite variety and blessedness. God is love without conditions. God is tender and kind and able to warm your soul, demonstrating in your life a complete and unquenchable restoration. God loves you first so you can love Him next, ending in your love being extended to the world.

Life on Earth has not gone south because of poor presidents or liberal agendas or the lack of a simpler time. The world has gone astray because of the victory of fear over love. The more you allow the world to make you afraid and conclude there is no solution, the more you help perpetuate the same. You remain powerless to shape the course of the world, but your true power resides in your decision to love. Every deliverance from bondage, every healing, every setting a captive free was done so in love. In fact, every good thing you ever did, every lasting impact, every difference you made, only did so because of your love. Love never fails and is the antithesis and antidote to fear. Love properly exercised and freely given brightens the hearts of men and adds light to a world engulfed in darkness.

The love factor is an unstoppable force. But, to have a true imprint in the hearts of men, it must be initiated and given by you. Love the unlovable. Offer people kindness. Be that sweet soul for people. Decide to care about them and be the one among a thousand that helped them. Don't give them all your money; give them all your heart! Don't concern yourself with what the world says. Concern yourself with what God says and, in so doing, set people free. People don't need unlimited riches; they need the right words at the right time from a heart of love; from your heart of love. Love has no complexity in it, no wrong motive, no pretense. Love not to be known as a lover, but because you already are...

Living love, working your love factor, you will find that life begins to take on a glow that encourages and refreshes your heart. Things begin to settle down on the inside. Peace will reign where anxiety once ruled. Your concerns will be that of others and you will finally be able to let go of *almighty self*. And God working in you as the ultimate source of love, will ensure that everything you need will be there before you can even ask for it. Odd as it seems, that is the true design, the Master's ultimate plan!

Are you unhappy, unfulfilled and empty? Does it all seem so futile and pointless? If so, it does so because your heart has been hardened and the softening is found in love. Get yourself directly to the source. Talk to God and tell Him how you feel. Open your heart to Him. Believe that He is and see if He will not reward and bless your decision. Everything you ever wanted to experience in life is found in love; in God who is love! Don't be afraid anymore. Use the love factor! Choose love!

As the gentle, spring sunshine and moisture encourages all living things to grow, while melting away the harshness of the long winter, you melt away the hardness of your heart by returning to love.

LOVE IS THE ONLY WHY

"I'm in all of it. ... I was there in her laugh but I'm also here in your pain. I'm the reason for everything. I am the why. Don't try to live without me, Howard. Please don't." ~ Aimee Moore, Collateral Beauty. Last night I watched a beautiful movie about a man (Will Smith) searching for answers following the death of his child. In his quest, he sought answers from death, time and love. Love's apt response for life was, "I am the reason for everything. I am the why..." Love will always be the only "why."

Behind every heartbeat in life is love. It is the life-giving solution to a world lost in emptiness and pain. It is the light that shines in the darkness. It is the warmth of a sunny day. It refutes fear and is the only motive that is always right. It is sought for by all and obscured for so many. It is ever-present and waiting behind very corner. It can make all it touches beautiful and can soften even the hardest heart. It will always be your only "why."

For all of the negative events that can happen in your life; for all the things that can go astray; for all of your sorrow and losses and pain, nothing takes away the joy of living more than the absence of love. You began your life full of love, both in receiving and giving. As your mother poured her love into you, you poured your love back into her. As your father's love flowed through his hand into your hand, your love flowed back from your hand to his hand as well. Living life with love was for you as natural as breathing. If you didn't receive the love you needed, you found others that would give it to you and you back to them. Love was your only "why."

Sadly, as you aged, you found that love wasn't as plentiful in the world. The people you interacted with had hearts that were hardened through difficulty and rejection. And, as they built up walls around their hearts in an attempt at self-preservation, you built up walls around your own heart as well. Like a callous on your hand, your heart became desensitized to love. Many find themselves groping through life looking for the love that already lives inside them, behind self-made barriers. In their numbness, they seek love in alcohol, in recognition, in admiration, in romance after romance. They aspire for wealth, extreme fitness, plastic surgery and anything that promises them the love they've been searching for all along, yet unable to see it because of the hardness of their hearts. They forgot love was their only "why."

Your hardness of heart wasn't something you intended, but rather a response to your own experience of life. As the world gnawed away at you, you couldn't perceive what was happening. You internalized its messages of guilt and shame. You accepted responsibility for every weakness and shortcoming and falsely concluded that there was something wrong with you. You became afraid to express who you really are and opted instead to portray yourself as someone else; someone you felt people would love. You carried around your failings like sandbags, refusing to set your own self free. You just couldn't imagine that you deserved any better. You never understood that your feelings are universal feelings, and even in moments of rejection, the people rejecting you needed the love as much as you did. For all people, love is the only "why..."

Finding the love that you feel has been eluding you, isn't in doing better, being better or working harder. It's not a function of discipline or reading books or in finding your soul mate. Love is manifested in giving. True love gives of itself freely and unreservedly, not by pretense, but in truth. You give out your love to other people and to yourself. You give love to yourself by giving yourself a break. You love yourself by deciding to no longer think disparaging thoughts about yourself and accept yourself for who you are. You cease giving love conditions to maintain and love yourself unconditionally. You love yourself by changing your focus from yourself, your stuff, your hang-ups, your frustrations, to other people's stuff and hang-ups and frustrations. You offer them love and unending forgiveness. You speak kindness and tenderness and sweetness and you refuse to speak otherwise. You remind them that love is their only "why!"

As the gentle, spring sunshine and moisture encourages all living things to grow, while melting away the harshness of the long winter, you melt away the hardness of your heart by returning to love. You don't need a wall to protect your heart, you need a heart that's full of love. Love is the life-giving source of the universe. God is love. Love climbs the highest mountains and swims the greatest depths. Love chooses the object of its adoration by decision, not a feeling, and thus gives and gives and gives. As you give, you receive back a thousandfold, for love is a generous giver. Love is the only "why."

Love is all around you, my friends, seeking life-giving expression through you. Don't refuse love its entrée to your heart, nor stifle its flow from your heart to another's. In love you will see again the wonder that is all around you. It is in your grandson's eyes, your wife's laughter and your mother's touch. It's on the pages of a good book, in the walls of your home and under your feet in your own backyard. It's in the wag of your old dog's tail and the embrace of a good friend. Love is forever the only "why," so be sure to notice her collateral beauty...

Love is the reason for everything...

Don't try to live without it.

WHERE IS THE LOVE?

How absurd it is to think that man is on the earth as the last stop on the evolutionary chain! Do you really believe that you are simply an offshoot from a gorilla, with less hair and the ability to process information? With all of our intellectual ability, sometimes we ain't so smart! Not only do you have the ability to think, but more importantly you have the profound capacity to feel. Dogs are affectionate, but you get the privilege to love. Love is the greatest thing in the world and without it life would screech to a halt. So, I ask you, where's the love, man?

Love isn't something that happens to you, love is something that you choose to do. It always amuses me when people act as if love just happens to your heart, because, you know, the heart knows... Your heart is you, you silly rabbit. When the conditions are all lined up, you choose to do it. So, what should you do when the conditions don't line up? You should love anyway. I don't have to tell you how wonderful life becomes when love is involved, right? Well, imagine choosing that experience at all times.

I can remember sitting through a class called, Power for Abundant Living. PFAL, the initials of the class, gained a permanent place in the form of a tattoo on my left forearm. That's how life-changing the class was for me. Above everything else, the class taught me about God's love and incredibly for maybe the first time, I learned to love myself. Even more incredulously, I learned that I had to love myself before I could love other people. But, here's where it gets tricky. Loving other people wasn't something that just happened to me because I felt a certain way. Love was something I had to choose to do, just like I chose to do with myself. And because I was so filled with God's love (which is synonymous with being filled with His Word), I did it like it was my job! I chose to be kind, tender-hearted and forgiving. I chose to build people up rather than tear them down! I was on the high road baby and everything started working out.

As the years rolled on however, I sort of forgot the most important part of my former success. Oh, I still knew God's Word, but I forgot the love part. God's Word without the love part is still true, but became hollow and empty in terms of my personal happiness. I had become religious. I did all of the behaviors minus the love. And when I reflect back on those empty years, I realize that instead of choosing to love, I was waiting to feel the love. And I waited for a long time... While you are waiting to feel the love (something the whole world participates in), life becomes all about you. Love is never all about you. God so loved that He gave, right? Well, I think God knows a thing or two about love. God is love.

You can choose to love at any moment in life. What does love look like? Easy, just think of someone you know who loves you. Well, what do they do with you? Do that! Love is interested in the object of its affection. Love notices and responds to what it sees. Love seeks the other's happiness and not its own, but always receives its own because you receive back what you give out. The more you choose to love, the more love you will receive. When you are choosing love, you are living where God lives. And within that wonderful, tender haven, you never have to fret and worry about getting your needs met because your needs start getting met before you even have to ask. Love is life on steroids.

So many, many people are wandering the earth desperately

seeking that elusive love when it is already in their heart waiting for the opportunity to come out. I don't care what your background is or how difficult your life has become; love is there waiting for you to choose. Choose love. But, and you can trust me on this one, do not wait for the feeling unless you have a lot of years to burn. Love isn't a feeling, it's a decision; a decision that produces a wonderful feeling. How crazy is it that the thing you seek so ardently, you already have? It's not the absence of love that has been screwing your life up, it's the absence of giving what you already have that's been doing it to you!

If you want love (and who doesn't?), you have to give it. Build, build, build. Bless, bless, bless. Stop being afraid and open your heart. We've all suffered while experiencing life to some extent because of the darkness that has prevailed at times. We've all gotten hardened and calloused. We've all been jaded, sadly increasing with age. But that wall you've constructed around your heart isn't protecting you at all. Instead it's preventing you from the experience called life that God intended for you. Yes, it can be scary. Yes, people will still run roughshod on it, but open your heart anyway. The rewards of love not only heal every hurt, but they offer the promise of a fantastic life; true power for abundant living!

Don't you dare wait for tomorrow to try it out. Do it right now! Give it to the person you see in this very moment. Shower it on your wife or your husband. It doesn't matter if they don't deserve it. You deserve it. Damn it man; doggone it woman, you deserve it! Pour it on your children and your grandchildren. Lavish it on your friends. Heap it on your co-workers. Overflow it on your boss. Love, love, love like your life and happiness depends upon it because it really does.

You are not an intellectual gorilla that manscapes, you are a wonderful human being with a heart. Open it! You are the top of the food chain not because you evolved over millions of years but because you have a heart of love from a God of love. Choose love! Give love! Open your heart...

TUNED TO THE FREQUENCY OF LOVE

I would like to give you some food for thought. What I am about to say is theoretic in nature, but so likely to be true. So, instead of presenting it as the absolute truth, I ask only that you run it through your mind and see what connections you make.

Much has been written about love and its powerful effect on how we live our lives. According to the Bible, God is love; perfect love casts out fear; love your neighbor as you love yourself, and incredulously, love *never* fails! You know already from your personal experiences that when your motive is love, things almost always work out. Love softens. Love warms. Love heals. Like I promised... food for thought.

What if God is truly a fantastic, unlimited energy source? So fantastic that He could direct His energy onto the sun and reflect it in the direction of the earth? What if, being the source of life, He put some of that energy into every living thing. And in turn, what if every living thing gave off some of that energy? And if you haven't already tuned out, what if us humans with our ability to think and feel have the ability to send and receive energy unlike any of the other creatures God made? What if in our thoughts, yes in our thoughts, we possess an uncanny ability to tune into certain energies and by doing so can make our lives blissful or miserable? Indeed, what if?

Much is spoken of concerning a person's energy. Some people have "bad" energy and you can feel it the moment you meet them. Dogs even have bad energy and other dogs react negatively to it without so much as a bark or tail wag. Other people have "good" energy and it too is apparent within seconds of meeting them. Assuming good and bad energy aren't inherent, maybe there is something a person does with their thoughts that produces that energy. Again, food for thought.

If God is a super source of energy, what if there is a frequency that He or *Love* operates at and that we can tap into the frequency? What if when we live and move and have our being with love as our motive, we tune into that love super-station and in so doing guarantee our own success? Much has been said already regarding vibration and that higher, loved-filled thoughts vibrate at higher frequencies than lower thoughts. So maybe, just maybe there is a reason that God tells us He is love; that perfect love casts out fear; that we are exhorted to love our neighbors; and best of all, that love never fails!

Some researchers have concluded that negative thoughts produce a different type of energy. That energy has been called lower, slower and even toxic. What if when we filled our heads with thoughts of fear and worry that we also tapped into an energy source; a source that is hell-bent on bringing difficulties into our lives? What if, huh? What if the Higher power (an interesting name) is infinitely greater in power than the lower source and is willing and able to move into action once we decide to tap into the right frequency? More (you guessed it) food for thought.

As human beings, God has given us an incredible privilege! We have the God-given ability to decide what we will and will not think about. If we decide to raise our thoughts to the frequency of love, we tap into something that we all have dreamed about. If we only knew it. It seems our biggest challenge isn't in deciding what to think and how to act, but rather in deciding to once and for all recognize that our lives and what happens in our lives are within the realm of our control by what we do with our minds. Have you ever felt like heaven's brass, as the saying goes? Could it be that when heaven's brass it's because our thoughts are brass and the treasures are made of gold?

All this theory (and truth) wouldn't be valid if it wasn't put to the test in the crucible of your personal experience. So, I'm going to lay down a challenge for you, if you choose to accept it. Tomorrow, or as soon as possible after you read this, decide to spend the day in love. Not just love for your loved ones, but love for every human being you come across. Love your co-workers (in your heart and in your words). Love your job no matter what it is. Love the people on the highway and love the people on the streets. Decide to love, then decide again and decide again. What if your love isn't reciprocated? So what! What we are interested in is you finding the right station where All-Love lives. I can assure you that if you do this, no matter what happens or who says what, you are going to have a fantastic day! If you continue it the best you can, you are going to have a fantastic life!

Run some love through your mind and truly see what connections you will make.

Love never fails...

WHY IS IT SO HARD TO
LOVE ONE ANOTHER?

Love, compassion, and understanding are all the underlying tenets behind every person that ever walked on Earth. So, have you ever wondered why folks find it so hard to love one another? There's a short answer, really... because they don't love themselves. Oh, sure, the world is full of people proclaiming copious amounts of self-love, but the real acid test of whether or not a person really loves themselves is, "do they love other people?" You can only give what you have, and if you can't share some love, you must not have love for yourself! That then begs the question, why don't people love themselves? Another short answer... because they have been taught not to! I think if you got inside most folk's minds you would find a merciless criticism machine that specializes in, "what is wrong with me." I don't have to prove that claim to you, do I? What do you tell yourself? How do you treat yourself? Would you be proud of the thoughts you think about yourself if they were broadcasted on the big screen? Being a fellow human, sharing your experiences on Earth, I would have to say probably not.

In the Bible, in 1st Corinthians 13, God tells us what love, His love, looks like. Love in action is certainly more than just saying, I love you. (Though that is also very necessary.) So here is a little summary of what that love of God looks like:

1. Love is very patient (long-suffering).
2. Love is kind.
3. Love doesn't burn for what others have and you don't have.
4. Love doesn't make itself appear better than others.
5. Love is not puffed up and proud.
6. Love doesn't behave out of character (like loving this one and hating that one).
7. Love isn't only interested in itself alone.
8. Love isn't easily agitated or made angry.
9. Love doesn't draw conclusions that are evil.
10. Love doesn't rejoice in wrongs received by others but rejoices in the truth.
11. Love protects and covers things.
12. Love always believes in good.
13. Love hopes for an expected outcome.
14. Love stands strong under pressure.

Love never fails!

Okay, I hope you are still with me! Love is clearly something you do with your mind. Love is a mindset that you decide to live in. You will find in life that your thoughts and your mindsets, and your attitude, play a huge part in determining how your life turns out. So why don't you love yourself, or at least continue to love yourself? Well, look at the list. Love is very patient or long-suffering. How are you Mommas with your two-year-olds? My guess is very patient. When they lose it, you don't! Why? Because you love them! So how about with yourself? Are you very patient with yourself, or do you demand flawless performance in every scenario? Maybe this old world has talked you into setting some unrealistic expectations for yourself? Love is very kind and tenderhearted. Are you kind and tenderhearted with yourself? Is your mind your friend or your enemy? It seems like you should always be on your side, since you are the only you, you've got! If you're not for you, who is? (You getting the picture?) Then, we need to venture into some things love is not. You will notice (if you are paying attention) that fear is involved in every negative characteristic. You envy what others have because you are afraid that you won't have. You try so hard to make yourself look superior because you feel secretly (and wrongly) inferior and are afraid as hell someone might find out! And on it goes...

So, if you would rather live in this world of prevailing hate and fear with love, why not change how you view yourself? Stop abusing yourself in the secrecy of your own mind and love yourself as God loves you. Stop criticizing yourself. Forgive yourself (even for that one big thing!) Quit measuring yourself against other people who you really cannot know that much about, and accept yourself for the wonderful person that God uniquely made you to be. Unless, of course, you have concluded that God has some flaws in his humanoid production line! Practice loving yourself and you will be hard-pressed not to share that love with other people. God has already graciously solved everything that was ever wrong with you and me forever by the accomplishments of His son, Jesus Christ. Don't you see? He knows the *crapola* that goes through our minds, and He solved for us what we could not solve for ourselves. He did it out of love! He did it so we could finally love ourselves! No matter what that angry preacher may have told you, God loves you in spite of yourself. That's real love...

So, how can you be a part of the solution and not be a part of the problem? Love yourself as God does, so you can share His love with someone else. The world needs love, man (and woman), and the world needs you to be the one that gives it. Don't wait on the other guy; you be the other guy (and gal)!

If you do this, you will find that all of your wrongs will be made right in a hurry. You will have what you need when you need it because you will have found the key to life ~ love!

ALL I WANT FOR CHRISTMAS IS LOVE

Christmas and the holidays in general bring back fond memories of times gone past; times filled with love and happiness and joy. It reminds us of the warm times we spent with our families; times when the people we ran into had a little more love, a little more kindness in their hearts. And yet for others, the holidays sometimes trigger sad feelings of loss and memories of loved ones who are no longer around. Or, they remind us of a better time; a time when things were simple and our lives were going the way we wanted them to go before we grew up and had to face a world that wasn't always on our side. Whether our memories are pleasant or painful, what we all really want for Christmas is love...

We can all remember those precious times when we were young, when we excitedly anticipated the big day when the mythical Santa came to visit and brought us the things that made us happy. Those days were all about ourselves, and we didn't take time to consider that someone was behind the scenes diligently attending to our happiness. We were completely unaware of the sacrifices someone was making to buy us the thing they really couldn't afford or how many stores they searched to locate the last remaining big hit, popular thing that every child had to have. And why did they go to all of the trouble? They did it simply to bless us. They did it for the smile on our faces. They did it out of pure, unconditional love...

Flash forward 30 years, and now we find ourselves the ones responsible for manufacturing the joy. Now we are the ones expending the effort, carefully planning for the big day, worrying that maybe we missed something or that maybe someone didn't get enough. And although we love a nice gift like anyone else, our real joy was found in the giving. Our true expression of love; indeed, any expression of love always involves giving. And so, we gave out of the love in our hearts and reveled in the joy that followed. Nothing brings a parent or a grandparent as much happiness as the happiness on the faces of those little ones. And in giving we found out what Christmas was all about. We learned that it is more blessed to give than to receive. And all that we gave, we gave out of love.

But, as we grew older with a few more years under our belts and we no longer had to get up at 5:00 in the morning, we began to see a greater lesson. When our family starts to show up at our house with their parcels and merriment, excitedly bustling around, talking more loudly than usual with laughter abounding, we look at their smiling faces, and we finally get it. These precious people, young and old, are what we really want. We treasure being around the people we love so dearly. We want to capture the moments forever. It's the people, can't you see it? It's the love we share expressed in mutual smiles and warmth in our hearts. It's the touch on someone's shoulder or the clasp of a hand. It's the laughter and goodness that follows our close associations. It's the hugs and the tenderness of families and friends that is expressed in mutual affection. It's your love and their love and shared love! It's the love...

If you find yourself unhappy at this time of year, or just don't seem able to capture the Christmas spirit, remember Christmas is just a day like any other day. It's not magical or blessed, it's just one day among many other days. The magic comes when you decide to stop making it about yourself; what you have and don't have; what you've lost and where things went bad, but instead make it about someone else. We all feel that pang at times of simpler days long gone, but don't let that discourage you. Living in this world, we all have access to other people, whether it be our family or our friends or that lonely lady who lives close by. So, you gather yourself up, set yourself aside for a minute, wipe the tears from your eyes and go love someone else. It's not so important what you give, but that you give even if all you have to offer is some warmth and good intention from the heart. I think you'll find that what everyone really wants for Christmas is love, love, love. Give love!

With the big day looming on the horizon, remember to give love. Whether you spent a fortune on someone special or made all your gifts yourself, what people will fondly remember is your love. Our great God is a God of love and, as such, made His love the priority of our hearts; of all people's hearts. Decide to love someone this Christmas. Decide to go out of your way to express that kindness and love. Get along with the difficult ones and give the sour ones a heartfelt pass. Love someone else with all that you are and see for yourself how wonderful love is. God is love. All I want for Christmas is love...

UNEXPRESSED LOVE

I had a great conversation with my adult son Joshua this weekend. We talked about how people, especially people that are close to one another, have such a hard time expressing their love, or for that matter expressing all types of good things they probably should be expressing. What is it about being kind and tenderhearted that causes us to take pause instead of moving forward? Why would we wait until people are sick or dying before we endeavor to communicate years of wonderful feelings we haven't ever shared, or at least haven't shared with any meaningful consistency? Why would your love for someone be left unspoken?

I remember some years ago adapting a Dale Carnegie principle regarding building people up to my immediate family. I called it, "I love you because..." The object of my little experiment was to make an opportunity for our family to say things to one another we may have never said before. Basically, each of us wrote on a three-by-five card the family member's name with the phrase, "I love you because..." to be filled in with some meaningful reason why we loved that particular person. We chose one person to be the receiver of our words and went around the table expressing why we loved that specific family member. Then, each person expressed verbally why they loved their sister or mother, etc. Once each person had shared to the family member, we moved on to the next receiver. Little did I know at the time, there would be such heartfelt emotion behind those words. Between the wine and the words there wasn't a dry eye in the room. We didn't just shed a teardrop here and there, but took part in some full-on crying in our deeply felt love for one another. In that moment, between tears, I realized something profound. We all loved each other so much but rarely felt permission to openly share those feelings. The love was always there, and the tears weren't sad tears at all, but we simply rarely said things like that to each other. Thank God we did it! (And for being the biggest part behind that little idea.)

So, if we feel it so strongly, why won't we say it? Is it because it makes us feel vulnerable? Do we fear it won't be reciprocated, ridiculed or made fun of in some fashion? All of us had a different upbringing. All of our parents had their own upbringing as well. In some homes, expressions of love flowed freely like water. In other homes those words were hard to come by. But, if those words were rare, it's hardly fair to blame your parents. Chances are those words were scarce in their homes as well. Imagine trying to feel comfortable expressing your love for someone if hardly anyone ever expressed those words to you. It's such a conundrum because though not expressed, we know that the love is there. So, we wait for some dire situation to force us into saying the things we haven't said before. It's like there is no time left to wait. But, here's a thought. The people you love so much need to hear those words now, and later, and often in-between. You cannot really lose by saying those things. Even if the person you love makes fun of your heartfelt notion, inside in their heart, underneath all of that cover and pretend toughness, they needed to hear it from you, right when you said it! Just say it!

It's so odd that in the world today, feelings of tenderness and kindness and love are shunned as if they represent weakness or perhaps aren't manly or appropriate. It's like to be a man you need to withhold your love in favor of toughness as a sort of preparation for the things your offspring (namely boys) might experience in the world. I can assure you, the best way to build someone up to face the challenges of life *is* with your love. You want your son to be strong? Shower him with love and acceptance. Ironically, few people have any trouble expressing their love to young children. Young children are safe recipients of our love. But, what about being a teenager or young adult negates that principle? Your 30-year-old daughter needs that expression of love as much, if not more now than when she was five. We all need it desperately. Your brother you grew up with, who drove you absolutely nuts, needs your expressions of love. Your father who didn't treat you right (God bless him as he was trying to figure it out also), needs your heartfelt expressions of love. Don't wait until they deserve it, do it while they don't deserve it. Do it now.

The only way to break the negative cycle is for you to break it. It really doesn't matter if you receive it first. You be the first to break the cycle. Shower people with your love and kindness of heart. Have you ever run into a truly kind person and left the better for it? You know what it did for you, right? So, you do it. Tell your wife you have being quietly residing beside for 30 years, how you feel. Tell her she is beautiful. Tell her what living with her has done for you over the years and the better person you are as a result of it. Tell her! Yes, I know she knows, but you tell her anyway! Your friend who always has your back and stands with you despite all your bullshit, tell them as well. It's not weird or out of place. It's weird not to tell them. You see, you and I have to be the initiators of the love. Take the first step. Don't make it odd or difficult or risky. There is no risk in loving someone. The risk is found by not saying what you feel when you feel it. That's the real tragedy.

Don't love in silence even though you both know the feelings are there. Love out loud! Say it, express it, do it. I love you because...

I'M IN IT FOR THE LOVE

"I'm in it for the love!" ~ said someone who is very special to
me (smile). But then again, aren't we all in it for the love?
Again perhaps, during the holiday season, we seem to get all
caught up in the Christmas "spirit." Some say it has something
to do with the birth of Jesus. Others say it's because there is
something special in the air. Maybe it's the family time we
have to look forward to or the memories of family times we
had in the past. No matter what our reasons may be, something is definitely different during this time of the year. Before
we figure out what makes this time of year so different, let's
talk about this illusive word "love" for a moment.

What exactly is love and why do we human-folk crave so
much of it? I think we can all agree that love is something that
comes from our hearts. It's that special something that we
have on the inside that is always trying to get on the outside.
The actual origins of love come from God Himself (surprise!).
The Bible says that God is love! He is not just the act of love
(though He has loving acts). He is not just love in His dealings
with us. He actually *is* love! Love warms our souls. Love encourages us. Love gets us to sacrifice for the ones we love and
the things we love. Love makes us stay up late and get up early.
Love presses us to find someone to love and someone who
loves us. Love guards our children, and love gives us the compassion to care for our aging parents. Love heals our broken

hearts and forgives those who do us wrong. Love feels sorrow for those in need, and love spurs our desire to help them out. Love gives and gives and gives and expects nothing in return, and the whole wide world is in hot pursuit of it! Have you ever stopped to think that maybe the whole wide world is really searching for God? (He is love, remember?) No force in the world is more powerful than love and nothing can stand against it! No one can resist it and no heart is immune to it. Love quietly helps us to get up after we fall, and love reaches out to those who have also fallen. Love is everything we need and everything we want.

So, back to our original thought ~ what makes this time of year so different from the rest of the year? What makes it different is we decide to love. Notice the characteristics of love? What is our focus during our beloved "ho-ho" times? For a short period of time, we get our minds off of ourselves and all our stuff and think about other people. We think how happy she will be when I buy her this special gift! We are kind to the guy on the street who asks for some cash (though we know he's going to buy some booze). We are a little nicer, a little more compassionate, and a little more forgiving because, after all, it's Christmas! Somehow, in some way, we manage to shift our focus away from our "almighty" self and share our heart with someone else. We seek their good, not ours. We give and give and give and expect nothing in return. And for that tiny span of time, our lives are that much richer, that much fuller, and so much more satisfying.

So, as you search the stores for that one thing that will make him smile or warm her heart, remember, it's the love in your heart you are letting out that makes this time so special. And as you revel in the warmth and the love you feel inside, why not decide to live that way every day? What your boyfriend really wants is your love. What your children seek isn't the train set or the dolls or the race track; it's your love. What your parents are looking for isn't the pricey gift; it's your love and affection.

At the end of the day, we all need that love. God is love, and the person that finds God (though He is never very far from any one of us) finds love and, for the first time in his life begins to love himself. And the greatest gift you could fathom for anyone you know in this life is to give them love. So, during the busy holiday season and indeed in every season, remember it's the love you feel that makes it all worthwhile. Love isn't limited in us but only to the extent that we decide to give it out! Love other people with all of your heart, and you will discover something wonderful and brand new ~ you will just be having the greatest time living; you won't know what to do with yourself! (smile).

I don't know about you but, "I'm in it for the love!"

LOVE THE ONE YOU IS

Some time ago I read a fantastic book called, "You Are a Badass" by Jen Sincero. It's one of those books that just gets you, and you're just not sure why. But, alas, she is the inspiration for this piece. Actually, she may be the inspiration for anyone suffering from an incessant need for outward approval, though the reasons be myriad. This is really a story about you and how you feel about yourself when no one is watching.

Something tragic has happened to you. You don't know it's a tragedy because you're stuck in the middle of it. You cannot see it or you would stop it immediately. You're pretty sure you feel good about yourself and there's nothing specific you can point at to know that something is wrong, but wrong it is. You, like the rest of us, live in a world that very narrowly defines who we should be; how we should look and what we should have achieved, by now. The messages come so often and with such frequency that we can't even keep track of what's happening. All we know for sure is that we are too fat, we don't have enough money, we aren't successful enough(?), in short that our real self comes up short (pun intended). The unsolvable problem is that we are foolishly measuring our self-worth by a standard set by the world, for the world, falsely promising us fulfillment in that same world.

Your self-value has absolutely nothing to do with anything outside of yourself. It is your self-value, for God's sake. The one determining your value was always you, is always you and will always be you! It's not based on a standard set by someone else; how could it be? You are unique in the highest sense of the word. There is no one the same as you, despite the similarities. What you have to offer and what you bring to the world cannot be offered or brought by anyone but you. But, instead of bringing you and betting on the cards you are holding, you fold before the game gets going. The world, huffing and puffing, looking confident and smiling smugly, quickly talks you out of playing your own hand. The moment you begin to feel yourself and start making some choices regarding your own direction, you entertain the naysayers and revert to being someone you are not.

As a long-standing member of the "approval seeking" club, I know what you are going through. You've learned, like I learned, that instead of being your real self, it is far easier to be who the people want you to be. You become a master of playing the role and you become loathe to disappoint. But, let me ask you a question. Aren't you wrongly concluding that the person you are isn't desirable and opting instead for a safe, outwardly approved version? Who can define success for you, but you? Are you happy? Are you content? Do you have value in your own estimation? Your opinion of yourself is the one that matters the most in this world.

What kind of cosmic hoodwinking could convince us to be at odds with our own self, our only self? What kind of trickery and treachery gets a person to think poorly of themselves and to measure themselves by any other factor than themselves? Can you even see the insanity of thinking that way? If you, my friend, are not actually for you, who the hell ever will be? If you aren't voting for you in the contest, how can you win? How can you achieve or succeed or find happiness or become fulfilled if you aren't even choosing yourself? I mean, man oh man, you can't even choose yourself? What happened to you that you could be so opposed to your own self?

The root of this self-destructive behavior can always be tracked back to guilt, shame, condemnation and generally feeling not so good about yourself. But again, the behavior is self-destructive meaning you, yourself are cooperating with the destruction. You bought in. You agreed. Somewhere along the line something or someone convinced you that your mistakes, your humanity; your susceptibility to error wasn't based on something outside of you, but rather pointed to something wrong with you internally. In accepting that fallacy, you started to become your own worst enemy. Instead of leaving error and evil and bad influence with its originator, you bought into the lie that you originated the troubles, yourself. And for that, you are being wickedly deceived. None of us would knowingly choose pain or difficulty or trouble. Instead we get pulled or pushed off track. We're human for goodness sakes and we all make mistakes. Once you have veered off course and made the mistake, it's in the books. You cannot change it or alter it or influence it. It's done and it's over with. It only lives on in your mind and even that requires your co-operation. In a sense, you cooperated with wrong by doing whatever you did and you continue to cooperate with wrong by harboring your mistakes in your mind. Any professional athlete knows that in order to remain a professional, you must move immediately to the next moment. Athletic catastrophe follows any memory of former errors made.

You may not be a professional athlete, but you are the professional of your own life. Well, you should be! Somewhere along the line, you have to choose you. You have to cast your all-important vote for yourself if you're ever going to approach the life you want to live. How much time do you have on this earth? How many chances do you get? You owe it to yourself to get on your own side. Stop playing a role and just be. Vote for yourself. Have confidence in yourself. Be 100 percent for yourself. If you can get there or even close to there, you will, for the first time in your life, find out something incredible and amazing. You'll find out that you do have something to offer and that you are indispensable. You'll discover that the thing you bring, no one else can bring, and bring it you will. As you bring it, you'll reinforce who you are and feel fulfillment in epic proportions. This is authentic living. This is the truth!

Love yourself, trust yourself, believe in yourself.

Love the one you is...

#LOVEYOURSELFMORE

I recently read a friend's Facebook status and her New Year's resolution, #loveyourselfmore. That little hash tagged goal spoke directly to the core of who I am. You see, of all the goals and plans and changes a person might undertake for the new year, the decision to love yourself more remains the foundation. How many of us really love ourselves unconditionally? How many folks even love themselves with conditions? Most don't and you know that's true...

You and I were designed to be creatures of love, from Love. Our hearts were supposed to be tender and sensitive to things and the people around us. We were created to have great peace and an absolute assurance and trust. Our lives were made to be joyful, overflowing with thankfulness for each new day. True love has no trace of fear in it, nor is it critical and fault-finding. Yet, that's not what people experience, is it? This old world runs roughshod on people's hearts and often we ourselves are the ones inflicting the pain!

I should offer that loving yourself more doesn't just mean accepting your bulging midline or the crow's-feet that surround your eyes. It's not just staring into the mirror and telling yourself, "I love you." It's deeper than that! It's something that takes place in your heart. It's something that needs to happen in the deep recesses of your mind. And because the world is always working you over, often imperceptibly, sometimes overtly, you need to fight back all the more. You have to learn to "hear" yourself, not loving yourself. You have to get really serious and determined about this love business!

Absent God and His goodness, the best you can ever do is learn to love yourself conditionally. In childhood, we all learned that if we chose certain behaviors, the adult responses were more favorable. And even with that in mind, we didn't always get the love we needed. It's not about blaming our parents, however, because they grew up under similar conditions and their parents before them, etc. Yet within that cycle, we became adults operating under the same faulty guidelines; the notion that love was based on "good behavior." Love isn't a reward for doing right. Love is a decision that precedes "doing right." Love is a choice we make and to love yourself is one of the most beautiful. But, you will never get to unconditional love until God gets involved. God is the source of unconditional love, and it is His love that finally convinces us to love ourselves without condition.

Attending a conference in New Orleans, I had to make a trip to Bourbon Street. I went with my colleagues to the infamous street and enjoyed the craziness that is that place. Yes, I saw the bead tossing and a record number of drunk people. And, as you might imagine, "when in Rome..." (smile). But, I saw something else as well. I saw great despair in the eyes of broken people living difficult lives. I saw the locals who weren't fortunate enough to be the tourists and who were not returning to a comfy hotel. I felt their desperation, and it's probably a good thing that I didn't have any cash in my wallet, as I would have emptied it all last night. I saw people who had given up on love a long time ago. I witnessed the end game of the world having its way with people and the ruination that goes with it, and I found it strikingly sad...

No matter your most sincere efforts to help people, you can't really help until you learn to love yourself first. You can't give out what you don't have. What you'll give out is what you've been giving yourself. The criticism and self-judgment you abide with won't stay inside, but instead leaks out and affects the hearts of everyone around you. Your pain and unresolved issues will inflict active pain to, and passive apathy with, everyone you encounter. Your negative feelings toward yourself and your secret lack of self-worth serves only to devalue the masses and breathe negativity and darkness into people's hearts; the very hearts that need your love the most. You won't consider the kind words because you don't hear them inside your own head. You won't convey safety to people because you certainly don't feel safe.

Can you imagine the change you can engender when you finally decide to love yourself ferociously, unequivocally and always? Can you start to see the impact you will have on everyone and everything when love comes first? Love heals people's hearts, not only medicine. Love changes behavior without compulsion. Love rescues and delivers and saves. Love grinds away the layers of cement that envelopes hearts and helps them begin to feel again. Love makes pliable the hardness; warms the cold; colors the grayscale; lights the darkness; repairs and mends; makes straight the crooked; fills in the gaps; encourages, builds and makes all things grow. Love is just the greatest thing there is, and you owe it to yourself to find it in earnest!

During our shenanigans on Bourbon Street, one of my new friends stopped to help a young guy who said he drew pictures. All he had was a ballpoint pen and some crinkled, white sheets of paper and following him was a ragged suitcase that appeared to be his home. He seemed to fade in and out of reality as he spoke and was largely inappropriate and, in most cases, vulgar. On and on he went with a sketch that seemed to take an hour. As we stood there, anxious to move on and end the madness, my friend kept mouthing, "He needs my help."

When he was done, she complimented his work and gave him $20, to which he exclaimed, "I love you." The drawing wasn't, by any means, spectacular, but the random act of kindness, love and compassion was! I was blessed to experience a person who truly loved herself and was more than willing to share that wonderful love to help someone else...

Love yourself more and so much more in the new year because you and this world desperately need it. "They need your help."

LOVE YOU LONG TIME

I was thinking the other day about my family and how well we all get along together. I mean, we genuinely enjoy each other's company! I wondered, "What is it that makes our family sing?" How did we get four children that not only hang out together but even live in the same apartments, with one married son nearby? It seems that many of the families I've witnessed work hard to get away from each other. The siblings don't 'sib.' Family gatherings are a tortuous affair to be avoided or at least softened with a shot or two of tequila. And it's usually not long after the alcohol starts flowing that this one is mad at that one, and that one is still mad at this one for some event that happened in 1982. Really? Is that what families are all about? Should the people who are the closest to one another reserve their good behavior for strangers and conclude that it's okay to say whatever to whomever because they are family? Again, really?

So, what is it that we do that others maybe don't do, and do we, in fact, have a secret that might benefit someone else? When we are together our words aren't always the most kind. We argue; we fight; we disagree passionately at times. We have strong opinions about everything. We gang up together on certain issues, and our heated discussions have been known to last three hours or longer. We might cry; we always laugh, and our volume is often off the chart. Yet, we get together again and again and again. Why is that?

Well, I think there are a couple of reasons actually. The first one, and arguably the most important one, is that we just plain old love each other. I suppose every family loves each other, but we carry that love in our hearts no matter what is going on. Maybe that's the spirit of God in each of us. We don't decide to love each other because the other person is behaving nicely and is deserving of our love. We love each other unconditionally and that's a whole different kind of love. Unconditional love has no conditions in it. Conditional love is chock full of rules. Conditional love demands behaviors and withdraws its love if those behaviors are absent. Conditional love has no tolerance for bad behavior. You either behave in the way that I think is right or I don't love you anymore; at least in my actions. Crazy huh? Conditional love chooses not to forgive, or at least not until sufficient penance has been paid to deserve it. In short, conditional love sucks! Family behavior is just too diverse and varied to hold up under the strains of endless conditions and expectations. Sure, we need some rules to function together, but we need unconditional love more than any rule. Interestingly, unconditional love doesn't require rules at all because love always has the other person's best interest at heart.

The next reason perhaps goes hand in hand with that unconditional love. We don't judge each other. We just don't! Judgment chaps our collective hides! Whether it's my son defending his friend or my daughter speaking up for her brother, we defer our judgments with a clear understanding of our own lives and foibles. Maybe each of us has participated in enough absurdity that we totally "get" absurdity from other people! In any case, we choose not to judge each other. We play together, and we sometimes "go hard in the paint," as my kids would say, but the end result is always precious, good times together with lasting memories for the future. We have enough trust in one another to be able to communicate how we really feel, and there's no reason to agree with something we don't think is right. And the reason we feel safe is because we already love each other no matter what!

Please don't think I'm saying my family is better than yours (I don't judge, remember?). I'm just acknowledging that we happen to be doing something right. It's pretty clear that unconditional love is something God had in mind when He came up with the idea of family! So, why not decide to love in that way? Why not carry that unconditional love over to your friends and everyone with whom you come into contact? You will instantly become a very popular person because all of us need that kind of love.

Personally, I'm grateful for my family. I couldn't have asked for a better group to live my life with. And, I can only imagine how many other people will eventually benefit from their love long after I'm long gone. That's a legacy worth living for!

Love you long time, my Washingtons... a long, long time!

YOU ARE GOOD ENOUGH

Today I had the privilege of attending the funeral service for one of our fallen law enforcement officers. As the speakers came up one by one, each one clearly a person who truly loved God, all offering heart-warming stories about their relationship with the officer, all had one common theme; namely concerns about not being good enough. These weren't people living on the fringes of society, committing crimes and taking advantage of their fellow man. These were people deeply concerned about doing the right thing, setting a good example and leaving behind a lasting legacy. Yet, they all echoed the same fear, one of not being good enough. So, my question for you is, are you good enough?

Ever since the beginning of time, man's heart has longed to be righteous before God. The true nature of man is goodness, and though he often struggles to accomplish it, his heart yearns to do right and to be right. It doesn't matter if a man loves God or rejects God, the wrongs he commits pain him and the good he does rejoices his heart. It is a universal condition, and because of that, the enemy of mankind works hard to exploit it. Imagine working hard day by day to please God, only to be left with a feeling that you somehow don't measure up. Therein is the rub... You don't feel like you measure up because on your own you could never measure up. Likewise, you don't feel good enough, because of your own works, you could never be good enough. God knows this and has made a way out for you and me!

Each of us was born into the world with the nature of wrong built right into our bloodstream. It was never intended that we start that way, but it is the way we ended up. Your very own life blood carries within it the seeds of error, sickness and death. You fall easy prey to temptation and wrong choices because the seeds of wrong live within you. But God, who did not intend this condition, made a way for you and me to live above it.

The way above it is to make the decision to get born again (Romans 10:9-10) and to accept God's free gift of righteousness; to accept Jesus Christ as your savior from sin; to accept his perfect walk before God to atone for your imperfect walk. True humility rests in understanding that you cannot lift yourself up by your own bootstraps. A humble heart is one that knows that it cannot, of its own accord, do anything! There's nothing humble about perpetually feeling bad about yourself. Humility isn't found in condemnation and feelings of inferiority. You certainly wouldn't want that for your children, so why on Earth would you believe that God wants that for His children? The reason people think this way is because that's what they have been taught. They have it drummed into their minds and scorched into their hearts that their walk before God, indeed their happiness before God, depends on what they do and do not do. And while we all know that doing wrong makes us feel bad, we fail to realize that attempting to do good or to do better has no natural end point. How good is good enough? How many good works are required to earn our own righteousness before God? Again, therein is the rub. It is the enemy behind this false logic, ever working to bring us misery and frustration.

In order to do good, you first have to believe you are good. The boy who believes he is a good boy will do good works because of his goodness. The boy who feels he is a bad boy will continue to do bad because of how he feels about himself. Oh, he may work to make himself good, but his good won't ever be good enough, and as a consequence his good works will end in resentment. God tells us that we are good, not from any works we have done, but because of God's goodness towards us; because of His love for us. It's the goodness of God that leads a man to a change of heart. God created His righteousness within us when we got born again leading unto good works. The good works we do aren't to be loved by God but because we already are loved by God! That's the truth...

In this short life, you cannot allow yourself to get trapped into the fallacy that you can, by your good works, make yourself good enough. All that belief will do is make you a slave, and not to God, for that matter. You'll spend your life rehashing some mistake you made 20 years ago. You'll dwindle away your days in self-evaluation and heart hardening condemnation. You'll be chock full of criticism and judgement towards others because of how damn hard it is to be you! It's not God's will for you to live that way. Life with God was never intended to be a checklist of requirements to accomplish before your little stamp book is full enough to earn a ticket into heaven. Instead, life with God was intended to be sublime, with you never having to earn anything from God, but rather living in the greatest freedom; free to love; free to give and free to serve!

I know the people I listened to today are wonderful people with a heart full of love for God. I just wish I could share with them a better way; a way where the focus of our lives is on God and His goodness, not on ourselves and how we might strive to be good enough...

You are good enough. You know how I know? Because God said you are...

A HARD HEART IS A HARD LIFE

Every problem you've ever had has a root cause. The root cause is the number one contributor to the effects you are experiencing. Yet, so often the negative things we are trying to escape come from a cause we have yet to discover. We don't find the true cause because it's hidden from view and, for that reason, continues to control our lives. We need to become serious about locating the cause to live the happy life we have imagined.

Your heart, the innermost part of your mind, is where your beliefs reside. Your beliefs, positive or negative, produce the circumstances and effects in your life. This is why God's Word says, "Guard your heart with all diligence, for out of it come the issues of your life!" Your issues are your results. And if you're like most people, you've got issues (smile)! Your heart, contrary to public opinion, is simply made up of your most predominant thoughts. Change your thoughts, change your heart, change your life. Can you see the futility involved with waiting for circumstance to change before you change your thoughts? You are producing an effect internally, then waiting for an external event to change it.

Your heart, in addition to being the innermost part of your mind, is very sensitive. It can be damaged quite easily. When it gets damaged, the human reaction is to build a wall around it. You build a wall because you are trying to protect yourself. You have pain and you want the pain to stop. I get it. But, ironically, building a wall around it produces just the opposite effect to what you are seeking. That sensitivity is where true life is found. A sensitive heart is not a weak thing, it is a great treasure. A sensitive heart is able to feel even the most minute change and is thus able to accurately discern truth from error. A sensitive heart is God's domain and where His abounding love can be found.

When you get caught up in error and wrong it has a deleterious effect on your heart. The most grand illusion ever played on mankind is the secret, surreptitious effect that wrong has on your heart. The adversary knows this very well and, as such, seeks to get you and I over into left field where the hidden damage can occur! Sometimes things that feel good can end up not feeling so good, if you know what I mean. Error, at its base, hardens your heart. You don't feel it like you don't know a thief has robbed you until it is too late. And to add insult to injury, in your hardened state you have less and less opportunity to recognize that something has gone wrong. You can tell that your heart has been hardened by how you feel about life. You'll have less happiness, less fulfillment in the joy of living. Things won't seem to matter anymore, and your existence will become increasingly cloudy. How many people do you know that live this way? Maybe you have been living this way! You just cannot seem to find any love, any joy anymore. That is the tell-tale sign of a hardened heart. You didn't start that way and you sure as hell don't have to stay that way!

Fear is perhaps the number one source of error that causes your heart to become callous. Fear is painful and as such again, you want your pain to go away. So, you opt for numb over pain, much like taking a *Percocet*. In your numb haze you don't feel any pain, but you don't feel anything else either. And a life minus feeling is not a life. Hurt people tend to hurt other people, and so the cycle continues. We need to get back to a sensitive heart, like the one we had when we were children. No wonder Jesus taught to believe with the heart of a child!

In order to successfully get back to a sensitive heart, you're going to need God's help. God looks on your heart and knows your heart. God sees what you and I cannot see! God knows exactly what "loony tunes" thoughts you have been entertaining and how to repair the damage. There are things that God exhorts us not to do, not because He seeks to control our lives, but because He understands the negative effects on our hearts and lives. In love, He tells us to get rid of anger; to eliminate fear; to not allow bitterness to take root in our lives. He instructs us to be kind, loving and tender-hearted. Kindness, love and tenderheartedness start first in our thought lives before they are played out in our reality. So, in order to find your healing, you need to open your heart. Open your heart to God in complete, unabashed honesty. I can assure you that God isn't freaked out by the insane things you've done, because He sees through your sin and error for what it really is; a heart that's been misguided and damaged and hurt. He will help you and heal you, with the only requirement being a willingness on your part. Open your heart!

You know deep down in your heart that you want to share your love and goodness with other people. You long to show them the real you without reservation or fear. You know there is a way you want to live and have been aching to live that way for many years. So, make the decision to live that way! Get rid of your fear of rejection and ridicule, and let your true heart out. Be sensitive and warm. Be honest with yourself and with others. Love in your words and in your deeds. Love even the unlovable, knowing that the unlovable are only so because their hearts have been hardened. Be a beacon of light in a dark world full of many, many broken hearts.

The root cause of your misery is your hardened heart. Make the decision to have a tender heart for from it proceeds all of the issues of your life. A tender heart can only issue in happiness for which the whole world seeks ardently. You want your life to change? Soften your heart and see for yourself if this life is not worth the living!

439

ARE YOU GETTING FAT?

Remember when you were 18 and ate everything that passed your way and never gained an ounce? Yeah, me too, but those days are long gone. Like you maybe, I recognize that the struggle is real. So, I started thinking, besides the cruelty of a snail's pace metabolism, what else is different? In complete honesty I have to admit, I'm doing some things that contribute to the problem. I sit at a desk all day long (almost). I have the resources to eat whatever I choose to eat and it's been said that I occasionally overindulge in the wine (smile). When it comes to eating and drinking and other enjoyable activities, my natural tendency is to let loose as I suspect many of you do as well. It's so easy to just let go and seems so hard to control yourself. But control is where the good stuff lives and this has nothing to do with your physical body!

Your mind is equally capable of getting fat. And much like your body, the fat doesn't show up from too many nutrients, but rather from too much junk. It comes from complacency and inactivity. It shows up in the form of uncontrolled thoughts and unchallenged ideas. It comes from letting go and just accepting whatever comes along. This may surprise you but your mind can get lazy. It was never designed to be that way. It was intended to be alive and vital, dynamic and energetic. It was pre-loaded to have a sincere love of learning; learning that never stops throughout a lifetime.

The popular notion of living an intentional life is the antidote to a chubby mind. Intentional means on purpose. An "on purpose" life is a life lived by decision rather than reaction. The world is entirely circumstance controlled. People decide they're having a good day by a few positive events and a bad day is born from a couple of negative ones. A problem at work morphs into a potential lost job and a snow prediction for the morning commute spells disaster. Sunny days equal happiness and gloomy Mondays are the worst thing ever. A pain in your side signals cancer even though you forgot you moved some furniture yesterday. This is no great surprise because we have been trained to think that way. Negativity is all around us. The news is negative. Twitter is negative. The people you interact with are negative. And sadly, negativity is considered the norm. If you are positive you are called naive. You just don't get it. But, I submit that no matter how much negativity you experience, it's not the way of truth. It's a grand deception on a monumental scale. It gets to you when you give in to it, like a bacon double cheeseburger at midnight. Intentional living chooses to "just say no" to negativity.

How many people do you know who have lost that spark in their eye? How long has it been since you felt alive and that life was worth living? I'm not talking about choosing life over death; I'm talking about overflowing and abundant life. Yet, we acquiesce and think that's just how life is... We traded in our value for something cheap. We've been riding the bike with the crooked handlebars for so long that we think they're straight. We fail to see that we adjusted to the wrong instead of fighting for the right. Even more spurious is the lack of thought employed in our choices, most evident during an election season. The media propaganda makes our choices and social media directs our minds. We believe the last thing we read and accept as true whatever someone shouts the loudest. You know why? Because our minds have fallen into decay from fast food logic and pre-processed understanding. We don't think anymore because we got fat!

So, how can you shed the pounds from your organ of mental perception? The simple answer is to learn again to think. The more arduous answer is to practice living in the moment and controlling yourself. Recognize what is going on in your head. What emotions are you experiencing? Which emotions do you no longer acknowledge? Have you worked around that broken door handle for so long that you fail to see it is broken? What isn't right? Where has your love gone? Where have you settled for less than you deserve? Which illness or sickness are you living with because a doctor said you have to when God has no limitation on what He can heal? What words have you stopped voicing in your relationship that you used to speak without hesitation? What? This is your one life, my friends, and you owe yourself the custom package!

Sometimes you fail to see what you need to see because you are living in the darkness. Turn on the light. Find out what God (who actually invented life) says. Unearth that dust-covered Bible and discover something you can depend on. If you don't know what to read, ask God for some help. That person will show up faster than a Jimmy John's sandwich! Get your mind back. Get your vitality back. Get your life back!

Being fat only lasts as long as you let it last. And again, I ain't talking about your body. Embrace your chubbiness and love yourself, but most of all take care of your heart, for from it proceeds all the issues of your life! (hcG for the soul!)

THE WOODBRIDGE WARRIOR EXPERIENCE

When I was a youngster, I had the most fortunate experience of my dad being transferred to Bentwaters/Woodbridge twin air bases near Ipswich, England. I was a 6th grader, highly impressionable and terribly concerned about being accepted by others. Like any military brat, I was learning how to move away from everyone and everything I knew and start fresh again. I always viewed it as a blessing that would teach me how to get along with anyone and give me an opportunity to reinvent myself again and again should the need arise. (Stateside kids never had it so good!)

Shortly after we arrived, I noticed there was something different about this place. Everyone seemed to get along. There were no apparent color lines or class distinctions. There were no cool kids vs. nerds, jocks vs. scholars, loners vs. socialites! We were just all there, all together and all loving every minute of it. In my later years I often tried to figure out what made the place so special. Was it because almost all of our dads had the same employer? Was it because there was an absence in disparity of pay? Was it because we all seemed to occupy the same base housing? Was it because we were all mostly Americans living in a foreign land together, where the foreigners actually spoke our language?

Whatever it was, and I have some deeper thoughts, the effect produced by the place was almost universal. I thought I was the only one that loved Woodbridge so dearly, before I stumbled upon MySpace and Facebook. But then, to my surprise, almost every person who lived there had a similar experience. I mean folks who were there when I was; folks who lived there before me and folks who arrived after me. How many of my dearest friends have told me that it was still the best experience of their lives? How many of our parents said the same thing? How many wished they could have lived there forever? How many? Now I know why I wept so heavily when it was time for reassignment... One of my earliest memories of talking to God was me telling Him tearfully, well it's just me and You again...

I look back with great fondness at walking through the woods to get to school. I remember what seemed to be the greatest teachers on earth. I practically lived at the AYA, playing ping-pong and foosball every day. And wow, what about the dances? What about the music at the dances? God, how I looked forward to those dances! I remember me and Matt Howell putting on our super clean threads, stacks and heavy doses of Hai Karate aftershave. I remember playing truth or dare on the busses to other base dances and French kissing a girl named Terry for the first time amidst a game of spin the bottle. If it wasn't Boone's Farm on the bus ride it was MD 20-20 in the woods. I'm still proud of playing on the soccer team wearing our England National Team jerseys via Coach Booty. I played baseball for the Eagles and went from being an also-ran right fielder to the starting first baseman for the All-Star team traveling to Germany. I hit a thousand balls on those tennis courts. I gave the pinball machine at the bowling alley every quarter I ever got! I dribbled that basketball at the gym and was in awe of Darrell Stacey and Big O! I was inducted into the stud-club by Dino Moya and then met Rico and Darren (2) and Ricky Love. Tony Lombardo was also in the club. I had girlfriends, whose names I will leave off for all the right reasons. Man, what a childhood!

So now, many years later in adult retrospect, I still ponder what it was that made that place so wonderful. It couldn't be that I was only in my formative years because my parents felt the same way. It wasn't the love era, but love was very present there. It couldn't have been living in a foreign country because almost all my friends were American. So, what was it? I believe it was God. I think He sent me to a haven where I could learn to love people and be protected from the things that jade other folks. I believe He taught me love and tenderness there that would be the precursor of the man I am today. He showed me a little slice of the Earth where your color, your money, your status didn't matter. He showed me how life really should be with people living together, loving each other and seeking the best from each other.

You may disagree with my conclusions and that is certainly your right, but how many of my fellow Warriors for Life love God? Maybe some don't, but they still were blessed to live in the haven!

Words probably cannot express how thankful I am for having grown up there. That place changed me in ways I can't even describe. And since then, I've never lived in a place so sweet. Don't get me wrong, my experience there wasn't my best until this day, because that God I whispered to many years ago, introduced Himself to me in the most profound and loving ways. I found the perfect wife and have the best family ever. I'm living a dream life! But good ol' Woodbridge certainly ranks as my number one place to grow up!

Thank you, God, for allowing me to grow up as a Woodbridge Warrior!

Signed,

A Warrior for Life

WHEN IN DOUBT, TAKE THE HIGH ROAD

Have you ever been in a situation where you are being nice or kind and someone takes a shot at you? You know what I mean. You are minding your own business and getting your stuff done with a great attitude and suddenly someone comes along and pees in your Cheerios! You were really having a great day; you were feelin' it and then, "KAPOW" someone pays back your love with nastiness or anger. In that moment of time; in that instant you have a choice to make. Will you take the high road or will you lower yourself to meet them on the low road? Sure, in the moment the low road feels good! Sure, you get mad and you can think of a whole lot of stuff to say, but after that moment is over with, where do you go from there? Don't you feel a little embarrassed; a little angry with yourself? Don't you really wish you wouldn't have let them take you there? But alas, there you went and here you are...

I had just such an incident happen to me yesterday. I teach a course on building relationships and was working on preparations to go and teach the course at our program in Northern California. After about four days of preparation, in addition to also having to carry out my responsibilities as the Program Manager in Utah, it became apparent that I had formerly sent out the wrong materials for the workbooks to the Program Manager (my peer) in California. It was a pretty serious error on my part because she had to print binders with about 300 pages in each, times 12 binders. Uggghhhh... So, after realizing my error I tracked down the cause to the new training disk I was using; which unbeknownst to me, had numerous chapters in the workbook mislabeled. So, I reached out to my compadre with a very sincere apology (high road) and offered empathy acknowledging what a burden I was placing on her (high road); offered to help make it right with her (high road) and apologized some more (high road). Well, much to my surprise she responded with some serious nastiness. She informed me in no uncertain terms that she was not going to spend any more time at Staples and did not have time for that crap! I repeated the above process acknowledging and apologizing (high road) which landed me an even nastier response, "I don't care if there was a problem with the disc, I'm a Program Manager and frankly don't have time to do this before next Tuesday!" As you can imagine, by now I'm thinking of quite a few "low road" comments like, "I have been preparing this crap for your folks (not my folks) for four days now and oh by the way, I share the same responsibilities you do in addition to what I'm doing!" (Followed by some angry swear words of course!) I chose otherwise and waited for a response. I waited and waited and waited, all the while telling my ego to hush and "no! don't you type that!" I had a choice to make. I could choose love and take the high road or I could indulge my anger and go down in the bushes for a fight. After some time went by and nothing appeared to be changing, I decided to text her. In my text, I apologized again and offered to help in any way that I could, stating again my understanding of what a pain in the a** this must be for her. Shortly thereafter, she texted me back and said she would make the copies for the training. But, I didn't stop there. I asked if that meant she still loved me (tongue in cheek) to which she responded, of course! No bruised egos, no hard feelings, no fractured relationship.

What did I learn? I learned that I just cannot lose when I choose the high road. Love truly never fails! Yes, I had to swallow some anger and you might even offer that I allowed her to walk all over me. But, I didn't feel like someone took advantage of me. Instead I felt like I chose God's love (for God's sake) and was subsequently rewarded with loving feelings and great satisfaction. That's not to say there aren't times when you have to draw lines or speak up; no, not at all! But, when in doubt, why not choose the high road instead? It's hard for folks to point fingers at you when you have chosen the high road. In fact, it's hard to even stay angry with someone who refuses to be angry with you (try it out sometime!). I don't know about you, but I'd rather end the day having chosen good than to succumb to evil. And, it's certainly no coincidence that when you set your mind for good, that trouble comes along. Something, somewhere is conspiring for you to make choices that end up only hurting you in the end.

So, instead of being overcome with evil, why not overcome evil with good? (Tadaaaa... Bible verse.) Why not choose love? Not because you are a wimp or spineless or afraid, but because it matters far more what God thinks than what people may think. And here's a promise for you, if you habitually choose the high road, soon you will find yourself living on it, and you will be one happy son of a gun!

When in doubt, take the high road...

I JUST DON'T MEASURE UP

I often hear people blame their difficulties on their parents and how they were treated when they grew up. You know the story, right? My daddy didn't love me! My parents didn't give me the love or encouragement I needed, therefore the troubles I'm going through today aren't really my fault, right? Daddy didn't treat me right, mommy didn't treat me right, and I was so young and impressionable! Well, my wife and I were on this topic today (enter good thoughts). How many folks in the world do you suppose really grew up in a totally loving, encouraging, God-inspired environment? Really, how many? Less than five percent, two percent? I think it is safe to say that the vast majority of people grew up with parents that were less than perfect, as becomes obvious when you have the privilege (or responsibility) to be a parent yourself. I believe parents often say and do things that hurt their kids because they aren't thinking about their kids; they are thinking about themselves. Welcome to the human experience!

So, what does that have to do with the mental malady called, "I don't measure up?" Well, quite a bit, actually. Living in the world, we are all subject to messages; messages that are always trying to convince us of one big thing. That "thing" is that we are not good enough. Not good enough to have good things happen in our lives; not good enough for God's love and protection; not good enough to be and do the things we dream of being and doing. If I was the enemy, that great opponent of mankind, and I knew that people's lives were lived in direct proportion to what they believed (expected) in their hearts, then it would make perfect sense for me to focus my energy on getting those same people to focus on themselves and what was wrong with themselves. Convince them to spend their days and nights rehearsing and cataloging all the things that weren't so good about them and how they failed to measure up! Then, as the ultimate dagger, convince them that they are not good enough for God's love and blessing in their lives. And, as a consequence of that, watch their believing diminish to beggar levels. And while they are experiencing a good case of the "not worthies," they are sitting ducks for similar insane doctrines like, "God wants you to be poor to keep you humble" and, "money is evil and it's better not to have any or at least not have much!" Hmmm...

So, we are left with the question, are we good enough? Do we deserve the best things in life? The answer, surprisingly, is not so simple. The answer is yes and no. God, who dreamed up the idea of people, knows that the basic cry of the heart of man is to be righteous before God; to be worthy of His love and goodness. It's in man's heart. Even the person who denies the existence of God still has to "make himself" right in order to feel worthy or deserving of good things. You can hear it in the things people say. "I try to live a good life!" "I give to the poor!" "I always try to give back!" Feeling worthy of good things has a huge impact on what people believe they can achieve and receive. Yet the problem is how can we become worthy? After all, if we are besieged daily with the message that we are not worthy or that we don't measure up, how can we become worthy? What can we do to measure up? Here's the yes and no part. No, you cannot measure up to become worthy on your own. You cannot! Do you hear me? Cannot! You cannot make yourself good enough. Oh, you can make yourself feel better, or you can make yourself feel righteous by doing righteous acts, but in that pursuit, you are going to find out the hard way that, that course has no end-point. Today's righteousness won't be good enough for tomorrow's righteous requirements, and so on and so on... This is the hamster wheel called religion. Give up this; say no to that; more discipline; more sweat; more sacrifice; soon God (or substitute Dad/Mom) will love me, right? It's a lost cause, folks. God, being all-knowing, knew that man in his fallen state could never live up to what it would take to make himself righteous before Him, so he did something spectacular. He made man worthy by something that He (God) did and not by what man did/does. He gave His perfect son, the worthy (and only guy that ever lived up to it) for the unworthy. He did it and He did it by His grace. So, yes... He made us deserving; He made us worthy! That's why He is God! He is cool like that!

So, what is our response? Stop trying to measure up! Stop trying to earn anyone's love! Love cannot be earned. Take the time to learn who God made you to be and walk out on what He said. Come on, man, you've already spent a 100 years listening to the wrong source (even if it came via Daddy). You have already accepted that foul message that said you didn't deserve to have or be anything in life. Don't fight that fire with more fire; pour a little truth on it and watch the flames flicker out. You show me an unsuccessful person (side-note: money ain't the only measure of success), and I will show you a person who doesn't see any value in themselves. You see, none of us have much value in just ourselves. Our value comes from God. If God says you are righteous and holy, then by God, you are righteous, and you are holy, even if the world never agrees with you!

Don't allow yourself to be a victim of the "measure-up" malady for another second. Take a look at the folks you see enjoying success and ask yourself, how righteous of their own works are they? All of us are about one misstep away from behaving badly, so don't be so hard on yourself. In fact, get your mind off yourself and on to what God has done for you in Christ Jesus. Shift your focus away from the impossible (becoming worthy/deserving) to the possible (God has made me worthy/deserving)!

And finally, don't be sad because Daddy didn't say he loved you; God is the best Daddy ever, and He is telling you He loves you right now!

You are worth it...

CHAPTER EIGHT
God

LET'S TALK ABOUT GOD

I recognize the obvious audacity in attempting to consider such a vast, important, indeed life-changing topic, but I will focus on what I know for sure. God is very likely not who you have been taught He is. You can learn who He really is according to His Word, but that's not a book you are just going to pick up and immediately understand. But, make no mistake, you *can* understand, and that is the purpose of today's one thousand words, give or take...

The largest point of misperception seems to center around this notion that God is somehow the moral police whose job it is to point out your sins and faults. I vividly recall taking some marketing clients to a college basketball game in Philadelphia when the topic of God somehow came up. I explained I was part of a local Christian fellowship. Immediately, both of them apologized for ordering beers and seemed distraught over how many times they may have cussed. What a shame! (I was buying - smile.) You see, how silly? As if God would somehow be opposed to having beers? Or, was God really offended about how they communicated with me? Really? I think we need to give God a little credit here. You don't think He understands the creatures he made? You think your use of an expletive is beyond God's tolerance level? It may surprise you to hear this, but all of that accusation and judgment you experience both inside your own head and at the hands of other people does not come from God. It comes from His opponent, the adversary who has done a spectacular job of convincing you otherwise. God has already seen your whole life through, so what surprises do you have for Him? God is not the moral police. God is not reminding you about your sins nor pointing out where you come up short. God sent His son to die for your sins so the subject would never be brought up again. That is love. That is who God really is...

Another great error in thought is the idea that you can be accepted before God according to your good works. In other words, if your good can somehow outweigh your bad before death, you will "make" heaven. Or, if you can work hard enough to be accepted by God, maybe, just maybe, He will help you out in life. You may not realize it, but that is a dangerous trap from which you will find it very hard to escape. Let's say something makes you afraid. Maybe it is fear that your children won't be okay. So, in order to earn a little protection from God you resolve yourself to "clean up" your life. "From now on, I'm not doing this or that anymore!" Then, because you are a human you are going to mess up again (trust me). You are going to feel really, really bad about messing up and resolve yourself to work harder to make God love you; to protect you. The harder you work, the more you will fail. Enter the hamster wheel of misery! In reality, God doesn't protect you because you are so good, but rather because He is so good! He is a loving Father. Don't you love your kids? Well, what shenanigans do they have to perform for you to love them? To watch over them? I'm guessing none! God isn't after your fear-based love, He is after your free will love! You love Him because He first loved you!

Our God is a God of grace; unmerited, unearned divine favor. He is the God of all mercy! He already knows you are going to come up short on your own and has made a way for you to win, and that way doesn't have a blessed thing to do with how good or bad you are! That's grace, my friends. God isn't your problem; He is your solution. He is the answers you've been searching for your whole life. He understands what you are up against in life and wants you to know how to do life successfully. And, by successfully, I sure as hell am not referring to all of the heaviness and misery associated with trying so damn hard to be good! Don't let anyone put you on that treadmill! All that behavior and wrong thinking does is force you to dwell on the world of sin and wrong and, as such, have no opportunity to change. It's a deception of unparalleled proportions. No one ever gets better or does better by focusing on everything they do wrong. Instead, more and more wrong is produced. You do not have to live that way no matter how much you were taught otherwise. God has already forgiven you!

How we ever let the enemy convince us that all fun and enjoyment in life is reserved for evil and that God's way is a way of perpetual boredom and avoidance of life is beyond me. Where do you think the notion of enjoyment and happiness came from? From evil? From darkness? From error? I can assure you that life with God is chock full of happiness and freedom and peace. God's job is to help you get rid of fear, not be the source of it. God wants to heal you, not make you sick or abandon you when you need Him the most. God does not want you to run from life, but rather embrace it and enjoy it to the full. Life with God produces joy! It is error and evil that is the source of ALL of your misery. God wants you to understand that and will lead you in the best way; the way that avoids it. Like any Father worth his salt, God wants you to know what's going on in life. He is willing to teach you if you want to learn. Don't spend another moment under the opinions and ideas of men, but rather seek the truth. The truth really will set you free.

God is life...

RELIGION AND GOD
(ARE THEY THE SAME THING?)

Let me begin by saying I'm not trying to bash your religion or the things you hold most sacred. I'm not making a case for one religion above another religion. I'm not saying everything your religion has taught you is wrong. Instead, I'm asking you a question; a question that may spell the difference between happiness and freedom and misery and obligation. Are you sure the things you do and say in the name of God are in alignment with what God says about Himself and your relationship with Him? Are your religious beliefs and your belief in God the same thing?

In my experience, religious people seem to be the most unhappy people on earth. They live and move and have their being ever fraught with some nagging sense of disapproval from a god whose requirements they can never live up to. They are guilty and condemned, always apologizing, always wrong, always convinced that what they do and say is inadequate and fails to measure up. They endeavor to live an impossible code with pleasures perpetually questioned and good times ever requiring caution. They sincerely love God but they conclude God doesn't love them. They are compelled to answer every accusation. Their motives are constantly under the microscope. In short, the people who should be the most blessed are often the least blessed with even the unbeliever outpacing their achievements. Yet, they love the God of all blessings.

458

How can this be?

The problem is found in not understanding the things that are important to God versus the things that are important to men. Religion's aim and focus is always man and what man does and what man doesn't do or what he shouldn't do. Religion's promise is the glorification of man's acts and man's experiences. In religion, men judge other men based on their behaviors and pronounce one man righteous and another man sinful. Religion seeks to elevate some and reduce the others. Religion is hard, damn hard! Religion teaches people to doubt themselves in favor of another's opinion. Religion smacks at the heart of God because it is not based on what God says. Instead, it is based upon the doctrines and commandments of men. God provides a good way to live, and religion adds to that good way by introducing requirements that God never intended. Religion puts burdens on men's shoulders. There is no love in obligation. That which you do that you do not want to do becomes a compulsion from which no one gets blessed. Giving without love as its motive becomes a religious duty where I scratch your back in the hopes that you will scratch mine. It's an exchange wherein you now owe me something. For centuries, men have engaged themselves in rituals and observances that make no sense to them. Yet, they continue in them despite it.

I say these things not to anger you, but rather to ask you to think for yourself. If doing God's will is so miserable, then wouldn't that make God miserable (God forbid!). Do you really believe that God is bland and rigid and narrow? Would it make sense for Him to be opposed to enjoyments that He invented the capacity to enjoy? Could He, being all-knowing, be illogical or whimsical? Would He ask you to believe in something you could not understand, or worse, try to make good things out of evil events? Our problem, our failure, is in discounting our human logic in terms of common sense. Would someone that reportedly loved me at the same time torture me or confuse me or punish me? Would He do inexplicable horrors to me and my family for some reason I can't yet understand? You see, it's not God who told us these things; religion did. Religion requests that we suspend our common sense in favor of so-called higher spiritual realities. Religion begs us not to think at all. In this way, religion controls and limits our experience of life. Men and women are herded together on paths leading to failure and loss. When something bad happens to someone, religion points that wrong back at man and how man is living or not living. Pretty soon you become responsible for all of the evils in your life instead of the true cause of your unhappiness and loss. Religion sucks, man, and I feel sorry for anyone who has gotten sucked into it.

In stark contrast, the things of God make perfect sense. The things of God aren't opposed to science; they are the forerunner to science. Someone made this world with all of its detail and symmetry. Someone invented the concept of love and forgiveness and kindness. Someone dreamed up the notion of human beings. Do you think you can surprise or shock God with your behaviors and the things you come up with? Is that sexual desire that God built into you really evil or just wrongly expressed? You see, religion gives God a bad rap. It turns Him into something silly and capricious. It makes Him impossible to please and not a loving Father at all. It turns your focus away from the God who alone can deliver you and places it back on yourself where you, by yourself, are powerless to do anything about your difficulties.

I offer these words in the hopes you can hear what I'm saying and be set free. All of those burdens you are living under; all of that guilt and condemnation; all of that focus on your own imperfection and weakness is not God's will at all. Instead, He asks only that you turn your focus towards Him. Don't suspend your logic; use your logic! Maybe all that super hard work you have been doing to get to heaven isn't a requirement to get into heaven at all. Maybe all of that denial of self and pleasure and fun wasn't something God said, but instead something that people said. What good is a Savior if you still have to save yourself? Why would Jesus have paid for your sins if you still needed to make a payment? The ways of God, the true ways of God, never hurt but only help you. God is a Father, and no one loves His children more than Him... You can escape the bondage of religion if you want to, and it starts and ends with God. Is religion and its dictates the same as a relationship with God? God forbid...

I love you without compulsion or obligation!

UNDERSTANDING GOD'S PERFECTION

In order for something to be perfect, it must be absolutely and completely free from all faults and errors. The smallest amount of defect renders a thing imperfect and though the shortcomings be minute and even imperceptible, if they exist, the thing in question cannot be considered perfect. God is perfect. He has no downside, no shadow of turning and no requirement for any give and take. Thus, the things of God must also be perfect, free from any admixture, free from darkness, and free from any heartache and pain. We speak of a perfect day, but what we refer to is a day that went well, though imperfect in many respects. Being able to begin to comprehend God's perfection, has the power to put us in touch with the right to every wrong; the elixir to any sickness; the solution to each and every problem.

There are more opinions concerning who God is than there are grains of sand on the seashore; than there are stars in the sky. Every group claims to know Him and are more than willing to share His will with you. Yet often that so-called will is fraught with illogic and puzzle pieces that can never fit. Truth cannot be one thing today and another thing tomorrow! God does not change His truth for the times or the circumstances. Truth is truth in every day. You can find it in a tulip and in a sparrow. It exists in and permeates the creation. It is complex, yet breathtakingly simple. It speaks to your heart in a poem. It soothes your soul in a song. It jolts and awakens your mind by both friends and your enemies. It has to, it must, because it is perfection. When you hear it, you already know it is true, though you don't know why you know it's true. It escapes your mind yet pre-exists in your heart.

Naturally, the whole system of God is also perfect. There is no whim, no injustice, no wrong in any form. The truth of God must then exist without contradiction, just as light has no darkness in it at all. Love works no ill to its neighbor because it cannot work ill. There is no fear in love because fear is the antithesis of love. Thus, the system of God, if it be of God, cannot work ill, make ill, or be ill. Nor can it promote fear, make fear or be fear. If fear exists, like it's counterpart darkness, then it must be absence of truth or light in some capacity. Trying to reconcile perfection with imperfection is impossible. Yet how many good men declare God's abounding love and with the same breath dole out His threatenings on unsuspecting mankind? Prayer to God for healing of a sickness He gave you is like begging the slave owner to stop whipping you. The question is rather, why the hell is he whipping me? What greater purpose could be found in such an act? An unjust beating is an unjust beating and ascribing something good to it is insane. Yet, men entertain this with God every day. Hurt is hurt and pain is pain. Calling pain good and hurt necessary might send you to the crazy house, but apparently never in the name of God.

So, you may now be wondering what it is I'm trying to say! What I'm saying is that once you begin to discern who God really is, you will axiomatically begin to love Him with all that you are. He is only good always and seeks goodness and love in all that He does. He doesn't punish people for their bad behaviors, evil takes care of that. He does not follow you around day by day waiting for you to slip up. He is not your conscience making you feel guilty for the mistakes you have made. Sure, you've been taught that but it just isn't true. God says, my people are destroyed for a lack of knowledge. It's what you don't know or what you "think" you know that has been killing you. You don't go to God for help or when you do by chance go, enter in sheepishly with your mind chock full of all your sins and errors. You ask without believing and in so doing ask amiss. I don't blame you for this because this is what you have been taught! The church did it to you. The Sunday school did it to you. Old Reverend Thus and Such did it to you.

You read the Old Testament and it scares you. You see a vengeful God wreaking havoc on mankind. What you don't realize is that in the Old Testament, the snare of evil had not yet been revealed. God never wanted all of the laws and commandments. The laws and commandments came because of the people and preserved for people a future opportunity for redemption. Jesus Christ could have never completely set you free if there wasn't something he could set you free from. The justice of God demanded it.

At the end of the day, there is only one True God, and He encompasses all that you could ever hope for and dream of in life. He is your sunny, perfect day. He is the love in the eyes of your grandchildren. He is the healing behind your doctor. He is the Miracle Gro for your flowers. He is the spring in your step and the smile on your face. He is indescribable joy and love and peace for a suffering and downtrodden world. He is who you thought He was when you were just a child!

If you can break yourself free from all the dogma and throw off the heavy shackles of religion, you will find Him, though He be not far from any one of us. You will discover that this life is worth the living, and that there is something fantastic behind this world waiting for you to tap in... Ladies and gentlemen, God is love!

MOTIVATED BY THE GOODNESS OF GOD

When something really terrible happens or there is some disaster, it always amazes me when people say we should try to find the good in the situation. What if there is no good in the situation? I think more often than not people don't understand why bad things happen and naturally try to find some "higher" purpose in the tragedy. It is very, very subtle, but the hidden message is that for some inexplicable reason, God is responsible for everything that happens to a person. If someone dies prematurely, they say that "God called him home" - despite the reality that all of us left living here on earth are besieged by great grief and pain from that horrible event. Seems like a higher purpose wouldn't be at cross purposes with everyone else involved, but hey maybe that's just me... Goodness and evil cannot come from the same hands any more than we could get apples from a pear tree. Yet because people don't understand (and that's no condemnation, because no one can go beyond what they are taught), they invent reasons and try to put good spins on bad things. Some would even go as far as to say that God is teaching us a lesson. Remember hurricane Katrina? Religious leaders (so-called) said God was mad at New Orleans and brought the disaster upon them. That would be kind of harsh, wouldn't it? What if 20 of God's kids lived there? How about five? What if there was just one? Oh, I know, the hell with 'em, they gotta learn! I trust you see some illogic here. The reality is that there are two great powers in the world today. One is named God, who is love, and all that is wonderful about life and one is named the devil, who is hate, and every evil thing that ever happened to a human being! Both are at work in our world today and both gain access into our lives by the things that we believe. If we believe lies, live in fear or are simply ignorant of spiritual matters, we get negative results in our lives; some small, some horrendous! In contrast, if we believe the truth, live above fear by believing and desire to learn spiritual matters, we get positive results in our lives; small blessings and 'oh my gosh' colossal blessings! There is no darkness in light and there is no light in darkness. If you don't learn anything else from reading this, learn that! We have, perhaps, depending on our age, all suffered at the hands of evil to some extent, so again there is no criticism of anyone, but rather a sincere willingness that we learn otherwise.

So, what does any of this have to do with the title? Well, a lot actually! The best way to learn ANY lesson in life is by experiencing the good, not the bad. Sure, because we tend to be quite hard-headed (smile), we learn lots of stuff the hard way, but that isn't God's way. God desires that we trust what He says and reap the results of that trust. Then, as we experience the good, we are more and more motivated to do more good. Can you see it? We are motivated by the goodness of God. (Here are two translations of Romans 2:4)

"Or despisest thou the riches of his goodness and forbearance and longsuffering; not knowing that the goodness of God leadeth thee to repentance?" (KJV)

"Or the riches of His goodness, and forbearance, and longsuffering, dost thou despise? – not knowing that the goodness of God doth lead thee to reformation!" (Young's Literal translation)

You see, the goodness of God actively leads us to a change of heart (repentance). This isn't talking about salvation here;

it's talking about our mindset. It is God's goodness that is ever extended towards us that causes us to want to change how we think or act. God will never, ever violate your freedom of will (that sadly comes from the other alternative). So, God, like any loving parent, wants your free will obedience to Him, and He just loves you and helps you and rescues you so that you will get to the place that you want to learn more about Him. In other words, He motivates you by His goodness. Don't we, as parents, pray that our kids will at least try doing what we said, so they can see a good result and be encouraged to get more good results? Well, God is no different! Being a God of love, He could not do otherwise.

So do your logical, common sense mind a favor. Don't spend any time trying to find apples on pear trees, they just aren't there! Don't look for good in bad or bad in good, they are mutually exclusive. Know in your heart that God would never send a disaster, tragedy or even a stomach ache your way to help you learn a lesson. Instead, pay close attention to the good things that are happening in your life, because that's where God is... joyfully and lovingly leading you back to Him, where you belong!

God is good always!

He ardently desires a relationship with you, not for you to prove something to Him, but to allow Him to prove something to you.

WHO IS YOUR GOD?

As I live this life, I'm consistently faced with many things that cause me to scratch my head, but nothing perplexes me more than the believers who don't believe. I should add, I recognize there are more viewpoints concerning God than there are wheat stalks in a wheat field, but one common grain sticks out every time. People just do not believe, it seems, in God's capacity to actually help them in their lives. They pray prayers not to get a tangible answer, but instead to soothe some psychological need or something. They follow rules of conduct or practice morality not to enjoy a positive result, but in order to hopefully escape some negative possibility. They attend meetings, not for encouragement or enlightenment, but to punch tickets during spiritual labor-day. It just seems so arduous and pointless. What good is your God if He lives a billion miles from you, unable and unwilling to help you with even the smallest of details of your life? What's the point of all of your hard works and sacrifices you do for your God, when at any moment He can pull the rug out on you for no apparent reason at all? Why even call Him your Father if He would do less for you than any earthly daddy would do? Why, people, why?

If there is one thing that annoys the holy bejesus out of me, it is going through the motions. It's like hanging out with people you don't enjoy. It's like laughing at jokes that actually offend you. It's saying bad food is tasty and asking for seconds. It's all ritual and acting and hypocrisy. So, why would anyone participate in that foolishness? Usually it's because of some fear or some rejection or some nebulous potential loss occurring. And, people do that very same thing with God. Instead of taking their shoes off and talking turkey with God, they reform their language to sound holy and dole out false platitudes before ever getting to anything real. And when they get to something real, they add so many qualifiers that it's probably hard for God to follow along (if it be thy will, if thou wilt have time, if you're okay with me having that, etc...). I have to tell you folks, something is wrong with that picture. I'm not being critical of your beliefs because I know someone taught you that stuff; I'm just asking you to rethink your shenanigans. If God is who He says He is, then I'm pretty sure He can see through all of our crapola. If He could create an entire world with all the life forms, it seems He might be able to fix something for you once in a while. If He is everywhere present, seems you shouldn't have to look up to find Him, nor assume any posture, neither go to any location to speak with Him. If He's your actual Father, seems like there wouldn't be much He wouldn't do to help you if He could, and reportedly there's nothing He cannot do! You see what I'm saying? Something is amiss...

Just by sheer logic, and I mean down to the guts of the matter, there ought to be some grand benefit to being God's kid; in being a believer. If there is no benefit, why in God's name should anyone choose it? Why would I spend time bestowing the virtues of God to you if God never did anything good for me? That's not being sacrilegious, that's being honest. Why would you tell someone you will pray for them while they're sick if you don't believe God can heal them? Why should you teach your kids about God if they get nothing out of the relationship but maybe a promise of a one-way ticket to heaven someday? Sure, heaven is most appealing, but what about today? Look, it has to be a helluva lot bigger than that, don't you think? The way most people believe God and who they think God is, if it were me, I would have chucked Him in a long time ago!

Well, good people, that is not who God is at all... God is everything you ever hoped He would be and then some! He ardently desires a relationship with you, not for you to prove something to Him, but to allow Him to prove something to you. He doesn't want your rituals and your rigmarole any more than you would want that from your children. Your behavior before Him and whether or not you sin was never His issue. You were born into this world dead in trespasses and sins, and there's nothing you can do by your own works; your foolish, pointless works, to fix that! All your focus on sin and mistakes does nothing more than talk you into doubting who He is and what He will do for you...

The real reason you never see Him in action or get to enjoy His goodness is because of one thing and only one thing - you don't believe Him. I don't mean believe "in" Him; I mean literally believe Him. Believing, true believing, is the polar opposite of going through the motions. It is the north when play acting a role is south. It's getting good and damn serious about getting your prayers answered! It's about an intimate relationship with your Father who is closer than your very breath. It is a reliance on Him opposing a foolish reliance on yourself. You can be a self-made man if you want, but how is that working out for you thus far? Life is big and serious and tricky folks and you were never designed to do it all alone. You never want your God to be yourself.

God, in His unending grace and overflowing mercy, doesn't expect much from you at all, really. But, one thing He does require is that you believe; as in flat-out, no questioning, no doubt; assured of a good outcome, peaceful, quiet believing. Your prayers are a conversation with Him, not a monologue or a speech. He knows the answer to your question and is most pleased to share it with you, if you believe He can and will. He, alone, made that body you inhabit, and He can fix any part of it at any time without a doctor or medication. There is no incurable with God! Sometimes your problems have developed over a long time, in much error, like gum deeply matted in the fur on your dog. And for you and your dog's hair's sake, it may take a little time to extricate you from your troubles. But, be assured, the repair was underway from the very first time you voiced your dilemma to Him and even before that. God loves everything about you, both big and small and has something great for you no matter the size of your issue. That is who God is, folks, and why He is everything you could ever want Him to be!

Do yourself a huge favor in this short life and stop searching for some mysterious cause or some silly behavior you need to fix and learn rather than how and what to believe. Your work; your real work, is to convince your stubborn, human noggin to believe what God says over and above what it looks like. And when you learn how to do that, you will find that God is exactly who He said He is... Then, you will love Him with all that you are, not because you are supposed to, but because it's your only logical, thankful response to Him for all that He is doing for you!

Just believe, baby, believe...

Once you start on your own quest for answers, you will see that you no longer need to live in fear, and that God is living and real and intimately involved in your life, if you want Him to be.

THE PROMISE OF A NEW YEAR

By all reasonable accounts, 2020 was a tough year. The Covid19 pandemic led to a lot of suffering for people and, in some cases, even death. Businesses struggled, some to never return. All manner of entertainment was curtailed, and eating out became a luxury limited to certain restaurants appropriately spaced. The sports we all love to watch were shut down, then brought back carefully with restrictions and little to no audience in attendance, played in bubbles and stadiums with cardboard cutouts. Work was conducted from home where possible, and we all became adept at video meetings (you're on mute!) Travel changed, shopping changed, and life changed as folks struggled to comply with mandates yet still participate in being a human. Yet, for all the damage done to people's lives during this past year, the most sinister of all was the sense of hopelessness, fatigue and generalized anxiety about how this was all going to turn out. The promised vaccine became our only hope as every sniffle and every cough warned us that we may have somehow gotten infected. Will 2021 offer more of the same, or is there something, anything we can do?

Ever since the beginning of time, mankind has been subjected to evil in its multifarious forms and disguises. Pandemics, like plagues, are not new. People being afflicted with sickness and dying prematurely are not new. Add to that catastrophes, unthinkable accidents (so-called), storms and floods and hurricanes and tornadoes, earthquakes and basically anything you can think of that succeeds in capturing and enslaving the minds of man. The reason man becomes enslaved by fear is because he has no avenue for safety, no answer of peace in the face of trouble, no help from anything outside of himself, or so he concludes. In the pandemic of 2020, the number one product for sale was fear. See it for yourself. If you wear a mask, a story comes along of a person who got it while wearing a mask. If you got past it somewhat, a story comes along about people with lasting symptoms that never go away. If you made it through with little or no symptoms, a story comes along of someone who got it again, this time only worse. Now, reportedly the vaccine is only partially effective, and of course, there's no guarantee a new strain won't get you as well! At some point it has to dawn on you that this shit has no logical endpoint that you can see, or so it appears.

Why do I recount all these things you are well aware of already? Because at some point you have got to get honest and recognize that you alone are virtually powerless against a carefully hidden spiritual opponent when you try to take him on with science, human willpower, your sense knowledge reasoning, and all of the smart ideas presented before you for your careful consideration. That's not to say that you don't do your best and follow recommendations, etc., but at some point, you have to break out of that fear hole and go visit your elderly parents! At some place you have to realize, without being foolish and cavalier, that the fear and worry became your problem. In some way that only you can define, you have to finally admit that this life with all of its potential pitfalls and dangers is too large to tackle on your own. God bless you for trying, but it's bigger than you, and it's bigger than me. The enemy of mankind has had thousands of years to hone his craft and he is damn good at it. How many people, do you imagine, are sitting at home right now, no longer living and experiencing life, scared to death to move, touch anything or go outside? Maybe you are one of those people. Don't despair, my brothers and my sisters; there is something you can do about it.

Since the beginning of time and eons before that, God has been well skilled in delivering, healing and rescuing His people. God knows how to solve every problem you have ever had because He sees what is behind your problem; the real cause. God has foreknowledge, which means He knows what is going to happen ahead of time; which also means He heard your prayer you just prayed long, long ago and did something for you to prepare what you needed. God is all-powerful and backs down to no one or no thing! And, since time began, He has been endeavoring to get that message to you; a message of love. He has, through a variety of different means, including the exquisite, perfectly ordered natural world, been seeking to get your attention. The perfection of the creation alone points to something vast and incredibly intelligent. Add to that all the little clues that come your way when you need them, including so-called happenstance and coincidences. Not even to mention the perfection of His Word, the Bible, that all seem to know about, but few seek to really understand. Yet man, arrogantly and incredulously, still endeavors to take life on, on his own. He reads and studies and researches solutions everywhere but the one place where the solutions exist. Again, God bless you if you are determined to go it alone. God bless you if you think you can, by your sincere efforts, crack the code and figure it out. But, as a humble human who knows his limitations, I'm here to say you aren't going to figure it out, absent help from God.

Do you want to make 2021 something awesome, enjoyable and blessed? Get God involved in your life. I mean really involved not just adding rituals or agreeing to go to church.

Reach out from your heart and get some help, the help you so desperately need. I don't know about you, but I need something more than a mask and the hope of a vaccine to help me sleep at night. God will hear your prayers, and He has been waiting for you to ask! He loves you more than you can comprehend and is more than willing to help you. Once you start on your own quest for answers, you will see that you no longer need to live in fear and that God is living and real and intimately involved in your life if you want Him to be. There's no problem or malady that He cannot resolve for you; none. Then, collectively we can believe for this scourge to finally be resolved and get back to living how we want to live.

Get some help, man. Get some assistance, lady. You ain't big enough to try and do this thing alone! God bless you; you just aren't! But God is...

WORKING HARD FOR GOD?

Have you ever seen the movie, "The End" with Burt Reynolds? There is a classic scene where Burt's character, after numerous attempts at suicide, finds himself in a large body of water with little hope of being able to swim long enough to save himself! So, he makes several deals with God, attempting to encourage God to rescue him. While being a hilariously funny comedy, the movie shows how many people view their relationship with God. Reynolds offers to keep the 10 commandments, after he learns them. Promises to be honest in business, etc. The message is obvious, if you do a lot of good stuff and obey the rules, God will help you out. But, if you mess up or sin, your shit is in the wind. How many of us are working so hard to please God in a misguided attempt to get something from Him?

The whole world, and I might add, every major religion, is wrapped up in that simple, yet complex lie. If you have ever been unfortunate enough to have tried it, you found out pretty quick that it was damn hard work! The more you work to earn something from God, the more you fail. The more you fail, the harder you work. When you finally think you've become good enough, you find out that your good enough apparently wasn't good enough, because something negative still happened. You analyze yourself deeper; find areas of potential error and set about to work even harder. It never even dawns on you that

God's willingness to help you was never based on your behavior in the first place. This is the message of almost the whole book of Romans in the Bible, but hey, who needs the Bible when you can just work hard?

Of all the dastardly, evil, discouraging, asinine, wretched, bull-crap, devious things people have been talked into believing, the most supreme of all is the absolute lie that you could do something to earn God's love, blessings and protection! Read that sentence again! You cannot earn it, never could earn it and never will be able to earn it. Even when you accept Jesus Christ as your Lord by believing God raised him from the dead (Romans 10:9-10), even then God reckons righteousness unto you because of your believing. Not by works, lest any man should boast. The only way you can ever get anything from God is by believing. Period. End of sentence. End of damnable hard works!

Do you want to please God? Do you want God to be pleased with you? Then believe Him! Do you need God's help in a situation? Believe that He can and WILL help you! Do you need to make a deal with Him? Never. Do you have to do good works to get His blessings? Heck no! In reality, God blesses you to motivate you to do good works, not the other way around. You have to give God a little credit here. He already knows all about you (and me) and still loves you. He already knows everything you are going to do (good and bad) and still protects you. His love for you always was and always will be unconditional. He doesn't have conditions; you do! He doesn't make deals - you do! He doesn't bless you because you are good enough; He blesses you because He's good enough!

The quicksand trap of that treacherous works routine is that as long as you believe you have to do something to get something from God, you will never get around to being fully persuaded in believing that what He said He would do for you, He will do! You are always going to be able to find something wrong with you, and you won't even have to look very hard. You, fellow human being, cannot measure up; it's impossible. So, for goodness sakes, stop it! It's a trick. It's a lie. It's wrong on every hand.

Look, I'm not trying to condemn you. I've played this game; far more than I am loathe to admit. It's subtle and it's obvious. It's clear and it's vague. It's a feeling and it's a thought. But, no matter how it manifests itself, it is a damnable lie! It contradicts God's Word. Whether it comes from your Preacher, your mother or your wife, it's a damnable lie, from a damnable source with damnable intentions to defeat you. It's not your conscience mysteriously chastising you; it's God's archenemy carefully crafting circumstances and conditions to talk you into something that isn't true with a further view to stop you from believing in and upon your ONLY true source of help!

At the end of the movie, Burt's character makes it out safely and quickly begins to break all of the deals he made with God. After all, he is safe now, and the deals no longer make sense. How profound, huh? He made it out alive and all of the deals he tried to make never did make sense anyway! So, if you are alive right now, and I'm assuming you are because you are reading this, stop trying to make a deal with God. Stop trying to trick Him into thinking you are better than you really are. Instead, be yourself, be honest and be true. Learn how to believe what He promised you. Stop thinking your behavior is a factor and just get your old stubborn brain to believe what He said He would do for you, without any conditions, clauses or contingency plans. He is that good people, and He is anxious to prove it to you!

Yeah, I still get caught up from time to time earning something God already gave to me, but when I do, I write a blog about it and somehow feel a little better.

Believing what God said is no harder than believing the

sun will come up tomorrow. Learn to believe God as you are, right now, and you will see what all believers see, God is faithful to those who believe. Are you working hard for God's blessings? I hope not, at least not anymore, anyway...

479

GOD'S JOB, YOUR JOB AND
HOW TO KEEP IT STRAIGHT

I find myself on a continual rant lately in regard to how God works with His children and delineating His job from our job. I don't think I can stomach another Facebook status that explains away a lack of results or an unanswered prayer by saying how "God works in mysterious ways" or that "God has a higher way or higher purpose for not answering a prayer." When it comes to prayers, the Bible says the following:

And all things, whatsoever ye shall ask in prayer, believing, ye shall receive. Matthew 21:22

This is often referred to as a "blank check" from God. As long as the things we pray for don't contradict God's Word [i.e., praying for temporary blindness to happen to the New York Giants during the football game - smile], God is more than willing to answer our prayers. In fact, God has left a *fill in the blank* that we can use for almost any situation in life. In essence, there is really no prayer that you can pray that God will ignore (as if He is too busy) or refuse to answer (as if He runs your life absent your cooperation) or is unable to answer (as if He cannot do something). However, if you will go back and re-read that verse of scripture above, you will see that it clearly outlines two distinct responsibilities to accompany prayer. Those responsibilities could be defined as "your job" and "God's job."

I'll start with God's job as that is the best part. Without going into potentially endless details about God, who is All-

Powerful, All-Knowing, Everywhere-Present, I will suffice to say that God has guaranteed that He will remain true to what He has promised in His Word. Just in case you haven't memorized all the promises, He promises to heal us when we need it, to supply all of our physical needs, bless us with His love, comfort us, help us get things straight when we are twisted, help us separate good from evil, so we can choose the good, and fill our lives with great abundance in every category of life. If you want to compare jobs, His is definitely the hard part! How He does His part really is none of my business. He does not need me to help Him with His part. He does not need for me to figure out how He will be able to do something. He is never caught off-guard or unaware of my needs. There's literally nothing in life stronger than Him, and there is absolutely nothing that He cannot do! (He specializes in things called impossible... as the song goes.) That, my friends, is God's part!

So, we are left with the big question, "what is your job?" What exactly is your part in this cooperative arrangement? Well, instead of trying to convince you with my winning personality and powers of persuasion, I will let God's Word do the "splaining!" Okay, back to the verse, *"And all things, whatsoever ye shall ask in prayer, believing, ye shall receive."* When you pray for something, it is "your job" to supply the required believing! Believing is something we do all the time. It's not mysterious or difficult, for that matter. We believe the news reports without even as much as a question. We believe the media and their outrageous claims without batting an eye. We believe the doctor, the auto mechanic, and the weatherman often with no corresponding evidence to support their assertions. But, when it comes to believing God we have a thousand "yes-buts" to enter into the mix. Our job is to simply take God at His Word and literally act upon the promise we seek to claim in our lives. Believing means to be fully persuaded in regard to some outcome. Fully persuaded means we have absolutely no doubt. If we doubt the outcome in any way, we have already decided the outcome (no result!). Most prayers that are offered up to God are, in reality, "wishes," as if by uttering the words to God guarantees a result. If we are honest with ourselves, we know whether or not we truly "believe" that what we pray will come to pass. And most folks, I'm sad to say, have such a vague, non-specific understanding of God that they aren't very confident that He can/will/is able to do the thing they are praying for anyway. So, how could they ever get any result? This life with God arrangement is predicated upon belief, and we cannot have accurate beliefs without God's Word. Life is just too big and complicated to guess our way through it! All of us fall short from time to time with our believing, but the remedy is not to work harder or try to take over His part, or explain away a lack of result with Facebook babble, but rather take the necessary time in God's Word to build our believing to a level that "s**** happens!" (stuff-smile).

So belief cometh of hearing, and hearing by the word of God. Romans 10:17

So, naturally, if we really believe something, then we are going to take the corresponding action. If you believed the roof was caving in where you are, at this very moment, you would no longer be reading this book! You wouldn't have to meditate or look for a sign; you would simply beat feet! It is like that with God's Word. If you believe God will do something for you (and He wants to more than you want Him to), then when it happens you aren't flabbergasted; you are thankful that He did it. And, every time you get a result you are that much more confident in Him for the next need. So, if you need a job, pray about it and then believe by getting your butt out there and looking for it. Sitting at home lamenting isn't believing; it's wishing! If you need healing, find what God says about healing and then do everything you can think of to get that thing resolved; then let God do His part and bring that healing to pass. Keep saying what His Word says and don't allow your feelings to contradict what He promised. Don't stop until it comes to pass! That's believing, that's power, that's what Jesus Christ came to make available to you!

So, don't get it twisted... You do YOUR job and let God do His job, and in the end you will see great deliverance in your life. Don't try to figure this thing out on your own!

God answers prayers... every day!

THE LIMITLESSNESS OF GOD

Do you remember when you were a kid and had that unrestrained enthusiasm for life? You were full of hope for the future and excited about how things would turn out for you. You believed that you had unlimited possibilities and could do or be whatever you wanted. Then, you got a little older and got introduced to the real world where things don't work out, and many good-hearted people took it upon themselves to educate you about being "realistic" and not to "get your hopes up" and convinced you to settle for a life of mediocrity. After all, who exactly do you think you are with your "pie in the sky" dreams? Life is difficult and filled with unsolvable problems, and there is nothing you can do about it. Or, life is not fair and no one gets out of it alive anyway. Sound familiar? I'm sure it does. Well, here is another newsflash: those people were wrong! When you were young and didn't know better (or supposedly didn't know better), you didn't put limits on things. You enjoyed your life; you enjoyed playing and having fun; you didn't worry about how your needs were going to be met, you just lived. Then, somehow, somewhere, in some way, someone talked you out of your hopes and dreams assuming that, that was maturity because long ago they were talked out of their hopes and dreams... That isn't maturity, that's a life that sucks! Sure, we all grow up and have to take on responsibilities that we didn't have when we were kids, but that doesn't translate to an adult life of misery. If that were the case no one should grow up, right?!

God intended for life to be a joy and full of blessings. God says that He desires above all things that we should prosper and be in health. Well, if he desires it then He certainly must be capable of carrying it out. We can be reasonably sure (sarcasm intended) that there is no power greater than God's power! BUT... and that's a big but, God is limited to what you and I expect and believe. God gave us free will, and part of that free will is being able to make decisions about what we are going to believe and accept vs. what we are going to refuse and reject. See what happened when you got all grown up? You stopped believing in the unlimited and settled for the limited, the finite, the supposed "real." You got real smart and your real smart reasoning said, "how can it be?" You traded in your youthful enthusiasm for that "same-ol, same-ol" that you saw the rest of the adults living in. In short, you got talked out of the truth that you unknowingly started life with. Hmmm... okay, you need some evidence?

At the same time came the disciples unto Jesus, saying, Who is the greatest in the kingdom of heaven? And Jesus called a little child unto him, and set him in the midst of them, And said, Verily I say unto you, Except ye be converted, and become as little children, ye shall not enter into the kingdom of heaven. Whosoever therefore shall humble himself as this little child, the same is greatest in the kingdom of heaven. Matthew 18:1-4

Children, little children, believe! They are humble little creatures. They don't have 50 arguments against what you tell them (well, before they reach age 15 anyway), they just accept things as truth and keep on moving. Now obviously there are limitations to the analogy because you can also easily talk them into giving you their lunch money (smile). But the point is, children are fantastic, little believers. They don't put limits on things and because they don't, they are just happy. If they have unmet needs, they are relentless about getting those needs met. They don't settle for "that's the way it is" or just move ahead unhappy and depressed.

So how about you and me? When did we get so smart that we believed something was impossible; some disease incurable; some desire of our heart unattainable? That ain't smart, folks! Case in point:

Jesus looked at them and said, "With man this is impossible, but with God all things are possible." Matthew 19:26

Seems like the smart thing to do is to put your confidence in the limitlessness of God! Let's be honest here, what you have been doing isn't working so well is it? That whole figure it out yourself thing is exhausting at best. Or how about that fear that besieges you day by day? Fear of disease, fear of not having enough, fear of poverty, fear of responsibility, fear of death, fear of the future blah blah blah, blah blah blah... Exhausting! God doesn't want you to be worn out by life. And, the reason you get worn out is because YOU ARE TRYING TO DO IT ALL BY YOURSELF! There is an easier way and that "way" you practiced freely when you were a youngster. That way is found in believing in the limitlessness of God and learning how to receive what He has already made available to you. That my friends, is the only way...

So, why not make the decision to learn more about Him. You will find that some of the silly stuff you have heard about Him simply isn't true! Our God is a God of abundance. He is a God of love. He is the originator of happy, peaceful, blessed, assured, successful, plenty and good times. (Let the good times roll....) He is quite capable of doing for you what you cannot do for yourself. He can do the impossible! He can heal, repair, restore or fix anything! He will give you the desires of your heart. He is God folks, and He is pretty awesome!

Decide right now that you will not spend another pitiful moment being a good, boring, dutiful, boring, almost dead adult (two borings don't make an exciting). Live life, man!

Experience life! Expect good things. Expect abundance no matter what the dum-dum economists say! Everything you excitedly thought about life when you were a kid is still true! All you have to do is get off the pedestal of "I already know" and humble yourself like the heart of a child.

May our wonderful, loving heavenly Father give you all the desires of your heart!

Hallelujah!

DO YOU BELIEVE?

In order to receive the good things you seek in life, you have to believe. It doesn't matter if you are a Christian or a non-Christian, everyone believes and everyone that believes, receives. Your true expectations for your life are your life, be it good or bad. There's just no getting around it. Believing is an immutable law that God established for all of mankind. Thus, it is in your best interest to learn "how" to believe!

First let's dispel a misnomer. Believing and faith, though similar are not the same thing. Faith is what comes when you become a believer. Faith removes the separation between you and God. Believing is what all people do. Believing is being fully persuaded in your heart that something is going to happen. When you doubt something will happen or allow "what it looks like" to discourage you, nothing will happen though you pray on your knees, in earnest, all day and all night! Prayers are not answered, not because God is unwilling; has another purpose; or it wasn't meant to be, but rather because of a failure on your part to believe. Every unanswered prayer has some semblance of this truth in it...

When it comes to believing, where the rubber meets the road is what you allow into your head and heart. Believing itself is not the power. Believing is the touchstone for the power. It is the necessary ingredient; the catalyst to tapping into the power, which belongs to God. Incredulously and with much grace, God is the one that brings to pass all things believed for regardless of the saint or sinner status of the one believing. Believing is the most simple thing in the world, best represented in the heart of a child. Children believe so easily because the world and all of its so-called wisdom hasn't talked them out of it (yet). You can learn to believe and apply the power that comes from believing into your life, right now, no questions asked.

Believing, as I mentioned earlier, is a full persuasion in your heart that something is going to happen. It is not a feeling. It is not some nirvana state you reach after meditation. It is therefore your job to persuade your pesky heart. Your heart's objections or negations have nothing to do with it, nor does any feeling of doubt or skepticism. Often, we foolishly accept our heart's skepticism as some kind of truth indicator. We think, "I don't feel like it is going to happen" and then foolishly conclude that is the end of the matter. But, like anything that runs at cross purposes with the truth, it is actually error. It is error built into us by the world. It is the lies of the five senses existence that define life as only those things you can see, hear, smell, taste and touch, a place God exists outside of... The way that God brings to pass the things you believe for is none of your business. What is your business is to believe and see it through to the end, until you have whatever it is you have been believing to have. What you believe for is entirely up to you and there is no limit. The limitations come from a world that is ruled by someone (or something) hell-bent on you not learning how to believe!

In order to fully persuade your heart, you have to work on it. One of the biggest and best ways to work on it is to refute those things that run counter purposes to it. In other words, stop considering what will occur if it doesn't happen. Stop worrying and churning about "how" it is going to happen and instead keep saying it "is" going to happen! Can you see that? Really? Understanding that, is the key for you to break through all that has ever held you back! You aren't aiming for good feelings, etc.; you're aiming for removal of the doubt! As a great man once said, "Every time you think about your situation or your condition, thank God that your answer and your release is coming." That is believing. Every time! Persuading your heart comes simply by successfully refuting the negatives that are assaulting it. (Yes, assaulting it!) Children believe so easily because they aren't battling mental strongholds of fear, doubt and unbelief. They aren't so damn smart as us adults and they are better for it.

It's peculiar to me, yet logical, that the best things in life simply are... and don't require arduous effort and toil to attain. The toil, the trouble, the thorns and thistles come from the wrong side of things, ever working to take away your garden of Eden! Life is hard because you don't believe. Sure, you are going to be assailed at times, but believing will cause you to win each time! That's when life becomes a blessing for you, when you have that peaceful assurance in your heart that you will always have what you need; that anything that goes wrong can be made right again and that by believing you will always have access to the power; the greatest power of which there is no rival! That is real life, my friends...

So, what is it you need in your life? What do you want? Get a clear, defined picture of what you want and hold onto that image no matter what. How long will it take? It will take exactly as long as it takes you to believe! The moment you believe, fully persuaded, it will come to pass. Stop asking yourself if you deserve it or if it is God's will or whatever else it is that has been successful in talking you out of receiving it thus far. Is it good? Is it beneficial? Will it bless you and make you happy? Will it meet a need for you and your family? Will it restore you to good health? Will it prosper you. Will it deliver you from bondage? Will it put a zest back into your step and make life worth living again? Then rest assured, it is God's will!

Do you believe? I do...

FLASHES OF LIGHT

There is no such thing as an ordinary life. Each one of us, uniquely made and different, have something to contribute to the world. We have the opportunity to offer what we alone do best and from whence we have no rival. In order to escape the mundane, the mediocrity, the humdrum that plagues the world, we have to find those flashes of light that lead us to our true purpose. And, while our purpose is inside of us, we need the light from the outside to guide our paths.

We all know that the sunshine does something positive to us. How many difficulties are immediately resolved in our minds just because the sun is shining? Gloomy days, also a part of life, remind us to seek the sunlight. Similarly, gloomy thoughts remind us to look for the light that warms and comforts us. Days, weeks and years spent in gloomy thoughts lead us unwillingly to the pain that is a life with no purpose, no point. Yet behind each dark cloud is the light that is always present, waiting for us to recognize it and embrace it. Our job is not to produce the light, but rather to seek it until we find it. The light that guides us is found in flashes of insight and understanding.

Those insights; the subtle beckoning of a change in direction or a suggested change in our thinking are all around us if we start paying attention. They show up in those moments of repose or when we admire the lifestyle of another person. It's found in the gentle appeals to something better inside of us;

some more sublime, sweet way to exist. The reason men and women fail to see the light is because they get trapped in some mindset, some hard, fast, habitual way of thinking that falsely presumes what life is and all that can be accomplished or enjoyed. The problem is that we but half live our days functioning by rote instead of seeking the new and profound in each day. Each day offers us the opportunity to live anew with fresh experiences and learning, but we've become so accustomed to our routines that we cannot discern it. And while the routines are necessary, they also serve to cut us off from a full life.

It seems many people as they age settle into certain patterns of existence. The days blur together because they are lived without inquisitive thought, without new learning, but instead with mindless repetition. Young people, still consumed with the idea of life, actively seek new experiences with a mind still bent on gaining a better view. Aging is not the issue, but rather the amount of time that has transpired to inculcate certain habits of thought. The light has not become less available, it's just harder to see with a fixed mindset. The light becomes diminished with our insistence on thinking we already know, thus closing us off from all that we do not know. It's not easy to break certain habits of thought, but break them we must if we wish to fulfill our experience of life.

The true joy of living is not often found in hallmark events, but in the mechanics of everyday life. The proposed destination is not the only part of the process. Learning to enjoy the journey is the paramount experience. The life that God has given us is infused with rich variety and opportunities for discovery and each day is pregnant with the possibility of new learning. For this reason, we have to unchain ourselves from our habitual behaviors. Get up at a different time. Choose a different route to work. Instead of arriving home from work to occupy the couch and the television for the evening, go for a walk in the park or meet friends on a weeknight instead.

One great hold back to a fulfilled life, offering your best "you" to the world is that tyrannical insistence on being whom everyone already thinks you are. People, in their attempts to classify and categorize us, assign us to some place in life usually described by a word or two. Instead of becoming more and more a rich cumulation of experiences, we allow ourselves to be assigned as, "the comedian" or the "drinker" or the "hard worker" when those aspects simply point to one portion of our existence. My wife exhorted me to stop posting pictures on Facebook of me drinking wine as over time I became defined as, "the wine guy" falsely assuming wine to be the point of my existence. And while I definitely have an affinity for fine wine, my greater affinity is for a passionate, experienced filled life.

At the end of the day, each of us have the privilege to be exactly whom we choose to be, not held in by the group's assessment. The magnificent uniqueness of who you are is encouraged and fanned by your experiences of life. Be the person you desire to be, spurred on by those flashes of insight, and refuse to be locked into to some minimalist viewpoint of who you are. Choose to walk a path designed for you and for you alone. Break free from the stumbling herd and live the days of your existence exactly as you desire to live them. Listen to music that inspires you though no one you know enjoys it. Make plans and goals too lofty for your present mindset and enjoy your incredible journey of becoming.

Your life is way too short to be anything less than exactly what you want. It is your one shot my friends, and the determining factor always was and always will be you.

HEAVEN'S BRASS AND
UNANSWERED PRAYERS

I was thinking today about how many people there are that
pray for things and how many people don't seem to get any
results. I'm not talking about hopeful, casual utterances, I'm
talking about sincere people with real needs who pray heartfelt prayers about vitally important issues. You know what I'm
talking about, right? Heaven's brass; nothing's happening...
nothing! So, the crucial, vital question is, why?

What I'm about to tell you may clash with your theology.
It may smack up against your preformed ideas. It may even
make you get a little angry, so just hear me out, okay? There
may be a multitude of reasons why your prayer life feels like
an exercise in psychology, but those reasons really center
around a few main points that I hope to make abundantly
clear.

First, let me clarify some general truths that you need to
understand. The answer to your prayer or lack thereof isn't a
function of God's decision. God isn't answering with a resounding "NO" because He has another idea or a better idea
or anything else that moves the believing responsibility from
you to Him. Sure, Father knows best, but Father, the perfect
One, doesn't make your decisions for you. He can enlighten
you, teach you and help you, but He isn't going to decide for
you. That always was and always will be your job. If my son

wants an Xbox, and let's face it they're expensive, I do my best to get him an Xbox. Imagine me giving him a board game and explaining why it will be better for him with some ethereal reason that doesn't make sense to me or him. Side-note* Nothing is too costly or too expensive for God!

Next and almost as important centers around the confused and erroneous notion that God answers your prayer based on your good or bad behavior. God is not Santa Clause; a fictitious story we make up to appease our children during the holidays. (I'm not mad at Santa and perpetrated the same stories....) Do you really think you could become good enough to somehow earn God's goodness? Lord, if that were the standard, we all would have forfeited answers to prayer yesterday! And, even if you are feeling particularly righteous today, how much further do you have to go to get to God's perfection?

The final "biggie" is entirely composed of your actual expectation. In your heart of hearts, what do you think is really going to happen? I mean the real you, not the Facebook advertisement version of you. Can you even conceive that God could actually do something about your dilemma, or are you simply throwing the words out there in hope that maybe, just maybe, the stars would align; your ship would come in; you would finally catch a break and whatever else goes along with happenstance and luck?

The truth concerning answered prayers and softening your relationship with heaven is found in alignment and agreement. You have to align your prayers with God's promises to you and agree with Him about it coming to pass. It's not a question of His will (no matter what such and such told you); it's a question of your belief. I'll say it another way. Do you know what God says He will do for you? (Seems logical to find out if you are praying to God.) If you know what His promise is to you, do you believe God can do it? If you believe God can do it, do you believe He will do it for you? In order for you to get an actual, tangible, solid, real answer to prayer, your response to all of those questions has to be a resounding "YES!" Not God's answer, your answer! God's answer is already yes!

Whenever and wherever your prayers do not come to pass, the answer will always be found in you (not in God); namely, are you in alignment with Him and are you in agreement with Him? I should clarify that by alignment I mean are your thoughts lined up with what He said? If you aren't careful, you take a statement like that and turn it into a religion. You start preaching that being in alignment means always doing everything right and before you know it you have the 1st Church of the Aligned Order. See above truth concerning earning God's blessings!

In order to receive anything from God, you have to somehow get your old brain lined up with the promise of God and become absolutely convinced that it will come to pass. What the situation looks like or what people say is possible or what has been scientifically proven to be true doesn't have a blessed thing to do with it. God's power and ability are unlimited! With God nothing is impossible. If He can raise someone from the dead, what can't He do about your dilemma? I'm assuming you aren't dead yet, are you?

I don't know how to say it any more clearly. Answered prayer is predicated upon your fully persuaded belief that God both wants to and has the ability, to do it! If it didn't come to pass (in terms of your life and not other people's lives) then you weren't yet fully persuaded! But, the fat lady hasn't sung yet because you still have time to get your old, obstinate mind fully persuaded. Your work in prayer doesn't involve becoming righteous, it involves working to become convinced. You have to get to the place where, in your mind, it has already happened. Begging, pleading and bargaining simply means you still have doubt and as such you still have some mental work to do. Welcome to the human condition. Welcome to the fight where you choose spiritual realties over five-senses appearances. When it comes to choosing to believe God, you cannot count on the senses evidence or signs or indicators. You just decide and joyfully see for yourself!

Believing God is simple, but not always easy. But, alas it's how it works and the system isn't changing anytime soon. Believers believe and if you are going to invest in prayers, you may as well learn how to do it effectively.

It may surprise you, but God wants you to learn this even more than you want to learn it. Would you expect anything else from the God of love you have been communicating with so persistently?

Get your prayers answered folks! That's what God wants for you in every situation. He's God people, and He answers prayers.

THE RELIGIOUS RIGHT
(AND LEFT AND UPPERCUT)

I have never been a fan of religion; any of them. Scratch that! I hate the stuff (swear word thought of but not typed)! Being an ardent lover of God and His son, my issues are never with Him. My issue is with religion and its man-made doctrines that drive men and women bananas. I have never met people more defeated and discouraged than religious folks. All day long trying to follow impossible rules, and impossible standards, stamped by men and issued as if from God directly. Discipline to no purpose. Denial to no end. The torture of human beings. They believe God is tempting them and then pray for deliverance from temptation. They look for godly meaning in catastrophes and disasters. They want to punish the wealthy for using people, but believing that God is using them! They are guilty for this; sorry for that; regretting this choice and hating themselves for that. And all this being done by perhaps some of the kindest and most thoughtful people in the world. The ones that actually care. The problem isn't the people, the problem is the religion that drives the people insane.

Assuming I may have already pissed you off, allow me to explain. Truth, if it is really truth, must have a logic to it. Illogical and true cannot mix. Think about it. God is angry with you for looking at that woman's butt, but He's the one that made it attractive to you (not me, honey... theory). God forbids you to defile your body with alcohol, yet Jesus' first miracle was resupplying the wine at the wedding. God gave you sovereign free will to choose for yourself, but occasionally uses you for His own ends. (Forgive me, Father; I'm making a point.) God makes you ill to test your faith, then asks you to pray to Him for healing. God made sex feel really good, then expects you to only do it to produce a child. I could go on, but now I'm annoying myself...

You see, folks, this ain't about me being right and you being wrong, or doggedly defending "my" way of thinking as superior to your way of thinking. This is about applying the test of logic to what you believe. IF God is perfect and all-knowing and all-wise, I'm thinking He is pretty dang logical (insert extreme sarcasm here). Perfection doesn't need to double-clutch and cough and sputter to make sense of the nonsense. But religion does. Sadly, someone has sold us a bill of goods. And that someone has done his job so well, his name doesn't even come up in the discussion.

I currently live in a very religious state. Is that so bad? Ummm no... I don't feel unsafe in my neighborhood. I leave stuff unlocked often. There's an excellent chance of a neighbor upon finding my wallet, actually returning it. People want to help us; take care of us and bless us. My state is one of the safest and cleanest in the nation because of the religion. Yet my state also has one of the highest rates of prescriptions for depression and anxiety per capita in the nation. You know why? It's damn hard to live that religion! Damn hard. I know because I got caught up in it myself. Someone, or a lot of someones, successfully convinced me that the love and protection I once freely enjoyed with God, required a much more complicated set of requirements than I had previously thought. You can get a lot of power over people if you can attach God's name to it. So, in order to stay safe, I succumbed and began a litany of ridiculous choices all founded and formed in religion much to the detriment of everyone I came into contact with. I became religious. And while striving so hard night and day to please God, my believing decreased, my prayers answered less, my results - non-existent. That it is until I had the good sense or maybe the God-inspired good sense to break free. Break free from God? Never... Break free from religion, yes!

So why do I write this, you ask? The religious folks don't want to hear it and the unbelievers don't believe anyway. Well, I wrote this for you. I wrote this for every person waking up each morning scratching their head and mumbling, ummm I don't get it. I wrote this for the good-hearted people out there killing themselves to earn God's love, yet missing it at every turn. I wrote this for the folks that don't believe the only two choices in life are to be evil or be religious. I wrote this for my children and my grandchildren.

The God whom I love and serve isn't into religion. He is into people and their hearts. Ninety percent of that malarkey you have foolishly assigned to God doesn't come from Him at all. It comes from religion and the minds of men. And ultimately, secretly it comes from that devious source of evil that seeks only to put you into bondage and torture you. Don't get mad at me, get mad at the enemy.

There comes a time in your life when you have to stand behind what you believe and say it. In the words of Emerson, "Let us advance on Chaos and the Dark."

There is a life with God that is sweeter than anything you may have ever experienced. And in that life, you will find that He is always logical and never religious. He is love folks, always.

ARE YOU BLESSED?

I have been feeling very blessed lately, so I thought it deserved some words on the page. 'Blessed' is one of those words that means a lot of things to a lot of people. There's the traditional 'blessed,' which usually refers to factors in life that almost everyone experiences like, "I got up today," or "I have a home to live in," or "I'm alive." Call me cynical, but it seems like people who utilize the term in this way usually don't seem very blessed. Yes, they are alive and living in a home, but not exactly blessed! Then there's the blessed that is always associated with doing the right thing, and since folks seldom always do the right thing... well, you get the point. Finally, there is the 'blessed' that I believe aligns more closely with the biblical definition, which refers to good ol' fashioned happiness and contentment. It's that inner sense that everything is going to be okay and if anything might not be okay, God is going to fix that in a hurry. It's a quiet confidence; an internal knowing, joyfully complete with a full anticipation of an awesome tomorrow! That is what it means to be blessed, and that's the only kind of 'blessed' I want to talk about...

Now, you might have thought the title was a setup, whereby I was going to point out how 'un-blessed' you are and prescribe the 'way' to get blessed, according to me. Nah, not so much. Instead, I want to explain what I have been doing differently lately that seems to have led to all these blessings I am experiencing right now. That's not to say you aren't doing these things, but instead simply a happy guy wanting to share that happiness with others.

Let's start by debunking a few myths. While it is marvelous to be alive and have some food and maybe a place to live, that's not exactly blessed. Something to be thankful for? Sure! But being alive is something we sort of had no choice in, right? Lots of good-hearted people are plugging away day by day with absolutely nothing with which to look forward. Life was never intended to be a perpetual chore to survive. Nor was life supposed to be a daily struggle for existence and a few shekels. We have all (myself included) had periods where we felt down and lackluster and felt like tomorrow would probably be just like today. There's no criticism in that. The criticism would come from acquiescing to that life and not getting serious about solving the puzzle.

Next, and probably the most perplexing myth is feeling like there is a never-ending list of things we have to do to perfect ourselves before that blessed day comes when we finally get what we want or get to fulfill our dreams. There is riddle like that one! The harder you try to be 'good' the more you fail at being good or the more you realize how much better you need to be in order to be considered good. Trust me on this one, your life is going to seriously suck if you get caught in that trap! Add to that the outrageous myth that purports that God will only bless you if you are good. You'll notice that in that scenario the one judging your goodness is usually some other person/leader who most likely isn't even doing the things he is asking you to do! Don't get me started! Follow that logic for a minute here. If God only blesses you or protects you when you are good, you're going to spend a lot of time not being blessed or protected. That is unless you have deluded yourself into thinking you can earn your way into God's good graces.

God, as your real source of blessedness (happiness), does not bless you because of how good OR bad you are. He blesses you when you do one thing and one thing only - believe. Therein lies the key to my recent blessing trail. I finally stopped cataloging my faults and shortcomings and stopped focusing on what I ought to do; should have done or shouldn't have done and moved my focus back on to the source of all my goodness - God! I got my head back into God's Word, to make myself good? Heck no! To be reminded about what it is that I should really be believing. Did you know that the purpose of God's Word is to give you right doctrine (how to believe rightly) and reproof (how to get back to believing rightly) and correction (how to get unstuck from doctrinal error from practicing error and get back to believing rightly)! Your life is truly all about what you are believing about yourself; your life; God and the world. It's so easy to get off track (believing wrongly) and to stay off course absent any true doctrine. But, once you start believing again you will find that all the wrongs become right and life returns to that sweetness you (hopefully) once knew.

So, what happened to me? I didn't get a new job or a new car. I didn't move into a new house. I didn't come into a pile of money or receive some tremendous award for human service. Nah... I got my head back on the right track. By becoming sinless? Haha, well, those of you who know me would dispute that one! Instead, I remembered that in order to receive anything from God, I had to believe and believing is easy once you learn (or relearn) the right things to believe!

Am I blessed? I think you know the answer to that one!

Living the blessed life...

LIVING ON THE PLUS SIDE OF THE LEDGER

This is a story about living without debt, but has nothing to do with your financial decisions. Rather this is summary of the greatest story ever told; a story about how to have a fulfilling and effectual relationship with God. But, I'm going to warn you right up front, if you are a fan of religion and religious ritual, read no further because chances are I'm going to make you angry. Naturally a discussion about your relationship with God will take more than a few words, but I'll do my best to give you the salient points and then you, my friends, can decide for yourself!

So, here goes... Anything that you do for God that you really, really don't want to do will ultimately be based upon fear. All kinds of things are said and done in the name of God are not only nutso and illogical, but are often far removed from the things God says actually please Him. Forced obedience is not obedience, no more so than when your kids do what you tell them because they are afraid of what you will do to them if they don't do it. And if you are honest, when you follow some commandment or refuse to partake in an activity because you fear negative consequences with God, you are acting out of fear. I'm pretty sure that you want your children to do what you say because they love you and trust you, not because they are afraid of you. Well, God is no different! Add to that a society that has ever-changing rules regarding what is a sin and what isn't, we are left with a real conundrum. But God is smarter than that...

This may surprise you, but God is well aware of the human condition. He knows how evil works, and He's well aware of the pitfalls that follow bad decisions. And, in the world of "anything goes," bad decisions still remain. Thus, in His infinite (and I don't throw that word around haphazardly) wisdom, He came up with a grand solution. For those of us that choose to believe, He did away with the sin problem once and for all. He knew we would never live up to His Word on our own. The first man, Adam, the prototype, didn't, so why would He expect that we would be any different? Yet how many of us think otherwise? How many of us do all kinds of shenanigans to "make" ourselves right with God? And have you enjoyed much success playing that game? For every good deed we do, we inadvertently do two things wrong. And even the good things we think we do often present with another layer of how we could have done better, and on that dastardly game goes. Have you ever noticed how angry and judgmental religious people are? Have a little compassion on them; that's a tough, tough game they are playing! Instead, God masterfully devised the ultimate solution. He sent His son as the Savior from sin. Jesus Christ, with all that wonderful freedom of will you and I have, decided to walk and live God's Word perfectly. Then after suffering the worst torture any human has endured, died, paying once and for all the price for everything that was ever wrong with you and me! He became sin for us so that if we chose to believe in him and that God raised him from the dead, we would be forevermore righteous in God's sight! Now think about that for a moment. Once you accept Jesus Christ as your Lord and believe God raised him from the dead, you are forevermore righteous in God's sight. And in being made righteous by God Himself, never, ever have to fear again coming up short in His sight. That's true freedom, folks... but it gets better.

Being now made free by God, you are now 100 percent free to choose how you live your life. Stay with me now! You simply cannot sin in God's sight. You cannot. Because you behave so well? Of course not! Rather, because you chose to accept God's sacrifice for you. Side note - if you revert back to earning God's love and protection with your good behavior because something made you afraid, you go back to the 'game of losers' that no one ever wins. And now, paradoxically, for the first time in your life, you truly have freedom to decide how you will live. When you're afraid of making God mad or losing God's favor, you aren't really choosing freely. I don't know about you, but I want my children's love and respect and trust to come from their hearts, freely and without fear. God is no different! He wants you to do what you really want to do. Don't you think He can see through your rituals? Can you imagine that He already knows your heart isn't in that behavior you are begrudgingly choosing? Really? He is God, after all... Now I'm not saying anything goes or do as you please through life. You already know that doesn't work. I'm saying stop doing stuff for God you really don't want to do. You aren't blessed, God isn't blessed, so why do it?

You and I, as believers, are living life on the plus side of the ledger. We cannot dip into the red because Jesus Christ already paid the price for us. You wouldn't pay more for something than it costs, would you? Well, that's what you do every time you try to earn God's favor! Don't go by what people say, go by what God says in His Word (you didn't think I made this stuff up, did you?). Don't rely on your Pastor or the TV or the Internet. Find out for yourself what God says in His Word. Not too long ago, dancing was a sin (smile).

Get off that high horse you have constructed over time and let God do for you what you were never able to do for yourself! A relationship with God isn't all about you (what you do and don't do, though the preachers beg to differ). Instead it's all about what God has done for you in Christ Jesus.

Breathe in the fresh air of freedom folks; where there is no fear. You deserve that, don't you think? Haha, well maybe not, but God made you deserving of it!

The question that begs for any human being; for anyone experiencing this thing called life; for anyone that has been sorely beaten and wounded by the world, is how can I gain access to this more than abundant life?

THE MORE THAN ABUNDANT LIFE

If you are like most people, I think you would be happy to live an abundant life. I mean, isn't that what we are all really after? We have a limited time to experience life on Terra Firma and subsequently limited chances to get it right. Before you know it you are celebrating your 30th birthday, then your 50th and suddenly, retirement looms just around the corner. In that space of years, you will have had the opportunity to make many decisions and choose paths that led you somewhere, both good and bad. If your choices were poor, you probably were forced to seek survival and felt like you had to settle for a mediocre existence. If your choices were mostly good, you may have even touched upon an abundant life. However, God's promise to you is that you can have a more than abundant life no matter what decisions you may have made in the past. Wouldn't you like to live a life overflowing with abundance in every facet and phase of life? Indeed, wouldn't you want to live a more than abundant life?

God's Word, the Bible, lays out the two primary forces working behind the scenes spiritually. One of them is called the thief and his objectives are always to steal, to kill and to destroy. The other one is God, and He sent His son Jesus Christ that we might have life and that we might have it more abundantly. (John 10:10) When you remove all the covers and peel back all of the layers, your life always boils down to the effects of one or the other. Those aspects of your life wherein you struggle; those places you just cannot seem to get it right, will always be the result of the thief who, by any means possible to him, has stolen something from you. He not only steals your prosperity, but he steals your health and your vitality and your enthusiasm for living. He steals the results of your efforts and labors. He steals your peace of mind. If successful and always in secret, he will steal away your life and cut short your days. And finally, he seeks to steal away your positive impact in this life and destroy all that was beautiful and good and noteworthy. He is not a cartoon character made up in the minds of men. He is a real, dastardly, dreadful being, separated from God, hating God and hell-bent on ruining anything or anyone he has access to in the world. Not understanding how he functions, how he influences decisions, and how he leads people astray is the total cause of every life not well lived. The total cause.

God, as the very source and originator of life, is quite the opposite. His desire is for you to live the more than abundant life. His will is for you to experience an over abundance in every facet and phase of life. As such, He wants to prosper you abundantly. He seeks to restore your health. He will breathe life and enthusiasm and vitality back into your existence. He promises to pay back the years the enemy has gnawed away from you. He offers you His peace that surpasses understanding. He works in you to protect you from all harm and danger in order to help you live a long and fulfilling life. And, while He is at it, He works to ensure the impact of your life is long-lasting and rewards you for all eternity in those things you did out of love with Him. This is the more than abundant total life.

The question that begs for any human being; for anyone experiencing this thing called life; for anyone that has been sorely beaten and wounded by the world, is how can I gain access to this more than abundant life? How can I tap into the power source; that most excellent power source? How can I turn things around in my life that have fallen off the rails? How can I escape my past life of failure and disappointment and enter into the ranks of those blessed and protected by God Himself? The answer is so plain, so unbelieving easy that people have missed it for a lifetime. The answer is to turn to the true God from idols. The answer is to learn how to live life as God intended it. The answer is to get born again; born from above! Getting born again means to get God's holy spirit inside of you; a spirit that never goes away no matter what foolishness you may engage in; no matter whatever you have done in the past or will do in the future. It means to get a permanent, unchanging, incorruptible connection to God that will never depart and will last throughout all eternity. It means to gain access to a power source that will work in you and with you to help you overcome all of life's challenges and difficulties. It is just the greatest thing ever, and it is yours for the taking.

In order to get born again, you have to access spirit how God says to access it. It has everything to do with your believing God and nothing to do with your good works. In this God has made it foolproof. You simply confess with your mouth the Lord Jesus and believe in your heart that God has raised him from the dead. For with the heart man believes unto righteousness and with his mouth confession is made unto salvation! (Romans 10:9-10) That is literally all that is required to get born again. Next, you have to learn how to operate that spirit of God born inside of you. It has nothing to do with feelings and has everything to do with what you believe. Once that spirit is born within you, you are born again. Then you can manifest that gift inside of you by operating the nine operations or manifestations of the spirit (I Corinthians 12:8-10). This is the victory that overcomes the world. This is the power you have needed all of your life. This is the difference between success and failure. This is the connection with God that will never, ever leave you. This is the more than abundant life!

Surely you want that! I know I did and will help you get there if you want it. Not only will you go to heaven, but you will have one hell of a good time getting there... This is the more than abundant life God is offering you! God bless you abundantly.

SURE, I SPEAK IN TONGUES,
DOESN'T EVERYBODY?

What I'm about to share with you may sound like the weirdest thing on earth. Speaking in tongues is so, so misunderstood (try Googling it). In fact, the world has done a bang-up job of convincing people that it is freaky and a thing you should avoid at all costs. But, in reality, it is just the greatest thing ever with the ability to completely and totally transform your life. Let me explain...

When believers were first born again on the day of Pentecost, they believed and received holy spirit on the inside. The spirit came with nine evidences or operations contained within it. One of those nine fantastic abilities is called speaking in tongues. Immediately after receiving the gift of holy spirit, the newly born-again believers spoke in tongues. Basically, speaking in tongues is the God-given ability to speak in a language you don't understand. Its purpose is to give you a lever in prayer that totally bypasses your understanding. Many, many of your issues and problems in life come from not knowing what to pray for or said another way, being unaware of the spiritual causes of your problem. Speaking in tongues was designed to cover those needs by having the ability to pray perfectly, absent any selfishness or senses reasonings. It sounds confusing, but it really isn't. You simply decide to speak in tongues in the language provided by God and those words will be exactly the best things to pray, though you don't understand it, provided you decide to do it.

Recently I came across a fellow believer on Facebook who was in the process of identifying 150 reasons to speak in tongues from the Bible. The idea intrigued me because I had always been taught there were 10 to 12 reasons. I started reading and researching the reasons. Wow, what a mind-blowing experience! I realized so lucidly that speaking in tongues was God's gracious solution for so many of the things that plagued me or diminished my life. Living on this earth, we all have a spiritual enemy working behind the scenes to thwart and retard our efforts. But, he is a spiritual entity and, as such, hidden from our minds and ability to see him in action. Without God's spirit and the capability to use the nine manifestations, we would not stand a chance. (Enter the futility that plagues the world!) Speaking in tongues, one of the nine operations, is the only one we can operate whenever we want, unlike, for example, revelation, which God gives at His prerogative as the need requires. Now here is where it gets very interesting...

Speaking in tongues builds us up on the inside; that I already knew. But, I assumed it built up my spirit and ended there. Further, I was taught that my mind is built up by God's Word, which is unequivocally true as well. However, there is a distinct carryover from spirit to my mind. Imagine, if my spirit was built up, since I cannot feel spirit, how would I ever know? But like all of the manifestations, it also works with my mind. The spiritual darkness that engulfs the world takes away our joy and happiness by assaulting us with negativity and drama. Speaking in tongues clears the path, so to speak and absent the hindrances, we feel fantastic.

Here's another example. Speaking in tongues gives rest to your soul. Have you ever felt weary and worn out? Speaking in tongues serves as a refresher to your soul. My spirit doesn't need refreshing because it is perfect and never tired. However, my soul needs refreshing and rest. Speaking in tongues provides that for me. My soul is not my spirit. My soul needs rest. Are you starting to see what I'm getting at?

Speaking in tongues quickens or makes alive our mortal body. How many times has your old body not been responding as you would like? How often is your body bothered by the things that are going wrong? Speaking in tongues brings life to your flesh and no amount of eating healthy or exercise, though necessary, can do more for you than God can. Do you hear what I'm saying?

Speaking in tongues offers you the opportunity to pray for things you need, that you have absolutely no clue that you need. God calls it our greatest weakness. When you speak in tongues for yourself or for the people you love, God fills in the true needs by your decision to speak in tongues. It is trusting in God with all your heart and leaning not to your own understanding. That's when all things work together for good, as the good book says.

The Bible also says God has not given us the spirit of fear but (a spirit of) power and of love and a sound mind! The power doesn't reside in your head, it resides in your spirit. Your spirit, built up and edified, comes alive with the power you need to overcome any trouble the enemy is throwing at you! Any difficulty, any problem, anything... It also comes with love and a sound mind, experienced and evidenced in your heart. It's like a love super-booster, pouring out from you like a river of pure sweetness. It's a profound ability to understand spiritual things and finally, for once in your life, understand spiritually what the heck is really going on!

Like anything you actively cultivate, it has fruit associated. The fruit doesn't show up right away, just like apples, but before you know it, you start seeing and experiencing the fruit. Guess what the Bible says are the fruit? Love, joy, peace, long-suffering, gentleness, goodness, meekness, temperance (self-control), and believing. Believing is how you can get things from God, and you have the ability to cultivate more of it as a fruit. You want more love? Speak in tongues much. You want the peace that passes understanding? Speak in tongues much. You want to be more meek or teachable? Speak in tongues much. You need more self-control? (and who doesn't?). Speak in tongues much. Our lack of self-control is often influenced by the dark side of seduction, and when you speak in tongues much, it builds you up and removes the sticky attachments. Suddenly you are finally able to get in control of yourself!

It is so, so big people! It is one of God's perfect solutions for you, and once you learn how you can do it as often as you want. Inspired by my learning, I've been going to the limits with it, speaking in tongues much, all throughout the day, when I can. (It doesn't replace my responsibilities like work - smile.) So, I can testify, it is drastically changing my experience of life. In fact, I think I'm tasting some heavenly fruit. But hey, don't trust me, try it out for yourself!

If you know how to do it, do it abundantly. If you don't know how to do it, reach out and I will help you get there. It's not freaky, my friends; it's part of God's perfection...

Sure, I speak in tongues, doesn't everybody?

THE FRUIT OF THE SPIRIT

For years and years people have spoken of the fruit of the spirit as if it actually referred to the fruit of good works. There's certainly nothing wrong with good works, in fact, the reason you have the spirit from God is so that you can perform good works. Or, I might say perform the best works! I believe the confusion comes from another verse of scripture that uses this same phrase. The verse says:

(For the fruit of the Spirit *is in all goodness and righteousness and truth;) Ephesians 5:9*

As it's stated here it certainly would lead you to believe that the fruit of the spirit comes from goodness, righteousness and truth. However, the word for "spirit" in the text is actually the word for light. It's the fruit of the light we are talking about here. This is simple to research for yourself or by even looking at other versions of the Bible. But here in the book of Galatians, the fruit of the spirit refers to the end result of cultivating your spirit. In order for anything to produce fruit it must first be cultivated. If you decide to plant yourself a peach tree, there are some steps you have to perform before you can actually enjoy the fruit. First, you have to plant your tree in good ground. You have to prepare the ground and you can't just plant the thing anywhere! After you've planted it, you have to care for it on a consistent basis, day after day. If you neglect it for a period of time, it may still produce some fruit, but the process will be hindered. However, if you diligently care for your tree, providing the best nutrients and water, eventually it is going to produce some good fruit. And, you already know that the fruit doesn't just show up overnight. That would be very nice, but it just doesn't work that way. You have to continue with your care of the tree until the fruit appears. Even then, there's a maturing that takes place before the fruit tree really kicks into high gear producing more fruit than you can handle. At that point, you have to find some friends and neighbors with which to share your bountiful crop. Pretty soon you become known in the neighborhood for your abundant peach crop!

The holy spirit living inside you follows the same process, with one exception. No matter how much you neglect your gift, it is never going to die off. It will just continue to be dormant until you start to provide it with the required care. God's seed in you, like any fruit-yielding tree, has contained within it all that you will ever need to produce the fruit. Therefore, your job is to cultivate your seed. You cultivate fruit by utilizing the manifestations of holy spirit, namely speaking in tongues. Speaking in tongues, day by day, builds up your spirit and, at a certain point, begins to produce fruit in your life. However, the fruit produced isn't limited to apples or peaches. The fruit of the spirit is everything you have ever yearned for in your life. It represents the most important things for a human being, necessary to thrive and to flourish! And, it can all be yours by making the decision to manifest the gift inside you. How incredibly simple and misunderstood this is in our world today. By confusing the fruit of the spirit with the fruit of good works, people think they must somehow become good enough before God will bless them with these fantastic realities. God does not bless you because of how good you are. God blesses you when you decide to believe Him. When you finally get around to believing Him, you begin to do exactly what He tells you to do, and you stop doing everything the world is always telling you to do. It is impossible for you to ever earn

God's blessings in your life! How good could you ever become? I have spent some time traversing that slippery slope, and trust me when I tell you, it is a painful, losing endeavor! You are not going to arrive at some place of 'nirvana' whereby you always do what you are supposed to do. You have the nature of sin in your blood. No matter how disciplined, how faithful, or how sincere you are in your personal efforts to earn God's goodness, you will never, ever, ever arrive at that place. Instead, like most of the "earn your blessings" folks, your end result will be nothing but condemnation and pain, coupled with critical judgment of yourself first and then other people. Your heart will become hard and calloused because the back-story to that behavior isn't God convicting you of sin, but rather the adversary's accusation being permitted to hold a place in your life. While you are feeling so self-religious and self-righteous, you will be completely off track from God and His love for you. That influence controlling your life and, if you are honest, making you feel miserable, isn't from God.

The things of God are always freely given to you when you believe, end of story! If you have ever felt the sting of condemnation and guilt, then you know it is not a motivator for good. It is the exact opposite. It just beats you down and takes away your confidence (believing) in God. What you need from God is His forgiveness and guaranteed assurance that He has made you who you are and that by your own self, you can do nothing! Understanding that reality finally liberates you from sin, which is a major point in the New Testament. You are now, because of what God has done for you, free to love; free to give; free to serve. You are completely, completely, completely set free by God because of the accomplishments of His son for your life. Your response? Speak in tongues abundantly, which is described as "giving thanks well!"

As you speak in tongues faithfully, day by day, as God's liberated person, you are cultivating the fruit of the spirit into your life. When the fruit shows up is God's business. Your business is to faithfully cultivate the fruit. So, what is the fruit of the spirit?

But the fruit of the Spirit is love, joy, peace, patience, kindness, goodness, faithfulness, gentleness, self-control; against such things there is no law. Galatians 5:22-23

Another way to say this is, what is the result of faithfully manifesting the gift? You get to enjoy your fruit! It is important to recognize that these fruit are an end result. They are not something you work hard to do; they are something that God blesses you with for acting on what He said to act on! This is a crucially important distinction! Fruit are a blessing from God to be enjoyed, not requirements for your behavior. For example, if you experience the love of God as a part of the fruit of the spirit, you will naturally share that indescribable love with other people. It will be there for you as a cultivated fruit. It is not a behavior you must strive to earn; it is a fruit you get to enjoy. Are you beginning to see how awesome this really is? This is your access point to the sweetest things in life. Your only requirement, if you want to use that word, is to enjoy and share your abundance of fruit. The peace of God that passes all human understanding can be yours as a cultivated fruit. In that sublime experience of God's peace, you will find that you really don't need anything else in life to make you happy. You will be totally and completely at rest on the inside. How many people have experienced this even once in their lives? There's so much more, but here it is, and it is yours for the taking. Speak in tongues much in your private prayer life!

It is a deep, heartfelt, inexpressible gratefulness for having a God
that never gives up on you even when you sort of give up on Him.

ON MY BIRTHDAY

As I reflect back on another trip around the sun, I cannot help
but be filled with great thankfulness and joy for the sweetness
that surrounds me in this life. As a youngster in college, a generous and loving man reached out to me and introduced me to
God. I should say more formally introduced me, as God and I
had many conversations in the past, but back then I only
hoped He was all that I thought He should be. Since that immortal day, my life has never been the same.

Back then I, like you, was full fear and trepidation about
life. And although I had all the vim and vigor that surrounds
youth, I was still pretty shaky about how it would all turn out.
I mean, let's face it, life can be pretty scary with loads of potential pitfalls. In college, I had some run-ins with a couple of
religious groups and I knew I didn't want that! I didn't want
anything that seemed designed solely to make me feel bad
about myself! Shoot, I didn't even know I was looking for
something, but apparently I was.

Then I took this class called PFAL (Power for Abundant
Living) and learned the Bible for myself. Holy shit, I found the
holy grail. I found a congruous *whole* that didn't cause me to
sneeze, cough or sputter! I found out that God was not only all
I had hoped He would be, but He was even better than that. I
learned that He is only good and never changes in His views
towards me. My life took off like gangbusters as I began to
shed fears like old skin. I was living on the high road, and the

sky literally was the limit.

Some years later, as my children got older and my purpose became less clear, I, like you maybe, sort of lost my way a little bit. I forgot about how good God was to me and began to see Him in a different light. Oh, He didn't change; I did! I learned from certain folks that the Way I knew and loved so much wasn't really as easy and free as I thought. I was taught rules and regulations and requirements that accompany maturity - so-called. And apparently, all those days I was living the high life were really just a figment of my youth, and real life, life with God was damn arduous and fraught with the danger of "blowing it" or worse. Welcome to the life suck club.

I found out the hard way that once you get captured by religion, the way back is difficult. That stuff attaches to your brain like oil, and you can't just wash it out overnight. In fact, it likely will claim years of your life. However obnoxious it begins, it seems less impactful as I imagine you get used to all of its claims. All you know is that you now have fear where you used to have love. In your desperation, you try to do good works hoping the Lord will start to like you again, as He did before. The harder you work, the less He seems to care, and you start morphing into those people you hate; the ones filled with self-righteousness but miserable as f*ck! You're definitely struggling, but God is still bigger than your malarky!

Then, not suddenly but surely, something or someone gets you back to God's Word; the Word that saved you and changed you and blessed you. And in your private quest, you, like me, begin to discover who God is again. You read what the Bible says, and you study what it says, and you begin to relish what it says, and just like that it dawns on you! The light at first flickers, then glows into full flame. All this bullshit you have been thinking and regretting and worrying about God is not true, and it was never true. You were taught incorrectly. You were led off course. You got sucked down a rabbit hole and lived there for way too long!

As you shake off the last vestiges of error, your heart wakes up. Your sleepy, numbed, slightly wilted heart comes back to life. You understand the profound significance of keeping your head in God's Word and putting nothing ahead of the truth of God's Word! You see, glory hallelujah, that it wasn't famous, charismatic men that saved you, but God via the supreme accomplishments of His son, carefully outlined in His Word. You catch glimpses again of not only who you are but who you have the potential to be! You feel like you got some power going on inside, and you need to let it out to help set others free; the free you cherished so dearly!

You may now be thinking this a sad story or a warning for how you live your life. It's not. What this is - is an ever-growing thankfulness and joy and blessed love between a son and his Heavenly Father. It is a deep, heartfelt, inexpressible gratefulness for having a God that never gives up on you even when you sort of give up on Him. It's indescribable joy that comes from the pure truth minus the religious admixture. It is 59 glorious years of life on earth with God as your backbone, your rock and your fortress. It is, "Life - you don't frikkin scare me anymore!" It's just the greatest ride ever, and I wouldn't change one piece of it!

You, like me, should learn about God and not allow the promoters of religious sacrifice to rob you of one of the greatest experiences you could ever have, not just now but throughout all eternity! God is not too good to be true, H; he is so good He is true! He is your first love that makes all your other loves that much sweeter... Choose God! Choose love!

I am one blessed individual...

CHAPTER NINE
Happiness

JUST ANOTHER BLOG ON
FINDING HAPPINESS

Of late, it has become more and more apparent that many of our notions of finding happiness don't really lead to happiness at all. Happiness isn't some target destination you can reach or some feeling you can acquire by your determination to think about being happy. In fact, the consideration and contemplation of happiness seems to cancel out its positive effect. And while happiness is greatly influenced by your thinking, it generally comes more from *doing* than from thinking at all...

There is, I'm sad to report, such a thing as too much thinking. This modern-day notion we have learned from the self-help, motivation and positivity age is that we somehow have to closely monitor our thoughts and then quickly change every thought over into a positive one. On the surface, this all sounds fine and dandy. However, when you stop your thinking and subsequent doing in order to evaluate and monitor, you sort of cease being and switch over to evaluating or judging. Now you, as yourself, are looking at yourself and making a determination about yourself. And how often are those self-focused, interior judgments good? Constantly checking in on yourself to see if you are okay is counterproductive to being okay.

Have you ever been completely absorbed in something like work and noticed how good you felt afterwards? Generally, it seems, the more focused you are in the present moment and what it is you are doing in the present moment, the better you feel. In these moments of ecstasy and bliss, you don't have to turn on your mental oven monitor to check if your happiness is ready. It just is and you have the pleasure of enjoying it. How many times have you been worried about some scenario and just couldn't get it out of your head? That is until you decided to mow the lawn and voila, just like that you feel better! Sure, these are simple examples, but they do point to an awareness that the best use of our minds is to accompany the activity we are engaged in, in the moment called now.

The polar opposite of simply being and doing is thinking and thinking and thinking. No one's life ever got better from over-thinking and analyzing and judging. Yet, we engage in it as if it is a responsible way to behave. The result of it is always "to do" lists for self-improvement and/or decisions to get up earlier, read more, drink less and the like. Hidden behind those noble efforts of goal setting and life betterment lies a subtle message that you are not okay just as you are. In the same way that religion questions your worthiness before God to control you and get your money, the self-help industry offers to improve you and make you okay as long as you buy the book, attend the seminar and buy another book! How can anyone ever simply "be happy" if they live perpetually in a state of "I'm not okay?"

In truth, it's not the analysis that is the issue, it's the judgment. It seems a person is the happiest when they can choose for themselves what they will and will not do. How many people really do what *they* want to do? Things are always modified and changed to fit in, be accepted, please him and satisfy her. We spend our days in anxiety ever trying to live up to some rules that someone else set-up for us to live. We don't trust ourselves and our judgment and thereby severely curtail our own happiness. Our minds become chock full of things we should do, shouldn't do and must do! It might be okay if *we* determined what those things are, but most often we are still living out someone else's rules for acceptability. Don't you just love and admire the people who do what they want to do and are not ashamed of it? Happy is the man who doesn't condemn himself for the things he enjoys! Indeed, happy is the man...

The essence of finding happiness is not in looking for happiness at all. Rather it is choosing to live in the moment, enjoying your choice of activities, accepting yourself just as you are and doing your own life! It's in making plans and pursuing dreams. It's in being fully present with the people you love. It's in flexibility, spontaneity and whim! It's in getting out of your own head while refusing to judge yourself, analyze yourself or berate yourself. It's in finally choosing to live your life rather than choosing only to think about it and judge it.

Happiness isn't elusive or hiding from you. Rather it is waiting for you to let go of all of your controls and ideas and simply let yourself be. It's all around you waiting for you to notice its presence. It's at your job, in your home, in the yard and at the store. It's in each moment of life spent doing and being and living. It's hoping you will set aside all of your judgments and comparisons and analysis long enough to notice, "I'm here" and "How happy I feel!"

Just another blog on finding happiness...

Notice carefully how there will always be some condition that isn't quite fulfilled; some destination to get to; some missing piece, which craftily informs your mind that you are not allowed to be happy yet!

HAPPINESS AND WHAT YOU MIGHT BE DOING TO 'EFF' IT UP

Ahhh happiness, the most talked about feeling in the whole world! Yet, for all that is inked regarding the subject, there is one thing that leads to its discovery and that one thing is you. Is happiness eluding you? Are your happy moments few and far between? Are you only truly happy when the circumstances line up perfectly? Can you even remember the last time you were happy? The answer to the questions is found within your own mind and within your own mind alone... Are you effing up your own happiness?

Happiness, substitute the word blessed if you're a believer, is such a simple concept and its attainment is always found within your grasp. Life doesn't make you happy; you make you happy. Favorable circumstances don't make you happy; you have already decided which circumstances make you happy. Material riches don't lead to happiness unless you have decided that they do. Happiness is not a mental state to be sought after, but a decision you are making every moment of every day. Even our great God cannot make you happy without your full consent! When you are unhappy, chances are you are doing something in your mind to eff it up.

Why, if happiness is so vitally important to us, would we consciously screw it up? Well, it's not so much a conscious decision as it is learned behaviors; learned ways of thinking we have unconsciously been programmed to adopt. Something somewhere is ever at work to steal away your happiness. Someone, unscrupulously scheming, behind the scenes, has been tirelessly chipping away at you day after day and night after night. He seeks to define your narratives. He, with help from the world's media machine, adeptly puts a spin on your perspective. He (or it) falsely outlines which conditions produce happiness and then makes sure you cannot meet those conditions. (You can never meet the conditions because the conditions are always a lie; a false portrayal.) You are not alone in your conundrum because what you are facing is the human condition, absent the truth. You are on a universal journey whereby how you vote determines the election. If you don't choose, the choice will be made for you. You eff up your happiness by allowing something or someone else to dictate the conditions!

Happiness is always very personal in nature. What leads to your happiness won't necessarily lead to my happiness, though the mechanics of being happy are the same. The world; the systems of the world, will always lead you into the dark cave. You end up chasing not what makes you happy, but what someone else says will make you happy. The amount of money you need to be happy will always be a little more than what you have. Instead of finding happiness in your relationship, there will always be something missing; something you wish you had; some trait you find less than perfect; something that informs you that you don't get to be happy yet. You can apply this formula to finding happiness in every aspect of your life. Notice carefully how there will always be some condition that isn't quite fulfilled; some destination to get to; some missing piece, which craftily informs your mind that you are not al-lowed to be happy yet! Please read that sentence again! You are waiting to be happy. You are waiting for conditions to line up. You are waiting for something that finally gives you permission to be happy. But, the only one impeding your happiness is you... waiting. You're effing up your own happiness by waiting for something else to produce it for you.

When it comes to happiness, it is something you must decide for yourself. Decide to be happy now, not just on the weekend. Decide to be happy at work. Decide to be happy in your relationship and behave as someone who is happy. Stop waiting for the future when conditions are right and you have everything you ever wanted. Look, you may one day have everything you ever wanted, but a lot of living will have transpired in the interim while you were waiting. Happiness in life is found in the journey, not the destination. Happiness is found not absent any challenges, but in overcoming the challenges. Happiness comes from controlling your thinking and refusing everything that confronts or challenges that happiness. Stop measuring yourself against impossible standards and enjoy your life. You are what you are today, the good and the bad, so you may as well make peace with yourself and live. Each day time slips away and your opportunities for happiness diminish as your time on Earth diminishes. Cherish what you have and where you are today. Hug your children. Spoil your grandkids. Kiss your wife/husband/boyfriend/girlfriend. Love the unlovable and help the folks who need the most help. Give your life your all with no holdbacks! Life is a treasure with happiness infused in the creation, if you are willing to see it! You may just be effing up your happiness by what you are refusing to see...

God, the source of all possible love and goodness, created human life with one grand intention, that His children would be happy. (If you're a parent, you know how that feels!) So, let Him show you what life and happiness is all about. You were not designed to figure everything out on your own! You were not built to pack around a world of worries and cares. It was never intended that you try to do life by your own human logic. Instead you were made to live with Him as your Daddy, casting all your problems on to Him. Then, after having done that, relax and enjoy your life! Allow yourself to be happy today and just trust Him to take care of everything in between. Allow yourself to be happy, today, right effin now!

Don't eff it up! (smile) I love you...

DESPERATELY SEEKING HAPPINESS

I don't know about you, but there are more opinions on finding happiness than there are stars in the sky. Some suggest that you turn your focus to yourself, prioritize yourself and choose yourself first. Others promote gratitude as the answer. A majority report it comes from doing the things you love. Many say that happiness is not a destination you reach, but rather something that occurs along the journey. Some offer that happiness is found in favorable circumstances. Indeed, there are a multitude of theories and ideas, but do they really work? Can you find the happiness you so desperately seek?

There are few things you can directly control in life. Circumstances change, people change, events ebb and flow. Some days you are on top of the world; other days nothing seems right. At times you feel totally in control, and other times completely out of control. Try as you might, control as much as you can, take no risks, choose maximum safety and still things go wrong; sometimes disastrously wrong. It doesn't seem to matter if you are a good person or a bad person, though we like to assume that bad people have it coming. Yet, bad things happen to good people as well. So, what is it? What are you supposed to do?

The only thing you can have total control over is your mind. Often the missing key lies in what you choose to do with your mind. I don't mean you should try to be happy when things are going bad for you. No, that's not realistic or reasonable. I'm talking more about your mindset. What is your default mindset? What do you think about when no one is watching? What thoughts, ideas and expectations are you rehearsing in your head? Do you even know? Or have you bought into the crazy idea that your mind thinks and concludes with or without your permission? It's sort of like when people say they can't shut their minds off in order to go to sleep. I'm here to testify that you can turn your mind off, or better quiet it down, once you begin to learn how to control your thoughts. Happiness is a result of consistently controlling your thoughts.

Think about the times in your life when you felt happy and blessed. Maybe it was a family vacation or on your wedding day, or when you graduated from college. Was it really the vacation in the tropics that made you happy, or was it your anticipation and expectation? I would suggest it was the latter. There are many folks living in the tropics that aren't working and are free to play who are miserable still! Why? Because of their negative expectation. How many people do you know who are always waiting for their happiness as if it is on a train and they are awaiting its arrival? They are waiting to be happy. They feel that once such and such happens, they will finally be happy. Maybe when they get the money or the job or the perfect spouse, maybe then the happiness will follow. In the interim, they remain suspended, waiting and waiting for some circumstance to finally line up or for their lucky break to at last arrive. You see, there are 260 workdays in a year, but only 52 Saturdays, if you get my drift. That's a lot of waiting...

There is a far better strategy than waiting. The best plan of action, yes action, is found in choosing to be happy right now, no matter what your circumstances are promoting as reality. Being enthusiastic and optimistic, indeed expecting good things is a function of your mind. The action is to control your thinking. Stop being run about from pillar to post, being blown about with every wind of doctrine. Stop basing your happiness on what things look like! Stop waiting and hoping and wishing and just decide to be happy. You might not have recognized it before, but it is the same thing you did the last time you felt happy, only you assigned your happiness to the pleasant circumstances. You don't need pleasant circumstances to feel happy. All you need is to control what you are thinking and when your thinking goes south, as it necessarily must, you have to change it back again. Your feelings, those great natural barometers, are simply responding to your thoughts. It's not magic or predestination, good luck or bad luck. It's not some mysterious force outside of you picking you for one or the other. It's you, my friend, and what you are doing with your mind...

Allowing your thoughts to default to your experience and taking life as it comes is a recipe for misery. The world we live in is fraught with negativity. Letting your thoughts run where they wish will lead you down the rabbit hole of mental defeat. Instead your solution, God's solution for you, is for you to take charge of that unruly mind and line it up with the things you actually want. You line it up! You control it! You make it get in line with the life you so desperately seek and then experience the joy of seeing it coming to pass. Do you know why life works so well for some people? Because they expect it to and you don't have to look any deeper than that. Do you know how to get blessed by God? Become blessed first and then the blessings will follow. Stop waiting on God. God is waiting on you!

The ability to control your mind is one of the greatest things God ever did for you. It is His solution in a world that seems chaotic and out of control. There's no need to beg God to change your life around. You change your life around by changing your thoughts around, not later on when it looks favorable, but right now in the midst of whatever. When the negative thoughts come, recognize them and change them.

And, if you really want to excel, if you want to tap into the abundant life, instead of the ordinary life, then find some positive promise of God that counters your negativity and change your mind accordingly. Say that, rehearse that, announce that, claim that. Soon you'll find your happiness increasing exponentially...

Are you desperately seeking happiness in your life? Have you already tried all the theories? Learn to focus and control your thinking. Decide first you are going to be blessed and enthusiastic and happy. Decide it right now today in this moment and keep deciding it though all hell should try to drag you back down. Don't spend another second waiting... Your feelings follow your thoughts and you are in charge of your thoughts. Be happy...

CONTROLLING YOURSELF TO HAPPINESS

The paradox of all paradoxes occurs when something that appears contraindicated leads to exactly what you are looking for in life. Happiness, often maligned and dismissed or over-exalted and worshipped, is found in control, not in letting loose; in reigning in, not in unbridling; in checks and balances, not in removing the boundaries. The good life demands you take charge of yourself. Control yourself to happiness...

I submit that the part of life you have failed to control, for whatever reason, is the primary contributing cause of your difficulties and your struggles. Corruption and deterioration have to find a way in and exist only when allowed or invited. Decay follows that which is not maintained, and control is that maintenance. The let loose life (and believe me, I've spent too much time there) lets loose both fun and pain. But, the pain always exceeds the fun in unfulfilled life and pervasive unhappiness. Sure, there is always a balance with religion being the polar opposite of ungoverned anarchy. Religion adds in checks where there are no checks and limitations imposed not for future bliss but for the intended misery of the occupant. Too much control strips life of its variety and blessings, ever pointing the one controlled to his own lack and deficiencies. Religion is not control but rather a fear-induced and fear-motivated attempt at escaping something thus far imagined or experienced, yet not producing a remedy but instead more fear! The control that leads to happiness is never found there.

Thought allowed to run rampant whithersoever it leads is

the bane of man's existence. It repudiates order and stands in active defiance to the system God designed for man. It results in a misery, then blamed on God, though encouraged and endorsed by the individual. No wonder as the message of the world is ever "all is to be welcomed" and "all may be experienced." While all things are lawful for me, all things are not expedient. Though God has made me free to do as I please, rotten and painful results help shape my future decisions. Thus, control is not engendered as a response to fear but rather as a humble attempt at locating what is best. Just as joy encourages perseverance towards the goal, control promises liberty and happiness, days with no end.

The question is not what is wrong with you but rather what category or categories of your life have you let go? What do you love so much that you over indulge in it? What vices have long since replaced problem solving or have promised peace by soothing and numbing? What thing pops up over and over and over as a lesson unengaged? If you are unhappy there is such a thing, promising you liberty yet putting chains on your soul. Controlling yourself isn't arduous, refusing to is. Control is nothing more than the discipline required to compete successfully. Once disqualified you're no longer eligible for the prize. Get the prize!

I have proven to myself as the ultimate fun lover and pleasure seeker that the more I loose the restraints the more restrained I have become. Yet the simple application of a diet or commitment to exercise or a sustained abstinence from that one thing, the happier I have become in increased proportion to my efforts. Yet my happiness hasn't followed some grand morality or complete change of being, but followed instead some small discipline I'm quite capable of achieving. Thus, the lesson is clear, check and balance that which you can check and balance and enjoy the unchecked blessings that accompany.

The starting point for you in your quest is to locate an area, decided by you and never by another, that you can apply some discipline to, such as, "no more of this thing on the weekdays," or "no sugar for three weeks," or "three times per week at the gym no matter what!" Do so, and you will find that not only do you immediately begin to feel better following your decision, but that the small decision starts to transcend into other categories of your life. It's as if God cannot get you to step seven until you have at least begun with step one and persisted through steps four, five, and six.

The happy fellow or happy gal you have been observing with eyes askant will, almost as sure as the sun coming up tomorrow, already be engaged in this process applying limits as required and learned. It's a mark of human maturity and seems hard to learn without having lived on the other side. Just as a child flitters from place to place with unbridled happiness, will also eat the whole bag of M&M's to their stomach's demise. It takes years lived to finally see, if you ever see, that control is not only expected but required.

Take the reins of your own life and leave no aspect of yourself in the hands of another! Let no good thing be relegated to chance and circumstance. Instead of railing and screeching at the conditions of your life, control yourself and those things applicable directly to you. If it is yours, address it. If you own it, care for it. If you're responsible for stewarding it, guard it and keep it and watch over it! Your body, like your car, can run a long time with little maintenance, but when it dies, it is really dead! But, a little care applied here and there, and most issues are simply resolved. Discipline is a choice, and a lack of discipline is also a choice. Choose wisely!

In short, "Be the boss of your own butt" and see if you don't have the best '*glutes*' in town!

THE HAPPINESS MYTH

Happiness is admittedly something we all desperately want in our lives, right? There's the "Happiness Advantage," "The Happiness Hypothesis," "The Happiness Project," and countless other books on the topic. Happiness is perhaps one of the most contemplated subjects in the world. And although there are many wonderful books that offer the elusive promise of enduring happiness, there's one thing I know for sure. Happiness is a dish best served...

I don't know if this has ever happened to you, but I found myself going through a "bit of a rough patch," as my British ancestors are wont to say. As a self-proclaimed promoter of happiness, I felt embarrassed to find myself a teacher who no longer believed in his own message. I analyzed my life, piece by piece, looking for an answer. I tried blaming others and their apparent lack of support for me. I made the usual excuses, "I'm so busy," "I need to get organized," "I need to finish unfinished business," etc., etc., etc. Maybe I just needed to start saying 'no' to other people's requests. And the more I searched for the cause the more lost I became. I thought I needed to be more selfish and devote more time to myself and what I wanted. Maybe it was not enough sleep or a bad diet, or maybe it was my thinking and not paying attention to what I was thinking about. I knew better than to blame God, so I thought maybe I wasn't devoting enough time to God or praying enough or studying. I searched myself from here to breakfast, and the more I searched the more unhappy I became. I became critical of myself and judged myself harshly, rehearsing my shortcomings and my faults. Maybe I just needed to get better at... Or work harder to... Or exercise more discipline with... And, in the end, only more of that pervasive misery.

Then something interesting happened. I received a call from a gentleman explaining that the Dale Carnegie franchise had returned to Utah and he wondered if I wanted to be a facilitator again. I vividly remembered how much I loved doing Carnegie classes, but I felt a hesitation in my heart. I couldn't explain it, but I felt like I didn't want to do it anymore. Yet I couldn't shake the memory of how much joy I felt doing the classes in the past. So, against my own feelings, I reluctantly agreed. Fast forward a month or so and I found myself sitting in an immersion class (accelerated), learning or relearning the principles again. At first, I was challenged and agitated because I knew I would be forced out of my comfort zone (that place I dwell in day by day where nothing happens!). But, I persisted and then it happened! As I made the long commute home, I recognized something that had been missing for a long time. Joy. Indescribable, all-encompassing joy!

What happened to me? What took place that moved me so suddenly from misery to happiness in just under eight hours? Well, while learning and practicing the principles in that unmistakable Dale Carnegie way, I finally took the focus off myself and on to other people. I practiced showing sincere appreciation and listening and seeing things from another's point of view. I became more interested in helping my fellow man than I was in helping myself. It was no longer about me...

One of the great paradoxes of life is that the more you seek the fulfillment of your own needs, the less they are fulfilled and the more you seek to take care of others, the more your own needs are going to be met. The Bible states it this way. The more you lose yourself for others, the more you find your real self. And conversely, the more you seek to find yourself, the more lost you become. Crazy I know, but oh so true!

Despite the multitude of claims circling around the globe today, focusing on yourself, and only yourself, can only result in misery. It has to; it must! Focusing on yourself as the great starting point for all endeavors almost guarantees a negative outcome, because all you'll end up with is yourself; full of flaws and mistakes and weaknesses. Focusing on yourself as an attempt to make yourself happy defies the laws of life. You want, you desire, you seek, but when done exclusively for yourself, it subtracts life, instead of adding to it. Conversely, when you seek the good of others (giving), the laws of life cooperate by returning back to you (receiving). It really is more blessed to give than to receive. Read this little poem that I think says it best:

The Man in the Glass

When you get what you want in your struggle for self
And the world makes you king for a day,
Just go to the mirror and look at yourself,
And see what that man has to say.

For it isn't your father or mother or wife,
Who judgment upon you must pass;
The fellow whose verdict counts most in your life
Is the one staring back from the glass.

He's the fellow to please, never mind all the rest.
For he's with you clear up to the end,
And you've passed the most dangerous, difficult test
If the man in the glass is your friend.

You may be like Jack Horner and "chisel" a plum,
And think you're a wonderful guy,
But the man in the glass says you're only a bum
If you can't look him straight in the eye.

You may fool the whole world down the pathway of years.
And get pats on the back as you pass,
But your final reward will be the heartaches and tears
If you've cheated the man in the glass.

~ Dale Wimbrow (c) 1934

And the only way not to cheat the man in the glass is by living your life in service to others.

So, if you, my friend, find yourself searching for the elusive happiness and finding misery instead, don't work any harder to find a way to give happiness to yourself, but instead find a way to give that happiness to someone else. And in so doing, you will find what every truly happy person has found; you have to give in order to receive. Happiness is a dish best served...

LEARNING HAPPINESS

The human mind is truly a fascinating thing, isn't it? Our brains have all this capacity to process information, classify, categorize and the like. We can store information; retrieve memories and even combine multiple ideas to form new conclusions. Yet with all of this unlimited mental technology at our fingertips, what do we do? We let the thing run on autopilot! You know what I mean. We opt for less thinking and let our minds run off of previously stored information. It's kind of like finding a good way to drive to work and then driving that way every day. That's perfectly fine I guess if our first conclusion is enduring, but what happens when there is a need for revision? Or, what happens when we are just plain old bored to death with that same route? I think that supplies an apt metaphor for human beings; a class I belong to with great pride. We learn things relatively early on in life (when the time seems ripe for learning) and sort of carry those ideas with us wherever we go. Of course, that is fine if those ideas are good or true but what if they aren't? What if we are applying a lesson of adolescence to adulthood, or worse a lesson of young adulthood to middle age? What if we have classified so much information that we just don't need to learn anymore?

My mom used to tell me over and over how smart I was. At some point, I believed her and now sit here typing with the intellect of a genius (hey, it's my story). Point being, that not all lessons previously ingrained need revision. However, many things do need revision. That black hole of negative conclusions we also formed, those babies need not only revision but elimination. Just because you have told yourself for 25 years that you have to struggle in life because of (________ fill in the blank) doesn't make it any truer than the first time you considered it! Just because Sally wouldn't dance with you at the prom when you were 15 doesn't mean that Sally wouldn't dance with you today; or that you are "unlucky" in love! Okay, I digress.... Life has been designed (passive voice intended) to function as one large, never-to-be-exhausted classroom with an infinite variety of opportunities for learning. Those opportunities are literally all around you. The issue isn't their existence but rather our capacity to see them. Seeing as God is the ultimate source of supreme intelligence, it makes sense to my little old brain that He might be constantly employed in teaching us stuff. Have you ever heard the phrase, "everything happens for a reason?" Well, I hate to be a "Debbie-Downer," but while everything happens for a reason is true, not everything happens for a good reason! But you see, our auto-pilot brain just accepted that expression and led us to believe that everything happens for a good reason! Now we find ourselves in the curious dilemma of trying to find the good in inherently disastrous situations, where no good thing exists. (Auto-pilot, numb brain, illogical at best.) The lesson in a terrible, negative consequence is to never do that "thing" again, not to try to find the good in it. God, who is light (and in Him is no darkness at all), doesn't need evil to teach you a lesson any more than you need to teach your children lessons by doing bad things to them! God, who is also pure love, seeks to teach you (and me) lessons that will help us win in life. He knows your issues; He hears your heartfelt petitions, and He has cleverly (understatement) placed things all around you to help you to learn. Your job; my job is to pay attention! But, before we have any shot at paying attention, we have to unload that giant weight called "I already know" and seek to understand. We have to humble ourselves and recall our "heart of a child" where we saw the most success. Have you ever been privileged enough to spend any time with a four-year-old? Those little boys and girls are fertile fields of learning. Sure, they can be easily led astray with their lack of life experience, but how many of us are being led astray because of (not in spite of) our life experience? How many of us have allowed our minds to idle down and simply stopped questioning things?

Interestingly, there is a huge, inescapable link between learning and happiness. Learning new things makes us happy. Rehearsing old things drives us nuts and sucks the very life out of us! In order to continue growing in life we have to continue learning. Can you even imagine that at age 51, you have learned all of the useful information there is to know? Silly huh? How about 74? Happiness, true happiness, comes from the adventure that is this life. And, it is proportionately as adventurous as is your capacity to want to learn. Thus, my advice to you is make the decision to learn again. Don't allow the "media-age" to define, classify and categorize your life! Twenty-year-olds aren't yet smart enough to know they can't do everything they think they can do. We should all be that smart, right? The truth is that you and I can do just about anything we think we can do, if we are willing to learn something new. We don't need to attend Harvard necessarily, but instead seek to understand. You can escape a "whole-lotta" trial and error if you get God involved. And God's middle name is "Happy" - so maybe we should start there? (not end there after 30 years).

At the end of the day, our happiness depends not so much on what we have, but rather on what we are learning. Life is an exciting adventure! "Clear eyes, full hearts, can't lose!"

HOW TO BE UNHAPPY

There are many things you can do to make yourself perennially unhappy. Unhappiness isn't something for amateurs to mess around with as it takes a serious daily commitment. So, if you really want to win at the game of losing, then this is for you!

If I wanted to be unhappy, I would start my day out past the time I wanted to get up, laying in the bed thinking about all of the things I did wrong yesterday. I would mentally rehearse where and how I went astray. I would berate myself for how fat I had gotten and question whether or not my hair was thinning. Then, I would hop out of bed with barely enough time to get ready for work. Because I didn't give myself enough time, lots of things would go wrong and end up making me late. Where's my damn blue tie?

On my commute I would feel agitated and distressed. I would pretend like the highway was mine and speed along cursing other drivers for having the audacity to get into my lane and not go at the speed I dictated. Up ahead there is a car in the fast lane going less than the speed limit, so I get as close to their bumper as I can without actually hitting them and cuss them out in their rear-view mirror! They flip me off in response to my behavior and I fly into a blinding rage. Just as I calm down, I notice someone was trying to merge next to me, so I speed up and tailgate the car in front of me, to make sure the bastards couldn't get in, no matter what.

Once I got to work late, I would head into the office with a sour, foul attitude. Mentally, I would point out which staff were ugly; which ones were fat and which ones were just plain stupid! When one of my co-workers came into my office, I would spend almost half an hour discussing how incompetent the leadership was, followed by some juicy gossip about one of the employees. Later in the morning, at the staff meeting, I would sit quietly at the conference table mentally comparing myself to the other leaders. I would lament on why I couldn't speak as intelligently as Bill and get angry over why everyone always laughs at Steve's silly jokes. I would literally grit my teeth anytime someone said something complimentary to the boss; effin, brown-nosers!

After lunch, I would dedicate myself to screwing around until the 'already too long' day was over. I would Facebook and Instagram, followed by a healthy dose of Amazon shopping. Hey, the stupid work can wait until tomorrow! Someone would call over to check on something I promised to get done, but I would explain in a highly frustrated tone why I didn't have enough time to accomplish things.

After another long commute, filled with slow traffic and my usual railings and flip-outs, I would get home and immediately dump a load of mental garbage on my family. I would corner my wife's ear and complain and fuss until dinner time. At dinner I would be sure to point out anything that wasn't quite cooked correctly. (I mean, she needs to know if the chicken is dry, right?) Then, after having a few drinks to unwind, I would pick a fight with her and begin to extol how unhappy I am with my life. I wouldn't take any responsibility for any of this because none of it is my own fault. If she didn't treat me the way she did, I could have been somebody! In fact, I never seem to catch a break like other people. I don't have enough money to do what I need to do, and I'm 10 times smarter than the wealthy people I know. And that's not my damn fault either. The cards have been stacked against me.

I wake up on the couch several hours later angry with myself for my behavior earlier. I pour myself into bed ready to begin the cycle anew tomorrow. I cannot wait for the weekend, when I can finally do what I want to do. But until then, everything sucks, everyone sucks and I guess deep down, I suck.

As I lay in bed trying to fall back asleep, I begin to question all of the decisions and choices I've made in my life. I fantasize about how things might have been if I married this person and moved to this state. I don't consider any of the good things I have accomplished because it doesn't matter as I could have done so much more. I know I'm deeply frustrated but it just doesn't seem like there is anything I can do about it. I remember the other day when some guy tried to talk with me about God, but I don't need that religion bullshit! I mean what could God do to help me with my crappy life? Doesn't He have big things to deal with like world peace and the starving people? I begin to drift off to sleep, exhausted and sad...

This, ladies and gentlemen, is how you make a career of being unhappy. Don't take any responsibility for anything, and for goodness sakes don't change what you have been thinking and doing. And if, by chance, there comes a point in your life when you want to choose happiness, then simply choose the opposite of all of this...

It's your life...

CHAPTER TEN
Musings

MONEY, MONEY, MONEY

This topic, the subject of this chapter, is decidedly abstruse, recondite, and arcane. We all want it, the more, the better it seems, but the mystery concerning it is monumental. It's the dirty little secret we don't discuss in public. It's something we think we understand, yet fail to understand. It can be the source of abundant pleasure as well as the source of copious amounts of pain. It's a perplexing riddle that is both easy to solve and impossible to solve. It seems to represent both status and power, yet actually personifies neither. It appears to be elusive and reserved for a small, closed group, yet once you have some it seems to replicate itself. It is the apparent cause of most people's problems yet portrays itself as the solution to most people's problems. It is the promise of the lottery ticket and the curse of having too much. Is it simply a means of exchange, or does it symbolize so much more?

In our culture today, money represents a means of exchange for goods and services. We usually don't have some cows for trade or bushels of wheat and barley. But, in America, we have money, cash in fist, dineros, dough. Money pays for the things that we need and want. If we do not have enough money, then we struggle in getting our needs met. Food costs money, homes cost money, cars cost money. Even our beloved fun and good times often cost money. Yet recognizing the vast impact money has on the quality of our lives, we fail to give it the priority it deserves. We harbor these confusing views concerning it. We have all heard the stories of the people that seem to have a lot of it and how reportedly difficult their life has become. Yet is it really the money that causes the problems or the failure on the part of the possessor to control themselves? In the United States we have an abundance of food, readily available and relatively cheap. And for this reason, we also have trouble with obesity. We can literally eat ourselves to death. We eat beyond our need or maybe beyond three people's needs and lament our sluggish and diminished state. It seems then again to point more toward the mindset of the possessor than the availability of the resource.

It has been said that money rules the world. But does it really? I think it would be fairer to say that money, as the means of exchange, determines in a large way just how happy you are going to be. Oh sure, we can all cling to the old adage that we don't need it, usually said by people that don't have it, as a sort of self-righteous stand against what it represents. But, I would submit that you still have to get your needs met. If you always have to say no to an activity or opportunity to do something, not because you don't want to but because you cannot afford to, you are doing yourself a disservice. You are erroneously concluding that money is something you cannot obtain or shouldn't obtain because of its so-called reported evils. But, what evil could be associated with a means of exchange? If you owned a chinchilla farm and paid for your needs with chinchillas, could someone accuse you of having too many chinchillas? Would anyone give you a solemn warning concerning the evils of having too many chinchillas and demand a reduction? You see, we've got it all wrong in this regard. The love of money is the root of all evil, not because money is evil, but because the love of it is, and loving it as the source (not a means) in your life leads you down a path replete with pain, suffering and misery. Like the rich person that cannot say no to things because they can afford them, or the obese person who cannot say no to food because it tastes good, the issue isn't the money; it is the lack of control you have over yourself. God is the source of our lives and the source of the money we need to buy things. Thinking He is opposed to you having more than enough money to get your needs met, to get your wants satisfied, to be able to bless and help others get their needs met, is not thinking soundly.

The point, if you haven't gotten it by now, is that it is your responsibility, with God's help, to crack the money code. Figure it out and figure it out quickly. Don't live out your existence with a growing list of unmet needs. Stop acting like it is noble to go without all the time. If your Daddy owns the cattle on a thousand hills, do you think He would be the one opposing you? And for God's sake, get it out of your head that you are somehow being greedy. People that are truly greedy never entertain the thought that they are being greedy. Instead, wonderful people like you and me are the ones that entertain it. Those of you who are parents, how do you handle getting your kid's needs met? I would submit, as a parent, that you would do whatever it took to get your child something they really wanted, let alone what they actually needed! You would spare no effort in figuring out a way to bless them. Well, how about God? Do you really think he is checking and stifling you to live below par; to settle for less; to go with your needs and wants unmet because the fulfillment of those things requires some dough? Hardly! Again, we have been sold a bill of goods...

Money is simply a means of exchange, and while you don't always need the money, but instead need the thing, there is absolutely nothing wrong with believing God to get the money. Money isn't evil, loving it and trusting it and worshipping it more than God is evil. I would guess that most people, not all people, have less money than they need and are selling themselves short in settling for less than what God, as The

Loving Parent, would want them to have. Raise your expectations. Cease from considering that your lot in life is to be meager and limited when God is unlimited! You already know, right now today, if you don't have enough, right? Well, there are lots of people that have more than enough; way more. The limit isn't God; the limit is you! Money, money, money! Get some! You need it...

THE DILEMMA OF THE THIRD DRINK

So a very wise and successful friend of mine posed the question, "Does THE THIRD DRINK really change us ... or in disguise does it bring out what indeed was always there?" An enticing question, I'm sure you would agree. I think I just heard Carrie Bradshaw saying it at the end of Sex and the City following her perpetual fight with "Big." Being an expert in the delights of a good Pinot Noir, I will frame my answer around my beverage of choice. If you are an avid wine drinker, and I say that to those wine drinkers who drink it simply for the pleasant purpose that God intended it (...He giveth wine that maketh glad the heart of man) and not necessarily to those in that sad, unfortunate class who drink it to mask their pain and misery in this life, then you will completely understand what I am about to say. Usually, the first glass of wine produces a sparkle on the inside that encourages us to talk and enjoy the people we are blessed to be with and in the reverie of those moments we gladly seek a second glass which seems to encourage more mutual sharing of fondness and kindness and love. But what about that third glass? Something odd seems to take place after that third glass, haven't you noticed? Somewhere, hiding within that third glass is a truth serum. We didn't know it was in there as it was deftly hidden, but somehow it manages to emerge. I'm not talking about that perennial sadness or the lament over lost dreams and opportunities. I'm talking about that idealist that lives in all of us. It's that guy or gal in there that knows exactly what they want and, in many cases, knows exactly what needs to take place to get to that ideal state that he or she has been dreaming about. But prior to that third partaking was simply lacking the *huevos* to say what they have needed to say all along. That idealist, always lurking just below the surface, wants to share love and kindness; wants to help lift others up and wants to relieve at least a portion of the misery that has been allowed to persist in those they care about the most. He knows the love he has withheld and seeks to remedy it. She knows her secret dreams and wants to share them with others without fear of ridicule and shame. And to this point, the only thing that has withheld them from speaking has been fear.

Fear is a spurious and deceptive animal. It seeks to lurk beneath our bold exteriors and convinces us that we cannot have our ideals. It tells us lies and half-truths about the things we earnestly seek and after getting us to accept those lies, succeeds in silencing our most noble and God-like aspirations. Fear is indeed our enemy and is always wrong in every category of our lives.

Back to our dilemma... what is it about that third drink that serves to loosen our tongues so adeptly? Well, that old, ancient beverage starts to lower those walls we have put up around our hearts and it no longer seems so unreasonable to say the things we have been thinking for so long a time. We can no longer contain that idealist and must give him or her voice to say what needs to be said. Is it delusion? Is it falsely heightened emotions? I hope not. It is instead, "liquid courage!" Lest you should stop reading now, the glorious point that shouldn't be missed in this well-meaning diatribe is that those things we wanted to say were there all along and Ol' Pino just brought them out! (Thanks Ol' Pino). Now of course Ol' Pino has a dark side, as anything does that is not enjoyed in moderation, in that by the fifth and sixth and ninth glass you are no longer an idealist but rather a drunk person seeking only some form of gratification!

So, "Does THE THIRD DRINK really change us ... or in disguise does it bring out what indeed was always there?" It brings out what was already there, my friend. It brings out what has been there all along...

Make today a day when you speak for the idealist and don't be satisfied with things the way they always have been...

Now this may surprise you, but God never promised that life would
be easy or that you would not have to deal with lemons
and sometimes grapefruits!

HANDLING LEMONS, GRAPEFRUITS
AND OTHER ANNOYANCES

Things often happen to us in life that annoy the bejesus out of
us. Whether it's harassing lemons or gigantic grapefruits;
small irritants or life-threatening situations, life isn't always
easy street. Now, if you are a member of random life club; believing that life is only what you can see, etc., and that there is
nothing behind it all, this surely will make no sense to you.
But, if you have the good sense to recognize that the design of
things is far too complex to swallow that story, then you may
want to invest the three minutes and hear what I have to say!

Life is spiritual, and behind it all is One wonderful loving
God who only gives good, and One rebellious lesser being who
only gives evil. Those two never intertwine. God doesn't do
evil ever, no matter the plethora of insane reasons people give
to explain why He does. The things that drive you "batshit"
crazy are by design and planned. They come from your personal adversary who is ever watching for things that might
defeat you and supplying a healthy dose of them on the regular. Not believing that and opting rather for the random life
theory makes no difference. It is what it is, and putting on
blinders won't change it.

Now this may surprise you, but God never promised that
life would be easy or that you would not have to deal with lemons and sometimes grapefruits! That's right. Often people are

afflicted because they have no idea what is going on in life and, as such, become afflicted. Are they bad people? Of course not, rather they just don't understand. It would be like playing tennis with a spoon. Until you learn that you need a racquet you are going to get your butt kicked. Other folks have their racquets in hand and still have to deal with annoyances. Why? Because that's how it is. Getting mad at the game doesn't change the game. What God did promise is that you can win and overcome anything that comes your way.

The great Apostle Paul prayed to God three times that those annoying, irritating, always in the way people would go away once and for all and let him do what God called him to do without the annoyances. But God told him that His grace was sufficient for him. He further said that His great ability was made perfect in Paul's inability to handle the situation. When Paul was weak in his own strength, he was strong in God's strength.

Often we feel the same way, don't we? We tell God, if you would just solve this thing, life would be good. We know He will help us solve it, but He doesn't just "magic" the problem away. You see, life just doesn't work that way. Imagine how stupid we would all become if every time we prayed God just fixed everything on the spot. I know I would be lounging on the couch praying for God to bring in money, food, wine and maybe someone to serve them to me. God doesn't violate the laws of life. He is going to help us solve it, but it doesn't always work on our timetable or in the manner we choose. Here's a thought... maybe God wants us to actually learn something. Maybe He wants us to learn how and why so we can be stronger next time. Maybe He is after our ultimate good. Now don't go south on me and conclude God is allowing us to suffer. Never! Instead, He is working with us, where we are, and teaching us the things we need to know. The difficulty, the annoyance, the dilemmas put us on our mental toes, don't they?

Nothing like a problem to get your mind focused and serious about a solution! Did God send the difficulty? NO! But He is at work within the difficulty to help us win. Does God want to help us solve it yesterday? Of course, He does. But He has the fantastic ability to know exactly where we are, what we believe and how to get us to where we need to be.

If you live long enough you are going to have some problems. You are going to be faced with situations that you cannot solve on your own. You are going to be tested (not by God)! The test, the problem, the annoyance isn't the issue. The issue is what you choose to do about it; where you go for help and how the thing ends. God's promise is that you can beat every dastardly, evil challenge that comes your way. You can. But in order to get the victory you have to be willing to learn something new. For example, God designed your body to heal itself once the cause (problem) is removed. However, you need God to remove the cause. Oh, you can analyze it and spend all your money on physicians, but God is always the one that removes the cause. He just needs some believing cooperation on your part.

So, the next time you find yourself challenged with some impossible dilemma, remember God specializes in things called impossible. There is always a solution, and I don't care what the doctor/the world/your friends/science says to the contrary. Your job is to believe God. Believe that God has your solution and that it is coming your way. Work with yourself where you are and be willing, at least, to learn something new.

This isn't Fantasy Island, my friends. This is real life; life with God, kicking ass and taking names!

When you find yourself holding lemons and grapefruits, give them to God and see if He doesn't send you the recipe for a victorious life.

ROUTINE ROUTINES AND THE DEAD TV HEAD

I recently heard of an anonymous study done on cell phone users across the country. In the study they found that 50 percent of people never travel more than three miles from their house. And add to that, the same people averaged only five places they traveled to throughout their week. Pretty sad, wouldn't you say? Get up; go to work. After work, go to the gym, go home, eat dinner, watch TV, go to bed. Shoot me now, please. (I felt bored just typing that.) There must be more to life than that, right? We all know that it is good to have routines, ways of doing things that eliminate wasted energy, like hanging your keys up on the key rack when you walk in the house so you don't have to spend 20 minutes looking for them in the morning. Or, figuring out what you are going to wear to work tomorrow before it's morning so you don't learn that your favorite jeans are in the washer. Or, putting your tools back in the toolbox so you don't have to use the butter knife for a screwdriver or your shoe for a hammer. But sadly, we tend to try to fit our whole lives into routines, and then life becomes... well, routine. Same thing, same system, same stuff, different day. No one really wants to live that way, do they? I don't!

So, how can we escape the mundane and the same-old, same-old? How can we use our time rather than finding things to occupy our time? How can we summon up the courage to actually turn the TV off? I know it seems weird, but there actually was a time when there was no TV. Scary, I know? What did people do? I remember years ago when my wife and I first got married and lived in a less than desirable little apartment. We were poor college students. One day the unthinkable happened; the TV broke! For a few days we stared at the spot where it used to be, above a small wooden table, and we greatly lamented its demise. What the heck were you supposed to do in the evening? We broke out the Scrabble and the Backgammon and played some games together. Can you imagine that? Married folks doing something together. This got my processor turning. How often do we participate in mindless television? I'm not talking about watching our shows or sports or things we enjoy. I'm talking mindless staring at the TV. Again, shoot me now!

This is no condemnation because I know how it happens to us. It happens the same way that we are coerced into driving the exact same way to work every single day. (At my house, if we run out of Dunkin Donuts coffee you would think someone committed a crime from my reaction - I digress.) We eat the same meals, go to the same Target, the same gas station, and we even do the same exercises at the gym. It happens to us because it is a whole lot easier to do things the exact same way every day. No thought required; no adventure; no scary unknown. We complain that we don't have enough time to work on our new book or our new job or our new hobby because... because we can't break ourselves away from Facebook, Instagram, our iPhone, our iPad or our cell phone or from tweeting (or from the TV in the living room, bedroom, bathroom, and kitchen). We have as much time as we have always had, but we don't see it being eaten away day after day, month after month. In fact, we don't see anything at all...

So, how can we escape the routine, the mundane, the boring? We have to do something different. We have to shake things up a little. We have to open our eyes and look around us. What's going on? What kind of life do we dream of but can't ever seem to approach? What do we want out of our next 24 hours? What do we enjoy? What makes our heart beat faster? What do we have to offer this world? What unique skill do we possess that can help someone's life get a little brighter; a little better; a little more hopeful? When I travel to various locations on business, I never actually turn the TV on. I exercise, I read, I write, I go out to eat and usually end up at the lounge. Interesting things happen at the lounge. After a glass or two of wine, people do something odd. They talk. They tell you stuff. Now despite having to sit through some endless, pointless conversations about seeds or the competitive nature of lettuce, some conversations are actually useful. Sometimes people want to learn about God or even unlearn some bologna about God. Some people tell you about their failing marriage. Some people give you advice about your marriage or your kids or your life, solicited or not.

You and I have to make up our minds to travel outside of our three-mile prison. We need to take a different road. We need to tear the iPhone from our fingers and talk to someone. Thirty minutes of thoughtful, meaningful conversation with your wife is better than five hours of mindless reality TV. Family discussions at the Washington household last for hours, and trump electronic entertainment times a hundred! (Just ask them...)

You want a better, more fulfilling life? Find yourself a human and talk to them. Who knows, you might share something that changes their lives forever, and lo' someone might even be able to help you as well.

In the words of that odd cat, Rick James, *"We're bustin out of this L7 square, we done braided our hair, we don't mind if you stare!"* And if that was too urban, just do something different!

Find a human... and talk!

HEY, I LIKE WAFFLES

Personally, I think the catch-all diagnoses of ADD and ADHD are over-diagnosed and subsequently prescribed. Now hang on before you toss out your Ritalin! Our modern-day theme for handling our issues seems to be based on being diagnosed with some condition, then being assigned to it entirely and then adding that you were born with it. I mean after all I was born this way, therefore there is nothing I can do about it... It is what it is, right? Absent a medical degree, but not absent some God-given horse-sense, folks are mighty quick nowadays to take away our personal responsibility. You see, if I'm responsible for something and I take responsibility, then I can also change something. But if I'm not responsible for it, then what do you want from me? I'm just a victim, powerless to effect any change. I believe that our minds are just that, "our's!" My mind goes where I tell it to go and it does not have its own agenda. I can turn it off; turn it down; change my thoughts; control my thoughts and focus my thoughts, if I want to. In fact, to achieve any success in this life requires that I learn how to focus. Mark Wallace, a minister and excellent friend said it best today, "Most people fail to get what they need from God not because they don't believe, but rather because they fail to sustain or focus their believing long enough to receive it!" In other words, they get distracted... Hey, I like waffles!

So, is this really about ADD or ADHD? (Wait... what were we talking about?) Oh yeah, this is about distraction. Being distracted has reached epidemic status in our world today. It used to be considered a character flaw, but now it seems to be almost revered. Weird huh? It has many code names that give it legitimacy. How about multi-tasking? Being an excellent multi-tasker means you can do several things at once. Of course, you don't really do any of those multi-tasks well, but hey, you get a lot of stuff done. There's hyperactive, which implies you are active times one hundred. Sounds promising. Preoccupied, busy, workaholic, all symptoms of a mind that is going in too many directions at once. Not good, my friends, not good. Our minds, absent a couple of doses of LSD, were designed to think one thought at a time. In fact, we cannot think more than one thought at a time, even if we think otherwise. Multi-tasking is nothing more than darting back and forth between duties. Moms are really good at it, however, but they also start feeling sleepy around 9:00 p.m. It's tiring, folks, really tiring! Now I realize you may not believe me on this one because you are just sure that having the radio on in the background while you work is helpful, so we should take a look at what God says about it:

If any of you lack wisdom, let him ask of God, that giveth to all men liberally, and upbraideth not; and it shall be given him. But let him ask in faith (believing), nothing wavering. For he that wavereth is like a wave of the sea driven with the wind and tossed. For let not that man think that he shall receive any thing of the Lord. A <u>double minded</u> man is unstable in all his ways. James 1:5-8

Surprising? In other words, when you are believing to get something or accomplish some goal, you cannot have a divided or distracted mind. You have to focus man! Otherwise, this old world is going to bat you around like an empty beer can in the ocean. Up real high - life is gooooooood, down real lowwwwww - life sucks again, up real highhhhhhh! Okay, you get it... This world is absolutely cram, bang full of distractions.

Go this way, no wait, go that way, no wait, why am I in the kitchen? What we need to do is to learn how to focus. If my dreams and goals are important to me, then I shouldn't give them up the first time it rains. I shouldn't give them up if it's never sunny again! But you know what happens. The circumstances of life paint a picture and my dreams aren't in the picture. So instead of staying put despite that picture, I modify my dreams to fit that picture that I didn't paint nor approve. Crazy, but true. God has many wonderful dreams for our lives and wouldn't you know it, they happen to be the same ones we have. What a coincidence - not! So again, my friends, our job is to learn how to focus. It's not good to be a double-minded man, angel on one shoulder, devil on the other. It's your life; it's your mind; it's your one shot on Terra Firma; make it happen! Why spend another day at the ice rink without your skates?

When the doctor tells you that you've got ADD or ADHD and will have a hard time focusing, thank him/her for the time and the Ritalin and get busy learning how to focus your mind! You can do it, or God would have never told you to do it!

Life is too short to wait for your empty beer can to arrive at some good destination! Pop open another beer and take charge of your barbecue! You can do it, you know why? Because... hey, I like waffles!

IT IS WHAT IT IS

As a burgeoning human being, you have this wonderful capacity not only to experience your life as it is, but also to imagine
what your life might become in the future. Being marvelously
unique, your awareness comes from within with all of the associations and connections you can muster based almost exclusively from your own perspective. Things that are labeled
good or bad to you, may represent an entirely different meaning to someone else. For this reason, it can be difficult at times
to perceive things as they really are absent your own internal
persuasions. Thus, in order to make any meaningful changes,
it necessitates you first see things clearly and accurately minus
all of the meanings you are likely assigning to those things.
Truly, when it comes to improving, repairing, healing or re-
storing any good thing, you first have to see it and accept it for
what it is. It is what it is...

Calling a thing a thing, as a famous lady once remarked, is
at the foundation of problem-solving any situation you may
find yourself in. Said another way, you cannot fix what you
refuse to acknowledge. Ignoring problems, glossing over bad
situations, refusing to accept that something is not right, only
leads towards difficulties and unpleasant times persisting. If
we are honest, we already know when circumstances have
gone south on us. We know when a good thing has lost its
goodness. Deep down, our hearts already know when there's

a disturbance; a misconnect; impediments and obstacles. The reason we fail to act on the obvious is because we desperately cleave to another narrative; one where things are still okay even though we know they are not okay. A narrative that assures us nothing has changed but instead has simply become familiar. And onward we trudge, inching ahead, hoping something or someone will make it all right. Our failure is in being afraid to see things as they already are. It is what it is.

It does not require a PhD or some other form of higher learning to recognize that nothing in life is static. Everything is ever in a continual state of flux. Living things are either growing or they are dying, but they are not remaining the same. Change isn't something to be afraid of as everything changes in one capacity or another. The key to successfully navigating the change is found in our willingness to observe what actually is, and then seek to make improvements or repairs or whatever the situation calls for at the time. People change, sometimes for the good, sometimes for the not so good. Circumstances change. Conditions change. You cannot apply the logic of 10 years ago to the scenarios of today. Neither can you compare yourself of today to yourself of the past, as the variables of today, though eerily similar, are not the same. Time and chance have happened to them all. For this reason, the only plausible way to endeavor is by addressing your life experiences now in the thousand-eyed present, not in the single-eyed view of the past. It doesn't matter what you did before; what matters is what you do now. It doesn't matter what used to work; it matters what works now. It doesn't matter who you used to be; it matters who you are today. Your problem is what it is today, and the only time to solve it is today. It is what it is...

If you would like God to heal your broken arm, you must first acknowledge that your arm is broken. If you want God to heal your broken heart, you have to admit to yourself that your heart is broken. It's not so much that over time things break, but rather that you are honest enough to accept what is, not what used to be. It is not being positive or renewing your mind to lie to yourself about your reality. Renewing your mind, like being positive, is about applying God's solutions to the things that plague you, those things that have become broken over time. How foolish it is to apply some cheery resolve to a problem rather than to see it and say it and determine within yourself to work it out. Insisting that you already know what to do or what you cannot do based on some tired, former assessment of a situation that has already changed a 100 times, leads only to a futile resolve to stay stuck, mired in some vague notion formed in the past. It is what it is...

Solving relationship problems, solving financial problems, solving achievement problems, solving health problems, indeed, solving spiritual problems requires that you finally allow yourself to see it for what it is. It doesn't matter if it is your fault or someone else's fault, the world's fault or the devil's fault. What matters most is that you stop being afraid to admit something has gone wrong and then take the steps to make it right. Why carry with you all of your former excuses and justifications, your rationales and myriad former failed attempts? Why insist on cleaving to a bad strategy that didn't work before and isn't working now? Why? Why not, while fully accepting and acknowledging the problem, try to see the situation through fresh eyes, with clarity, focused not on continuing to be right or begrudgingly absolving yourself of any responsibility, and choose not rather to locate the remedy, no matter the cost? Sometimes the solutions are right there in front of you, patiently waiting for you to release what was in favor of what is. It is what it is...

At the end of the day, we all want to be happy, to be fulfilled, to be blessed. We all want deepening and enduring love. We all want to succeed and to prosper, and to live life to the absolute full. This life is far too short to continue tripping over our own selves and our own stubborn refusal to see things for what they really are. With God's help we can solve anything, heal anything or recover anything that has become broken or damaged over time.

It is what it is, but it doesn't have to stay that way...

DECEIVED...

The problem with being deceived is that you do not know you have been deceived! At its core, in order for any deception to be effective, the person subject to the deception has to remain unaware of the deception. There's little profit in informing someone they have been deceived, because in their deception they usually don't believe you anyway. So why bother discussing such a subject given that there's so little return on your investment? The point is that the deception only lasts as long as there is no information exposing the deception for what it is. This is the exposure. Have you been deceived? Probably!

As I've penned many times before, life is spiritual at its base. Spiritual verities, though often referred to and lauded, are typically misunderstood. They are misunderstood because man needs a standard of truth outside of his own reasoning to separate truth from error. Absent any standard of truth, man is ripe for deception. God does not say that His people are destroyed because they have a spiritual enemy. He says His people are destroyed for a lack of knowledge. It isn't what man knows that defeats him. It is what he doesn't know, or worse, what he thinks he knows but doesn't really know that defeats him. Ignorance is never really bliss! No person that begins to dabble with illicit drugs, for example, perceives that there is something evil behind his pursuit. Instead, he relies on his feelings and his newfound discovery of an exciting hidden world he wasn't aware of before. In this new world there is promise of discovery and insight, indeed awareness he never experienced before. His experiences are generally positive and fun and certainly nothing to be concerned about. He assures himself he has things under control and knows what he is doing, that is until that which he allows begins to show itself for what it really is, and usually by then occurs too far down the road to escape. And like a fish trapped on the hook or a bird caught in a snare, by the time the trap becomes painfully apparent, it's too late. This is the story of life lived by what appears as opposed to life lived by what is actually true.

It has been said that the secret to the adversary's success is the secrecy of his moves. As a testimony, most folks don't even believe there is an adversary. They brush it aside as religious fantasy, all the while being sorely pricked and assaulted by that same source. They fail to see that the life they live is influenced by two sources, one good and one evil. One source promises life, life lived more than abundantly in every regard. One source seeks only to steal, to kill and to destroy. One source encourages and enhances life. The other source diminishes and hinders and thwarts life. Every problem you have ever had, small and great, minor and major, inconsequential and catastrophic, comes from one source. Every sickness, every disease, every life cut short, every life lived in bondage, every torture, every war came ultimately from that one evil source. I say that not as a criticism for those suffering or to blame those unjustly victimized and targeted, but as an exposé and urgent appeal to see things for what they really are. If you are suffering, if you are having a tough time, if you are struggling in any capacity, the source of it is ultimately evil, and it is not God's will for you to live that way! There is a way out, a real source of escape, but it requires that you humble yourself to what God says is true, instead of spending your life trying to figure it out on your own. The reason your spiritual opponent gains ascendancy in your life is because you remain ignorant of his devices.

All of us living in this world are subject to the same contest, the same fight. I am not exempt and you are not exempt. I lose the fight sometimes just like you lose the fight sometimes. I get deceived like you get deceived. Being a Christian, indeed a child of God, does not guarantee you will win the fight, ultimately, yes, but not necessarily in the day by day. The only way to win the fight is to see through the deceptions, and the only way to see through the deceptions is to learn what God says is true in opposition to what the enemy says or portrays as true. The systems of the world are set up and carefully schemed to convince you of things that aren't true. It doesn't matter how smart or confident you are; it matters what God says is true. In fact, your spiritual opponent is counting on your own ego to lead you astray. You cannot go by what you think or how you feel, or what your parents may have taught you. You cannot depend upon your finite, limited five senses reasonings to discern truth from error. You cannot depend upon your life experiences or your previous successes or failures. You can only depend on one thing, and that one thing is the truth of God's Word.

God invented life and, as such, knows exactly how it can be lived. Thinking you have to try and just survive life, or that life sucks for everyone, or that is just the way life is, when it is not good, is to be deceived. With God's love and help you can solve every problem that ever confronted you or portrayed itself as unsolvable. You can overcome any barrier, every hurdle, all obstacles that ever showed up in your path. You can be healed, restored, uplifted, rejuvenated, revitalized or whatever it is you need to be blessed and to be renewed in your one precious life. It's not about quoting scriptures and claiming God's goodness in your life. It's about seeing and proving it to yourself. It's about a real and true source of help and answers and solutions. Otherwise, why bother? Lord knows, life is too short to live in perpetual defeat!

Have you been deceived in your life? Chances are if you aren't living blessed and victorious, happy and excited about life, the answer is yes. Don't stop there however. God is alive and well and chock full of the answers and solutions you need to win against your spiritual opponent. He is just waiting for you to ask.

"SHOULDA, WOULDA, COULDA…"

"You don't understand. I coulda had class. I coulda been a contender. I coulda been somebody, instead of a bum, which is what I am, let's face it." (On the Waterfront, circa 1954) Sorry for using an old movie reference, but how many times have you engaged in the shoulda… woulda… coulda mentality? I cannot think of a mental state more pointless or more damaging than focusing on what you should have done, would have done or could have done, when you already done did it! (bad grammar used for emphasis…). The laws of life being what they are, none of us can go back in time and change one iota of what happened even five minutes ago, no matter how much we wish we could. Oh, I feel you - I also wish I coulda, but I can't. So why even bother to do that to ourselves?

Let's start by understanding what you "shoulda" done. First, you cannot judge your 'past' decisions in light of your 'present' understanding. Let me say that again; you cannot judge your 'past' decisions in light of your 'present' understanding. All of us make decisions about various things, and we make those decisions based on our understanding in that present moment. For example, you get into a bad habit of going out to the club and having drinks and then driving home. You know it's not a good idea really, but you feel you aren't totally impaired and can handle it. After all, nothing happened the last four times you did it. Then, with some wrong thinking conditioning in place, you try it again, expecting the same result and with sirens whistling, you get pulled over. You fail the breathalyzer and get a DUI! Ouch, license suspended, large fine, can't get to work, court dates, etc., etc. You made a bad decision based on your thinking at the time. Maybe you "shoulda" known better, but we will get to the 'shoulda' later. The reality is that you made a bad decision and got burned for it. It happened! Now, I am guessing that you gave some serious thought to taking that chance again (at least I hope...). In other words, you might not make that choice today knowing what you know now. But the choice you made back then... you already made. Now, here's where the self-abuse really kicks in. You spend the next six months or however long you remain license-less, kicking yourself for being so stupid, so ignorant, so reckless! Why? Can you hear me? Why? You already made the mistake and, in this case, already paid the price. Lamenting, kicking yourself, beating yourself, berating yourself, does absolutely nothing to remedy the situation, and does not in any way make you a better person. You weren't a bad person to begin with! You made a bad choice, suffered some pain and learned a tough lesson. End of story. The rest of the self-flag-ellation is not the voice of God, my friends, it is you condemning yourself for an event you cannot undo. The voice of God would actually tell you to *let it go* because Jesus Christ paid the price for every foolish, silly, lamentable, wrong, grievous, wacky, crazy, perverted, heinous thing you or I ever did! Did you get that? Every wrong thing. So, in God's sight, what's important is not what we 'shoulda' done, but rather what we do right now. God typically won't turn back the hands of time (though He did do that once in the Bible, in a different context) no matter how much we beg. (Trust me... been there, done that.) So, spare yourself some lost time and just let it go. Learn what you can learn and move on.

Woulda is a similar animal to his brother shoulda. How many times have you thought about what you would have done? How about how very different things would have been if only you would have gone to school, would have paid more attention to him/her, would have earned more money, would have worked harder, studied more, gave more effort... if only, if only and more if only. Okay, you know what I'm going to say, right? You know today what you know today because of what you learned yesterday and the day before and the day before... ad infinitum (without end). You cannot possibly put your wiser today brain in your less wise yesterday brain. Just like you "can't put an old head on a young body." Please forgive the cliché. I used to lament the fact that I should have taken to writing when I was 25 instead of the present age, but you know what? I did not have the capacity to organize even *one thought* when I was 25, let alone many thoughts. So, you know what you know, when you know it, not a day before and not a day after. Capiche? You arrive when you get there, not when you are almost there or after you are already there. You did what you wanted to do at the time because it made sense at the time. Sure, now you would have done it differently, but alas now was not then. Be a little kinder to yourself and stop doing that. If what you would have done is still that important, do it now! If you can't do it now (I mean really can't... i.e., play professional baseball), choose another passion and do that now! Really...

Okay, so if you aren't totally lost in clichés, fragmented words and similar word sentences by now, let's get to the last but certainly not least beast, "the couldas." Of the three, the 'could have beens' are the worst. They are the worst because they represent regrets. How sad regrets are, you know? Sad, but unprofitable in every way. Logically, what can I do about something that could have been, but wasn't? There is no end to what could have been, is there? In the end, what I wanted to do - I did. What you wanted to do - you did. It may have been a poor choice; an uninformed choice, a deceived choice, an immature choice, a selfish choice or a silly choice, but in the end, we chose it and it is what it is. Regret is poison to your soul; a poison that corrupts the beauty of today. If you regret not telling your children more how much you loved them, tell them more now. If you regret not telling your mom how much you loved her when she was alive, trust me, if you love her that much now, then you loved her that much then, and she knew that even if you didn't say it as much as you wished. If you regret that you never went to college, go to college now. Do you get it? Don't poison yourself with thoughts of what could have been, instead embrace today; embrace your life right now and do the thing now! Now is all we have, my friends, right now. Life just doesn't last long enough for regrets...

Replace all of those pointless "shoulda... woulda... couldas" with the life you are blessed to live today. Live today as if it is your last and be everything you ever wanted to be right now. The world needs your goodness today. The world needs your love today. The world needs your achievements today. Be kind to yourself, love yourself and don't spend a moment in the past. In the end, that's the only thing that you 'shoulda' 'woulda' and 'coulda' done!

WHY AREN'T YOUR TOMATOES GROWING?

In the Spring, I planted a garden. Last year's garden sucked, so this year I took the time to make up the chemistry of the soil in detailed proportions. After proudly planting my tomatoes and telling them I loved them and so forth, I turned them over to God. (Well, sort of....) I planted them in full sunshine and faithfully watered them every day. After about six weeks of growing time, I noticed that my tomatoes were decidedly puny. Their leaves were yellowing like they needed more water, so I added more water. This went on for several more weeks with less and less results. So, I did what everyone does that is at a loss for answers. I Googled that sh*t! Mr. Google gladly informed me that the most common reason for stunted growth in tomatoes is "too much" water. Imagine, water makes them grow, but you can get too much of it. Yet, this story isn't about moderation; it's about roots, deep roots.

Apparently that guy on TV that talks about watering your lawn less, was right. The more you water something, the less the roots have to dig down. The shallower the roots, the weaker the plant. The deeper the roots, the more robust the plant. So, I started thinking, humans grow also, but only if they have well-developed roots. The question that begs becomes, how deep are your roots in the things that are most important to you? Do you take the time to understand why things happen or do you simply grab for more of the things you *think* will make you happy?

This precious life we live is all about understanding. Not understanding how things really work is the cause of **all** of your difficulties. When you are challenged with some circumstance of life, do you quickly grab the next clichéd bottle of water or do you look for the well where the water never runs out? The truth is ever the truth, and it shows itself in a million combinations. Error only offers a quick fix that doesn't really fix at all, but serves simply to salve the wound in the moment. Men's theories, men's ideas, men's philosophies always fall short because man is woefully unaware of all of the variables. Most of the time, the effect wasn't produced by the cause you had in mind, but another cause of which you remain ignorant. Understanding is therefore, getting to the true cause.

In every field of life, we devote ourselves faithfully to understand, especially in those things we deem most important except for one. We have failed to understand life and the One behind it. And it's no wonder because there are more false ideas about God than about anything else! (By design, I might add....) It's like my son said to me today, "If something feels bad and unpleasant, it probably is...." Things that are contradictory and inconsistent beg for further inspection. If someone teaches you that God is love, yet also tells you He sometimes randomly kills the people you love, I would think that deserved some further inspection. But no, what do you do? You try to accept it by faith or explain it away as a mystery or something. Turn the sprinklers on; you just need more water.

Life is not random, my friends. Every effect does have a cause and although you don't yet understand it, doesn't mean you can't understand it if you really want to know! Just think about your life for a moment. Think about the earth and all of the things in it; the perfection, the symmetry, the beauty. Why does that forest or that beach cause you to feel tranquil? Why doesn't the skyscraper do that for you? Why do you have nerve endings in your fingers and not in your hair? How can you see images in your mind? Well, it's actually a chemical reaction! Okay, but a damn complicated one, don't you think?

The reality behind this life is spirit. You can't detect it by your five senses, but you can get to it by your heart. Every one of us have something in us that beckons us to understand; to find and love its Creator, until the old world talks us out of it. Every one of us recognize the truth, even if we can't always explain it. It's in the lyrics of a song, the words in a poem, a line in a movie and on it goes. But, when you've heard it, you know it even if you cannot express it in words. Truth is un-changing but it's not always on the surface. You have to dig for it. You have to want it and expend the effort to get it. You have to sink your roots down in something substantial if you really want to grow. But, like a tomato, you can't make your-self grow. You simply get the conditions right, sink your roots down deep and the One who causes the tomato to grow will cause you to grow as well.

People spend their whole lives giving themselves to every-thing and everyone and never get to the true cause. We get so busy, so preoccupied, so caught up in our present dilemmas, that we forget to seek out the cause. We get scurried away with false causes and things we cannot possibly effect. We wrestle with intangible concepts like making sure the earth has the resources we need to keep living, never imagining that the One who created the earth may have thought that through!

Instead of wasting away your life; your one precious life with endless and pointless activity, take some time and serious effort to understand. Ask God to teach you! Ask God to make it plain. Ask God to get someone on your path that can help it make sense for you. He invented eyelashes for goodness sakes, don't you think He might have something for you? Oh He does and He wants you to get it, even more than you want to know it! And, He's been looking for you for years!

Well, I did something crazy. I stopped watering those to-matoes and made 'em dig. I still loved them, but they had to do their own work. They did their job and now we got 'maters for days! Do you need tomatoes? I got more than I can han-dle...

WHAT I LEARNED PLAYING GOLF

I had the privilege this past weekend to host our annual golf challenge for the Utah brothers and sisters. The challenge was renamed the Steven B. Kelly Memorial Challenge to forever memorialize my brother-in-law, Big Steve, who is gone from us way too soon. Having finally gotten serious about learning the game, I had been taking some lessons and felt like I might actually escape the beginner phase and play some legitimate golf. Boy was I wrong! I was arguably almost the worst player out there. One brother suggested that I might want to get my money back from the golf pro! (smile). But I learned something on that fateful day, and it's worth writing about here...

Golf is only as hard as you tell yourself it will be. You cannot take lessons and commit yourself to a game and at the same time verbalize repeatedly how much you suck; how unlikely it is that you will make the shot; how challenging the damn game is and on and on and on. What you think is what you say and what you say is exactly how it is going to play out. No sport, upon your early encounters, is easy, and to assign yourself failure before you fail is to work against your own best interests. Golf, like any sport, has fundamentals you have to master. Once you have mastered the fundamentals, which never happens overnight, you will gain confidence in your abilities to do it right. But, dogging yourself for not having mastered them yet is foolish and serves only to ensure you will continue to lose. The reason you do so much better at the driving range is because you have not assigned the same importance to every shot, and instead relax and swing the damn club! Life is very similar in that you are only going to learn when you decide to just swing the damn club!

The things you tell yourself have a huge impact on how things are going to play out. When you are learning something new, things will be difficult and feel uncomfortable. You are going to flub up and foul up and f*** up! That is how life works. You may have spent your whole life thinking something is true or reliable, that isn't true at all. It's not knowing how everything works that matters, but rather your ability to adjust, change and learn something new. The real measure of your success is not how well you do in the things you have mastered, but how willing you are to learn something new and master that as well. The best things in life aren't the things you may have thought they were. There are principles and mindsets and behaviors that accompany the best life and those things are not at all what the world says they are. The world's offerings are shiny toys that glisten and shine and promise but fail to deliver. They are sparkling bundles of nothingness that leave you hungry, empty, unsatisfied. You must persevere with right principles (the right swing) until you have mastered them, leading to unending joy and happiness.

In addition to the affliction you put upon yourself is the affliction you allow from others due to your over-reliance on their opinions of you. Once you become concerned about what others may think about you, you quickly lose sight of what you think about yourself. You become a performer in someone else's contest. The moment you look for your competitors, you lose the race. You don't play for the crowd; you play for yourself. You are competing both for and against yourself. Once you have entertained the mistake, the mistake is about to occur. Your job, your responsibility, your necessity is to not play against yourself. You have to prove to you that you can do! Your challenge is not with others; it is with yourself. Your job is to win yourself. If others ridicule you or take shots at you or doubt you, you don't endeavor to prove them wrong; you prove yourself right! You own your own failures and mistakes fully and completely. You allow yourself to not know yet while committing yourself to know eventually. It's not where you are now, but where you end up. You seek for the mastery of yourself, and whether the crowd approves or disapproves matters little. You have to answer to yourself!

You will find, if you are paying attention, that you are not fighting the world, you are fighting what it is you are thinking about yourself. The world cannot make you into anything without your consent. It's the man staring back at you in the mirror whose opinion counts most. Do not allow circumstances or situations to define who you are and what it is you are capable of in life. It's not the crowds or your best friend or your husband or wife who decides who and what you are; it is you! Fight for you. Believe in you. Stand for you! You can do or be anything you want, no matter what has gone on in the past. The only limitation is you...

Life, like golf, can be a very challenging game. You are going to hit some balls into the water. You are going to whiff on some of your drives and the ball will only travel about 15 feet. You are going to sail some 10 foot chip shots into the abyss. You are going to three-putt and four-putt and have a scorecard worthy of the garbage can. But, the real essence of life isn't found in your failures, but rather in what it is you learn from your failures and where you go from there. Golf is only as hard as you think it is, and you owe it to yourself to recognize your progress and determine in yourself to finally figure it out! Don't be seduced into working against your own best interests. The enemy you are fighting against is you! Win the fight.

See you on the links...

The divide that assaults our nation is only successful because people have stopped thinking like human beings and instead allowed others to do their thinking for them.

A NATION DIVIDED

I cannot think of another time, at least in my lifetime (Civil War excluded), when our nation was so polarized and divided. The crisis we face as a nation isn't so much based on our differing beliefs as it is on the apparent lack of capacity to consider that nothing is really black or white. Republicans aren't entirely one thing, and democrats entirely another thing. And while there is a far right and a far left, most people can be located somewhere within the range. People are not exclusively evil nor exclusively good. Humans are not completely strong or completely weak, with all of us having combinations of both mixed in. Liberals have conservative beliefs, and conservatives entertain liberal ideas. To consider that everything must be one thing or another thing is to be deceived. The reason such ludicrous logic is even considered today is because people have stopped thinking for themselves, and instead given themselves over to hurtful ideas and concepts that seek to corral the masses into one camp or the other. To be a human is to be exclusive, though sharing many of the same values and beliefs. Our nation is divided because we no longer trust our own hearts, and instead look to others or to a majority to clarify what it is we should believe. Such things shouldn't be so...

The profound beauty of our country is found in the freedoms we enjoy to be able to choose for ourselves. We are free to worship as we see fit. We are free to speak out against injustice and wrongs done to our fellow man. We are free to publicly and peacefully gather and demonstrate. We are free to vote and choose who we feel best represents our beliefs and, further, who will stand up for our beliefs and ensure our rights are protected. Yet sadly, that is not the America of today. It is not our nation today because we, as a people, have been led off course; far off course. We no longer vote for our ideals, but instead cleave to party loyalty and, as such, are ripe for corruption and exploitation. Our elected officials don't represent us; they represent special interest groups (code name for money) and support things they do not really support. They are no longer outraged at injustice (any injustice) and choose rather to go with the party flow. Facts and realities are blindly ignored and called "fake news." Rather than adhering to the old Bible adage, "ye shall know them by their fruits," we ignore the fruits and call the light darkness and the darkness light. We rely on the news outlets to tell us what to believe rather than provide information that informs *how* we should believe. We trust no one and, most regrettably, our own thoughts and hearts. We are a nation divided because we trust the media machine more than we trust what we know is good and right and beneficial...

Democrats, republicans, liberals are all names constructed to identify beliefs we all have about how people should be treated, what our priorities are and what types of laws should be in place to further and protect the things that are right and chastise and correct the things that are wrong. But, that is not our nation today. Instead of identifying with people as individuals, we identify with people as groups; good groups and bad groups and in so doing dehumanize one another which leads, as surely as the sun rises, to unspeakable hatred and atrocities done to one another. Instead of witnessing a cruelty, and feeling strongly that something should be done to resolve it or to make things right, we instead cleave to our labels and affiliations, adamantly rejecting the suffering of others because the suffering is not happening to us. We have been talked out of our basic human compassions for one another in favor of supporting the majority we have chosen to affiliate with. When a black man is clearly victimized and murdered, instead of being infuriated about it, we seek to point out his character flaws and compare it to atrocities done to our own group. Our failure isn't found in choosing which group to stand with, but instead no longer being capable of recognizing an atrocity was done! We behave like sheep following not our own inclinations, no longer our own constitution, but whatever "our" completely polarized group says is okay. We are a nation divided because we stopped noticing individuals and opted rather for the labels and factions we've been talked into accepting...

If we say we feel badly for a marginalized group, we suddenly become "lib-tards" crying about things that don't matter, like human lives and human suffering. We throw out all-or-nothing ideals that suggest all poor people are lazy and assumes that all people began with the same opportunities and advantages. We bemoan any welfare program designed to help people in an emergency, yet welcome a stimulus check, extended unemployment benefits though they be programs with a difference in name only, coming from the same source, in an attempt to help people through the same issues. The real question we should ask ourselves is why we are so pissed off with the notion that, at times, people need help in life. Pull yourself up by your own bootstraps only seems to apply when they aren't your boots that need some help! Those of us that have learned the value of hard work, who have been blessed with opportunity, who have learned some basic principles of life, owe a profound duty to those who are not so fortunate. Not because they have earned it, but because we have it to give. We are a nation divided because we have stopped caring for and having compassion for others, a principle our country was founded upon...

So what is the conclusion of the whole matter? Stop being such an asshole, mean-spirited and cruel and return to helping others. Quit spewing out words of hatred that aren't really your words, but instead the words of a cruel enemy seeking to take down all that is beautiful about America. Republicans, democrats and liberals don't make America great, God does, and He does it by taking care of people, all people, regardless of any label that has been applied to them. And He asks us to do one thing, namely love our brothers as ourselves... The divide that assaults our nation is only successful because people have stopped thinking like human beings and instead allowed others to do their thinking for them. It was never me versus you. It is good versus evil, and it's time we stopped letting evil win.

Let's get back to being the America that was great...

CONCLUSION

THE END GAME

When I first began writing "Just Some Good Thoughts," my aim was only to provide a vehicle by which good thoughts of all kinds could be shared with people in order to uplift their spirits. But, the more I wrote, the more I recognized that I wasn't just offering something nice to think about, but instead something true and reliable and sure from which any reader might recognize those areas of their lives that were not so good and thus seek something new, something different, something outside the established framework from which most people find themselves trapped. People unknowingly and often knowingly have accepted a life that is mediocre, defeated and sad. They wrestle with the same demons year after year, deflated and weary, privately begging for something better, something closer to the life they envisioned as a child when life was still pregnant with possibilities and hope for a bright future. Yet life and time and difficulty besieged them all perpetually and consistently until they finally gave in to the wheel of things, persuaded that the life they were experiencing was real life and that nothing better existed for them. It is for those poor souls I write and will continue to write, not as a chastisement but rather a remedy, indeed the solution to all that ever ailed them. To that end, life is so, so much more!

As someone vitally concerned for people's happiness, which admittedly began as a quest for my own personal happiness, I find it a shame how far below par good hearted people have been forced to live. The world, with all of its advancements and progress, offers no real help. All of the lightning-fast technology and clever inventions, and scientific research promising to answer the question, "why?" still leave the heart answerless, afraid and unfulfilled. Bad things happen to good people, and evil men appear to prosper and succeed. Life just doesn't make sense. For every person, there are at least a thousand opinions broadcasted and shared as truth, leaving man confused and bewildered. Every answer given is not a real answer but a fabrication, a red herring, something from which an unthinking person might find temporary solitude. But is it really solitude? If even one part breaks down, then aren't all parts broken down? Is it possible that their truth has holes in it or that their perfection is also fraught with imperfection? If something is true, then it must always be true in every circumstance and under every condition. All the rest is error, error compounded upon error, lies upon lies, treachery on top of treachery. It is no wonder that people have given up on goodness and the possibility of a fulfilling and happy life. The life they live is not happy, at least not with any lasting permanence. Instead, it is fleeting and temporary and founded upon whether or not the sun is shining today, or that circumstances have at last lined up to some good end. In this, I submit to you, dear reader, that the life you have imagined does exist, though it be deeply veiled from the mind of the casual observer. The real essence of life isn't found on the surface, but exists deeper down where the gold and treasures are to be found.

You certainly don't need me to clarify this for you, as you have been living your own experience of life. You have been heretofore wading through the muck and mire on your own. Inside, in your private heart, you know that something is missing. You know life cannot consist of merely making the most money and gathering for yourself the most toys before you die.

You know precisely where you struggle, but you don't know exactly why. You know when and where you are unfulfilled. You know how your heart aches for unconditional love and a world where love and kindness hold first place. And on those rare occasions when you have dared to let that warming and consoling love out, the world has punished you for it. Quickly you have been forced back in line with the masses to a life of meager expectations and poor results. You count yourself happy because at least you don't live the life of such and such. That is not to say that life is without struggles, as it must be for a time, but rather that every struggle may be won and every obstacle surmounted once you find the source, the real source of life. The trouble, which seems far too light a description, is that you are seeking life without engaging the Author of life. You don't seek the Author because you are inherently evil, but instead, because someone or something has deftly hidden Him from your view. The same thing that secretly fills your life with misery and impossible dilemmas is the same one that has deceived you. In his craftiness, he has convinced you of a lie, a thousand lies, whereby all he engenders is falsely attributed to God. The very notion of God causes your skin to bristle as you contemplate the painful, boring existence that supposedly encompasses life with Him. Instead of learning of Him, as Adam did, you hide yourself in the garden from the only One that could ever give you help. This is man's only real dilemma, whether to reach upward or continue to seek within. Oh, my friends, God exists, and He is only good always.

The journey you are on is similar to the journey all of us are on. We all have been blessed with one very short and rapidly passing life. We have only one shot at this thing. There will be no great by and by until there is first a great here and now. This is our one life. This is our only opportunity to learn what we need to learn and ultimately win. No matter your present age, there is no plausible, rational reason for you to remain a fraction of your true self. It is not just how life is, no matter how many times that has been drummed into your head. There exist real, solid, substantial, concrete solutions to your problems. I'm not talking about religious, pious platitudes whereby the exclaimers still suffer the same fate, the same defeats. I'm not promising answers and help merely as a psychological pacifier that assuages your mind for a moment, until the next hardships arrive. I'm talking real answers, real help, real and enduring solutions. I'm speaking of vast intelligence, unlimited power and ability, all founded upon the basis of love. And He exists for you...

My thoughts for you, my just some good thoughts, are that you find the life you have been missing. That one day it dawns on you that you do not have to keep living the way you have been living, that you don't have to go along with the status quo and relegate yourself to a meaningless existence. That the good life you dream of is a present tense reality and not the stuff of fiction and feel-good novels, that you experience the fullness and blessedness from which life was created to be in every facet and phase of your existence. And, finally, that you find the God that made you, though He be not far from any one of us. You owe it to yourself to live your best life. You owe it to the people you love to be a vibrant, lively proponent of life. You owe it to all of those sad, poor souls you can help after you have found the way. That, folks, is the ultimate end game, a life that is not only wonderful now, but one that will last forever. This is your promised end game of which all humanity privately seeks. This is it...

Just some good thoughts...

ABOUT ATMOSPHERE PRESS

Atmosphere Press is an independent, full-service publisher for excellent books in all genres and for all audiences. Learn more about what we do at atmospherepress.com.

We encourage you to check out some of Atmosphere's latest releases, which are available at Amazon.com and via order from your local bookstore:

Finding Us, by Kristin Rehkamp

The Ideological and Political System of Banselism, by Royard Halmonet Vantion (Ancheng Wang)

Unconditional: Loving and Losing an Addict, by Lizzy and Adam

Telling Tales and Sharing Secrets, by Jackie Collins, Diana Kinared, and Sally Showalter

Nursing Homes: A Missionary's Journey Through Heaven's Waiting Room, by Tim Eatman Ph.D.

Timeline of Stars, by Joe Adcock

A Boy Who Loved Me, by Wilson Semitti

The Injustice in Justice, by Charmaine Loverin

Living in the Gray, by Katie Weber

Living with Veracity, Dying with Dignity, by Alison Clay-Duboff

Noah's Rejects, by Rob Kagan

A lot of Questions (with no answers)?, by Jordan Neben

Cowboy from Prague: An Immigrant's Pursuit of the American Dream, by Charles Ota Heller

Sleeping Under the Bridge, by Melissa Baker

The Only Prayer I Ever Have to Say Is Thank You, by M. Kaya Hill

Amygdala Blue, by Paul Lomax

A Caregiver's Love Story, by Nancie Wiseman Attwater

Taming Infection: The American Response to Illness from Smallpox to Covid, by Gregg Coodley and David Sarasohn

The Second Long March, by Patti Isaacs

Me & Mrs. Jones, by Justine Gladden

Echoes from Wuhan, by Gretchen Dykstra

Through Her Eyes, by Maheen Mazhar

ABOUT THE AUTHOR

Tony Washington was born in Leicester, England, the birthplace of one of his most influential writers, James Allen. Growing up as a child with the US military he had many opportunities to connect with people from all over the world, learning they all had most of the same challenges in common. He later learned the truth concerning God's Word through a class called Power for  Abundant Living, leading to a lifetime pursuit of helping people with varying challenges to find freedom, help, and relief from God through the pages of the Bible. He received training as a minister and earned an MBA in Health-care Administration. An avid writer and lover of writers, he began writing a blog called *Just Some Good Thoughts* from which the materials in this book were developed. He is a firm believer that truth is simple, and it is error that is difficult. When he is not writing he can be found seeking the sun, traveling, playing golf, and enjoying time with his friends and family. He currently resides in Salt Lake City, Utah, with his wife of thirty-nine years.